DATE DUE

JAN 17 2002			

D0369239

The Search for Equity

The
Search

Women at Brown University, 1891–1991

for
Equity

Edited by POLLY WELTS KAUFMAN

BROWN UNIVERSITY PRESS
DISTRIBUTED BY THE UNIVERSITY PRESS OF NEW ENGLAND
HANOVER AND LONDON

FRONTISPIECE: Women's studies majors at
the 1986 Commencement, in front row, from
left: Letitia Allen and Heather Findlay.

Photography by John Forasté, University
Relations, *frontispiece,* p. 14, 31, 142, 182,
258, 242, 308. All other photographs
courtesy Brown University Archives. Index
by Nicole Cunningham. Printed in the
United States of America.

Library of Congress Cataloging-in-
Publication Data
The search for equity: women at Brown
    University, 1891–1991 / edited by
    Polly Welts Kaufman.
        p. cm.
    Includes index.
    ISBN 0-87451-570-X
        1. Brown University – History. 2.
    Women – Education (Higher) – Rhode
    Island – History. 3. Educational
    equalization – Rhode Island – History.
    4. Women college teachers – Rhode
    Island – History.
    I. Kaufman, Polly Welts, 1929–
    LD638.S43 1991
    378.745'2–dc20   91-24346
                                            CIP

*For the women of Brown
as they enter their second century*

C O N T E N T S

TABLES AND CHARTS

Dᴜʀɪɴɢ ᴍʏ ʏᴇᴀʀs as Nancy Duke Lewis University Professor at Brown I became attached to a university as I never have before or since. I loved the students and the openness of the curriculum; I thrived in an atmosphere of intellectual experimentation with colleagues committed to stretching the bounds of knowledge and to including students as collaborators in our efforts; I learned how rewarding teaching could be when students took education seriously. But above all, it was my immersion in Brown's history, in the history of women at Brown, that enriched my experience and sealed my attachment to the university.

The history of women at Brown is a remarkable story, full of determined, outspoken, clever women who first made room for women at an all-male institution and then carved out a larger and larger space for them. Sarah Doyle, the principal of the Girls Department at Providence High School, and her associates pushed and pushed until they won admission for the first group of women in 1891. Then they pushed some more until funds were raised for a building. Sarah Doyle minced no words when she told a small gathering (that would become the Rhode Island Society for the Collegiate Education of Women) in 1895:

> This is the day of education and women must be educated . . . Under President Andrews, the education of women at Brown University is well under way. It is our duty and privilege to help in this work and we can best help by providing a suitable building for these women students. Now, how shall we proceed to raise the money?

When the money was finally raised (it was a slow and laborious process), Doyle gloried in the success and in the fact that Rhode Island women now had a college of their own:

> Today marks an era in the education of women in the State. No longer need they stand at the door of the temple of knowledge, but may enter and be ministered unto at its shrines. What an immense gain has been achieved in the intellectual training of women since Hannah Adams, a hundred years ago, expressed her idea of heaven to be a place where women would have their thirst for knowledge gratified.

Doyle ended this, her speech at the dedication of Pembroke Hall, with a powerful vision of women's future. When I first read her words I was inspired, even thrilled, by the way they linked the future to the past in a long tradition of women's history. I still find them inspiring:

> We dedicate Pembroke Hall to the service of women who, like Mary Somerville, or Maria Mitchell, shall prove their ability to grapple with scientific problems; to women like George Eliot and Elizabeth Barrett Browning, who will enrich the literature of the world by their imagination; to women like Florence Nightingale and Dorothea Dix, who will practice and teach the Christian spirit of love. We dedicate, nay we consecrate it to the highest, holiest womanhood.

This was the speech in which Doyle also referred to women's sphere as one of "infinite and indeterminate radius," a phrase I have never stopped quoting since I read it, now more than ten years ago. That phrase sums up for me the purpose and experience of women's education at Brown, through its ups and downs, its setbacks and advances as they are so carefully and well detailed in this book.

It was precisely the expanding sphere of women's education and of their potential for unlimited competence and achievement that both delighted and frightened university administrators. President Barnaby C. Keeney complained loudly (and teasingly) that Dean Nancy Duke Lewis had proof that her women students did better on average than Brown men. Like Lewis, women deans regularly pointed to the academic success of their students in order to secure more support for the college, but their arguments were not always welcome. The opponents of coeducation in earlier years, those who insisted that the Women's College be renamed Pembroke in 1928 to distinguish it as much as possible from Brown, and some of those who fought the final merger in 1971 did so out of fear that the radius of women's sphere would become so "infinite and indeterminate" that there would be nothing to distinguish scholars except their individual achievement. If more women succeeded than men, what would happen to the claim that men were intellectually, socially and in every other way superior, better fitted for "public" roles, better able to organize and run the world? A sphere of "infinite and indeterminate radius" might, after all, be no sphere at all. Those who felt that social order depended on the separation of the lives and activities of men and women found this a threatening prospect indeed.

Others, of course, welcomed the idea that a women's college could equalize the conditions of women and men in relation not only to the pursuit of knowledge, but also to careers, social service, and politics. These people not only promoted equal education and then coeducation, but they also worked to put women in positions of power at the university – as administrators, tenured professors, and members of the corporation. Their efforts, sometimes successful and sometimes not, sometimes permanent and sometimes only temporary, are described with great interest in these pages.

I don't want to keep you from these pages any longer. This book is a great treat to read; it is chock full of information and new readings of women's history at Brown. It is a book Sarah Doyle would approve of, I think, for it is unsparing in its honesty, honest in its critical judgments, at once critical and celebratory about its subjects. I learned a great deal I hadn't known before; I also revisited women who had become old friends; I smiled at examples of great courage and frowned at forgotten instances of discrimination. Mostly, though, I found enormous pleasure in reading this history, a history that has not ended with the centennial celebration, but that goes on and on. The authors of the chapters have worked long and hard and they have come to love this history; many are students or former students, there are also alumnae among them. Their work is itself an example of how deep is the commitment of Brown women to their education and to their university. That commitment has been evident for a century and it persists to this day. The question of how infinite is women's sphere has not yet been, perhaps will never be resolved, but we can count on Brown women to continue to offer imaginative and inspiring answers to it. They will also, through their words and actions, deepen our understanding of how liberating it is to be allowed to push beyond all imaginable limits a sphere whose radius is ever more "infinite and indeterminate."

JOAN W. SCOTT
Institute for Advanced Study
April, 1991

Brown women have progressed
from undergraduates to Brown
Corporation members: Mary
E. Woolley, left, and Anne T.
Weeden, first graduates of the
Women's College in 1894;
Ruth Harris Wolf, Class of
1941, former Brown trustee,
chief marshal at the 1991
Commencement.

POLLY WELTS KAUFMAN

W̲HEN WOMEN FIRST entered
Brown one hundred years ago, the university was an all-male institution
with 125 years of history and tradition behind it. At first, Sarah E. Doyle
and the clubwomen of Rhode Island who pressed for women's admission
expected women students only to attend classes and earn Brown degrees.
One hundred years later, Sarah Doyle's figurative daughters are integrated
into virtually all the functions of the university. The history of women at
Brown is the story of the expansion of women's awareness of their potential for becoming legitimate participants at every level of a university. It is
also the story of women's subsequent challenge to the status quo as they
sought entrance into succeeding levels of power in a male-dominated
institution.

This collection of essays describes women's ongoing search for equity
at Brown University. The one hundred year mark is an appropriate time
to assess the extent of their progress. Quantitative gains are the easiest to
enumerate. Nearly half of the 5,560 undergraduates and 40 percent of
the 1,560 graduate students are women. The number of women in the
alumni body is growing faster than the number of men. Of living alumni
in the classes graduating since 1971, the year of the merger of Pembroke
with The (men's) College, 44 percent are women. Although their numbers
are increasing, women comprise only 23 percent of the faculty, and hold
only 16 percent of the total tenured positions. Women hold some important
administrative posts. The dean of The College and half of the associate
deans are women, as are the university librarian, the chaplain, the registrar, the university counsel, and the director of alumni relations. Only one

quarter of the members of the Brown Corporation, the governing board, are women, but a woman currently serves as the treasurer of the university.[1]

Qualitative issues are more difficult to assess. The "Coed Study," as the 1980 report from the corporation's committee studying the effects of the merger has come to be called, identified a drop in achievement and academic self-confidence during college among women as compared to men undergraduates, even though women entered Brown with higher secondary school records. A survey of the Class of 1988 by the Office of the Dean of the College indicates that the drop in women's achievement may have leveled off, except in the fields of mathematics and the physical sciences. Women undergraduates, however, still attest to the continuation of different standards for men and women in social life and in classroom dynamics, areas directly related to the development of self-esteem.

Although present undergraduates may consider one hundred years too long a time for women still to be working for equity in any institution, Brown's record on integrating women into all university functions compares favorably to the performance of similar institutions. The improved position of women at Brown, however, did not occur automatically. As their awareness of new issues unfolded, succeeding generations of Sarah Doyle's daughters worked to open one door after another at Brown.

The Variety of Brown Women Seeking Equity

The differences in their methods reveals a wide spectrum of Brown women who searched for equity. Enthusiastic Rhode Island clubwomen and new Brown alumnae claimed space in the name of the advancement of women and spearheaded the fund drives that built the Women's College campus. A well-mannered firmness marked the approach of alumnae who pushed for representation on the Brown Corporation for nearly forty years before they succeeded. The corporation turned down the Alumnae Association's petition for a woman trustee in 1927, seven years after women were granted suffrage in national elections. Their candidate, Mary E. Woolley, Class of 1894, M.A. 1895, had impeccable credentials. Not only was she one of the first two women graduates, she was also the president of Mount Holyoke College. Fifteen years later alumnae won the right to vote for alumni trustees but the candidates were still all men. Although the corporation named Anna Canada Swain, Class of 1911, to the Board of Trustees in 1949, representation remained token until another generation of alumnae hammered out an agreement in 1965 that allowed women to run for positions on the Board of Trustees.[2]

The vocal demand of radical women of the sixties, propelled by the civil rights movement, ended the separate social system for women and was the impetus for the merger of Pembroke College with The College in 1971. Supported by a revived women's movement, qualified women faculty who were denied tenure secured their goals by taking the university to court with a successful affirmative action suit in 1977. Women faculty and administrators in the 1970s and 1980s, committed to improving the undergraduate experience for women, developed separate support structures for women, including a women's center for undergraduates, a women's studies major, and a nationally-recognized center devoted to teaching and research on women. Presently, a coalition of Third World students is working for the addition of women's studies courses with a multi-cultural perspective and women Odyssey Fellows are partners with faculty in the process of integrating multi-cultural material into existing courses. Recently, women undergraduates have called attention in dramatic ways to the need for the entire university community to address what they view as a persistent problem of sexual harassment and assault.

Yet it can also be said that women could have been denied entrance at every level of the university, no matter how hard they pushed, as they were at many comparable institutions. It was only twenty years ago that women undergraduates first attended Yale, Princeton, Dartmouth, Amherst, Bowdoin, Franklin and Marshall, Colgate, and Trinity. Radcliffe women did not receive Harvard degrees until 1965. As for tenured faculty members, women at Yale and Harvard, for example, still comprise less than 10 percent.[3] The climate at Brown for the acceptance of women has been more positive for several reasons.

Economic factors supported the rapid growth of women undergraduates at Brown to approximately two hundred in 1898 and five hundred by the late 1920s, even though the university continued to maintain a proportion of between two and three men to each woman. The admission of women to Brown allowed the university to expand without decreasing the quality of its students. Although the ratio of women to men was maintained until parity was reached with the merger in 1971, the number of women at Pembroke College jumped to nine hundred after World War II and reached twelve hundred in 1970.[4]

One can also look to Brown's traditions to explain its relative openness to women. Founded in 1764 with a liberal charter, Brown has always prided itself on its commitment to diversity. Several Quakers on the Board of Trustees in the 1880s found it difficult to deny women access to Brown and gave their support, the poet John Greenleaf Whittier for one calling it "a matter . . . of simple justice."[5]

The Brown Corporation's appointment of Elisha Benjamin Andrews as president in 1889 created a window of opportunity for the entrance of women into Brown. Although he supported higher education for women,

Andrews was also anxious to increase the size of the student body, which had hovered around 250 for thirty-five years. By the end of his presidency in 1898, he had increased Brown's enrollment to approximately one thousand students, including two hundred women undergraduates and about one hundred graduate students, one third of whom were women.[6]

The demand of the people of Rhode Island that women be educated at Brown was another deciding factor. Local families did not see the need for their daughters to leave the state for higher education when there was a perfectly good university close to home. In 1888, thirty Rhode Island women who traveled to women's colleges outside Rhode Island referred to themselves as exiles and offered their experiences as a reason for Brown to accept women. Brown was the most acceptable place in the state for a college education at the time: Rhode Island Normal School offered only a two-year course and the University of Rhode Island was not founded until 1892, the year after women were first admitted to Brown.

Brown women also withstood the national backlash against coeducation in the first decade of the twentieth century caused by a fear that the rush of women into higher education was feminizing the college curriculum and driving men away from the study of liberal arts. Although Connecticut's Wesleyan University had preceded Brown by twenty years in accepting undergraduate women, after 1909 it refused to accept women students, prompting its alumnae to seek a more hospitable location for women's higher education. With the support of the city of New London, they founded Connecticut College for Women which remained a separate women's college until the admission of men in 1969.[7] Tufts University, the University of Rochester, and Western Reserve University abandoned their coeducational beginnings to set up coordinate colleges on separate campuses with separate classes for women taught by the same faculty who taught the men. When the number of women in the graduating class at Stanford equalled the number of men early in this century, a quota of three males to one female was adopted.[8]

Although the Women's College in Brown University was a coordinate college from the beginning and the university maintained a fairly constant ratio of women to men, there was no retreat. Women, who took upper level classes with men on the Brown campus from the beginning and had always received a Brown degree, gradually attended more and more coeducational classes until separate classes for women virtually disappeared during the 1940s. Women graduate students, who also entered in 1891, attended coeducational classes from the beginning.

Despite economic factors, Brown's liberal tradition, and the demand of Rhode Islanders for women's higher education in their own state, the admission of women to Brown still would not have been achieved without the energizing ideals of Rhode Island's clubwomen. Women would probably still be vastly underrepresented on the Brown Corporation if the alumnae had not organized to change the system of election to the Board of Trustees. Without the student outcry, women might still be subject to a social system separate from men and continue to view themselves as subordinate to their male peers. Without the challenge by women faculty to the university's promotion policies, women would not hold one quarter of Brown's faculty positions. The women at Brown today owe a great deal to the women who came before them.

The intent of these essays is not to detail the history of the Women's College in Brown University which became Pembroke College in 1928 and merged with The College in 1971. The reader is referred to Grace E. Hawk's *Pembroke College in Brown University* for that story.[9] Rather, each of these essays examines the efforts of women to define their relationship to the various components of the university, beginning with the simple objective of preparing for Brown examinations. As women opened each door, succeeding generations found other doors needing to be opened before women were accepted as truly legitimate members of Brown University. It is the contention of this work that until women as a whole achieve equity on all levels of such institutions as universities, they will not become fully-functioning members of society. As the two essays on the lives of Brown women after college demonstrate, the university and the broader society have been greatly enriched by incorporating the talents, skills, and commitment of educated women.

Expanding Goals of Brown Women

When the Rhode Island Society for the Collegiate Education of Women assumed the responsibility for enabling women to become students at Brown, they wanted to retain some control over the quality of the experience of the undergraduate women. They proceeded to raise the funds for Pembroke Hall, an elegant building named for the college, founded by a woman, that Roger Williams attended at Cambridge University.[10] In her speech dedicating Pembroke Hall in 1897, Sarah Doyle, who inspired and directed the fund-raising campaign, made it clear that the women of the Rhode Island Society expected Brown to prepare women to be scientists, like astronomer Maria Mitchell, poets like Eilzabeth Barrett Browning, and social reformers like Dorothea Dix. In the original library of Pembroke Hall, a frieze personifies women in Grecian robes as the fields of knowledge, the arts, religion, and motherhood. Its creation was suggested and supervised by the society's secretary, Amelia S. Knight.[11]

The prevalent fear that coeducation would not only feminize collegiate education but also masculinize women and even reduce their physical ability to bear children had to be addressed by the new Women's College. The Rhode Island Society, deans, students, and alumnae worked together to create a separate women's culture at the college. Of foremost importance was the development of physical education in order to lay aside fears that college women would develop physical weaknesses leading to infertility. Thus in 1906 a second building drive resulted in the opening of Sayles Gymnasium, a fully-equipped facility for women complete with popular bowling alleys paid for by the new alumnae.[12]

Women were essential to the success of funding drives to expand the Women's College campus. Two dormitories, Miller Hall and Metcalf Hall, were added in 1910 and 1919 and, in 1927, the graceful Alumnae Hall, its very name signifying recognition of the determination of alumnae to develop the Women's College. It contains a large lecture hall, the Crystal Room for smaller intellectual and social gatherings, a lunchroom, and rooms originally designed for student activities. Women students so enthusiastically created extracurricular activities that Women's College deans worried that either students' academic courses would suffer or their health break down. Together, students and deans assigned points to various activities, keeping students within a stated maximum, but their enthusiasm for their own college continued undiminished.

When the name change to Pembroke College was advocated in 1928 by male undergraduates chafing from what they perceived as the stigma of coeducation, women students, proud of the college they helped to create, accepted the new name. They were used to being called Pembrokers after the name of their hall. A few alumnae, whose memories were longer, disapproved of the new title because it was Brown University they had worked so hard to enter, and they wanted the world to know that they still received Brown degrees. They were somewhat placated by the retention of Brown's name in the full title: Pembroke College in Brown University.

The women's college at Brown was known as Pembroke College for more than forty years. Students believed they had an ideal combination: the academic advantages of a university combined with the opportunity to run their own campus life and extracurricular activities without competition from men. The campus was completed with the opening of Andrews Hall in 1947 and Morriss and Champlin Halls in 1960, all dormitories.

As the college developed into a residential college, reaching out beyond Rhode Island and New England for students, the deans and students developed an elaborate social system, entirely different from the system regulating the lives of male undergraduates. Although the ostensible reason for a separate social system for women was to ensure the safety of women students, the underlying message the students received was that women were dependent and needed someone else to regulate their lives. The demand by women students in the sixties that the college should no longer serve *in loco parentis,* or play the role of parent, led to the end of a separate social system for women and ultimately to complete coeducation and the end of Pembroke College in 1971.

Because the merger happened so quickly, there were inevitable losses. Many alumnae thought they had had the best of both worlds under the coordinate system and felt disconnected from Brown. Women students lost all their separate support systems, useful ones as well as restrictive ones. Although the committee set up to advise on the merger recommended the development of a women's center, none was forthcoming. The women's community at Brown, with the support of some alumnae, began to agitate for a women's center and the completion of the funding of the chair for a woman professor begun by the bequest of Nancy Duke Lewis, dean of Pembroke from 1950 until her death in 1961. At first the Chaplain's Office funded a part-time director of a new woman's center. Named for Sarah Doyle, the center opened in the house across from Pembroke Hall that had been the location of the Pembroke Alumnae Association before the merger. Eventually the university appointed a full-time director. A fund-raising drive led by Ruth Harris Wolf, Class of 1941, established the Nancy Duke Lewis Chair for a woman professor.

Until the 1960s it was entirely possible for a woman undergraduate to complete her Brown degree without ever studying under a woman professor, making it difficult for any woman to picture herself in that role. The funds raised for the Nancy Duke Lewis Chair brought visiting women faculty to campus or supported existing faculty in the 1970s, although the chair was not fully funded until 1983. In 1980 Joan Wallach Scott became the first Nancy Duke Lewis professor to come as a tenured professor from the outside. With Elizabeth Weed, then director of the Sarah Doyle Women's Center, Scott raised funds from private foundations to establish the Pembroke Center for Teaching and Research on Women in 1981. That year the women's studies major was also developed. Two years later, the Center added an advisory board, the Pembroke Center Associates Council, made up of alumnae. The Christine Dunlap Farnham Archives, devoted to the history of women at Brown and in Rhode Island, was organized in 1984 after the death of Christine Dunlap Farnham, Class of 1948, the first chairperson of the Pembroke Center Associates Council.[13]

In 1977 the class action suit filed on behalf of the women faculty by Louise Lamphere, an anthropology professor who was denied tenure at Brown, resulted in the signing of an agreement, called the consent decree, between the university and the women faculty members named in her suit. The numbers of women in each department on the Brown faculty were to be increased until they approximated the availability of women in that discipline for positions, a number connected to the proportion of women holding Ph.D. degrees in that field. With the signing of the agreement, it became virtually impossible for any woman student to graduate from Brown without having studied under a woman professor.[14]

The Present and the Future

As women continue to probe society for the underlying causes behind unequal opportunity, their search for equity at Brown and similar institutions will continue. In the past decade, women undergraduates have focused attention on a double standard that they perceive still exists between men and women students and between women students and some male faculty. Although there has been steady improvement since the 1970s, women still find an inequity in the allocation of resources to women in athletics and financial aid.[15] In an effort to analyze the roots of inequality, half of the women members of the Class of 1990 took at least one women's studies course while they were at Brown. The number of women on the faculty continues to rise, but faculty women believe the situation will need continual monitoring as soon as the court vacates the consent decree. Although six of the fourteen elected alumnae/i trustees are women, some alumnae have noticed that women's total representation on the Brown Corporation of one quarter has remained stationary for more than a decade during the time that the proportion of women in the alumni body has risen to 36.5 percent.

Sarah Doyle's daughters, who in 1991 include 18,780 living alumnae, have more than met her expectations. The final two essays in this collection only begin to document the contribution of Brown alumnae to society. Brown women graduates are confronting some of society's toughest problems. Nearly eight hundred alumnae are serving as physicians, with a similar number working in the legal profession. Fifty have been ordained as ministers or rabbis. Both students and alumnae volunteer to help AIDS patients. Alumnae are working on such environmental issues as the protection of endangered species. Through community action, they have changed laws to provide for the education of children with special needs and to strengthen gun control. Brown women are well represented in the arts, education, journalism, and business.

Alumnae also serve the university, dispelling the fear that women would not contribute to maintaining the university's financial well-being. Women trustees hold positions on the important Advisory and Executive Committee. Both the outgoing and incoming presidents of the Associated Alumni are women. Since 1972, when Doris Hopkins Stapelton, Class of 1928, became the first woman to receive a Brown Bear for sustained outstanding service to the university, the Associated Alumni has awarded twenty-one of the fifty-seven Brown Bears to women. Women have served as chairs of the Brown Annual Fund in four of the past ten years.[16] Alumnae are also helping to build the future student body. In a survey of women in the classes with reunions in 1990, a majority of respondents graduating since 1950 who volunteer for Brown listed as their major activity the National Alumni Schools Program in which they interview and introduce prospective students to Brown.

Brown alumnae recognize the contribution Brown has made to their lives as well. When the women who were surveyed were asked to name the turning points in their life paths, it was attending Brown that ranked at the top of the list. The investment in the future made by Rhode Island clubwomen one hundred years ago when they facilitated the entrance of women into Brown is of incalculable value today. Both Brown and the broader society have profited enormously as a result.

NOTES

Special acknowledgements to the Class of 1958 whose gift of a revolving fund to be used for Brown publications made this book possible. The editorial support for the entire project of the following people is gratefully acknowledged: Ruth Burt Ekstrom, Class of 1953; the Christine Dunlap Farnham Archives Committee consisting of Sophie Schaffer Blistein, Class of 1941; Doris Hopkins Stapelton, Class of 1928; Mary Holburn, Class of 1950; and Teresa Gagnon Mellone, Class of 1939; the staff of the Pembroke Center for Teaching and Research on Women including Barbara Anton, Elizabeth Weed, Elizabeth Barboza, and Karen Newman; Karen Lamoree, former Christine Dunlap Farnham archivist; Martha Mitchell and Gayle Lynch, Brown University Archives; Christine C. Love, Class of 1970, director of alumni relations; Robert Reichley, executive vice president; Professors Mari Jo Buhle and Maurice Glicksman; Dean Karen Romer; Associate Director of Athletics Arlene Gorton, Class of 1952; Rebecca Wakefield, faculty statistician; and Marjorie B. Houston, assistant secretary of the corporation.

    1. The women are: Sheila Blumstein, dean of The College; Merrily Taylor, university librarian; Janet Cooper Nelson, chaplain; Katherine P. Hall, registrar; Beverly Ledbetter, university counsel; Christine C. Love, Class of 1970, director of alumni relations; and Marie J. Langlois, Class of 1964, treasurer of Brown University.

    2. As president of the Alumnae Association in 1927, Nettie Goodale Murdock, Class of 1895, had recommended that the alumnae ask to be represented on the Board of Trustees in 1927. Almost forty years later, her niece, Elizabeth Goodale Kenyon, Class of 1939, was elected as the first alumnae trustee.

    3. Michele N-K Collison, "20 Years Later, Women on Formerly All-Male Campuses Fight to Change Their Institutions' 'Old Boy' Images," *The Chronicle of Higher Education,*

12 December 1990, pp. A23–24.

4. Walter C. Bronson, *The History of Brown University, 1764–1914* (Providence: Brown University, 1914), pp. 454, 485. Enrollment figures from 1928–1987 are taken from a compilation by Louise Newman from Brown University annual catalogs.

5. Three women applied for entrance into Brown in 1871 and another in 1874. Bronson, *The History of Brown University*, pp. 1, 450–51.

6. Ibid., pp. 428, 454, 485; *Historical Catalogue of Brown University* (Providence: Brown University, 1950). See also Chapter 5 of this book.

7. Women were accepted at Wesleyan again in 1970. David Potts, *An Earnest Enterprise: Wesleyan University, 1831–1910* (New Haven: Yale University Press, forthcoming), Chapters 4 and 6; Gertrude E. Noyes, *History of Connecticut College* (New London: Connecticut College, 1982), pp. 9–13, 178.

8. For two classic statements of the fear that feminization would drive men away from the study of liberal arts, see the address of Charles R. Van Hise, president of the University of Wisconsin, before the Association of Collegiate Alumnae [now the American Association of University Women] in Boston, 6 November 1907, published in the *Educational Review* 34 (December 1947): 504–20, and Frederick W. Hamilton, president of Tufts College, in "Co-education," *Journal of Education* 66 (7 November 1907): 485–86. See also Barbara Miller Solomon, *In the Company of Educated Women* (New Haven: Yale University Press, 1985), pp. 58–61; Lynn D. Gordon, *Gender and Higher Education in the Progressive Era* (New Haven: Yale University Press, 1990), pp. 43–44.

9. Grace E. Hawk, *Pembroke College in Brown University, the First Seventy-Five Years, 1891–1966* (Providence: Brown University Press, 1967).

10. The founder of Pembroke College, Cambridge University, England, was Mary de St. Pol, wife of Aymer de Valence, Earl of Pembroke. Hawk, *Pembroke College*, pp. 27, 275.

11. The frieze, sculpted by H.L. Hubert, is in two classrooms on the second floor of Pembroke Hall. Female representations include the muses, genius, agriculture, medicine, engineering, navigation, crafts, law, and commerce. See clippings on the dedication of Pembroke Hall in the Rhode Island Society for the Collegiate Education of Women folders, Christine Dunlap Farnham Archives, Brown University. In later years, the society was affectionately referred to as "the society with the long name."

For a similar drive a few years later by clubwomen to raise funds to allow women to enter the University of Rochester, see Gordon, *Gender and Higher Education*, p. 24.

12. Dr. Edward H. Clark started the controversy when he published *Sex in Education: or, A Fair Chance for the Girls* in 1873 [reprint edition, Arno Press, 1972] to document cases of college women whose reproductive organs became inoperative because of required studies and the tensions of college life. He was immediately refuted in a series of essays edited by Julia Ward Howe in 1874, *Sex and Education, a Reply to Dr. E.H. Clark* ... [reprint edition. Arno Press, 1972]. Coupled with the fact that only 50 percent of the first generation of college women bore children, Clark's thesis gave women educators much resistence to overcome.

13. A research guide to the Farnham Archives was published in 1989: Karen M. Lamoree, *Research Guide to the Christine Dunlap Farnham Archives* (Providence, Brown University, 1989). For the importance of women's centers and women's studies as an approach to transforming the college curriculum in order to provide equal experiences for all students, see the following articles in Carol S. Pearson, Dona L. Shavlik, and Judith G. Touchton, *Educating the Majority: Women Challenge Tradition in Higher Education* (New York: Collier Macmillan, 1989): Peggy Means McIntosh, "Curricular Re-Vision: The New Knowledge for a New Age," pp. 400–13, and Jane S. Gould, "Women's Centers as Agents of Change," pp. 219–230.

14. For comparative data on the progress of women on college faculties, see "Faculty Women: Preparation, Participation, and Progress" in Mariam K. Chamberlain, ed., *Women in Academe: Progress and Prospects* (New York: Russell Sage Foundation, 1988), pp. 255–73.

15. Between 1975 and 1980, undergraduate women received 35 to 40 percent of financial aid given to Brown students from both the university and outside sources. In 1988–89 and 1989–90, women received 42 percent of the money allocated for university scholarships. Kate Garrett and Jane Hitti, *Piecework: Women's Lives at Brown,* Sarah Doyle Women's Center, 1982, p. 69; recent years supplied by the Brown Financial Aid Office.

For an analysis of some of the ways college women are treated and respond differently from college men in campus and classroom settings, see "The College Experience," in Chamberlain, *Women in Academe,* pp. 15–33, and "Reconceptualizing the Way We Think and Teach" in Pearson, *Educating the Majority,* pp. 265–361. See also the example of Brown professor Anne Fausto-Sterling and graduate student Lydia L. English in "Women and Minorities in Science: An Interdisciplinary Course," *Radical Teacher* 30 (Spring 1985): 16–20.

16. Anne Jones Mills, Class of 1960, is the outgoing president of the Associated Alumni and Gail E. McCann, Class of 1975, the incoming president. The women who served as chairs of the Brown Fund were Norma Caslowitz Munves, Class of 1954; Claire J. Henderson, Class of 1961; and serving two terms: Marie J. Langlois, Class of 1964.

INSET: Sarah E. Doyle, founder of the
Rhode Island Society for the Collegiate
Education of Women, the women's club
whose fund raising assured the establishment of the Women's College.
The first page of the account book for
the Rhode Island Society's successful
campaign to build Pembroke Hall.

Rhode Island Society for the Collegiate Education of Women.

The Women's College Fund Committee
became incorporated Sept. 18. 1896 under the name
of the Rhode Island Society for the Collegiate Education
of Women, Sarah E. Doyle President, Louise Prosser
Corresponding Secretary and Amelia S. Knight Treasurer
The accounts of the Women's College Fund
balance of $15796.51 was transferred
account of the Rhode Island Society
Collegiate Education of Women

Amelia S. Knight Treas.

The balance of 15796.51 noted
above is composed of the following
items which are fitted in the
ledger.

Diman Memorial Fund
Collegiate Alumnae Fund
Interest
R.I. Women's Club Fund
General Subscriptions

Paid for sundry expenses

CHAPTER I

The Women's Club Movement Creates and Defines the Women's College

by KAREN J. BLAIR

THE CASUAL OBSERVER of the Providence city skyline on November 22, 1897, would have noted the impressive church spires, State House dome, factory smokestacks, and the buildings of Brown University on top of College Hill which bespoke the strength, ambition, and success of Rhode Island's forefathers. The prominent position of University Hall at the crest of College Hill symbolized more than a century and a quarter of higher education for men in Providence. It was connected by College Street to the bottom of the hill and the First Baptist Meeting House whose parishioners had founded Brown in 1764. Less readily identifiable would have been a three-story brick structure on Meeting Street between Brown and Thayer Streets on the periphery of the Brown campus. Nevertheless, an impressive crowd of individuals, many of them women, gathered there on that cold autumn day to dedicate Pembroke Hall, the first official home of the Women's College at Brown University. The celebration marked the official recognition of the Women's College of Brown University and signaled the beginning of an important era of higher learning for the bright young women of the state and beyond.

Just as surely, however, did the event represent the culmination of a generation of cooperative effort among the state's women, united in all-women's societies and clubs, to ensure a place for women within Rhode Island's most distinguished educational institution. The tenacity, ingenuity, and idealism of the clubwomen, as evidenced by the admission of women to the college, was every bit as hearty as that of the industrialists, legislators, clergymen, and professors who had made their mark on the urban landscape. When Providence educator and clubwoman Sarah E. Doyle handed over to Brown University President E. Benjamin Andrews the keys to Pembroke Hall, the city's associated womanhood knew they had achieved the dream of their lifetimes, the establishment of an institutional haven for the development of young women's minds, a resource to steer the twentieth century. As the delighted young beneficiaries declared at the time, "It was as though the gates of Heaven had opened to us."[1]

How distant this event must have seemed, four years before, when the first women students, only a half dozen in number, actually appeared to begin instruction under the aegis of the university. Thanks to the new and enlightened administration of President Andrews, women were first permitted to take the same examinations that Brown offered to its male enrollees in the fall of 1891. Nettie Serena Goodale of Pawtucket High School and Elizabeth Rowena Peckham, valedictorian from Bristol High School, arrived on October 1, 1891, at the University Grammar School, near campus, to review the course work in French with Professor Asa Clinton Crowell, in order to prepare for the test.[2] Andrews had prepared for this moment in advance by plucking able Rhode Island high school students from the ranks and alerting them about the possibility of admission. When he addressed the graduation at Bristol High School in the spring of 1891, he became impressed with fifteen-year-old valedictorian Elizabeth Peckham. He invited her and her mother to his home to discuss the likelihood of women at Brown and alerted her to be prepared for instruction.[3]

In the afternoon of the first day of study, Goodale and Peckham were joined by four ambitious pupils: Mary E. Woolley, Clara E. Comstock, Maude A. Bonner, and Anne T. Weeden. These pioneering women were confined to study with sympathetic professors of Greek (Charles Edwin Bennett), math (Henry Parker Manning), French (Asa Clinton Crowell), and Latin (Walter Goodnow Everett, who would marry Clara Comstock). These cooperative professors had accepted the president's invitation to duplicate their regular instruction for the women for the grand sum of seventy-five cents an hour. Barred from the regular university classrooms, they met in make-shift settings, at first in rooms of the University Grammar School, which was lit only by natural light. When October's early nightfall inhibited the afternoon exercises, President Andrews permitted them to adjourn to his office in University Hall. The new year found the women meeting in the state normal school building. When that grew unsatisfactory, the women studied at 235 Benefit Street until Pembroke Hall, their own brand-new building, was ready in 1897.

Thus, in 1895, a handful of powerful Rhode Island women, with President Sarah Doyle at the helm, appealed to the state of Rhode Island to incorporate a new women's league – the Rhode Island Society for the Collegiate Education of Women (RISCEW). By tapping the financial resources of Rhode Island women enrolled in women's clubs, RISCEW would raise the money to erect the building on property donated by Brown University. The members would direct architect Alfred Stone to design a structure for recitations, a library, and gatherings of college personnel, surrender it to the university, and then continue to serve as "godmothers" to the women students and their deans by providing them with basic services, niceties, inspiration, and new campus facilities. This they would do for six decades, with their responsibilities diminishing as they transferred their power to the growing body of alumnae of the college they helped to create. When the Women's College, renamed Pembroke College in 1928, was collapsed into Brown University in 1971, RISCEW disbanded itself. The story of the admission of women to Brown, signaled by RISCEW's erection of Pembroke Hall, is the story of the strength of the women's network in the city of Providence, which reached throughout the state to make a place for women in higher learning. The values of this network, particularly of its flagship, the Rhode Island Woman's Club, would be transferred to the women students of the new college.

To those determined to increase women's educational advantages, it became clear quickly that haphazard facilities were unsatisfactory to meet the needs of the growing number of Rhode Island's daughters prepared for higher education. A structure was needed, yet the corporation which governed Brown University was unwilling to make the financial and educational commitment to erect a structure befitting the new intellectual paths the young women were to forge. The need for a permanent place to launch women's education at Brown was met by the same women who had attempted to pressure the Brown Corporation's members, for decades, to allow women to share higher education with Brown men. The women, allied in women's societies and associations, under the capable leadership of clubwoman and high school educator Sarah E. Doyle, rose to solve the dilemma and fund a facility for women which Brown University would accept, and thereby officially sanction the permanent presence of women on campus.

The Training of a Leader

Who was the dynamic leader who could wrest thousands of dollars from Rhode Island women in the space of two and a half years, plan and supervise the building of the hall that would ensure a place for women at Brown University, welcome students to occupy their very own center, and steer an association which would carefully nurture women at Brown until their place in the university was secure? Undoubtedly there were those who referred to Sarah Elizabeth Doyle as the mayor's sister. Certainly Thomas Arthur Doyle was Sarah's older brother and he directed City Hall in Providence from 1864 until his death in 1884, except for the years he served as a senator in Rhode Island's General Assembly. Such an association, however, underestimates the two careers which Sarah Doyle built for herself. Sarah was both a leading educator for forty-six years and also the premier clubwoman of Rhode Island for the same space of time. Her talents played no small role in building alliances among the late nineteenth century women of Providence and leading them to demand a place for young women at Brown.

Sarah E. Doyle was born in Providence, the third of seven children of bookbinder Thomas Doyle and Martha Dorrance Jones Doyle, on March 25, 1830. She attended local primary schools, including the Elm Street Grammar School, and entered the Girls' Department of Providence High School in its first year, 1843. She was graduated three years later. The woman most responsible for the admission of women to Brown University never attended college herself. Instead, she began a career, over four and a half decades long, of teaching girls, first in private schools, and, beginning in 1856, in her alma mater. She served as principal of the Girls' Department from 1872 until her retirement, at the age of sixty-four, in 1892. So devoted were her pupils to her that when they decided in 1894 to form a club of Providence school teachers "for mutual assistance and culture of its members, especially in the line of their professional work," they called it the Sarah E. Doyle Club and raised one thousand dollars annually for her pet project, scholarships for young women at Brown. They also commissioned a portrait of her by one of the most renowned woman painters in America at the time, Cecilia Beaux.[4] Doyle's devotion to her students, lovingly reciprocated, signals her talent at nurturing the best in the women around her.

Busy as she was with her career as a teacher and administrator, Doyle's biography would be half written and omit the source of her and her club sisters' strength if it ignored her other passion, the work of women's voluntary associations. She had her hand in a staggering number of them, not as a casual participant but as a leader. In so doing, she shaped her own philosophy of life and instilled her own values into the budding Woman Movement of Rhode Island.

Doyle joined the Rhode Island Woman Suffrage Association shortly after its founding in 1868, thereby labeling herself as a strong-minded woman, committed to the political equality of women in an era which still dismissed the members of the female sex as second class citizens. She also endorsed the award of $1,500, left over in 1877 from Rhode Island's Woman's Centennial Committee, to help found the coeducational Rhode Island School of Design (RISD). Doyle, a charter member of RISD, served as its secretary for twenty-two years, from 1877 to 1899. This role points out her high regard for the cultivation of beauty in the Victorian era and her support for training women to enjoy self-support by designing tasteful objects for daily use in American homes.

Doyle pressed, too, for women educators to win clout within their professional associations once they had entered careers, and in 1884 was the first woman to preside over a session at a meeting of the National Education Association, a forum she continued to use to press for women's educational advancement. Likewise, she participated in the Woman's Group of the Naples Table for zoological studies when it met at Vassar College. A church woman, she took on the presidency of the National Alliance of Unitarian and other Liberal Christian Women at the First Congregational Church in Providence in the early 1890s.[5] Not insignificantly, she also founded and volunteered generously in the work of the Rhode Island Woman's Club and the Rhode Island State Federation of Women's Clubs, in addition to RISCEW.

Sarah Doyle formed an ideology about women's changing roles in late nineteenth century America, developing it out of her experience and observation. It came to be shared by most of her sisters in women's clubs. While the society in which she lived revered women for their domestic and maternal roles, and perpetuated political, economic, and social inequities to maintain them, Doyle believed that women were capable of transcending those constraints to shape a full life of independence. Her vision included women's self-support, holding useful public lives, exercising trained minds, solving problems creatively, devising efficient work habits, applying humane values to social problems, and engaging in public activism to improve an unjust world. Doyle insisted that a woman alone could not marshal the necessary forces to defy social expectations and overturn the limits on her ambitions. Women needed to cooperate with like-minded sisters, in schools, in associations, or at the workplace, to achieve the skills, confidence, and power to press American institutions to change to incorporate women's full participation in the world outside the home.

Doyle and most other nineteenth century advocates of the Woman

Movement felt, however, that although they wanted women to enjoy all the advantages that men had, they expected women to spend them differently. She believed that men and women were not and should not be equal. She was not so conservative as to advocate the traditional lot of household drudgery. In fact, she lobbied to assist women in learning to dispatch domestic tasks with greater efficiency. But she did share the widely-held societal notion that women were more intuitive, virtuous, loving, and sensitive than men and less competitive and aggressive. She expected that women's vision of a harmonious, gentle world, if institutionalized, could temper men's acquisitory and individualistic approach to life and create a more balanced, humane society, one which served the have-nots as well as the successful entrepreneurs and professional men.

Although the schools and clubs women had developed separate from men's arose because of women's exclusion by men, women sought to praise and protect the differences between the sexes perpetuated by the separate spheres. The clubwomen, then, should not desire admission to men's institutions, where their special gifts would be ignored, trivialized, or trampled, and their access to leadership roles would be squelched. Instead of pressing for entrance into the men-only Hope Club, Union Club, or University Club, they should create their own clubs, where women defined the goals, ran for office, and learned how to speak in public, organize committees, launch fund-raising campaigns, publish newsletters, issue press releases, and, in short, to take charge of their own affairs.

Neither did Doyle nor her constituency idealize coeducation in high schools and colleges. They championed "coordinate" education instead, whereby women and men shared the same curriculum, professors, and campus, but resided, studied, and socialized separately. This guaranteed two oftentimes contradictory impulses – the vitality of the differences between men and women while, at the same time, maximizing women's access to skills and intellectual experiences heretofore monopolized by men and denied to the "fair" sex. Doyle herself embodied this dichotomy. She dispensed her administrative authority with the confidence of one comfortable with power. Her demeanor was described by Mary E. Woolley, who attended the Girls' Department at Providence High School under Doyle's principalship and who herself would become a leader in women's higher education. Doyle, she said, had acquired "a manner so direct as to seem almost brusque" and had acquired the confidence, strength, fearlessness, and power more commonly displayed by the men of her generation. On the other hand, Doyle's fairness and gentleness, her willingness to share all she knew, to nurture the women around her, and dedicate herself to human service "with integrity like the rock of Gibraltar" won her the life-long admiration and even devotion of the "daughters" her position permitted her to influence both in school and in women's clubs.[6]

The Founding of a Club for Rhode Island Women

Perhaps the women's club on which Doyle had the greatest impact was the Rhode Island Woman's Club of Providence, of which she was a founder in 1876 and president for its first eight years. The club, which continues to meet, began when six women gathered at the home of Elizabeth Kittredge Churchill to establish Providence's first "social and intellectual centre where ladies of the most varying tastes could find congenial companionship."[7] The other founders included Fanny Purdy Palmer and Sarah Dean, although Mary E. Eddy and Mrs. Louis J. Doyle signed on quickly.[8] These women sought to create an institution which would permit them to study and discuss topics women had not generally considered before. So unbecoming was this occupation to a world which expected women to devote themselves single-mindedly to domestic responsibilities, that the club was unflatteringly nicknamed "The Society for the Prevention of Domestic Industry." Yet so popular was the plan that almost one hundred women, middle-class, white, and Protestant, had signed on within the first year.

The members tended to be of two types. One third were career women, generally unmarried educators. The others were wives of the city's business, professional, and political leaders, living in comfortable neighborhoods, enjoying sufficient assistance with domestic responsibilities to permit a pastime of clublife. They were generally mothers whose children were grown, leaving them free to devote twenty afternoons a year, between the months of October and June, to the examination of eight designated subject areas – art, literature, music, science, education, politics, sociology, and domestic economy. The career women were often teachers, like Doyle, although Fanny Purdy Palmer, Elizabeth Churchill, and Anna Garlin Spencer published several books during their lifetimes and Spencer became the first woman minister in Rhode Island.[9]

Both the wage-earning and non-wage-earning members had made peace with defying the traditional assumption that "woman's place is in the home," to devote their spare time to shaping urban institutions to build a more humane and just municipality. Many members did not confine their organizational activity to the Rhode Island Woman's Club. Churchill and Palmer were active in the Rhode Island Woman Suffrage Association and Women's Educational and Industrial Union of Providence.[10] Former abolitionist Elizabeth Buffum Chace and her daughters, Mary and Lillie

(Elizabeth), also active suffragists, resigned from the Rhode Island Woman's Club early on, when its members decided not to admit Black women to the membership.[11]

In many ways the Rhode Island Woman's Club served as a vehicle to provide its membership with the skills they would have acquired in college had an institution of higher learning been available to them. Furthermore, the club curriculum acquainted its "students" with the major contributions that their sex had made to civilization, a concept which today forms a significant component of women's studies programs. From its beginning, the club members demonstrated their commitment to using the Rhode Island Woman's Club as a forum to strengthen the opportunities for women in their world and for their own self-education and self-development. They demanded that each member take her turn in researching, writing, and delivering a paper on an assigned topic, either before the general membership or in a subsection devoted to a particular special-interest topic. Everyone shared responsibility for engaging in serious discussion of the matter at hand. In addition, the club offered hands-on experience in holding office, working on committees, and using parliamentary procedure. At the first anniversary celebration, the club secretary boasted that "the ladies speak more readily, and with great animation and confidence" and that this was achieved because "timid persons learned to discuss questions before a few, and, in time, gained self-possession, which enabled them to do the same before the club."[12]

Insofar as possible, the membership honored creative women of their day, inviting them to come to the meetings to present their ideas.[13] Sometimes they invited illustrious women from Boston or even farther afield to speak before the club, but the RIWC prided itself on how infrequently it turned to men to entertain the assemblage, although they did hire a Brown University professor to instruct the interested clubwomen in botany.[14] The subject matter the women addressed also illustrates their commitment to present women's past, present, and future contributions to society, as when they discussed such individual political figures as Charlotte Corday and Isabela of Castile, writers Elizabeth Barrett Browning and George Eliot, as well as the education of Hindu women, suffrage, the relation of women to business, the industrial education of women, and prostitution.

The club also assumed a leading role in inspiring the women outside the membership to take strength from the role models everywhere in America who were stretching the definitions of acceptable behavior for nineteenth century women. Only three months after the founding of the Rhode Island Woman's Club, the members extended an ambitious hospitality in inviting the Executive Committee of a fairly new and forward-looking women's organization to confer at their club. The Association for the Advancement of Women, founded in 1873, brought several leading women reformers to Rhode Island to plan their annual convention.[15] Rhode Island Woman's Club members attempted a still grander effort in 1878 when they hosted the annual conference of the organization. This enabled women and girls of Providence and the vicinity to attend several days of presentations by numerous singular women. Among the speakers who heralded women's abilities were astronomer and Vassar science professor Maria Mitchell, syndicated journalist Martha Lowe, New York clubwoman Jane Cunningham Croly, educator Anna Brackett, and anthropologist Alice Fletcher, all providing thoughtful remarks on the importance of women's involvement in affairs outside the home.[16]

Unwilling to selfishly monopolize the joy of learning, the members very quickly devoted themselves to bringing learning to the wider community. They went to the public schools to urge the decoration of classrooms with reproductions of paintings by old Masters from the European tradition. They also supported the creation of traveling libraries to reach teachers, children, prisoners, residents of state asylums, and all of Rhode Island's citizens who desired access to materials on health or domestic science, for example, by donating books, magazines, and scrapbooks to a volunteer-run system.[17] The club library activity required wide cooperation among clubwomen, steady funding by them, and bridge-building with governmental and educational agencies and institutions. It paved the way for the clubwomen's ability to play a key role in providing higher education for women at Brown University. But first the RIWC would need to become part of a broad network of other Rhode Island women who emulated the RIWC by founding similar groups, many of them devoted to the same principles and goals.

In an effort to enhance the nurturing of club women's talents, members perceived that a homey clubhouse, planned, owned, decorated, and maintained by the members, would provide a warm environment for the cultivation of women. Members yearned for such a place immediately after the club began.[18] Such an atmosphere was a long time in coming, however. The Rhode Island Woman's Club changed its residence seven times before the members were able to erect a place of their own. The women moved into Churchill House on George Street next to the Brown campus in October 1906, thirty years after the club's founding, having committed themselves to providing a permanent space for Brown University women first.

The Rhode Island Woman's Club was a forerunner in the explosion of women's clubs at the turn of the century. It was the building of a network among them that assured the success of their goal to install women at Brown University. In a list compiled for the World's Columbian Exposition of 1893 in Chicago, over one hundred organizations were catalogued, attesting to women's enthusiasm to meet with one another to accomplish social reform in a sociable environment. In Providence alone, women had founded an impressive range of literary and civic reform societies,[19] in addition to those devoted to suffrage, music study, patriotic activity, academy and normal school alumnae associations, temperance, church and missionary work, charitable and philanthropic efforts, working girls' welfare, and the Young Women's Christian Association. Throughout Rhode Island, the story was the same, encompassing such varied causes as Indian aid, cycling, a home for aged colored women, and the Watchemoket Free Public Library.[20]

Having learned within each club the value of pooling assets – financial, creative, intellectual – to create a force to bring about change for women, the club members came to view broader and broader federations of women's clubs as a logical, indeed necessary, culmination of their drive to amass the clout to effect the social changes they had prescribed as a result of their study of American life, including opportunities for the formal higher education of women. Thus, thirty-two Rhode Island clubs allied themselves with the National and later the International Council of Women, an organization founded in 1888 to link women "along all lines of social, intellectual, moral or civic progress and reform." Not only did the Council of Women create a link between Rhode Island clubwomen and their sisters around the world, but it also facilitated cooperation between the Rhode Island women in their home state. Thirty-two women's organizations, including those devoted to suffrage, temperance, and others meeting societal needs, embarked on an alliance to further their progressive beliefs.

The following year, the RIWC delegated Sarah Doyle to go to New York City to attend the conference which would precipitate the formation of still another giant women's federation. The General Federation of Women's Clubs, an alliance of women's culture and civic reform associations, which would grow to a force of nearly one million clubwomen by the mid-1920s, formed to provide a staggering advocacy force for social reform.[21] At its 1889 meeting, Doyle agreed to serve on the committee which drafted the organization's constitution.[22] The federation's emphasis on solving social problems through voluntary efforts would widen the scope of Rhode Island club activities.

In February 1895, when seven Rhode Island women's clubs, including the RIWC and the Sarah E. Doyle Club, banded together to form a Rhode Island State Federation of Women's Clubs, the local counterpart to the nation-wide General Federation of Women's Clubs, the alliance gave further impetus to address the concerns of all members of society. By the turn of the century, the Rhode Island federation had grown to contain seventeen clubs, representing 1,414 members. The act of moving several women's clubs, representing thousands of members, in concert, polarized a network essential for the realization of the clubwomen's plan to allow women access to a Brown University education.

Far from abandoning the early commitment to women and to education, the "university for middle-aged women," as clubs were sometimes called, now had acquired vast experience in bringing social institutions around to absorbing women's demands. Club life turned out also to be a school of hard knocks and their routes toward municipal reform had prepared them to take on such institutions as the university. Rhode Island clubwomen, denied a college education themselves, were following with excitement the surge of acceptances by women into more and more experiments in higher education during the 1880s. Not only had Bryn Mawr College recently opened to provide rigorous academic opportunities for women of Pennsylvania and Mount Holyoke College been transformed into a woman's college from a seminary, but in New York City Barnard College for women was established in 1889 in association with Columbia University. In Cambridge, Massachusetts, women studying at the Harvard University Annex saw a charter create Radcliffe in 1894. They observed that thirty Rhode Island women, desiring an education beyond the two-year teaching preparation which Rhode Island Normal School offered, left the state to study at the new women's colleges.[23]

Clubwomen Call for the Admission of Women to Brown

Now clubwomen in Rhode Island were prepared to call for the advantages of higher education for women in their state. Certainly regional pride should move local boosters to action, to provide advanced study for the Ocean State's women. The clubs, secure by now with their power, launched a campaign to persuade the corporation which administered Brown University to make a place for women. Their array of tactics was stunning. First, they considered the idea among themselves. The Rhode Island Woman Suffrage Association, for example, in 1881, invited Helen MacGill, the first woman to receive a Ph.D. in America, to speak before the membership on her post-doctoral experiences as a student enrolled at Cambridge University in England. Hers was probably the first public call in Providence for the admission of women on equal terms with men.[24]

In 1885, a deputation of ladies visited Brown University President Ezekial G. Robinson to impress upon him the desire of Providence women to have women enter Brown.[25] Next, the members of the RIWC invited Robinson to appear before the club to sound him out on his commitment to women's education. In addition, Professor Elisha Benjamin Andrews and his wife, Ella A., a woman devoted to Providence's Free Kindergarten Association who served as its president, soon to be the president and first lady of Brown, were also entertained by the club and quizzed about their attitudes toward women at Brown. Trustees of Brown, including Arnold B. Chace, also discussed the matter with the assembled members of the Rhode Island Woman's Club. In order to build a record that there was interest among Rhode Island's brightest women in obtaining a Brown education, Sarah Doyle advised her prize pupil, Alice D. Mumford, to apply for admission to Brown. Mumford, like other women before her, met rejection, but served to build a record that women desired the educational opportunities offered by the university and were qualified to do so.[26]

Not only did the clubwomen use personal interchange to pressure for admission of women to Brown, they also used financial leverage. Taking a memorial fund which had been established in 1881 to commemorate the service of Rhode Island Woman's Club founder Elizabeth Kittredge Churchill, the club initiated a $1,500 scholarship for women "should they be admitted to Brown." Individuals like Elizabeth Buffum Chace pressured her husband, Arnold B. Chace, a member of the Brown Corporation, to permit women to obtain a higher education in Rhode Island, and saw the support of several Quaker members surface, including that of Richard M. Atwater, poet John Greenleaf Whittier, Albert K. Smiley, and George Howland.[27] Some other members, non-Quakers, also asserted their approval for women at Brown. These included Alvah Hovey, William E. Lincoln, John C. Sockbridge, and Thatcher Thayer.[28]

Despite their polite but steady pressure under the Robinson presidency, clubwomen saw only slow movement on the question of women at Brown. Even with the oft-quoted support of Whittier who urged the admission of women to Brown as a matter "of simple justice" in 1881, no change was in the offing. In discussions among corporation members of the late 1880s, enthusiasts did not overcome the naysayers. If Robinson admitted that Rhode Island women preparing to be teachers expected their universities to save them the expense of studying out of state, he still rejected the idea, on the grounds of the danger of mixing young men and women at an "inflammable age" and because of the financial burden a woman's program would create.

In 1887, the corporation seemed to step forward by endorsing the idea of accepting women, but only if a donation of $150,000 were made to meet the necessary costs. This figure, prohibitively high, would be exposed as a widely inflated estimate for serving women's educational needs when clubwomen provided facilities for women for a fraction of the cost. The financial stipulations would be abandoned with new administrative leadership. Robinson, finally impressed with the system for women's education which he observed at Cornell University, simply admitted, "In a general way I am in favor of it, but at my age I do not wish to undertake it."[29]

With the accession of President Andrews to the Brown University presidency in 1889, the clubwomen hoped for a more sympathetic ear. Andrews seemed to be a braver supporter of women's education. As soon as he took the reins, twelve women met at the home of Mrs. J.J. Fry to formulate plans to impress the administration with the seriousness of women's intention to see their daughters win access to university-level training. While no immediate results came of the meeting, Mrs. Fry later contributed considerable sums to Pembroke Hall and left two thousand dollars to the Women's College in her will.[30] Andrews had inherited, however, a corporation, faculty, alumni, and student body ambivalent about taking on the financial and moral support of a women's college coordinated with Brown. The male students, debating the question in the student newspaper throughout the 1880s, had anticipated and criticized the women who "would turn half-masculine because they have been trained like men." They heralded the "colleges of our grade" which "have all set their faces against the admission of women," and insisted that "a modest young woman" would prefer an all-women's college, like Wellesley or Smith. They also feared the distraction that young women would bring to campus. "If I met on the campus and in recitation and in society, the right kind of girls – the womanly, tender, emotional kind – I am afraid I might get interested in something besides study."[31] Professors echoed the same reservations. Dr. Edmund B. Delabarre remembered that "none of the faculty with whom he came into contact had any great enthusiasm for the admission of women to the classes of the University."[32]

The alumni, too, addressed the question and provoked many reservations about the desirability of women on campus. When the class of 1880, at a ten-year reunion, polled its members, Zechariah Chafee reported that only four alumni in his class approved the admission of women on an

An unfinished Pembroke Hall provides a backdrop for the Women's College Class of 1900.

equal basis with men. Still, he suspected that a woman's annex, with a
modified curriculum, "better suited to the needs of women rather than
identical to that studied by the men," might pass muster with his classmates.[33] The corporation, like the alumni, was hardly unanimous in its
support.

President Andrews Lends Support

Even though President Andrews would take some tentative steps to open
Brown's doors to women, it was not until he joined the Rhode Island
clubwomen that any permanent success could be achieved. They had the
will and the skills to bankroll an actual facility for women to launch their
entry into higher education. Before he called in the women, he took only
modest steps. In 1891, he allowed women to take the same entrance exams
and college exams as men with no reference to the question of providing
formal instruction or granting a Brown degree to the women who passed
the tests. Having passed the first hurdle with no major objections, Andrews
felt emboldened to permit women to prepare for the exams at Brown. He
invited professors who had the time and inclination to duplicate their
lessons after hours to teach the women enrollees for additional wages.
In June 1892, Andrews asserted that Brown would award a degree to a
woman who passed the exams, bestowing the university's special distinc-

tion on the capable women who passed, with or without professorial tutoring.[34] Rhode Island women had one foot in the door. Yet Andrews knew that only financial support would secure the permanent admission of women to Brown. He appealed to the public for a half million dollar donation to facilitate the abandonment of make-shift arrangements and to create a woman's coordinate college with Brown University. If he expected a rallying of Rhode Island's philanthropists, he was disappointed. His appeal sat, unmet.

When Andrews recognized the power the clubwomen could wield to bring about their desire for young women's educational advancement, he took his most effective step. With some trepidation, he gambled that a meeting of Providence clubwomen, under the direction of Sarah E. Doyle, would yield a mechanism to find the funds necessary to enable women to play a full part in Brown University. His wife Ella invited eighteen leading clubwomen of the state, many of them from the Rhode Island Woman's Club, to the Andrews home on January 31, 1895. Admonishing the four women students serving tea to "look and act their prettiest in order that the distinguished guests be well disposed toward the project,"[35] he breathed easier when the women decided to form still another women's organization. Called the Committee for the Women's College Fund, it was created for the specific purpose of tapping the women's network to raise funds to erect a woman's building on a piece of land Brown donated on Meeting Street. Only when a separate woman's classroom building was erected and paid for through private donations, would Brown accept the facility and the coordinate education of undergraduate women which it implied.

From Andrews' point of view, Doyle was the ideal person to lead the campaign to create the structure which would install women at Brown with permanency. Because she had just retired from her long career as an educator at Providence High School, she was free to devote herself to the project fully. She had invested a quarter century in public life and was the uncontested leader of the city's Woman Movement. She was not only in touch with the newest ideas but also was one of the most progressive-thinking individuals at the heart of the women's network. Finally, the university had just bestowed the highest honor on her which it had ever awarded to any woman. Brown's first honorary degree to a woman went to Doyle in 1894, in recognition of her long service to Rhode Island's women. Since no one was better connected with the forces likely to raise the money for a new institution of higher learning for women, Doyle was also the most likely candidate to arouse sympathy and dollars expeditiously to establish women at Brown.

As for Doyle, why would she be willing to devote her retirement years, ultimately twenty-five in number, to this project? It is likely that she consented to use her influence and numerous acquaintanceships for the cause of women's higher education because her own life's work had convinced her that this was the most useful culmination of her powers. In her decades of high school instruction, she had met a great many young women who had demonstrated capabilities and ambitions like those with which she had been endowed. But she and they had had to develop their talents without social sanction or institutional support. Now Doyle wished to provide a better, richer atmosphere for future generations of women.

Only rather late in life did Doyle and her women friends come to find a solution to the omissions and limits in women's lives. Only in women's clubs had women built for themselves a safe environment where they could drink in new knowledge, meet the greatest thinkers of the day, and learn to discuss ideas freely and unselfconsciously, by gaining the confidence, gradually, to speak up and build new structures for examining history, life and culture, including an appreciation of women's accomplishments. In clubs, women had come into contact with contradictory opinions they could come to respect. They were provided with a path that directed them toward occupations of value to themselves and others. All this they had accomplished in the company of other women of good character, serious intent, kind spirit, gracious demeanor, moral perspective, jovial attitude, and steady energy. But why should a woman have to wait half a lifetime to build her mind and character? Doyle wanted Providence's daughters to begin their lives with these advantages, to consolidate early a foundation from which to build a rich life, rather than cultivating their best qualities too far along in life to spend them generously. She knew that only an elect few could afford to leave Rhode Island for such opportunities. Because Doyle believed that a Brown education could do all this for women, she embarked on a new career, of using Brown University to launch a modern enlightened womanhood. To succeed, she used all the gifts she had developed.

A New Women's Club Funds Pembroke Hall

The group which Doyle steered to fund a new women's college at Brown University was renamed The Rhode Island Society for the Collegiate Education of Women (RISCEW) when its growing treasury warranted incorporation in September, 1896. RISCEW's membership consisted of several

Frieze of women personifying the fields of knowledge and the muses, given by the Rhode Island Society, adorned the first library in Pembroke Hall.

trustees, including Sarah E. Doyle and Mary E. Woolley, from the first graduating class, Anna Metcalf from the fourth graduating class, and Louise Prosser Bates who, in 1893, joined Lucia Clepp in being the first woman to receive an A.M. from Brown.[36] RISCEW had immediately gone about raising building funds from other clubwomen of Rhode Island, filling the record books of Treasurer Amelia Knight, who was also the president of the Rhode Island Woman's Club. They circulated a flier asserting the endorsement of President Andrews and the newly-appointed women's dean, Louis F. Snow, and captured the pocketbooks of clubs and clubmembers throughout the state. The treasury books of RISCEW reveal the painstaking fund raising among women, dollars carefully contributed from personal savings and club accounts, previously earmarked for other purposes, none as noble as the creation of a suitable building for women at Brown, one whose existence would force the university to formally and fully accept women on the Brown campus.

The women's club network all over the state responded to the plea for funds to make young women's dreams come true. The treasurer's accounts document steady and generous sums. Sarah Doyle collected $131 from twenty-two members of the RIWC in spring 1896 and $195 more from fourteen others at the following club meeting, including ten dollars from her own pocket. The first day of January 1897 finds $71.50 from the RIWC, another $60.16 a few weeks later, and $16.75 more in early February. At the May 1896 meeting of the Sarah E. Doyle Club, a donation of twenty-five dollars was made. Twenty-five individual women at the meeting also gave $180 and at the July meeting, another twenty women came prepared to give $135. Clubwomen's contributions would be steady, on behalf of their namesake, the prime mover of this operation. (After her death, in 1922, the club established a memorial fund in her honor and contributed its contents to the cause she so relentlessly heralded.) The Pawtucket Daughters of the American Revolution contributed five hundred dollars; chapters in Westerly gave twenty-five dollars, and in Woonsocket fifty dollars. The Woman's Suffrage League of Pawtucket sent ten dollars and the Collegiate Alumnae Fund, the Providence branch of the Association of Collegiate Alumnae, sent one thousand. No female in the state was considered too young to contribute. The "Young Women of Pawtucket High School" sent twenty dollars and "Little Women of Pawtucket," collected fifty dollars. Individual women came forward: Elizabeth Buffum Chace gave two hundred dollars. RIWC members and, from the first and second classes of women at Brown, Mary Woolley and Clara Comstock, gave twenty-five dollars. The fund-raising did not abate, even on the day of the dedication of the building itself. Dean Emily Jane Smith of Barnard

College, who had traveled from Manhattan to make an address at the dedicatory event, contributed fifteen dollars for the worthy cause.

Men were approached as well, and urged to contribute in the name of a woman they wished to honor. Rhode Island Senator Nelson Aldrich gave one hundred dollars. When the Ladies' Circle of the Roger Williams Circle was approached, the *Organ of Congregation Sons of Israel and David* urged that "The Jewish ladies must not stand back from a movement appertaining to women's education. Think earnestly and respond generously."[37] Families were also approached to make contributions to Pembroke Hall in memory of important women in their families. Jesse H. Metcalf gave five thousand dollars in memory of his wife, Helen Adelia Metcalf, mother of Eliza Metcalf Radeke. Contributions of over one thousand dollars were made to honor Mary Miles Aldrich, Abby Greene Beckwith, Mary Ann Shaw, Eliza Howard Slade, and Sarah Benson Tillinghast. These six names are memorialized on a commemorative plaque in Pembroke Hall.

Success was achieved quickly. Building began almost immediately and in only two and a half years, when $14,000 had been collected, the building was completed and formally dedicated. The building, finally costing $37,601.06, was named Pembroke Hall, to honor the college which Rhode Island's founder, Roger Williams, had attended at Cambridge University in England. It had been founded by the widow of the Earl of Pembroke, Maria de St. Paulo, five hundred years before. Finally, in 1896, when the success of the building drive was certain, the Brown Corporation legislated the founding of the Women's College and defined it as being part of the university.[38] Once RISCEW paid for the new building, women were officially welcomed at Brown.

The dedication of Pembroke Hall, on November 22, 1897, was probably the most important day in Sarah Doyle's long and busy life. How proud she must have been to survey the structure which housed recitation rooms, a library and reading room decorated with a special frieze commemorating the contributions of women, a lunchroom, gymnastic facilities on the spacious top floor, lockers and dressing rooms in the basement, and spaces for social and religious activities, including debating clubs. Before her, while she stood at the dais, were her fellow RISCEW members. Today, they would pour tea and serve refreshments in the library, as ready to do whatever needed to be done as they were the day they had agreed to raise among their acquaintances the huge sum of money necessary to erect this fine building.

Doyle and the rest of RISCEW were justifiably proud of their accomplishment. Together they had mobilized the resources to provide young women with a start undreamed of. RISCEW's members, after all, knew what Brown's 157 undergraduate women did not yet know – that women had innumerable and immense talents, that many barriers existed among society's institutions and individuals to stifle the development and expenditure of those talents, and that those constraints might be overcome if women banded together to assert their strength in concert. The dedication of Pembroke Hall represented the collective effort of Rhode Island's activist women to ease the paths of their daughters, granddaughters, and great-granddaughters. It was the moment they had worked for all their lives.

The Rhode Island women's gift of an intellectual and social haven for women at Brown University came with strings attached. In turning the facility over to President Andrews for the long use of young women, Doyle articulated her expectation that the university would now assist in the higher education of young women and that the new students would now work to discover their genius and to return the favor just bestowed upon them by serving their society fully. "We dedicate Pembroke Hall," Doyle declared, "to the service of women who, like Mary Somerville or Maria Mitchell, shall prove their ability to grapple with scientific problems; to women like George Eliot and Elizabeth Barrett Browning, who will enrich the literature of the world by their imagination; to women like Florence Nightingale and Dorothea Dix who will practice and teach the Christian spirit of love. We dedicate, nay, we consecrate it to the highest, holiest womanhood."[39] The young women who would now use Pembroke Hall owed to themselves, their sex, their society, and most assuredly to these dedicated godmothers, their best efforts to become all that they might be.

Clubwomen Continue to Develop the Women's College

While its most dramatic achievement is embodied by the opening of Pembroke Hall, RISCEW's work was not completed with the dedication of the building. Its members, remaining loyal to the work of easing the intellectual and social experiences of the young women at the college, lost no opportunity to keep before the Rhode Island club community the importance of continuing their support for higher education of women. Their values defined that higher education; they worked to make certain that it met their ideals for women. At the first of what became an annual breakfast of the Rhode Island Federation of Women's Clubs, for example, many women offered toasts to the future of womanhood, but Sarah Doyle came forward with one to the "Higher Education of Women in Rhode Island." In 1911, she urged the federation to provide a scholarship for young women at Brown University.[40] She successfully encouraged her namesake club, the Sarah E. Doyle Club, to donate scholarship money. The RIWC continued to offer a scholarship in honor of Elizabeth K. Churchill.

If RISCEW remained determined to involve Rhode Island's clubwomen in maintaining support for the new women's college, it also established stronger protections for women through the hierarchy of the campus administration. It became evident early on that a formal mechanism for communication between RISCEW and the Brown University administration was necessary to assure that women would enjoy the considerations which were their due. A forum had been created in 1895, when five RISCEW members formed an Advisory Council, which reported RISCEW progress on behalf of the Women's College to the Brown Corporation and additionally sought to broaden the assistance the corporation might offer to the women enrolled there. During the infancy of the Women's College, the RISCEW representative detailed for the corporation both grand plans and minutiae, clarifying both their attention to the general status of women and the fine points of their comfort. The women reported on their purchase of chairs for the lunchroom, announced the donation of new land on Meeting Street, sought permission to grade the land for a tennis court near Pembroke Hall, and reported their payment of insurance on the hall, as well as sharing new strategies for fund raising.[41] The women also attempted to persuade their male colleagues to mitigate the inequalities on the campus, urging a "consideration of what legal steps can be taken to throw the competition for prizes open to the women of the college upon the same conditions as they are now open to the men."[42]

In 1906, the brand new Alumnae Association was permitted to add two additional representatives to the Advisory Council. This change seems not to have altered the type of interaction established previously between the women and the corporation. Whether the elected alumnae representatives had been graduated only five years before they served, or twenty, they supported RISCEW's efforts to cultivate additional donors of land, buildings, or money for the use of women at the university. And despite the hard work of fifteen years, RISCEW's members remained unrelenting in their assumption that the women enrolled deserved as much from their Brown experience as did their male counterparts, that the corporation and administration needed to be pressured to share as many of its resources as possible and eradicate its barriers to equality, and that the women's volunteer community would continue to use its skills, as fund raisers, networkers, role models, and nurturers of new generations of women students, in order to ensure that the dream of cultivating women's talents would come true.

The dedication of Pembroke Hall merely signaled the beginning, then, of RISCEW's efforts to address the issues of women in higher education. They began, at once, to agitate for more space. They saw women get their first dormitory, Slater Memorial Homestead, in 1900, a gift of Mrs. Horatio N. Slater; in 1907, the Sayles gymnasium was dedicated. Not only did RISCEW make donations to their facilities, but they also attended to the comforts of the young women enrolled. Members held an annual breakfast to honor the seniors and hosted receptions for the women deans.

Anne Crosby Emery, a Bryn Mawr Ph.D., became dean in 1900 and served until her engagement in 1905 to Professor Francis G. Allinson necessitated her resignation. Lida Shaw King, who had studied at Vassar as well as Brown and made a name for herself in the field of archaeology, held the position of dean from 1905 until 1922. During her tenth year of service King received a generous gift from RISCEW. The members raised a five thousand dollar fund for the arts. Now King was able to carry out RISCEW's ambitions to provide students with enrichment beyond the basic curriculum, to "provide certain cultural entertainments for the students for which there was no provision."[43] RISCEW held teas for alumnae and dignitaries visiting from other women's colleges, to keep forward-looking women in touch with one another. They met with the president and dean to keep abreast of student needs. They launched a campaign to provide an endowment to put the college on firm financial footing. RISCEW also honored Brown's women, as when it delegated Sarah Doyle to attend the inauguration of Mary Woolley, Brown's first and shining graduate, as Mount Holyoke College's president in 1901.

RISCEW's members never tired of identifying new problems that required solutions. Ever vigilant to carry forth clubwomen's determination to secure all rights and privileges for women students, Mary Woolley introduced the proposal that women should be admitted to Phi Beta Kappa at Brown. While women were not invited to join the honor society for men at Brown, they saw RISCEW press for the creation of a special chapter for women.[44] As early as 1901, RISCEW also created a loan fund, permitting needy women students to borrow money until they could repay the organization and permit the funds to be lent to someone else.[45] This assistance, in conjunction with the Rhode Island Woman's Club's Elizabeth Churchill Memorial Fund and additional grants which became available, enabled many women to enroll who would not otherwise have done so. Many of the original members continued to transmit their club-nurtured ideology to the women's college until infirmity prevented their activity. Both Doyle and Amelia Knight, the founding officers in 1895, worked on until 1918. Their successors, however, were no less untiring in their efforts, maintaining the useful programs and establishing new ones, such as a campus landscaping venture, when necessary.

Alumnae Organize to Support the College

RISCEW, for all its dedication, did not work alone to assure the comfort of the women at the Women's College at Brown University. The Andrews Association formed in June 1900 was comprised of alumnae who volunteered to pay one dollar dues and participate "to conserve and promote the interests of the Women's College in Brown University." They raised money for campus women's needs, subscribing to journals and newspapers[46] for the Pembroke Hall Library.[47] The organization also met with the dean and Advisory Council for the Women's College to keep abreast of women's college activities and plans. Anxious to protect their Pembroke Hall charges, they compared its resources to those of other women's colleges and investigated whether women were welcome in the Brown Alumni Association. The members also prepared a survey of possible careers for women graduates.

After five years, the Andrews Association automatically transformed itself into the Alumnae Association, representing every woman graduate of Brown University. They did so in 1906 when the Brown Corporation granted alumnae representation on the Advisory Council for the Women's College. The first two presidents of the Andrews Association, Charlotte Tillinghast, Class of 1896, and Martha Clarke (Williams), Class of 1895, served as the first alumnae on the Advisory Council. The organization provided professors' salaries for courses on elementary logic and psychology. It funded an annual lecture, reading, and, after 1913, musicale. In 1909, it initiated a scholarship fund. Women expanded their network beyond Rhode Island, forming new clubs in New York, Boston, the Connecticut Valley, Albany, and Washington, D.C., and purchased gifts for the women's library. They sent silverware and fine tea sets, the Pembroke Hall clock, and trees to decorate the campus. They provided bowling alleys, and a maintenance fund for them, in the new gymnasium. In 1914, they performed a play on campus, *The Critic,* to raise money to buy a drop curtain and drop set for the budding Thespians enrolled. So successful was the Alumnae Association in raising money for campus women, notably for the gymnasium in 1907, that Doyle voiced the suggestion, dismissed vehemently, that RISCEW disband. Even if Doyle felt women had successfully implanted the clubwomen's blueprint on campus, her co-workers sought to continue to offer a presence to ensure its protection and perpetuation.

Still another organization gained a foothold in Rhode Island to improve educational opportunities for women, the Rhode Island Branch of the Association of Collegiate Alumnae, the forerunner of the American Association of University Women. The ACA was founded in Boston in 1882 by Marion Talbot. In 1892, Eliza Greene Metcalf Radeke, a graduate of Vassar in 1876, founded the Providence branch.[48] A voluntary organization open solely to that exclusive band of women who had graduated from accredited colleges throughout the nation, it assumed the same supportive role in the city that other women's organizations did on the question of women entering Brown. Meeting at 235 Benefit Street, the temporary women's facility at Brown, they had helped to press for the admission of women to the university. Once the goal was accomplished, they funded a scholarship for a Rhode Island woman who wanted to attend the Women's College at Brown University.[49] The group immediately sponsored public lectures, featuring speeches by woman professors from the "Seven Sister Colleges" who addressed the importance of higher education for women. The programs netted one thousand dollars, which the members donated to the Pembroke Hall building fund. The women courted and were courted by President Andrews and Dean Snow via club receptions. They strengthened the deepening community determination to plant young women firmly on the Brown campus. Steadily, members continued both to encourage Brown's institutional efforts to educate women and to isolate individual cases of needy girls who required the financial and moral support of the club's membership.[50] In 1914, the Alumnae Association of the Women's College achieved eligibility to become a member of the ACA under the organization's guidelines.[51]

Despite the continuing interest of Rhode Island women in Brown's female students, the consensus was that RISCEW still had work to do. Clubwomen's goals – to respect the capabilities of women, to satisfy their hunger for knowledge, to enable them in their effort to hone practical skills by surveying resources, collecting information, applying findings in order to create change for women and for all society – these goals the members continued to transplant from clubhouse to women's college. Indeed, as long as women were associated with Brown University, the women's society which had delivered them into that world would protect them there, insofar as possible. The society would help the college women to grow, unencumbered by a limited vision or mean resources, with the freedom to gain as rich an intellectual and social experience as the university could offer. Brown women have continued to profit from the wisdom and zeal of their nineteenth century godmothers for more than a century.

NOTES

1. See Grace E. Hawk, *Pembroke College in Brown University: The First Seventy-five Years, 1891–1966* (Providence: Brown University Press, 1967), pp. 6–10.
2. Rosemary Pierrel, "History of RISCEW," 1971, Christine Dunlap Farnham Archives, Brown University, p. 4.
3. Hawk, *Pembroke College*, p. 7.
4. Grace E. Hawk, "Sarah Elizabeth Doyle," in *Notable American Women* (Cambridge: Harvard University Press, 1971), v. 1, pp. 515–17, hereafter cited as *NAW*; Obituary, *General Federation News*, 3 April 1923: 5; Obituary, *Providence Journal*, 22 December 1922. The portrait now hangs in Sayles Hall, a building facing the college green.
5. Charlotte Field Dailey, *Rhode Island Woman's Directory for the Columbian Year, 1892.* (Providence: Rhode Island Woman's World's Fair Advisory Board, 1893), p. 101.
6. Grace E. Hawk, "Sarah E. Doyle: Gifted Organizer of Pembroke's First Friends," *Pembroke Alumna* 42 (April 1967): 4–7.
7. Rhode Island Women's Club, *First Annual Report*, 1877, p. 4.
8. Sarah Dean, an educator, died shortly after the plan coalesced.
9. Churchill published *Overcoming* (Boston, 1870) and *Bethlehem* (Pennsylvania) *and Its Surroundings* (Providence, 1878). Palmer began writing for a county newspaper in New York State at the age of fifteen or sixteen and soon developed a huge career. She contributed verses and stories to great numbers of periodicals and wrote several books of nonfiction, verse, and plays. Spencer published widely in both scholarly and popular journals of her day and wrote several books, among them *Woman's Share in Social Culture* (1913). See Louis Filler, "Anna Garlin Spencer," *NAW*, v. 3, pp. 331–33.
10. Mrs. Louis J. Doyle served as vice-president of the Prisoner's Aid Association; Mrs. J. W. Tillinghast was secretary for the Home for Aged Men; Mrs. Jesse Metcalf served on the Women's Centennial Executive Committee of Rhode Island in 1876. Churchill was also a leader in the Women's Christian Temperance Union.
11. Jane Levine, "From Club to College: The Rhode Island Woman's Club and the Founding of Pembroke College," *Pembroke, A Journal of Feminist Studies* (Spring, 1982): 53. See also Jane A. Levine, "Separate Politics in the Rhode Island Woman's Club Movement, 1876–1910," B.A. Honors Thesis, Brown University, 1981.
12. Rhode Island Woman's Club, *First Annual Report*, 1877, p. 6 and Sarah E. Doyle, "History of the Rhode Island Woman's Club, 1876–1893," in *Seventeenth Annual Report*, Rhode Island Woman's Club, p. 50.
13. The city of Boston, in particular, was a rich source of women speakers. Ednah Dow Cheney, founder of a Women's School of Design in the 1850s, came down to open the very first meeting of the Rhode Island Woman's Club with a presentation on the work of Albrecht Dürer. When travel was impossible, the members had to be content to read papers prepared by distant women.
14. The members made exceptions only for Carroll Wright, Boston expert on conditions of working women, and the Rev. Augustus Woodbury of Providence, who spoke on women of the Bible and Shakespeare.
15. The expressed purpose of the AAW was "to consider and present practical methods for securing to women higher intellectual, moral, and physical conditions, with a view to the improvement of all domestic and social relations." See Papers of AAW, Arthur M. and Elizabeth Schlesinger Library, Radcliffe College, Cambridge, Massachusetts.
16. Jane Cunningham Croly, "Rhode Island Women's Club," *History of the Women's Club Movement in America* (New York: Henry G. Allen, 1898), p. 1060.
17. The system was finally absorbed by the state Board of Education in 1911.
18. RIWC, *First Annual Report*, p. 7.
19. Among them were: Arderhebiah, Embreaso, Four-Leaf Clover Club, Providence Federation of Teachers, Fortnightly, Mothers' Club, Sorosis, Read, Mark and Learn Club,

Sarah E. Doyle Club, Saturday Club, the Council of Jewish Women, the Catholic Woman's Club, and the Vincent Chautauqua Literary and Scientific Circle, and a local branch of the International Sunshine Society. For a survey of their work, see Karen J. Blair, *The Clubwoman as Feminist: True Womanhood Redefined, 1868–1914* (N Y: Holmes and Meier, 1980).

20. In Charlotte Field Dailey, ed., *Rhode Island Woman's Directory for the Columbian Year, 1892* (Providence: Rhode Island Woman's World's Fair Advisory Board, 1893), is a long list called "Organizations Governed by Women."

21. The organization claimed three million members in 1924, but most likely had seven hundred thousand dues-paying members at the time. See Alice Ames Winter, "President's Speech," *General Federation of Women's Clubs Seventeenth Biennial Proceedings,* 1924, p. 139.

22. For this, and for her additional labors on behalf of the federation, Doyle was named a national honorary vice president of the General Federation of Women's Clubs in 1912.

23. Namely Mount Holyoke, Wellesley, Smith, Vassar, Barnard, Radcliffe and Bryn Mawr Colleges. "Thirty Exiles from Rhode Island," *Providence Journal,* 2 July 1888.

24. Anne Tillinghast Weeden, *The Women's College in Brown University* (Providence, 1912), p. 8.

25. Sarah E. Doyle, "Dedication Address, November 22, 1897," p. 11, Farnham Archives.

26. Pierrel, "History of RISCEW," p. 1; Hawk, *Pembroke College*, pp. 9–10.

27. Weeden, *Women's College*, p. 7.

28. Hawk, *Pembroke College*, p. 274.

29. Weeden, *Women's College*, p. 8.

30. Ibid., p. 11.

31. Hawk, *Pembroke College*, p. 20.

32. Ibid., p. 5.

33. Ibid., p. 19.

34. Linda Eisenmann, "Women at Brown, 1891–1930: 'Academically Identical But Socially Quite Distinct'" (Ed. D. Dissertation, Harvard University, 1987), p. 2.

35. Pierrel, "History of RISCEW," p. 6.

36. Other trustees were: Amelia S. Knight, Juliette P. Comstock, Eliza G. Radeke, A. I. C. D. Ames, Rebekah B. G. Goddard, and Ella Andrews. Other members included: Sarah L. Danielson, Anna M. Wheaton, Nancy A. Dyer, Susan C. Sawyer, Lucretia G. Chace, Emily R. Matteson, Susan A. Ballou, Eliza H. I. Barker, Julia E. Smith, Josephine Angier Binney, Isabel Harris Metcalf, and Eliza Greene Chace.

37. "To Our Ladies," *The Organ of Congregation Sons of Israel and David* 1 (21 February 1896): 1.

38. Hawk, *Pembroke College*, p. 46.

39. Sarah E. Doyle, "Dedicatory Speech," p. 15, Farnham Archives.

40. Report, Rhode Island State Federation of Women's Clubs, 25–26 January 1911. Rhode Island State Federation of Women's Clubs Papers, Rhode Island Historical Society.

41. Minutes of Rhode Island Society for the Collegiate Education of Women, 1 March 1907, 3 March 1899, 11 March 1898, 8 March 1898, 4 April 1898, Farnham Archives.

42. Ibid., 4 April 1898.

43. Hawk, *Pembroke College,* p. 66; Marion Shirley Cole, *The Women's College in Brown University: Its Progression and Expansion* (Providence: RISCEW, 1917), p. 30.

44. Hawk, *Pembroke College*, p. 51.

45. Cole, *Women's College*, p. 31.

46. The journals included: *Outlook, Scribner's, The Critic, Review of Reviews, Master's in Art, Atlantic Monthly,* and the *Providence Daily* and *Sunday Journal.*

47. Andrews Association, Annual Reports, Farnham Archives.

48. Radeke took graduate courses in art at Brown from 1903–1904.

49. Marion Talbot and Lois Kimball Mathews Rosenberry, *The History of the American Association of University Women, 1881–1931* (Boston: Houghton Mifflin Company, 1931), pp. 76–7.

50. "A Brief History of the Rhode Island Branch of the Association of Collegiate Alumnae, January 1892 to May 1905" and "History, January 1892 to March 1946, Organized by Terms of the Presidents," in Papers of the Rhode Island Branch of the Association of Collegiate Alumnae, held by the officers of the club.

51. These required school-affiliated member chapters to demonstrate strong institutional support for women in higher education, including an endowment of over half a million dollars, adequate laboratories, libraries and other appropriate facilities, and a rigorous curriculum taught by well-qualified faculty. Talbot and Rosenberry, *History of AAUW*, pp. 76–7.

CHAPTER 2

"Freedom to be Womanly": The Separate Culture of the Women's College

by LINDA EISENMANN

W HEN ANNE CROSBY EMERY assumed the deanship of the Women's College in Brown University in 1901 as its first female dean, she took the college by storm. Her personal charm, poise, intelligence, experience, and attentiveness presented a combination that awed the women students. They were lavish in their praise of this first woman leader in their midst:

> We hug ourselves and say with delighted wonder, "This is our Dean, our very own, this graduate of Bryn Mawr, this Bachelor of Arts, this Master of Arts, this Doctor of Philosophy, this European Fellow of her year, this first holder of the office of 'Secretary to the President' of Bryn Mawr, this first President of Self-Government, this Dean of Women and Professor of Classical Philosophy at Wisconsin, and now our very own Dean?"[1]

Emery was not unaware of her potential influence on these students and the rest of the Brown community. In fact, she took as a challenge the need to create a unique place for Brown's women within the all-male university. Her effort, along with the work of successive female deans and other advocates of women's education at Brown, nurtured a separate female culture built upon the strengths of the Women's College even as it chafed against the limitations placed upon it by the university. It is a story

Costumed members of the Class of 1897, as sophomores, ready to initiate the freshman class. Front row from left: Ruth S. Devereux, Martha S. Briggs; middle row: Clara Whitehead, Ida E. Hawkins, Anna L. Metcalf, Sarah M. Osborn, Mary A. Brownell; back row: Josephine A. Beane, Bertha B. Grant, Minnie H. Hough, Linda Richardson, Jessie G. Tiffany.

of female leadership and student response that pursues two strands: one, the ongoing effort to define women's place at a university geared toward men; and two, the women's own work to foster a separate culture within the sphere prescribed for them.

Many people at Brown did not see any limits around women's sphere. In fact, President William H. P. Faunce, who succeeded E. Benjamin Andrews, a man notably devoted to the women's cause, ostensibly applauded the freedom given to women through the coordinate arrangement.[2] In his inaugural address in 1899, Faunce explained the unique value of the women's separate social life:

> When the collegiate life of women is left free to organize itself, neither excluded from the privileges of men, nor forced into their social tradition – and the latter is now our danger – it will create its own ideal, and around it will crystallize all educational activity. In this realm imitation is suicide, and freedom to be womanly is the only safety.

It is doubtful that Faunce recognized, either in 1899 or throughout his thirty-year presidency, any ironies in offering Brown women the "freedom to be womanly." Yet Faunce presumed, as did most men and women at the turn of the century, a somewhat narrow view of what "being womanly" entailed. In a college environment like Brown's, it meant that women could share the men's curriculum and facilities, but always with the understanding that men's needs came first. Society's expectations about the social behavior of "womanly" college students were very clear: collegiate women must be courteous, pleasant, studious, unobtrusive, and above all feminine. After all, as Faunce asked, what could be more abhorrent than "a mannish woman."[3]

But neither Faunce nor his contemporaries necessarily held these views as a way to belittle or deprive women. Rather, the nineteenth and early twentieth-century view of women's nature asserted that women were in fact morally superior to men and that women's presence in a domain like the college would naturally civilize and improve male behavior.[4] When Faunce offered women the freedom of a separate campus, then, he truly wanted women to build their own feminine version of collegiate life. That the women of Brown, like their sisters on other campuses, satisfactorily built such a separate life does not obviate the fact that these women always lived with the tension of defining their place within a male university nor that the life they built was created with fewer resources and often tepid institutional support.

Historian Linda K. Kerber has highlighted this dual nature of women's freedom – a forced separation, but one that allows for the creation of a separate culture – in her discussion of the "instrumental" and the "prescriptive" aspects of woman's sphere of activity.[5] At Brown, women clearly saw the instrumental possibilities in the prescriptive separation of their Women's College. They continually combatted the men's challenges to their presence – some subtle, some overt – and they fought for their continuing fair share of resources. But at the same time they worked to turn several limitations of their situation into advantages.

This chapter tells the story of how women converted three of those handicaps into assets. First, Women's College deans supplemented the restricted curricular flexibility of the coordinate arrangement by adding new opportunities outside the classroom. Second, local women and alumnae continued to provide fiscal and emotional support to help overcome the inadequate physical and financial resources of the Women's College. Third, the women deans parlayed the existence of a student body dominated by commuter students into a diverse population enhanced by an active, unique campus life. This story describes how the Women's College – through its deans, the members of the Rhode Island Society for the Collegiate Education of Women (RISCEW), the Alumnae Association, and the students – exercised the "freedom to be womanly" over the first four decades, concluding with the ambiguous meaning of the change of name to "Pembroke College" in 1928.

Supplementing the Separate But Equal Academic Ideal at Brown

The aim of coordinate education at Brown University was

> to offer to all properly prepared women precisely the same examinations, the same courses of study, under the same teachers, the same degrees, the same opportunities in every respect that the University offers to men, but to preserve the distinct social life of a separate college.[6]

The ideal, then, was a separate but equal educational experience. In practice, the coordinate plan dictated that nearly all of the women's coursework was taken on their own campus, of which Pembroke Hall was the academic and social center. Course offerings by the male faculty were of three types: required courses taught at the Women's College (these were duplicates of the men's required courses); elective courses with a large enough female enrollment to warrant offering them separately on the women's campus (duplicates again); and elective courses on the men's campus in which, by permission of the instructor and the women's dean, small numbers of women studied alongside the men. In addition, a few female faculty members were employed to teach biology (hygiene) and physical education.

Limited flexibility in the women's curriculum was in some ways a benefit to the Women's College. Because the university insisted that the women follow the same entrance and degree requirements as the men and that they earn the same degree, Brown women never had to fight for the opening of certain courses or for the right to a university degree, as did the women at Radcliffe, for example.[7] In fact, the superior male faculty of Brown University was always cited as "the outstanding advantage" of the college's affiliation with Brown.[8] A question remains, however, about this supposed advantage: could the particular needs of female college students be addressed within a prescribed male curriculum? The answer suggests mixed success.

Although some early concern existed about the quality of the women's courses, it appears that over time the women experienced the same academic rigor as the men. In 1897 RISCEW asked its secretary for an analysis of the women's coursework. She reported favorably that

> with only one or two exceptions the courses at the University are open to such women as are prepared to enter them; and that of the thirty courses offered at the Women's College, in only five does the instruction materially differ from that in corresponding courses at the University, and in none is it of decidedly inferior quality.[9]

President Faunce concurred with this assessment, explaining: "So far as regards the curriculum, the women are on exactly the same basis as the men: there is no coddling whatsoever."[10] In fact, the women succeeded quite well with this curriculum, earning better grades than their male counterparts. The "academic group lists" of the 1920s which reported the final cumulative grades for seniors revealed that the Women's College consistently placed a greater percentage of its seniors in the upper academic groups than did the men.[11]

It is unclear how openly male professors and students welcomed their female classmates over time. In the early years, when female students were oddities on campus, they tried to attract as little attention as possible. Nettie Goodale, Class of 1895, recalled the advice of both the dean and their much-admired classmate Mary Woolley to be "inconspicuous" and "dignified" as they went to classes on the men's campus. Yet these new students attracted attention nonetheless, and were greeted with a call from the men:

> Here she comes,
> There she goes,
> All dressed up
> In her Sunday clothes.[12]

A woman from a later class recalled not enjoying those classes on the men's campus which had only one or two other female students: "We didn't like that too much. When the professor should call on us and we didn't do very well, all the boys would snicker. (She laughed) Oh, they'd snicker anyway."[13]

But even in the beginning, women students objected when certain aspects of the forced separation threatened academic parity. Mabel Potter, Class of 1897, chronicled early student life in dozens of letters to family and friends. She describes the anger of women students in mixed classes when they discovered "a scheme on foot for the girls to take exams separately instead of going up on [the] hill." The women were "all up in arms – every girl without exception" at the notion that they were to be treated differently in this important and symbolic aspect of their education. Potter describes their campaign to interview and then convince all their professors of the wrongheadedness of this plan; just when they succeeded with their teachers, the women were vindicated at finding a notice that the plan had been cancelled.[14]

Potter was also not shy in confronting the university president when she felt that women were shortchanged. She writes to her family of buttonholing President Andrews on the hill to ask why women could not have a gymnastics program. Although Mabel was disheartened by the president's explanation that "it could not be arranged," she expressed considerable pleasure in being seen walking with the president by Brown men.[15]

The first three female deans of the Women's College – Anne Crosby Emery, Lida Shaw King, and Margaret Shove Morriss – all recognized the limitations and the possibilities inherent in their peculiar situation.[16] The women's curriculum and their academic experience were "equal" to the men's, yet the women also were expected to create a collegiate life based on "womanly ideals." These three female leaders each approached the challenge from two directions: they worked to enhance the women's curriculum, even though such opportunities were small, and they bolstered the academic offerings with a strong set of extracurricular activities, which in turn fostered the separate female social life of the Women's College.

Emery was aware of the limited "freedom" allowed her in shaping the curriculum of the Women's College, but she also understood her ability to influence the students. One of her efforts to differentiate the women's curriculum – one that ultimately did not persuade the students – arose in 1902 when a "kind friend" of the college offered a gift to create a Department of Household Economics at the Women's College. This offer arose during an era in which the proper training for college women was a source of debate. One side came from M. Carey Thomas, president of Bryn Mawr

College, who championed the view that as serious scholars women could and should follow the same classical curriculum as men. But a round of concern had been prompted by Dr. Edward Clarke and others who predicted dire physical consequences for women who followed a strict academic regimen. These concerns had encouraged educators – like those at Brown – to plan time for rest and physical activity in the women's curriculum.[17]

But the appearance of household economics on women's campuses offered a solution to preparing college women for their inevitable roles in the home. At Brown, both Faunce and Emery expressed delight at the opportunity to fund such a venture. As the president explained, "Women should be made to feel that there is nothing nobler than the maintaining of an American home."[18] At least one course had always existed at the college to focus on issues of women's biology and hygiene. With money in hand, plans now proceeded to create a full four-year course in household economics, complete with elementary and advanced work in anatomy, physiology, bacteriology, embryology, and ecology.[19]

Members of RISCEW, who served as advisors to the college in the early years, had expressed some initial doubt about the appropriateness of domestic science in the college curriculum. They were won over through a presentation by Ada Wing Mead, former instructor of biology at the Women's College, who emphasized the intellectual possibilities of this new women's profession. Mead cited the work of Ellen Swallow Richards in Boston who envisioned the field as one to effect better sanitation, nutrition, and health for the community.[20]

This professional conception of domestic science did not succeed at the Women's College. After only one year, Emery expressed her disappointment over low student enrollment; only eight students had been ready with the prerequisite background courses. The dean remained optimistic, however, noting that twenty-five women had registered for general anatomy in the fall. Emery's enthusiasm was not rewarded with increased enrollments, however, and after 1903 the course was scaled down to a two-year program. By 1904–05, with enrollments continuing to suffer, the original four-year proposal became merely a year-long course in the Comparative Anatomy Department. Over the next two decades, the course repeatedly changed title and emphasis. Eventually, it landed in the Biology Department as a two-term general biology class, with the focus on sanitation and hygiene shifted into physical education classes.[21]

The trail of the course in hygiene/household economics/biology illustrates the school's attempt to provide some sort of training for women's presumed role in the home and community. Yet, like many other women's colleges which tried to incorporate this program, Brown found difficulties in sustaining the academic nature of household economics. As Faunce explained in 1904, "the problem of giving such a course dignity and power as an intellectual discipline is one not easily solved."[22]

Little evidence exists to explain why students at Brown steered away from the household economics curriculum. They may have disagreed with the premise of the course, preferring not to prepare themselves for careers as homemakers. But, in a newspaper editorial, one of the editors suggested another possibility for the low enrollments, asking "shall we all be content to leave this course entirely out of our consideration just because we dislike science?"[23]

Extracurricular Activities Express a Student Culture

Except for this effort to differentiate the women's curriculum, Dean Emery exerted most of her influence on women outside the classroom. One of her first efforts, centered around her belief that students had potential waiting to be tapped, was the creation of a student government at the Women's College. Like the leaders of the Rhode Island women's clubs, who encouraged their members to develop intellectual and political skills through club activities, Emery saw student government as a vehicle to enhance women's leadership skills, especially at a time when so few self-governance opportunities existed for women. Although the notion of student self-government was new to college campuses at the turn of the century, Emery had experienced its success at both Bryn Mawr and the University of Wisconsin. Amid the skepticism of Brown's president and faculty, she implemented the new idea at the Women's College where students accepted the change quite readily, seeing it as only one step in the dean's overall philosophy of trusting her students as scholars and women.[24]

Emery also used the daily compulsory chapel service to express and model her philosophy. Graduates readily recalled some of her "cardinal teachings": the importance of "work done squarely, and unwasted days"; the need for "an absolute sincerity in seeking truth, and fearlessness in speaking it," and for "a gaiety that shall make life richer for oneself and happier for others."[25] Above all, Emery was appreciated by students and colleagues alike for her ability to model an educated woman who was nonetheless charming and feminine.[26]

Another of Emery's efforts to foster a female collegiate life like that she had seen at Bryn Mawr was to create a gathering place at the Slater Memorial Homestead, the College's first dormitory, where she lived. There she conducted her popular biweekly "Universe meetings," extracurricular gatherings for students and faculty at which "we discuss anything from 'the destiny of the human race' to 'feminine demonstrations of affection.'" Much testimony to the intellectual inspiration of these meetings exists in the students' writings, where they affirmed that "it does us good to think of these deeper subjects."[27]

Emery's tenure at Brown was quite brief, however. After only five years she resigned to marry Francis G. Allinson, professor of classical philology at the university. Although the students bemoaned the loss of their dean, they were neither surprised nor resentful of her decision to leave. In fact, her marriage seemed to show them a perfectly acceptable path for a college-educated woman, a way "to fulfill another sphere of woman."[28] She remained in Providence, however, as an influence on the Women's College, serving again as dean in 1920–21 and in the fall semester of 1923.

Lida Shaw King, who succeeded Emery, had a different relationship with the women students, preferring to exercise her influence in a less personal way. For example, when she felt obligated to speak to the students about the issue of women's suffrage, her approach and her effect were hardly the same as Emery's would have been. One graduate remembers the dean's caution, as she asked students to bring no guests to her chapel talk that day and not to speak to the press. King then explained of women's suffrage that "she believed it would come; she didn't like it, but she thought it was part of the future." The student recalled, "From my four years of daily chapel this is the only one that I remember distinctly; she must have felt strongly and in spite of her reticence, made her point."[29] The issue never excited much attention on the campus, however.

Although King's service as dean lasted more than three times longer than Emery's, much less student comment about her survives. However, it must be remembered that Emery served in an era when close faculty-student relationships were the norm and when exuberant expressions of female friendship were common. The 1910s, which comprised the main part of King's tenure, witnessed a lessening of such open affection.[30] Also, Dean King's mental health declined toward the end of her deanship, and student memories from that time are not especially flattering.[31]

During her tenure Dean King focused on upgrading the cultural life of women students at the college, and like Emery, she worked both within and outside the academic curriculum. In the classroom, King tried to bring more music and art into the women's course offerings. Like Emery, King also found her best success in extracurricular efforts. She exposed the students to new influences by bringing outside speakers to the chapel talks. A representative sample included Jane Addams, who spoke in 1911; the secretary of the National League of Women Workers, who spoke about social and educational clubs for women who worked; a professor from Wellesley who made "a plea for graduate study" as the students' next step after college; and missionaries who made frequent visits to speak about their worldwide travels.[32] In honor of King's retirement, RISCEW created the Lida Shaw King Decennial Fund to continue to provide the music

Anne Crosby Emery Allinson, dean of the Women's College, 1900–05, 1920–21, 1922–23.
BELOW: Lida Shaw King, dean of the Women's College, 1905–22.

courses, lectures, drama exhibitions, and other artistic endeavors that Dean King spent so many years bringing to the campus.[33]

To King's successor, Margaret Shove Morriss, who became dean in 1923, fell the responsibility of guiding students through "the Jazz Age," a time when colleges burgeoned in size, and career opportunities for women (and men) began to grow. Morriss found more success than King in building these changes into the curriculum. A few courses such as "Application of Social Principles," "Social Work in Times of War," and "Child Welfare" appeared during the 1910s and 1920s, as women began to craft the field of social work. But always faced with a stringent men's curriculum, Morriss put most of her efforts to show women new opportunities into extracurricular activities.

Morriss also added two career-oriented innovations, both of which attracted national attention: a vocational bureau and an orientation lecture series. The vocational bureau consisted of job counseling and a personnel service to help students seek jobs that met their interests and skills. The orientation series, later called "Freshman Lectures," was designed to "consider the problems of the educated woman," especially in helping students with "their future adjustments in the world outside the college walls."[34] The dean opened the series with a talk on "College and the Future," which was followed by such topics as "The Higher Education of Women" and "Wives, Mothers, and Education."[35]

Over the first four decades, each of the three women deans also had the services of the members of RISCEW and the Women's College Alumnae Association to help them inform students about career and home opportunities. The alumnae, for example, actively used the student newspaper, *The Sepiad,* as a forum to explain their work and research. Alumnae contributed notes about marriages, births, and new jobs, as well as lengthy pieces on their work. Articles in 1912, for example, included a piece by an 1896 graduate on the National Recreation Association and its movement to create playgrounds, a discussion on Talladega College for Negroes in Alabama by an alumna teaching there, and a long article about a graduate's work in the research department of the Women's Educational and Industrial Union in Boston.[36] And like RISCEW, the Alumnae Association had members who were married and at home, as well as those who were single and employed, so that both models could be represented to the students.

Margaret Shove Morriss, dean of the Women's College and Pembroke College, 1923–50.

Continuing Support by RISCEW and Alumnae

The women of the Rhode Island Society and the Alumnae Association played major roles in sustaining the female culture of the Women's College. Besides providing career information and role models on a campus with few adult females, the two groups provided ongoing financial and emotional support for the college during the first forty years. In fact, the "freedom to be womanly" that was granted through the inadequate financial support of the university actually fostered a women's culture at the college by heightening the need for both RISCEW and alumnae involvement as well as for creative interpretation by the women deans.[37] The battle to run a strong women's institution was fought on two fronts: while the deans worked to create a female collegiate life, the women's advocacy groups supplied the funds and support.

The Rhode Island Society, created in 1896 for the purpose of "aiding and promoting the higher education of women in Brown University," took on both the financial and the emotional challenges of fashioning a Women's College in Brown University.[38] At its start, the effort to educate women at Brown was completely self-supporting; the university opened its doors, but the women literally needed to erect their own building behind those doors. The completion of Pembroke Hall was their first, impressive success. Only one year after its incorporation, the society had raised enough money to give the Women's College its first permanent, physical presence on the Brown campus – a presence that signalled women's intention to secure their own place at the university, even if they had to provide their own funds.[39]

Because the Women's College was such a small, peripheral effort at Brown in its early years, RISCEW assumed a great many roles in its charge of "aiding and promoting" higher education. During the time when the college's administration consisted of only President Benjamin Andrews and Dean Louis Snow, RISCEW was visiting committee, planning board, fund-raising arm, loan fund, and social committee all in one. In 1898, when Andrews and Snow recognized the need for help with the women students, an Advisory Council for the Women's College was formed, consisting of five members of RISCEW. In fact, that Advisory Council and its successors over time did their best to suffice for women's long lack of representation on the Brown Corporation.

In addition to its administrative support, RISCEW quickly recognized the continuing need to bolster the insecure financial relationship of the Women's College to the university. A typical example of their involvement occurred as early as March of 1898, shortly after Pembroke Hall had opened its doors. Flush with the success of erecting the building, RISCEW asked the corporation to provide funds to grade and plant the grounds around the new hall. A society committee reported back that the corporation "does not feel it has any funds to expend for this purpose at the present time."[40] A precedent was quietly set; immediately the society began plans to raise money for this and numerous other women's needs over time.

Financial support for Women's College buildings was the most visible of RISCEW's contributions. After Pembroke Hall, the society spearheaded the drive to build a women's gymnasium, completed in 1906 through the gifts of alumnae and Frank A. Sayles. Always aware of the importance of women's physical presence on the campus, the society also created an endowment fund that would continue to support the small cluster of buildings that was growing around Pembroke Hall. The need for women to raise their own buildings would continue over time: Miller and Metcalf dormitories, as well as Alumnae Hall, would all be built through women's fund-raising efforts.

Financial issues extended to the students as well. Hearing from the Advisory Council that some women students were experiencing difficulty in paying their bills, RISCEW in 1900 began a loan fund which continued until 1941, serving as one of the organization's strongest ties to the Women's College over time. The fund also symbolized the nature of the relationship between RISCEW and women undergraduates.[41]

Eventually, as the body of Women's College graduates grew, the Alumnae Association began to supplement and then supplant the advocacy roles that RISCEW had played in the early years. Like the society, alumnae supplied many of the fringe benefits that were needed at the college: they held teas and luncheons and built bowling alleys for student use. On the intellectual side, they sponsored lectures, created the Anne Crosby Emery Fellowship for one year of graduate study by an outstanding senior, and, recognizing a need that graduates felt especially strongly, paid the faculty salary for one course each year at the Women's College.[42]

With the substantial financial support of long-term benefactor Stephen O. Metcalf, the alumnae also built the beautiful and impressive Alumnae Hall in 1927, filling a long-acknowledged need for a social center on the campus. This large building enhanced the reputation of the Women's College, both in its immediate environment and throughout the country. The executive secretary of the Alumnae Association noted with pride that "a group of Rochester alumnae, making a survey of college buildings, were advised by every woman's college not to build until they had seen the Alumnae Hall at Brown."[43]

This reputation had taken a long time to build, however. For many years the Women's College had seen its lesser resources and its size compared unfavorably to both Brown and to the established women's colleges of the Northeast. The Women's College at Brown was smaller, younger, more urban, and less free-standing than separate women's colleges like Wellesley, Vassar, and Smith. Yet the Women's College had been created as an affiliated school for good reason: the clubwomen and other supporters of women's higher education in Rhode Island had wanted to provide not just collegiate training to local women; they also wanted the power and prestige of Brown University made available to women. When the coordinate arrangement proved to be most feasible, those supporters took what was offered and spent their efforts in strengthening the fledgling Women's College.

Building a Women's Culture Amid a Diverse Student Body

Even though supporters of the Women's College at Brown faced a situation of limited resources, small size, and uncertain status within the university, its advocates did not apologize for their institution. Rather, taking a cue from the initial creative approach of Dean Emery, these supporters steadfastly continued over the decades to view the college's deficiencies as assets to be exploited. When facing limited finances, the women focused on building support networks; when looking at its small size, the students emphasized possibilities of a closer community; and when considering the mix of students who presented themselves at the Women's College, the deans lauded the opportunities for new cultural influences. Each of these approaches in turn reinforced the female culture on the women's campus.

Dean Emery began with a concern for developing character, that all-important virtue to turn-of-the-century educators. To do so, she relied on

> a necessary student life, rich in wholesome activities, which, on the one hand, develops the sense of responsibility and communal feeling, and on the other stimulates and widens the imagination, and makes the mind more plastic to the influences of learning and of culture.[44]

At a new school like the Women's College, size and limited resources were strong obstacles to building such a "necessary life." Emery, however, encouraged her students to see the positive sides of those problems. The success of her continued encouragement can be seen in an editorial on college life in the women's student newspaper:

> We hear a great deal about the disadvantages of our college – that it is a city college, that it is small, that it is poor financially. It is often compared with

the great wealthy women's colleges, with their broad campuses, their great dormitories and a dormitory life where the girls have no interests but college interests, their laboratories and libraries and chapel.

Some of these disadvantages were actually "blessings in disguise," this student argued. For example, being at a city college "keeps us more aware of real life. It would be far easier to ignore the problems of life on the beautiful campus at Wellesley than it is when one is waiting for a car on North Main Street." Likewise, the poor financial situation and small size could give students "a greater sense of individual and collective responsibility." Not only that, the author explained, the newness of the Women's College gave each student a part in "establishing its reputation and in creating ideals and an atmosphere worthy to be lasting." Finally, the small size provided even the average student an opportunity "to make a place for herself instead of being lost in the crowd."[45]

Another student recognized a Brown woman's tendency to compare her school unfavorably with other women's colleges. She, too, looked for the special qualities of her institution, and chastised her peers:

> We see how readily and eagerly a Smith girl or a Wellesley girl goes to look up another girl from her own college. Would we do the same by our girls? What is there to hold us together while we are in college and to make college of real and vital interest to us after we graduate?

Her answer lay in putting into college activities "all that we possibly can; let us try to know each other better, to share each other's lives more, to make our college seem more real to us."[46]

The college activities that these students relied on were those developed by Anne Emery and her successor Lida King. Following on student self-government and the Universe meetings, Emery encouraged the establishment of numerous college organizations and activities that would build a women's student life on the separate campus. She was quickly rewarded by the sense of loyalty to class and college created by these efforts. In January of 1902 *The Sepiad* — itself quite a noteworthy creation — assessed the state of college affairs:

> Within the last year and a half, the social life of the college has broadened; . . . the various series of concerts, readings and lectures have proved of social as well as intellectual value. In the line of organizations our growth of late has been remarkable. The past few months have seen the rise of a student government association, a magazine, a dramatic club, and a new Greek letter society. The source of this increase in activity is the wave of college spirit which has lately swept over the Women's College.[47]

In fact "college spirit" became the rallying cry for Women's College students. Without it, a student "is missing the greatest good of college life, the opportunity to broaden her character by entering into sympathy with the interests of others."[48]

The need for "sympathy with the interests of others" had been obvious on campus from the beginning, and it, too, created a challenge for the deans of the Women's College. Because of its status and location, the Women's College at Brown attracted a large number of both commuter and first-generation college students.[49] The college served this clientele happily, recognizing that it owed its existence to the continuing support of local women and men. Yet as time went on the Women's College sought to extend its influence to a national audience. This situation of serving a local clientele but seeking to increase its drawing power characterized both the Women's College and the university over the first few decades of the twentieth century.

The university had always drawn a large number of its students from the local area. On the men's campus, one-half to one-third of the students came from within twenty-five miles of Providence. Over time, a concerted recruiting effort aimed at students from distant states succeeded so that by the 1920s nearly one-half of the men's class hailed from outside New England.

The interest in drawing distant students existed on the women's campus, too, but the increase in non-New England students was far less dramatic. In 1900 all but 9 percent of the thirty-six female students came to the Women's College from within twenty-five miles of Providence; even by as late as 1925, 29 percent of the 135 women attended from the other New England states but only 5 percent from outside New England itself.[50]

The Women's College never lamented the large number of local students; but, always aware of the need to expand its appeal, the college undertook both local and national publicity efforts. The national recruiting effort, headed by both the president and the deans, was often phrased in terms of the benefits it would bring to the local clientele of the college. In discussing the need for a women's gymnasium, for example, RISCEW noted that parents seriously considered the opportunities for physical education at a college for women. Only by providing such opportunities at Brown, they argued, could the college hope "to draw students from a distance; and only by bringing together women from different localities can a college surround its students with broadening influences."[51] Faunce was more explicit: "The College can do most for the young women of Rhode Island when it offers them companionship for four years with students from wide ranges of territory, inheritance, and position."[52]

Even though most of the early women students were from Rhode

Island and southern New England, they nonetheless constituted a mix of backgrounds. The college was also divided into two major groups: commuters (called "city girls") and boarders. The deans realized the issues inherent in these differences, but once again, as they had with concerns over the college's size and its youth, the deans turned this mixed student body into an educational advantage. Writing in her newspaper column in the late 1920s, Emery provided a carefully crafted answer to the question, "Do you think it is worth the difference in expense to send a girl away to college, instead of sending her to Pembroke?" Recognizing that so many in her local audience could hardly send their daughters elsewhere, Emery affirmed that "nowhere in the country do girls receive better intellectual training than at Pembroke College." She then went on to explain the advantages for some students in living away from home and being forced to stand on their own feet among strangers, as she had learned in her own experience at Bryn Mawr College. Emphasizing the value of communing with many types of people, Emery said, "I would always have young people, boys and girls alike, know that their own traditions and habits are not the only ones in existence." Thus everyone clearly benefited from the mix at the college: the students "from away" were learning for themselves, at the same time as they helped the local women by exposing them to new ideas and behaviors.[53]

Deans and students alike recognized that many Women's College students chose Brown because it was near home and frequently the only school they could afford. Once again, however, they framed this circumstance as a benefit. Emery explained that, unlike students at other schools who "come from home well provided with material things," these Brown women were dedicated workers "whose one aim is the pursuit of knowledge."[54] Students agreed, emphasizing the democratic nature of their school: "We are not for the most part wealthy girls, . . . and that helps us attain a spirit of democracy."[55]

Such a mix of students did raise issues on the campus, however. The deans' response had been to create a strong collegiate culture in which the extracurricular life would foster unity. In fact, the class suppers, freshman initiation, sophomore masque, junior prom, and senior Ivy Day celebrations had all worked to unite students with both classmates and college. But leaders on the women's campus also recognized how the physical space available to them could influence the female students. As historian Helen Horowitz has explained, the architecture of women's colleges often reveals assumptions about female students' need for protection or for a homelike atmosphere.[56] Pembroke Hall had obviously provided the first and strongest sense of place for women on the Brown campus; when dormitories were finally added to the campus, replacing the hodgepodge of housing arrangements for the boarding students, a new opportunity to influence women appeared.

Comments surrounding the opening of Miller Hall in 1910 as the first real dormitory reveal people's visions about the effect of the physical campus on the students. Faunce noted, for example, that a dormitory is much more than housing for female students; it is "the center of a home atmosphere, appealing to the domestic instincts of the students, as the gym appeals to the physical, and Pembroke Hall to the intellectual."[57] Others agreed, with one student asserting that the "artistic success" of Miller Hall would provide "a lasting influence upon [my] whole life."[58]

The same opportunities were seen in the opening of Alumnae Hall in 1917. As Dean Morriss summarized:

> Alumnae Hall's most potent influence will be in the beauty with which it surrounds the students. Living in an atmosphere of beauty, of grace of line, of richness of color, they will gain a grace and richness of spirit that only lovely surroundings can impart. It will mean that city students will now receive much that they have lost through leaving the campus every day.[59]

The fact that "city girls" were targeted as the real beneficiaries of the new building highlights the continuing need to draw these commuter students into the life of the college. For all the growing class and college spirit, the numerous "city girls" at Brown did experience their collegiate life in a different way from the boarding students. As one commuter from the Class of 1928 explained, "We lived sort of in a different world, I think, than the dorm girls because they had a closer relationship with one another."[60] For commuters, college life inevitably took on a different flavor when combined with "the home life":

> For them, college means extra work and extra pleasure; it means a little studying tucked in here, a recitation tucked in there, and above and around and between, the usual home and social duties to which they have always become accustomed.[61]

For several years the emphasis on the unifying power of the campus life succeeded in drawing together students of different backgrounds. Over time, however, the extracurricular demands became too strong for many at the college and in fact threatened the academic focus of the institution. By the 1910s students were suggesting that the social schedule, when combined with academic work and home responsibilities, was in fact overwhelming them. Because of so many demands, activities were understaffed, prompting even more calls for student participation. As students noted, in this case the small size of the school worked against them: "A small college is not merely a large college on a lesser scale."[62] That is, they could not simply divide up the work of all the organizations and expect all to be performed adequately.

Dean King began to notice the strain on students' ability to manage their time and involvement. In 1907 she created a committee to recommend solutions to ease "the strain of office-holding and committee work." The group's study resulted in the "point system" which assigned a number of points to all offices in student organizations. Major offices such as the presidency earned twenty points; minor ones, five. No student was allowed to accrue more than thirty-five points. This system, designed to limit students' extracurricular participation, stayed in force through the 1920s.[63]

Both Dean King and President Faunce were beginning to worry that student activities were taking on a life of their own – a life that detracted from the academic side of college. Faunce urged students and faculty to "keep first things first, and to subordinate petty 'student activities' to the main and real business of education."[64] Dean King took stronger action to eliminate the distractions of student activities, shocking the community with her move to abolish women's fraternities.[65]

By 1911, fraternity life was in full swing at the college. Seven fraternities existed, all of them social organizations except Alpha Beta, which retained its original focus as a literary club. Two-thirds of the women were fraternity members. Most of the groups held weekly meetings where students and alumnae socialized, and several fraternities rented off-campus space for their permanent gathering spots. The "rush season" for freshmen was one of the most exciting times on the campus.

Dean King had been concerned about the fraternities for several years and tried to exert some control over their flurry of activity. Her concern, as she explained to RISCEW in 1911, was over a growing division among the college's students: "The rivalry to secure the largest and choicest number led inevitably to competition, disputes and even distrust among the fraternities." In addition, those students who were not pledged felt discrimination, "and this feeling affected their attitude toward the College," lessening their loyalty.[66]

Initially King asked the fraternities to disband voluntarily, but following the failure of that attempt, she was able to convince the groups to withhold one rush season so that only sophomores could be pledged. Even as that effort was underway, King and the college's Executive Committee took the stronger step of prohibiting any new members. The die was cast; the next year, in 1912, fraternities at the Women's College were officially disbanded.[67]

The fraternity decision caused huge dissension on the women's campus. Besides seeing their own social system violated, women were also angry that no such action had been taken to force the men to disband their organizations, although fraternities had been accused of having the same disruptive influence on the men's lives. The men's dean for years had expressed concern over the Greek societies and had tried to limit their purchases of off-campus housing. However, the men's societies were not disbanded; in fact, by 1926 they still claimed fifty percent of the male student body as members.[68]

Challenges to the Collegiate Culture

The dissension caused by the fraternity decision symbolized how a social life created at the Women's College to bind its students together was in fact beginning to divide them, and at the same time to take on an importance all its own. The belief of the early students that all classmates could participate equally in college activities was probably always unrealistic, given people's outside demands and interests. Yet exhortations to show "college spirit," and challenges to those who did not, were continuous on the campus.

Uncontained growth of extracurricular life was becoming a big concern on campuses all around the country by the 1910s and heightened during the 1920s. Historians who study college life have suggested that the 1920s witnessed the rise of a widespread youth culture, based on an idealized conception of the social excitements of college life.[69] Several changes on the women's campus hinted at the shift from an academic to a social focus. The Athletic Association, for example, emerged as the strongest group on campus, deposing the Christian Association of the earlier era. The student newspaper and yearbook, too, shifted their emphasis from a discussion of students' academic interests to a stronger focus on their social lives.[70]

Many of these changes could be attributed to shifts in the student population. After World War I college enrollments soared, partly from an increased belief in the efficacy of collegiate training and partly from the rise of a new youth culture. The greater numbers brought new types of students to the campuses. More middle-class students, as well as Catholics, African-Americans, and children of recent immigrants, especially Jews, were ready and eager for college training. For the first time, many colleges could not accommodate the numbers of well-prepared students who presented themselves for admission. As Faunce noted at Brown, "the increase in the number of students in the University is beyond our desire or our capacity."[71] The era of selective admissions had begun.

With the new opportunity to choose a student body, many of the private colleges resorted to a claim of their "privilege," based on the notion that they were training the nation's leaders. As Faunce explained it, that privilege allowed a school like Brown to make distinctions among applicants depending on those students' adherence to the university's ideals:

> The American college is solemnly bound by legal and moral obligation to preserve its own identity, to be loyal to the ideals of its founders, and to receive at any one time only so many students of alien tradition as it can properly assimilate and guide.[72]

This "alien tradition" usually referred to most of the newcomers to academe.

Neither the language Faunce used nor the privilege he claimed was unusual for a private college president in the 1920s. As Marcia Synnott and David O. Levine have documented, the Ivy League and other private colleges all struggled with selective admissions during that decade, and most employed a quota system – either openly or subtly – to limit the number of racial and ethnic minorities on their campuses. Synnott found Brown to be somewhere in the middle in terms of its welcome to these minority students. For example, in a study of the percentage of Jewish students at thirty private schools in 1918–19, Brown ranked seventh from the bottom, with only 2.9 percent Jewish students, thirty-four out of 1,140 undergraduates.[73]

Although the numbers of Jewish, Catholic, and African-American students were not large on the Women's College campus, some of those students expressed feelings about their acceptance among students and faculty at the college. Oral history evidence suggests that Jewish students felt some discrimination, although it was not overwhelming. A Jewish graduate from the early 1920s said that she experienced "never one bit of discrimination." At the same time, however, she acknowledged that being Jewish "made a little bit of difference." She and her Jewish friends were not invited to fraternity dances until their junior or senior years, for example, and they did most of their socializing at the Jewish country club off campus.[74] In 1921 a branch of the Menorah Society was started on the Brown campus, and that club sponsored some dances for its members.[75]

Another female Jewish student compared ethnic concerns with racial problems on the campus in the late 1920s. She recalled the story of an African-American friend who had encountered an "interracial problem" at Brown, and who told her friend with a sigh, "Oh, things are awfully hard for colored people. I wish I was Jewish." Her classmate replied, "And at that time it wasn't so easy to be Jewish."[76]

The African-American friend at Brown was Rosa Minkins, Class of 1920, one of four sisters who graduated from the Women's College between 1919 and 1936. Rosa and her sister Beatrice had strong views about the discrimination they had experienced at Brown in the early decades of the century. The sisters came from an African-American family of unusual prominence in the Providence area. Both of their parents were college-educated, and their father had been the city editor of both the *Providence Tribune* and the *Pawtucket Times,* positions which connected him well with politicians and leading citizens of the area.

Rosa and Beatrice both felt that instances of racial discrimination were not numerous on the campus. But Rosa noted that Blacks were not allowed to live in the dormitories at the college, a fact she discovered in her freshman year when an older student, "fair skinned and quite lovely," was found to be Black and asked to leave the dorm. Rosa also recalled being denied permission to attend her junior prom by Dean King, a decision that was reversed through the efforts of Rosa's father and some of her classmates.[77]

Rosa's Jewish colleague recalled another time when their classmates were not so supportive, an incident which perhaps helps explain, although not excuse, Dean King's action. She remembered a college dance which required students to sign up ahead if they planned to attend. The women who came without dates could then choose partners from among their female classmates. Rosa's friend recalled the incident:

> So Rosa signed up that she was going. As soon as she put her name on, the other girls didn't want to exchange dances with her. So, they kept crossing off their names from the list. And I recall that so vividly. And, when so many names were coming off, Rosa decided to knock herself off. So she scratched her name out, and all the names went back on the list, you know. And then I remember she came, anyway. She didn't exchange dances with them. She came with a white man.[78]

This Jewish student said of the experience, "It left a big impression – more so than the Jewish problem ever did."[79]

Fear of Coeducation Leads to a New Name for the Women's College

Besides the changes in the composition of the student body, the decade of the 1920s also brought about changes in women's relationships with the male students. At Brown as around the country, male and female college students of the 1920s turned more of their attention to each other as they turned away from the academic life. Dancing, drinking, and partying assumed great prominence in the college life of "the roaring twenties."

Although the women at Brown had always been interested in the men, their earlier involvement had been somewhat more formal, with women's visits to the men's campus usually restricted to class sessions, for example.

In many ways the male/female relationship at Brown resembled a sibling rivalry, and the comments of both women and men suggest the type of teasing characteristic of brothers and sisters. Some women understood that familiarity lessened men's and women's appreciation of each other. When asked why the men looked down on their female classmates, graduate Ethel Humphrey suggested, "I think propinquity. Somehow it didn't seem as attractive." Like a brother unable to see his sister objectively, a Brown man might find it "much more exciting" to seek female dates from another college.[80]

Of course there were many women students who enjoyed the attention, even the teasing, they received from their "brothers on the hill." Charlotte Ferguson Roads, Class of 1924, laughingly recalled that, "I didn't ever feel the tension. If I needed anything, I would rather get attention than feel the tension!"[81] Some women felt that the dislike between men and women was all feigned, citing the preponderance of Brown/Pembroke marriages as evidence. Their feeling is confirmed by statistics from the catalogs of the university which suggest that the number of Brown/Pembroke marriages was quite high: between 1895 and 1930, these marriages constituted 20–30 percent of the total marriages in any given class.[82]

The reason Brown men worried publicly about openly sharing their facilities and privileges with the women was their fear of "the stigma of coeducation."[83] These men believed that outsiders who saw women around the campus would assume that Brown was a coeducational school, and that, they affirmed, would be the end of traditional Brown:

> If it were [coeducational], the great majority of the present undergraduates would not be here – if it becomes such, it will not only change the standards for which it has stood for so many years but it will also lose the support of many of its most powerful alumni.[84]

Thus even as the men and women expressed more interest in dating and partying, concerns about coeducation heightened. The president of the men's Class of 1922 fired a salvo against perceived coeducation in an address to the Brown alumni when he coined the phrase "the Pembroke problem" to note his concern over women's prominence on the campus.[85]

The battle lines were drawn more sharply during the 1927–28 school year, centering around an editorial campaign by the men's *Brown Daily Herald* to change the name of "the Women's College" to "Pembroke

College." The name change had been proposed before, appearing as an occasional issue before the Executive Committee of the Women's College between 1911 and 1927. Sometimes the proposal had been offered by President Faunce, who sought "a unique name, easily pronounced and printed, and of real historical significance."[86] Dean King was also known to favor the change but for a different reason, apparently believing that the current name implied to outsiders a greater level of financial support by Brown than actually was the case.[87]

No action had been taken on the proposed name change in either 1911 or 1913, although by the latter year the source of opposition became clear. As the Executive Committee explained, "It is the sense of the meeting that the name be changed but that in deference to the views of some of the alumnae the decision be postponed for the present."[88] Over the decade of the 1910s, alumnae argued for retaining the name under which they were graduated. Part of their opposition symbolized their fight to be recognized as loyal daughters of Brown. As Sarah Doyle argued pointedly, "Would the Corporation change the name of the University without submitting the question to the Alumni?"[89]

The other part of alumnae objection centered on their concern that the Women's College was being pushed away – symbolically and literally – from its close connection with the university, a connection that had taken years to build and refine. The alumnae argued for the power of a verbal association with Brown through the college's name. Alumnae Association president Elsie Straffin Bronson, Class of 1904, clarified some of the concern in a passionate appeal to the college community in 1911, urging people not to be swayed by the desire for a "more convenient" name. She compared the situation of the Queen of England who must always be introduced by her lengthy but proper name. Bronson noted that "some say she is hampered by the lack of a convenient and distinctive name. What – hampered by the fact that wherever she is named the phrase that shows her power must be spoken?" As for the Women's College, Bronson suggested that

> thousands might hear of Pembroke College and straightway forget it, as a new and obscure little college, perhaps unworthy of the name. Many of those same thousands would remember and respect The Women's College in Brown University, knowing it to be unmistakably grafted upon the sturdy Brown stock and nourished by Brown traditions and ideals.[90]

Precisely why the *Brown Daily Herald* editors chose to reopen the question in 1928 is unclear, but they proclaimed in a long and prominently displayed "open letter" in their January 11, 1928 issue that after years of misunderstanding and misinterpretation, the *Brown Daily Herald* believes that the time is ripe to define clearly the status of the Women's College in Brown University in relation to the men's division.[91]

The men denied any wish to sever the relationship between the two schools or to diminish the attachment of the Women's College to the university. Rather, they argued, the women's school had been hindered in the past "from attaining a distinctive and individual development" by its bland name; the new name would provide "the recognition it rightly deserves."[92] In other words, the "freedom to be womanly" demanded a freer rein.

The editors of the *Record,* the women's newspaper that had replaced the *Sepiad,* not only printed the *Herald*'s letter, but agreed with it, using even stronger language:

At present the Women's College is a greedy parasite. Not content with nourishing itself by the superior facilities afforded by the University, it demands a name which will indissolubly connect it with that University. Blindly, it lives, weak and dependent, seemingly without the mental powers of a higher organism.[93]

In this 1928 battle, many alumnae held to Elsie Bronson's earlier position, believing that women's relation to Brown must be clear in the college's name itself. Yet current students evinced less interest in the issue, and the *Record*'s editors appeared to believe the Women's College needed the independence of a separate name. Most students from the era claimed little recollection of concern over the name change, explaining that the college was often referred to as Pembroke already because of Pembroke Hall. As one graduate recalled in an oral history: "If there was [much debate], I was completely unaware of it." Classmates agreed, claiming "we were a little bored at the whole idea. They said, 'they decided to change Pembroke's name to Pembroke.' It was just an administrative thing."[94]

Students at the college seemed less threatened by the change of name than did alumnae. The similarity to the alumnae/student split on the issue a decade earlier suggests that women's sense of truly being a part of Brown changed after they were no longer physically on the campus. Perhaps the sense of belonging to the university was easier to feel when students were attending classes and moving about the campus, even with the formal restrictions. Once having left, however, the tie to Brown symbolized in the name "Women's College in Brown University" seemed to attain a stronger significance. Yet, when the corporation finally voted on the name change in 1928, the proposal sailed through with very little attention on or off the campus.[95] Until 1971, after another student movement demanded the abolition of a separate college for women, women undergraduates belonged to Pembroke College in Brown University.

The male students' push to change the name of the Women's College coincided with their other public challenges to women's prominence on the campus during the 1920s, challenges that were less an objection to women's presence than they were to the impression of a coeducational Brown. A national backlash against women's participation in higher education appeared to be playing out at Brown as well. After decades of women's steady advances, the 1910s witnessed several campus retreats from coeducation as well as a growing interest in separating male and female students.[96]

To some extent, the huge changes in student populations that appeared in the 1920s encouraged male students to assert their hold on traditional college life. That is, as new types of male and female students – African-Americans, ethnics, Catholics, and Jews – arrived on campuses after World War I, lines were often drawn in an attempt to maintain the old boundaries of college life. At Brown, as at other colleges, this challenge of growing numbers of women and ethnically-identified students in the 1920s seems to have been met by a closing of the ranks by the traditional male student body, an effort perhaps symbolized by the Brown men's interest in clarifying their relation to the women's college through a change of name.[97]

The women, too, reacted to the changes they saw in their campus. The old sense of unity, fostered so fervently by Dean Emery and Dean King, no longer sufficed to bind together a student group that was diversifying over time. The breakdowns in college spirit that Lida King had sensed in the 1910s were heightened throughout the 1920s by more students of different backgrounds and interests. Brown women certainly were not alone in their need to redefine collegiate life by 1930. Campuses everywhere were reorienting themselves to new students who sought new careers, seeking merely the advice rather than the close guidance of their faculty.

Brown women faced the 1930s with heightened problems, specifically the ambiguity of a new name and a shifting relationship to the male campus. In exercising their "freedom to be womanly" over the first four decades, Brown's female leaders and students had skillfully built a woman's institution that had weathered the uncertainties of a coordinate arrangement. Despite their success, however, women's formal power on the Brown campus was still limited: there was only one significant woman administrator; there were no women faculty who taught men; and there were no women on the Brown Corporation. And now the very terms of that relationship were changing. The challenge of women's search for equity at Brown continued in the decades to come.

NOTES

1. Speech of the senior class president for 1901, reprinted in *The Sepiad* 1 (June 1901): 72.

2. Andrews resigned his presidency twice, once in 1898 and then permanently in 1899, in a dispute with the Brown Corporation and the community at large over his stance on the silver standard. The case attracted national attention because of perceptions that Brown was impinging on Andrews' academic freedom. Faunce succeeded Andrews in 1899 and served until 1929. For a discussion of the Andrews controversy, see Walter C. Bronson, *The History of Brown University, 1764–1914* (Providence: Brown University Press, 1914), pp. 461–468.

3. William H.P. Faunce, "Inaugural Address," *Inauguration of William Herbert Perry Faunce, President of Brown University, October 17, 1899* (Providence: Brown University, 1899), p. 38.

4. See, for example, Ronald Hogeland, "Coeducation of the Sexes at Oberlin College: a Study of Social Ideas in Mid-Nineteenth-Century America," *Journal of Social History* 6 (1972): 160–176.

5. Linda Kerber, "Separate Spheres, Female Worlds, Woman's Place: The Rhetoric of Women's History," *The Journal of American History* 75 (June 1988): 9–37.

6. *Announcement of Courses,* The Women's College in Brown University, 1901–02. This language first appeared in this catalog and was used as standard phrasing for several years thereafter.

7. See Sally Schwager, "'Harvard Women': A History of the Founding of Radcliffe College" (Ed.D. Dissertation, Harvard University, 1982).

8. See, for example, Dean Margaret Morriss' article on "The Affiliated College" in *Alumnae Record,* 1927–28, unpaginated.

9. *Minutes of the* RISCEW, 3 January 1898, Brown University Archives.

10. Faunce, quoted in *Minutes of the* RISCEW, 2 November 1903.

11. These lists were published yearly in the *President's Report.* Results for the Class of 1927, for example, showed that women had twice the percentage of men in the top two academic groups, and only one-fourth the percentage of men with a "D" average or lower. See *President's Report* for 1928, pp. 74–77.

In the early years, faculty comments suggested that the women performed better academically than the men. See, for example, the *President's Reports* for 1893 through 1899.

12. Nettie Serena Goodale Murdock, "To a Group of Alumnae, November 5, 1944" (typewritten), p. 5, in Christine Dunlap Farnham Archives, Brown University. Mary Woolley went on to become a professor at Wellesley College and later, president of Mount Holyoke College from 1901 to 1937.

13. Oral history interview with Isabel Ross Abbott, Class of 1922.

14. Mabel Potter, in two letters to her mother, 14 December 1893 and 15 March 1894, Farnham Archives.

15. Potter letter dated 1 October 1893, Farnham Archives.

16. The terms of the deans of the Women's College were: Louis F. Snow, 1892–1901; Anne Crosby Emery, 1901–1905, 1920–21, and fall semester 1923; Lida Shaw King, 1905–1922; Margaret Shove Morriss, 1923–1950.

17. The "kind friend" was not identified publicly, although the gift was acknowledged and discussed in Faunce's *President's Report* of 1902, p. 25. See, for example, M. Carey Thomas, "Present Tendencies in Women's College and University Education," *Educational Review* 25 (1908): 64–85. Dr. Edward H. Clarke, *Sex in Education; or, a Fair Chance for*

the Girls (Boston: James R. Osgood and Company, 1873; reprint ed., New York: Arno Press, 1972).

18. Faunce in *Minutes of the RISCEW,* 2 October 1905.

19. The 1902–03 catalog for the Women's College contains the full plan.

20. Mead's presentation is recorded at length in the *Minutes of the RISCEW* for 7 December 1903. Her report is recorded verbatim, in fuller detail than most reports to the society. Earlier, less favorable discussions had appeared in the *Minutes* for 7 April 1902 and 4 May 1903.

21. Information is from the *President's Reports* and annual catalogs of the Women's College.

22. Some women's institutions around the country experimented with a household economics curriculum at the turn of the century. See Elizabeth B. Young, *A Study of the Curricula of Seven Selected Women's Colleges of the Southern States* (New York: Teachers College Press, Columbia University, 1932) and Barbara Miller Solomon, *In the Company of Educated Women: A History of Women and Higher Education in America* (New Haven: Yale University Press, 1985); *President's Report,* 1906, p. 29.

23. Free Press article in *The Sepiad* 4 (June 1904): 169.

24. Editorial, *The Sepiad* 1 (October 1901): 20.

25. Students' recollections of the Dean's address, quoted in *The Sepiad* 5 (June 1905): 126.

26. For example, the senior class president of 1905 called Emery "the embodiment of the ideal" of college culture. See *The Sepiad* 5 (June 1905): 126.

27. See, for example, editorial in *The Sepiad* 1 (May 1901): 60–61.

28. Quote from Anne Tillinghast Weeden, *The Women's College in Brown University: Its Origin and Development* (Providence: Standard Printing Co., 1912), p. 24.

Several Brown students from the early classes at the Women's College also married Brown professors or student assistants who later joined the faculty. Information gleaned from the 1934 *Historical Catalogue of Brown University* reveals eleven marriages between male professors and female students from the classes of 1895 through 1930. See Linda Eisenmann, "Women at Brown, 1891–1930: 'Academically Identical but Socially Quite Distinct'" (Ed.D. Dissertation, Harvard University, 1987).

29. Frances Foster, Class of 1909, in a handwritten reminiscence, dated 25 May 1970, in manuscript folder in Brown University Archives.

30. Solomon, Helen L. Horowitz, and Paula Fass all suggest that by the 1910s and 1920s college students' relations with their professors were much less significant than in earlier times. Men and women students began to turn to each other more, encouraged by a growing national youth culture. See Solomon, *In the Company of Educated Women;* Horowitz, *Alma Mater: Design and Experience in the Women's Colleges from their Nineteenth Century Beginnings to the 1930s* (New York: Knopf, 1984); and Fass, *The Damned and the Beautiful: American Youth in the 1920s* (New York: Oxford University Press, 1977).

31. For reflections on Dean King see, in the oral history collection of the Farnham Archives, interviews with Anonymous, Class of 1920; Gladys Paine Johnson, Class of 1913; a joint interview with Alita Bosworth Cameron and Rowena Sherman Allen, Class of 1914; and Charlotte Ferguson Roads, Class of 1924.

32. See *Minutes of the RISCEW,* especially 11 November 1915 and 6 December 1915.

33. Examples are from reports in *The Sepiad.*

34. Morriss, quoted in *Journal of the American Association of University Women,* April 1927, p. 96. News of the orientation series was also reported in the newspaper *The Boston Traveler,* and in the national journals *The Survey* and *School and Society.* See Scrapbook of Clippings from Newspapers Outside Providence, Brown University Archives. The Vocational Bureau was cited in *The Journal of Personnel Research* 5 (September 1926): 221.

35. Texts for several of these lectures are available in a manuscript file on Orientation Lectures in the Brown University Archives.

36. See volume 13 of *The Sepiad*.

37. Chapter 1 in this volume shows how the women of the Rhode Island Society transferred their energy and their values from the club movement to the Women's College in its early days.

38. See "Articles of Incorporation, 8 September 1896," in *Records of the* RISCEW, Brown University Archives.

39. In fact, the pattern of women "buying their way" into universities by providing buildings or endowments was rather common in the nineteenth century. For examples at Johns Hopkins University, Radcliffe College, and others, see Solomon, *In the Company of Educated Women,* and Margaret Rossiter, *Women Scientists in America: Struggles and Strategies to 1940* (Baltimore: Johns Hopkins University Press, 1982).

40. *First Record Book of the Committee to Build Pembroke Hall,* Brown University Archives.

41. 1926 Loan Committee Report, quoted in Rosemary Pierrel, "Address to the RISCEW," delivered by the dean of Pembroke College as the society disbanded on its 75th anniversary, 19 April 1971, Farnham Archives. The original of this Loan Committee Report is not extant in the records of the RISCEW.

42. In 1907 the alumnae announced a five-year plan to pay the faculty salary for one course per year at the Women's College, an annual expense of $400. See *President's Report,* 1907, p. 38.

43. Report of the Executive Secretary in *Alumnae Record,* 1928–29, p. 19.

44. Emery, "The Present and Future of Coeducation," in *Selected Essays* (New York: Harcourt, Brace and Co., 1934), p. 186. (Essay originally published in *The Nation,* 1909.)

45. Free Press article in *The Sepiad* 7 (April 1907): 28–30.

46. "Let's Put More In, and We'll Get More Out!," *The Sepiad* 8 (February 1908): 27.

47. Editorial, *The Sepiad* 2 (January 1902): 18.

48. Editorial, *The Sepiad* 1 (November 1901): 19.

49. The numbers of commuter and boarding students changed over time, especially as available on-campus housing increased. Even in 1924, when Miller and Metcalf dormitories plus a few smaller buildings were open, more women lived at home than at the college (219 at home, 208 in other arrangements). See, for example, Dean Morriss' report in the *Minutes of the Executive Committee,* 17 November 1924.

50. Eisenmann, Table 4, Geographic Origins of Pembroke and Brown Freshmen, 1895–1925, in "Women at Brown," p. 147a.

51. *Minutes of the* RISCEW, 1 February 1904.

52. Faunce in *President's Report,* 1910, p. 27.

53. From 1926 until her death in 1932, Emery (then Mrs. Francis Allinson) published a daily newspaper column called "The Distaff" in the *Providence Evening Bulletin.* These articles are collected in three volumes of scrapbooks in the Brown University Archives. Unfortunately, the columns are not dated, although they do appear in chronological order. This quote is from a column entitled, "A Practical Question About Choosing a College For a Girl – An Attempted Answer," in Distaff Scrapbook, volume 2.

54. Emery quoted in *Minutes of the* RISCEW, 2 May 1904. In this talk she compared Brown women favorably to the students she had known at Bryn Mawr and Wisconsin.

55. Free Press article in *The Sepiad* 7 (April 1907): 28–30.

56. Horowitz, *Alma Mater.*

57. Faunce, quoted in *Minutes of the* RISCEW, 6 December 1909.

58. Editorial in *The Sepiad* 11 (December 1910): 5.

59. Morriss, address at dedication of Alumnae Hall, reprinted in *Alumnae Record,* 1926–27 (unpaginated).

60. Oral history interview with Sarah Mazick Saklad, Class of 1928.

61. Speech of the senior class president, in *The Sepiad* 1 (June 1901): 25.

62. Editorial, *The Sepiad* 10 (December 1909): 19.

---

63. See, for example, the section on "Offices and Eligibility" in the Student Government Association rules in the 1908–09 *Handbook*, pp. 13–14.

64. Faunce in *President's Report*, 1920, p. 28.

65. Greek organizations at the Women's College were always called "fraternities" rather than "sororities," beginning with the formation of Alpha Beta as a literary organization in 1893.

66. King in *Minutes of the RISCEW*, 4 December 1911.

67. Information about the fraternity decision can be found in Frances Foster, "The Fraternity Question At the Women's College," *Pembroke Alumna* 42 (April 1967): 11–13, and in Grace E. Hawk, *Pembroke College in Brown University: The First Seventy-Five Years* (Providence: Brown University Press, 1967), pp. 72–74.

68. Concern over the destructive influence of the men's Greek societies was expressed almost every year by President Faunce or Dean Otis Randall in the *President's Reports*. The 1914 and 1915 reports are especially illustrative of their concerns.

69. For a good discussion of the changes in college life generally in the 1920s, see Fass, *The Damned and the Beautiful*; Horowitz, *Alma Mater*; and David O. Levine, *The American College and the Culture of Aspiration: 1915–1940* (Ithaca, NY: Cornell University Press, 1986).

70. *The Record* (the student newspaper which replaced *The Sepiad*'s news efforts in the 1920s) indicated some dissatisfaction with the Christian Association, especially that it had become too "goody-goody" and emphasized religiosity at the expense of religion. See, for example, *The Record* for 24 February 1926 and 12 May 1926. For a discussion of these changes in both the women's yearbooks and their student newspaper from 1920 to 1930, see Eisenmann, "Women at Brown," pp. 219–222.

71. Faunce, *President's Report*, 1924, p. 9. Between 1919–20 and 1924–25, the undergraduate enrollment at Brown increased from 1,207 to 1,872.

72. Faunce, *President's Report*, 1927, pp. 6–7.

73. Table 1.1, "Percentage of Jewish Students at Thirty Colleges and Universities, 1918–1919," in Marcia G. Synnott, *The Half-Opened Door: Discrimination and Admissions at Harvard, Yale, and Princeton, 1900–1970* (Westport, CT: Greenwood Press, 1979), p. 16. See also Levine, *The American College and the Culture of Aspiration*, especially chapter 7.

74. In deference to this graduate's wish that some of her comments in her oral history interview not be attached to her name, she will not be identified here.

75. The Menorah Society was a campus organization, like the Catholic Newman Club, created at college campuses around the country to enhance the social life of Jewish students. *The Record* mentions the creation of the Menorah Society at the Women's College in 1921.

76. Oral history interview with Gertrude Eisenberg Fagerson, Class of 1921. For more information on Jewish women's experience at Brown, see Karen Lamoree, "'Why Not a Jewish Girl?': The Jewish Experience at Pembroke College in Brown University," *Rhode Island Jewish Historical Notes* 10 (November 1988): 122.

77. Imogene Minkins graduated in 1918, Rosa in 1920, Carolyn in 1932, and Beatrice in 1936. Rosa and Beatrice spoke about their feelings in a speech which is included in the oral history collection of the Farnham Archives and also described in an article by Katherine Hinds, "The Minkins Sisters: To Be Young, Black, and Female at Brown in the 20s and 30s," *Brown Alumni Monthly* 82 (April 1982): 23–24, 41.

78. Oral history interview with Fagerson.

79. The Minkins sisters' experience at Brown was not unusual for many of the eastern women's colleges of the era. Like Brown, most of these schools took only a few African-American students at a time, but rarely so many that any systematic racial policy was developed. Commenting on the attendance of African-American women at predominantly white women's colleges, W.E.B. DuBois said in 1926, "On the whole, the attitude of northern institutions is one which varies from tolerance to active hostility." Of the 13,000 Black college students in the United States at that time, only 1,500 or so attended predominantly white

institutions. See discussion of DuBois in Solomon, *In the Company of Educated Women,* p. 143. A listing of the male and female Black students at Brown compiled in 1966 found that twenty-two Black women and forty-one Black men attended the university between 1900 and 1930, and only after the mid-1920s did more than one Black woman attend in any one class. See list compiled by Dr. Carl Russell Gross, based on university records and his own personal knowledge, "Black Graduates of Brown and Pembroke," in Brown University Archives.

80. Oral history interview with Ethel Mary Humphrey Anderson, Class of 1929.

81. Oral history interview with Roads, Class of 1924.

82. See Table 6, Brown/Pembroke Marriages, Classes of 1895 to 1930, in Eisenmann, "Women at Brown," pp. 268a and 268b.

83. This phrase was used in an editorial in *The Brown Daily Herald,* 12 January 1928, and the same idea was expressed frequently.

Linda Kerber discusses the widespread nature of this "fear of feminization" in "Separate Spheres, Female Worlds," p. 37.

84. Editorial from *The Brown Daily Herald,* Commencement Issue, 1922, reprinted in a scrapbook presented in 1928 to the Brown Corporation. The scrapbook, in the Brown University Archives, contained letters, articles from the student newspapers, and other articles on "coeducation" gathered from local newspapers.

85. Chapin Newhard's address is reprinted in the *Brown Alumni Monthly* 22 (April 1922): 245. I am grateful to Mary Ann Miller and her fine study of the name change for directing me to several of these sources. See Miller, "The Pembroke Problem: Defining Women's Place in Brown University, 1891–1928" (B.A. thesis for honors in American Civilization, Brown University, 1981).

86. Faunce, *President's Report,* 1911, p. 24.

87. King spoke on the issue to the RISCEW, *Minutes of the RISCEW,* 4 March 1907.

88. *Minutes of the Executive Committee of the Women's College,* 29 May 1913.

89. Letter from Sarah E. Doyle, Chairman of the Advisory Council, to the Executive Committee, 31 May 1915, in *Minutes of the Executive Committee of Brown University,* 8 June 1915.

90. Bronson, in *The Sepiad,* 12 December 1911, p. 21.

91. *Brown Daily Herald,* 11 January 1928, p. 1.

92. Ibid.

93. Editorial, *The Record,* 11 January 1928.

94. Oral history interviews with Saklad and Humphrey.

95. When Margaret Morriss reported on the name change in her 1929 annual report, she said, "There were many speculations on the part of the administration as to the effect of the change of name, but, contrary to expectations, it apparently created little comment or talk." She also added her own analysis: "It seems as if the change had come naturally at a time when the College was ready for it." Morriss in *President's Report* 1929, p. 21.

96. Coeducational Tufts University, for example, created the coordinate Jackson College for its women in 1910 after a sharp decline in male enrollments was attributed to the growing presence of women on the campus. Wesleyan University, the University of Chicago, and the University of Wisconsin all took steps to separate women or to eliminate coeducation. See Solomon, *In the Company of Educated Women,* especially Chapter 6.

97. See Synnott, *The Half-Opened Door,* and Levine, *The American College.*

From Coordination to Coeducation: Pembrokers' Struggle for Social Equality

by L O U I S E M. N E W M A N

I N 1 9 2 8 , T H E S A M E Y E A R that the Women's College in Brown University was renamed Pembroke College, William Faunce, president of the university, reaffirmed the official policy regarding the education of women: "We are determined that through the present and future there shall be no coeducation [at Brown]....Coeducation would change the entire tone and temper of both the college for men and the college for women, and neither alumni nor alumnae will ever desire it."[1]

Yet, by the late 1960s undergraduate education at Brown was coeducational in everything but name, and in 1970 the Pembroke Study Committee confirmed what was already well known: "by their own choice and assertiveness, women students have drifted toward integrated university activities rather than to strictly female pursuits." A majority among the committee recommended that the Pembroke and Brown administrations be combined, and following a vote of the Brown Corporation on June 4, 1971, Pembroke College was merged into The [men's] College and ceased to exist as a separate administrative institution.[2]

Equality in education for men and women at Brown University has had a complex history and has proved to be an elusive goal. At no point in this history has there been general agreement on how to define or implement such an ideal, although equality was generally thought to have at

Nancy Duke Lewis, dean of Pembroke College, 1950–61, awards a cup to Alice Manchester Chase, president of the Class of 1905, for the class's 100 percent participation in the Pembroke Scholarship Fund at the time of their fiftieth reunion.

least two dimensions: academic (or what happened in the classroom) and social (what happened on campus, outside the classroom). In the 1890s, Brown's original plan was to provide women with the same education as that offered to men, although in separate classes on a separate campus. This plan was formally organized as a system that came to be called coordination. By the early 1900s, educators at Brown had formulated an educational philosophy to justify the practical arrangements, arguing that coordination was neither coeducation nor separate education but a new and better system that offered women the best of two worlds: a university faculty in a women's college setting. Thus women were to have access to the "same courses of study, under the same teachers, the same degrees and the same opportunities in every respect that the University offers to men" – all of this within a separate, different, and distinct social environment.[3]

Three periods divide the transformation of women's education at Brown from a coordinate system to a full-blown coeducational system: 1928–1960, when a distinct women's institution was maintained and supported by administrators, alumnae, and students alike; 1960–1971, when students criticized the rules of the social system and challenged the authority of the Pembroke deanery, thereby precipitating the merger of the two colleges; and 1971 to the present, when many students, alumnae, faculty, and administrators have worked together to reintroduce certain institutional aspects of the women's culture that disappeared when Pembroke College was dismantled.

The Separate-but-Equal Women's College at Brown, 1928–1960

From the beginning in 1891, Brown and Pembroke deans worked steadily to establish a separate institution for women with a distinct identity and image, its own social life and social regulations, and separate extracurricular clubs and activities. Brown's undergraduate structure consisted of the men's college, known simply as The College, and the Women's College, renamed Pembroke College in 1928. Each college was headed by a dean and had its own personnel in admission, financial aid, housing and student activities, counseling, and placement or career planning. Although Pembroke College had its own separate administration, it shared Brown's faculty and ceded to Brown full responsibility for hiring and promoting faculty members and setting academic policies.

Throughout the 1930s, 40s, and 50s, students at Pembroke enthusiastically devised and supported traditions that were separate and distinct from Brown's, with the understanding that these were instrumental in fostering independence, self-confidence, and leadership among women.[4]

Certain social organizations, open to women only, included all Pembrokers automatically: the Brownies, which organized the major social events; the Student Government Organization, which enforced the social regulations, curfews and parietals governing women's comportment on campus; and the Student Christian Association, which fostered Christian religious practices and values. Even into the 1950s, most extracurricular activities were segregated by sex, with the exception of such organizations as the Brown-Pembroke Chorus; the Brown-Pembroke Orchestra; Sock and Buskin, the dramatics group; WBRU radio station; and Brownbrokers, a group staging an annual musical.

Certain organizations explicitly fostered leadership and philanthropic values: the Campus Chest, begun in 1947, coordinated fund raising for different charities; the Question Club, composed of representatives of each major student organization, organized freshman week each fall; and the Leaders Conference, comprised of the presidents of all the women's organizations on campus. Pembroke also produced, separately from Brown, many of its own publications: *Pembroke Record,* a weekly newspaper; *Brun Mael,* the Pembroke yearbook; the *Freshman Handbook,* a guide for new students; and the *Freshman Directory,* which had pictures of the entering class and transfer students.[5]

Like students at other northeastern women's colleges, Pembroke students willingly, even enthusiastically, administered the intricate social system that governed their behavior and social activities and kept track of their whereabouts on and off campus.[6] This social system remained much the same from the 1930s through the early 1960s and consisted of curfews, sign-out procedures, and parietals. To stay out past 10 p.m., students had to sign out for "lates" or "double lates," which extended the curfew to 12:30, 1:30 or 2:30 a.m. Parietals specified the hours during which men were allowed in the common rooms of the women's residences. For most of this period, women were not allowed to have men in their rooms, nor were they permitted to visit men in the Brown dormitories, except on special occasions and during specified hours. All of these regulations kept track of students' whereabouts, it was said, for the women's physical protection, but they also served to preserve the reputations of Pembroke students. These policies were crucial to upholding the school's status among other elite colleges.[7]

During the 1920s, a decade of increasing prosperity for women's education overall, the number of applications to Pembroke rose sufficiently to permit the college to take more control in choosing its students. Previously, most students who had been admitted had a diploma from an accredited preparatory or high school and a letter from an official attesting to an upright character. In the 1920s, the Pembroke Admission Office began requiring applicants to fill out formal applications and attend an on-campus interview, and the administration strove to create a national reputation.

Admission officers took notes on the physical attributes and ethnic backgrounds of prospective students. Remarks like "looks too Italian" or "has obvious Jewish features" appeared in interviewers' assessments of candidates, who nonetheless were accepted.[8] In 1936, the admission forms were changed: the new forms asked specifically for the candidate's race, nationality, and religious affiliation. The dormitories, in which there was a perpetual shortage of space until the 1960s, were largely reserved for white, Christian women. An official quota limited the number of Jewish women allowed to reside on campus, although local Jewish "city girls" were accepted without restriction.[9] African-American women were admitted in very small numbers, and were excluded entirely from the dormitories until some time after World War II.[10] Similar practices characterized most elite colleges at this time. There were also evident divisions among the student body, which students recognized and articulated as divisions between the "city girls," who were from the environs of Providence and lived at home, and the "dormitory students," who were mainly from families throughout southern New England and metropolitan New York.

The Women's College continued to attract students who as a group consistently outperformed the male undergraduates at Brown.[11] But President Faunce feared that Brown's reputation was being tarnished by a mistaken notion that it was a coeducational institution, and Pembroke administrators were keenly aware of the college's perceived inferior social status in relation to other elite women's colleges. Thus, the deans at Pembroke made a concerted effort to "improve" the social background of each entering class. As one alumna from the class of 1932, looking back on her college years, remembered:

> what she [Eva Mooar, director of admissions] was looking for ... [were students] from the upper classes.... She tried to get well-to-do people from New York, and she tried ... very hard to up-grade the place....We were ... taken, by Dean Morriss, to tea, to learn how to serve tea, to learn how to sit and drink tea.[12]

Given this environment, it was important for all Pembrokers to adhere to traditional "womanly" social customs. Rules governed students' comportment on campus and in the dormitories. Students could not wear pants on the street, unless they pinned the legs up and covered them with a coat so that it looked as if they were wearing skirts. They were only permitted to smoke in certain designated areas on their own campus.

The environment created to foster "gracious living" included sit-down dining, where some students held campus jobs as waitresses; and formal, dress-up dinners held twice a week, to which Pembrokers could invite guests, followed by demitasse in the dormitory living rooms with housemothers. Many students agreed that smoking and drinking in public was unladylike behavior. Even as late as 1960, an editorial published in the *Pembroke Record* declared: "Pembroke pedestrians certainly look most unfeminine and poorly mannered with cigarettes hanging out of their mouths. In addition to this fact, a girl smoking a cigarette while walking outside does tend to cheapen herself."[13] As one student of the late 1950s asserted, "We must take advantage of our time at Pembroke to become both enlightened and womanly."[14]

Throughout the 1930s, 1940s and 1950s, Pembroke students took great pride in their theory and practice of self-government and self-discipline. To a very great extent they obeyed the rules, and rarely, if ever, appealed the Dormitory Council's decisions to the dean.[15] In the spring of 1952, Pembrokers further strengthened their own responsibility for maintaining behavioral standards by creating an Honor Code, requiring that all students upon their arrival take an oath swearing to uphold the code.[16] The Honor Code serves both as evidence of students' attempts to foster a sense of belonging to a separate, distinct, privileged community of women, as well as proof of the difficulty students had in achieving this goal. As one student described the rationale for the Honor Code: "Traditions and Pembroke seem to go hand in hand. . . . They bind us all together somehow, for although we may never all know each other, we are each, through our [shared College] traditions, a part of the whole that is Pembroke."[17]

The existing arrangement that assigned responsibility to Brown's administration for academic affairs and to the Women's College administration for social affairs was questioned by a group of senior women in 1926. Pembrokers' dissatisfaction with the system, however, was not expressed as opposition to either academic or social separation, but rather as a critique of Brown's refusal to recognize the academic relevance of women's differences from men, and of an institutional structure that permitted women insufficient control over the development of their own academic programs.

A report by a group of senior women in 1926, written on behalf of the entire female student body, summarized the state of affairs as follows:

Today . . . the chief emphasis is on athletics . . . on dramatics and other extra-curricular activities, and on social life. Much has been said in late years of the training of the student by association with her fellow students; training her to take her place as a member of society through . . . such things as the

College newspaper and the Debating Union; training her to be an executive and leader through her management of College organizations.[18]

And while the student committee acknowledged that extracurricular activities should have their place in the life of a college student, they believed that "the emphasis upon them is undue" and argued that priority should be given to "things intellectual," on teaching women to think, not simply to amass and regurgitate information at recitations. The report offered searing criticisms of male professors who treated women students with "contemptuous paternalism" and younger male instructors who were "dogmatic in their statements and often insulting in their manner."[19]

The students' report then reviewed the curriculum, department by department. What emerged from their review was an appeal for changes that would accommodate the special needs of female students, most of whom, the students argued, were preparing for future lives that were structured differently from those of their male peers.[20]

The report also criticized many departments in which women were enrolled in large numbers for being under-staffed or poorly organized (psychology and philosophy), for not offering enough different courses to comprise an interesting concentration (history, music, philosophy, botany), or for offering courses that were too easy or boring (foreign languages, music, biblical literature, and education). Only the Biology Department was praised and it was singled out as an exception: it was described as "well manned" and "offering among the best instruction."[21]

As the existence of this report indicates, new questions had arisen by the mid-1920s as to whether an *identical* education was in fact an *equal* education. For the first time, students and administrators began to argue that equality in education should not mean offering women the same education as that offered to men. A new formulation appeared in official Pembroke documents, in which equality in higher education was conceptualized in terms of "usefulness" to women.

In 1928, Dean Margaret S. Morriss explicitly entertained the notion that educational equality might not have to involve exactly the same intellectual training for women and men. In Morriss' words, the coordinate college was in a particularly good position to "undertake experiments which will suit the separate needs of both sexes.... It may even offer different intellectual food to its students," secure in the knowledge that "the same degree at the end of the four years' course guarantees equality."[22] An external survey, which the university contracted to assess all aspects of university life, reiterated Morriss' views: "It has been abundantly proven in the last half century that women can compete successfully with men in college classrooms and laboratories. There is no longer any necessity to keep on repeating the demonstration by insisting that the studies they pursue shall be identical with those followed by any group of men ....The Committee ... would like to see Pembroke ... undertake a progressive experimental revision of its offerings, guided solely by the need and desires of its own students."[23] In other words, the university recognized that it was departing from its earlier understanding of educational equality. In the beginning decades of its history, the identical aspects of men's and women's education had been stressed, and the differences minimized. Now, the differences between men and women students were emphasized and attempts to address these differences were presented as an indication of the university's progress towards implementing educational equality.

Efforts to develop special programs of study for women in home economics and teaching met with limited success, however, and these were eventually discontinued or cut back in the 1920s as a result of financial pressures and lack of student interest.[24] For several decades, Brown also offered women a five-year B.S. program in nursing, but this too failed to attract students and was eventually phased out in the early 1960s.[25]

During the early 1930s, as financial strains of the Depression mounted, the Brown and Pembroke administrations permitted more and more women to take courses with men on the Brown campus, rather than organize additional sections for women on the Pembroke campus. This change, although presumed at the time to have been a financial decision resulting from an increasing shortage of funds, nonetheless came at a point when educators were no longer insisting that women receive the same training as men, when it was increasingly understood that women students were not in competition with male students because they were not preparing themselves for the same careers as men. Simultaneously as an equal education for women was being defined in terms of a different education, the fears that had previously led to segregating the sexes lessened, and separation was cast aside with little feeling of regret.

World War II consolidated the trend towards increased coeducation in academic affairs. The relative scarcity of undergraduate men on campus during the war continued to encourage the merging of sections and extracurricular activities. The size of Pembroke grew rapidly during the war years, from roughly five hundred students in 1940 to more than seven hundred in 1945, as President Henry Wriston (1937–1955) suspended the quota in order to make up for the increasingly low numbers of male applicants. In 1947, the official quota for Pembroke was increased to nine hundred students.[26] Because enrollments in science courses dropped precipitously as male students left Brown to enlist in the war and because there was a perceived need to train women for the war effort as quickly as possible, Brown encouraged Pembrokers to complete the requirements for the Bachelor of Science degrees in chemistry, physics and engineering.

The war made an impact on Pembroke College in other ways as well. Dean Morriss participated in special war-time organizations, serving as the only woman on a special committee of the American Council of Education, acting as a consultant to the Secretary of War, and as president of the New England Association of Colleges and Secondary Schools. After returning from a national conference held to discuss the role that educated women might assume during the war, Morriss reported to Pembroke's Advisory Committee: "I left the conference with two very definite impressions. One was that the need for women workers, especially for educated women, was urgent in many fields....The second impression was that Pembroke College was better equipped to meet this need than almost any other woman's college in this part of the country....The problem is how to make the student body appreciate the need."[27] Morriss tried to take advantage of an opportunity to prepare women for professions that historically had been closed to them. For example, in 1944 and 1945 she encouraged students to participate in a three-semester training program in engineering being offered by the Pratt-Whitney Aircraft Corporation in East Hartford, Connecticut. Pratt-Whitney provided tuition, room and board, and a monthly allowance for those students it accepted, in exchange for one year of employment after graduation. Graduates received a Brown engineering degree.[28]

Despite Morriss' efforts, students were reluctant to enroll in these new courses. Only fifty-four students, or roughly 10 percent of the student body, participated in them the first year they were offered. After studying data she had collected from the registrar, Morriss concluded that there had been "no significant change" in the concentration choices of Pembroke students, "except a growth in Psychology and perhaps in Economics." Enrollment in the sciences remained low, and the nursing program still did not attract many students, only four to five per class. Morriss admitted to having done everything she could think of to "bring more pressure to bear on the students for a different type of concentration during the war emergency," but "without much success."[29]

Despite Morriss's belief that the war had failed to increase women's interest in non-traditional majors, a longer-term perspective permits a different assessment. In each of the three classes to graduate in 1945/46, there were more women majoring in the physical sciences, mathematics, psychology, economics, and political science than in all the other subjects combined. By contrast, for the Class of 1948, art, music, English, sociology, history, philosophy, and foreign languages outran all other subjects. These findings suggest that when fewer numbers of men were on campus and when women received encouragement from their deans and professors, greater numbers of women ventured to major in the sciences.[30]

The rapid growth in the numbers of women on campus and their increased participation in previously all-male courses, clubs, and activities during the war produced a sense of uneasiness among some men at Brown, particularly when the men's newspaper was forced to merge with the women's paper. One male editor of the combined student newspaper, *The Herald-Record*, expressed his concern over the fact women had gained access to more of Brown's facilities. With some bitterness, he wrote: "We at Brown realize that we must share our swimming pool, our professors, our classes, our book store and our Newspaper with Pembroke girls....We realize that soon the name of our Alma Mater will change to Brown College in Pembroke University."[31] After the war, however, the temporarily merged activities separated again.

Pembroke continued to attract better qualified students than Brown in the 1940s and 1950s, and Pembrokers outperformed their male colleagues scholastically, even in coeducational classes. The deans of Pembroke College during this period – Morriss who served until 1949, followed by Nancy Duke Lewis from 1949 to 1960 – repeatedly noted that Pembrokers were getting elected to the academic honor societies at a much higher percentage than their numerical representation in the university warranted.[32] In the Dean's Report for 1956–57, Lewis stated that she found these statistics particularly interesting "in the light of the current discussion as to the effect of coeducational classes upon the academic performance of women." Brown's administrators were forced to take cognizance of the fact that teaching men and women side-by-side in the same courses had not resulted in women performing less well than they had when they had been taught in separate sections.[33]

But Lewis had no more success than Morriss in getting Pembrokers to major in the sciences, which many educators at Brown and elsewhere in the 1950s took to be the ultimate test of whether an institution was indeed providing an equal education for women. For the years 1955–59, a very small number, thirty-nine women, entered one of the Sc.B. degree programs (not including nursing), and only eleven finished.[34] Lewis, a mathematician by training, was greatly disturbed by these statistics and identified some reasons why Pembroke College had difficulty getting women to concentrate in mathematics and science. After stating that Pembroke women were not attracted to science and mathematics, she explained that an

> additional factor which cannot be overlooked is the discouraging and sometimes disastrous experience that many very able girls have in their first year science courses at Brown. In my opinion, this is partly due to a psychological attitude created by the generally accepted campus opinion that women should not continue in science...but more largely to the fact that the girls are thrown immediately into competition with boys who have had more and better preparation in science.[35]

According to Lewis' analysis, this was the down side of coeducation in academic affairs: the intimidation of women by male students and male professors in subjects in which women's high school preparation had not been as good as men's. As a solution to this problem, Lewis proposed creating separate freshman sections in science for Pembrokers only, but this idea was not implemented.

The attempts to encourage Pembroke students to engage as equals in academic programs so clearly designed and earmarked for men may also have been undermined by an existing social system that nourished contradictory values for women students, a problem Pembrokers shared with women students nationwide. Although students were told to learn independence, self-reliance, and leadership in separate extracurricular activities, they were not expected to put this knowledge into practice when it came to interacting with men. When socializing, if not in the classroom, they were to relinquish authority and defer to men. This was especially true when it came to dating Brown undergraduates, who as escorts, were made the protectors of women. The extent to which Pembrokers were encouraged to relinquish authority to men is evident in the record of punishments kept by the Dormitory Councils in the 1940s and 1950s. Normally, Pembrokers who returned to their residences after curfew were punished with "social discipline." But if the lateness could be attributed to actions taken by an escort (Brown men's proclivity for getting flat tires was a standing joke among students), then the Pembroker was excused and forgiven.

While the social system frequently brought women and men together in dances and parties, these events were always chaperoned. Whether a student had a date was public knowledge, as social custom required that an escort arrive at the residence, stop at the desk on the ground floor, and announce himself to the student in charge for the evening. This student would then phone up to the appropriate hall and announce the escort's arrival. Pembrokers complained about the lack of privacy and that there were very few places on campus where they could go on informal dates. Although in the 1950s, Pembrokers were prohibited by the social code from exhibiting affection in public, when it came time to say good night to their escorts, couples would kiss and embrace on Andrews Terrace outside the main dormitory.[36]

Partly because male students outnumbered female students by roughly two and one-half to one, Pembrokers had little difficulty securing dates, and freshmen were "rushed" with invitations during their first semester. Many Pembrokers felt pressure to find a husband while they were at Brown, and it was not unusual for women to be "pinned" or engaged in their junior and senior years and to marry soon after graduation. In this period, a remarkably high number of women from each Pembroke class – on the

Students on bells, from left: Roberta Eiriksson, Class of 1961, and Marlene Drummond, Class of 1962.

order of 30 percent – eventually married Brown graduates. One alumna remembers that around graduation time, even as late as 1968, a list of the names of Pembrokers and their fiancés were posted by the mailboxes in Pembroke Hall. A second list, "which was clearly auxiliary" was also posted: this one indicating the names of Pembrokers who had been admitted to graduate schools.[37]

The deans working in Pembroke's administration sometimes approved of and sometimes were worried by their students' conventional social behavior. For example, Alberta Brown, dean of admission, proudly described the student body of the 1950s as "largely from upper middle class homes, setting a fine standard of ideals, conduct and achievement." Dean Lewis agreed with this description, adding: "today's student body is made up more largely of 'nice girls from nice families,' is more conservative in conduct and in ideas, and has a more cooperative and cordial relationship with the administration." But she also found the conventionalism of some students disturbing and worried about the increasing tendency of undergraduates to marry while still in college. Lewis feared that early marriage "prevent[ed] the graduate from entering into exciting study" and was concerned that Pembroke graduates of the 1950s were not "entering the demanding fields of Medicine, Law or College Teaching," but were "seeking positions which in many instances are far beneath their abilities."[38] "There may have been a time," Lewis declared in her Dean's Report for October 1959, "when newly opened careers for women contained some threat to the American home. That this threat did not materialize is obvious today, and we are faced with another and quite different problem, namely that of lifting the sights of our young people, particularly our girls."[39] Tragically, Lewis died prematurely in 1960 and so did not live to see the social revolution in which Pembroke students of the next decade participated.

Events Leading to the Merger of Pembroke and Brown, 1960–1971

By the early 1960s, classes were fully coeducational, but Pembrokers continued to live under a separate social system, in which their personal lives were carefully supervised. A few organizations and activities were still reserved for Pembrokers only: the Pembroke Social Organization (the successor to the Brownies); the Pembroke Council (the vestige of the Student Government Association); the Athletic and Recreational Association; a few singing groups; and two student publications, the *Pembroke Record,* a semi-weekly newspaper, and *Brun Mael,* the annual yearbook. College-wide, mandatory convocations, replacing chapel, were held twice a week, and women lived on a separate campus, with curfews and parietal hours still in effect. Many extracurricular activities, however, had already become or were becoming coeducational: the academic and athletic clubs, the drama, choral and orchestral societies, and the radio station. Although the *Pembroke Record* and the *Brown Daily Herald* continued to operate separately, women could serve as reporters on either staff.

As time went by, most students supported the movement toward coeducational extracurricular activities, although initially there was some ambivalence on the part of Pembrokers. For example, students active in the University Christian Association, formed by the merging of the Brown and Pembroke Christian Associations in 1958, felt that the association had become more effective as a result of becoming coeducational. But they also acknowledged that the change "has magnified one problem – that of meeting interests and needs peculiar to the Pembroke campus."[40] The Pembroke administration was also ambivalent, as the new dean of Pembroke, Rosemary Pierrel (1960–1971), looked upon the increasing prevalence of coeducation in social activities with a sense of foreboding: "Certainly, a measure of such cooperative activity is highly desirable and should be encouraged, though these tides should be carefully examined lest the individuality of Pembroke College gradually leak away."[41]

Rosemary Pierrel, professor of psychology, dean of Pembroke College from 1961–70.

With the exception of a separate mandatory physical education program, greatly resented by most Pembrokers because a much less stringent one existed at Brown, and a required course in freshmen fundamentals, which students now derisively referred to as the "training for ladies" course, Pembroke College no longer had any separate courses of its own. There was one faculty, still predominantly male, one curriculum, and one degree. But the deans of Pembroke still continued to supervise an elaborate social system, while men at Brown were free to come and go as they wished. This tension between academic freedom, associated with Brown,[42] and social restrictions, linked with Pembroke, eventually proved to be too great. Some Pembroke women strenuously criticized the social system of Pembroke College and the authority of the Pembroke deans, turning to male administrators at Brown for allies.

For the first time in Pembroke's history, a vocal minority of students in the 1960s expressed the view that the social system was oppressive and sexually discriminatory. In the context of the social movements of the 1960s, many of the rules and customs upholding the standards of "ladylike" behavior, ranging from the requirement that skirts be worn to dinner to forbidding students from living off campus, seemed increasingly outdated and no longer within the legitimate purview of college authority. Some students adamantly opposed this transfer of authority from parent to dean, a system that was known as *in loco parentis*. As one student wrote in a "Letter to the Editor" to the *Pembroke Record* in 1962:

> The College attempts to conform us to a set of social strictures which many of us feel are unjust and, what is more important, not a part of the university's jurisdiction over us . . . . The only solution to this difficulty is to make the rules few, liberal, and well-defined, and to allow as many students as possible to decide their own rules by permitting them to live off campus. College graduation should not be the dividing line between a sort of advanced adolescence where one conforms to arbitrarily established social and moral tenets and the adulthood of self-determined conduct.[43]

In the 1920s through the late 1950s, Pembrokers worked through the Dormitory Councils and Student Government Association to uphold and enforce the system of curfews, parietals, and dormitory rules they were sworn to obey under the honor code. By the early 1960s, however, more and more students resented these restrictions on their behavior and began to find ways to circumvent the curfews. In 1961, Dean Pierrel abolished the Honor Code because students could no longer be relied upon to report their own or others' violations. As one student remembered, "we all learned to juggle the rules early: simply don't record the male guest in the parietals book and no one will ever know he's there; after curfew, come in the back door . . . . [Even this] soon lost its popularity. People learned that it was easier to stay out all night."[44]

The college's explicit attempts to teach students how to act like "ladies" was met with contempt, anger, and resentment by some students. During freshman year, all students were required to strip down to their underwear and have a photograph taken so that their posture could be evaluated; by the late 1960s many students found this a humiliating experience.[45] Students also resented having to take the required course in freshman fundamentals. As one student of the late 1960s remembers:

> They taught us how . . . to walk straight – we were supposed to practice with books . . . . They gave us exercises that were supposed to help us with our menstrual period . . . . That was what the Pembroke deanery's perception of what a well-rounded woman was: one that understood the social graces and was attractive.[46]

Having maids in the dormitories also made some students feel ill-at-ease, as it reminded them that they, the students, were now entering a college community that supported and reinforced the dominant racial and class hierarchies of American society:

> The maids were all local Black women, from Providence . . . . I always felt very guilty about having them come in . . . . I was just as happy when it was abolished, sorry that they had to lose their jobs, but it was something that really made me feel uncomfortable. But that was Pembroke in 1968.[47]

By the mid 1960s, Pembroke was suffering a full-blown "identity crisis" – as one student called it. Numerous articles appeared in the *Pembroke Record* discussing the "good, bad and neutral" aspects of Pembroke's distinct institutions. The "good" institutions were identified as those that gave advice to women undergraduates or enabled them to participate in activities without competition from men. The "neutral" institutions comprised the special traditions and social events that Pembroke had developed over its history, such as the Father-Daughter and Mother-Daughter weekends, in which Pembrokers were invited, but not required, to participate. Included in the category of "bad" institutions were "an overestimation of the value of 'a residential college,' a petty and restrictive system of curfew regulations, and a contradictory and ambiguous means of enforcing these regulations."[48] Even so, as late as January 1970, when students were asked why they had chosen to come to Pembroke, many gave the decades-old reasoning that Pembroke provided the best of two worlds: as a women's college it offered the opportunity for women students to gain confidence and independence in assuming positions of leadership in all-female clubs and activities; as part of a coeducational university, women students benefited not only from having a prestigious faculty, but more importantly from having men in their classes.[49]

During Rosemary Pierrel's tenure as dean, students discussed with intense seriousness whether a more "liberal" system would harm Pembroke's reputation by attracting a "different kind of girl."[50] The majority of students continued to believe that the social system was "designed as a protective system, not primarily as a rigid guard of student morals," but by the mid 1960s, some students were expressing doubts about the sincerity of the administration's avowals that the system was merely for their safety.[51] In October 1962, when Pierrel suspended three students for violations of the social code against the recommendation of the students' Honor Court, approximately three hundred students, or roughly one third of the Pembroke student body, attended a meeting to voice their anger and suggest other, less severe, punishments.[52]

During the next few years, student leaders desperately tried to make adjustments in the social system that would make the rules palatable to the student body.[53] Students demanded and won an extension of senior privileges to juniors, which entitled upperclassmen to stay out one hour past the regular curfew on weekend nights. The Student Government Association also experimented with harsher punishments – imposing fifty-cent fines for minor violations and "put[ting] the teeth back" into social discipline, by prescribing it during the weekends.

The critical issue, however, was the women students' desire to live off-campus. By this time, sufficient housing on campus was available, and all students were required to live either in the dormitories or at home. Although an overwhelming majority, over 80 percent of the student body, resided on campus, students repeatedly asked that seniors be allowed to move off-campus as a means of avoiding the restrictions of the social system in their final year. In 1962, after consulting with Pembroke's Advisory Committee, Dean Pierrel refused to grant seniors permission to do so, expressing concern for students' health and safety and fearing that there would be a loss in mature leadership that would be detrimental to the college.[54] Later Pierrel assented, permitting thirty seniors over the age of twenty-one (one-tenth of the senior class) to move off campus on a trial basis in 1966–67. However, the dean did not excuse seniors remaining on campus from the sign-out procedures, parietals, and curfews.[55]

In the summer of 1966, Pembroke suddenly announced that it would enforce the regulation that forbade students from using a man's apartment as a legitimate address when they signed out overnight. The rule had always been on the books but had not been enforced the previous year,[56] and an informal poll taken by the *Pembroke Record* revealed that about a quarter of the senior class had ignored the rule when they were juniors.[57] On September 20, 1966, Pierrel suspended a Pembroke student for violating the sign-out rule and staying overnight in a man's apartment. Students immediately protested that the administration had violated her rights by suspending her without trial, and objected vehemently to the practice of using suspension, which they called an "academic" punishment, for what they termed a "social offense."

For many students, the ban on signing out to a man's apartment pointed up the falseness of the Pembroke administration's claim that the social system existed merely to provide for their physical safety. They came to believe that their disagreement with the Pembroke administration really centered on conflicting views of what constituted moral behavior for unmarried women. If safety were all there was at stake, students reasoned, it would be more important to permit them to sign out to where they actually were sleeping, instead of forcing them to lie about their whereabouts.[58] This incident convinced many students that the real issue was not safety, but control over their personal and sexual lives.

Relations between students and the Pembroke administration deteriorated to such an extent that on November 14, 1966, President Ray Heffner set up a committee to review student conduct and make recommendations concerning the social system at Brown and Pembroke.[59] The Magrath Report, published in the following spring,[60] supported most of the demands Pembrokers had been making over the past five years. Most importantly, it affirmed Pembrokers' rights to have a substantial role in "determining the policies and procedures impinging directly and exclusively upon them," and agreed that "disciplinary sanctions for the violation of rules should not be imposed without affording students an opportunity to avail themselves of procedures that make the disciplinary hearing procedurally fair." The report cautioned the Pembroke administration against using suspension and dismissal too freely, recommended "that there be no prohibitions attached to sign-out destinations," and agreed that all Brown seniors who desired it and all Pembroke seniors who had parental permission be allowed to live off-campus.[61]

With respect to Pembroke's curfews, the Magrath report suggested a graduated curfew system, with "definite curfews" for freshmen, "relaxed" curfews for sophomores, and no curfews for juniors and seniors. Although curfews were relaxed as a result of these recommendations and coeducational dining was introduced gradually, beginning in 1969, many Pembroke students demanded more "liberalization," by which they meant more freedom from the deans' authority in social and personal matters.[62]

Students at Pembroke increasingly felt estranged from the women in charge of Pembroke College, whom they considered overly conservative and of another generation.[63] Many of the top administrators at Pembroke had been at the college since the 1950s, all of them had grown up in an era when premarital sex was considered immoral, and only one of these women was married.[64] From the students' perspective, the deans of Pembroke were not ready to accept that times had changed, and that the students of the 1960s were more politically engaged than previous generations. Many had traveled through Europe, had worked to get ROTC off-campus, had called for more African-American students and faculty; had participated in the Vietnam War protests, and had taken part in marches on Washington. Some deans in turn were dismayed by the increasing degree of student activism on campus and tended to blame Brown men, especially those on the staff of the *Brown Daily Herald* and in the Cammarian Club (Brown's student government) for "whipping up" the emotions of Pembrokers.[65]

The Pembroke Admission Office had become a focal point of student criticism as early as 1961, when a few students concerned about the low number of African-American students at Pembroke formed a committee to work with the admission office in recruiting more Black women to the college. Despite the increase in enrollment of Black women from two in 1963 to thirty-five in 1968,[66] many students remained suspicious that the admission office was screening out political activists, unconventional artists, Blacks and ethnic minorities, and working-class whites. Students in the 1960s saw these practices as morally reprehensible, and formulated their critique of sexual separation along with criticism of racial segregation. The impact of the national civil rights and women's movements occurred simultaneously on campus. African-American women at Pembroke active in both national movements helped organize both the Black students' walkout of 1968 and support for the merger of Pembroke and The College.

"Segregation of the sexes" and "special treatment" for women, the terms that were employed without perjorative connotations in the 1920s through the early 1950s, took on new meanings. Separation, whether of the races or the sexes, became a suspect arrangement. For example, students challenged the separation of advising facilities for men and women. At Pembroke in the 1960s, there were several types of advising services available to women: academic counseling undertaken by Pembroke's deans, resident fellows, and senior assistants; and job counseling, undertaken by the Pembroke Placement Office. The Pembroke administration believed that these arrangements provided students with advice tailored to their special needs, as counselors attended to the problems women faced in combining marriages and careers.[67] Many Pembroke students, however, wanted to reorganize counseling services university-wide by establishing one office to handle all advising (academic and job-related) for both Brown and Pembroke students. They recommended hiring at least two deans, one male and one female, so that women students could be advised by either men or women.[68]

Instead of seeing separate offices as a way to provide counseling specific to their needs, students believed this arrangement perpetuated the unequal and discriminatory treatment of women in employment. Students' perceptions, at least, were that employers wanting to hire executives usually recruited at Brown's placement office; when employers came to Pembroke, they were looking to hire secretaries. Students believed that the Pembroke Placement Office provided information primarily for "traditional" women's occupations and that "business-oriented" students had to go to the Brown Placement Office to obtain information and interviews.[69] Thus, the existence of two offices indicated to many Pembrokers that the university was not offering them the same or equal career services, but was fostering sex-segregation in the work place.

In December 1968, African-American students at Pembroke organized a walk-out to protest the policies of the admission office. In a statement released to the press, they stated that they would "no longer function under the present policies of the administration ... which prevent a representative number of black women from being students at this institution and perpetuate the status quo, e.g., producing white students totally ignorant of black people and the black situation in America." Eventually, with the assistance of Black students at Brown, these students won a concession from the Brown administration that beginning with the Class of 1973, enough Black women would be admitted to constitute at least 11 percent of the entering class, the percentage of African-American people in the U.S. population at large. The students also called for the hiring of a Black admission officer to oversee this process. Both Pembroke and Brown hired Black admission officers to implement the new guidelines. But within a year, the Black woman employed by Pembroke resigned amidst great controversy, claiming that the college had not hired her in good faith and was refusing to follow her suggestions.[70]

In the aftermath of these protests, acting president Merton Stolz appointed a committee in November 1969 to consider merging the two separate administrations at Brown and Pembroke.[71] The Pembroke Study Committee eventually set forth "goals of the university for the education of women." These goals, the committee declared, "should be, in part, the same as those for men, in that women should have the same options for

study in any field of learning represented at the University, for participation in any activity available to the campus community and for experimentation with any of a variety of life styles." But the committee also argued that to achieve educational equality, women would need "special treatment" that could only be assured if separate institutions were maintained. To quote from one of the committee's reports: because of the "persisting insensitivity among many of the male members of the university community," a separate "organization that speaks for women" was required so that women "would not lose the advantages that they have gained and become lost in a male-oriented environment."[72]

Because Pembrokers objected to being separated out and treated differently from male students, however, a majority of the committee eventually changed their minds about the need for separate facilities. Unable to reach a unanimous decision, the Pembroke Study Committee made two final reports to the new president, Donald Hornig (1970–1975) in November 1970. Nine members, including the chair, Professor Elizabeth Leduc, all four students, and two members of the Brown Corporation, signed a Majority Report, which recommended the merging of all offices to form one united undergraduate structure to be administered by a single dean for both men and women. The Majority Report also recommended that the number of female undergraduates at Brown be increased until the ratio of men to women was one to one (the ratio at this time was 2.43 to one) and that the number of women on Brown's faculty be substantially increased in order to provide adequate role models for female students. Finally, the Majority Report called for the establishment of a women's center, "to be charged with the development of special programs for women … [and to] act as a research center and data bank for the special problems of women in society."[73]

Fearing that the education of women would suffer if a separate administration was not maintained to safeguard women's interests, four members of the committee, among them Rosemary Pierrel, the dean of Pembroke, and Sophie Blistein, president of the Pembroke Alumnae Association, Class of 1941, signed a Minority Report calling for continued study of the matter. This group declared that "The students think all problems will be solved with the merger of Brown and Pembroke and this is just not so."[74]

Most of Pembroke's administration and many alumnae opposed merging the undergraduate administrations, doubted the university's

Beverly J. Hodgson, Class of 1970, the first woman to be editor-in-chief of the *Brown Daily Herald*, now a judge in the Connecticut Superior Court.

commitment to providing for the "special needs" of women students, and distrusted Brown administrators' statements regarding their willingness to hire and promote women to high-ranking positions in a merged administration. Throughout the history of Pembroke, alumnae had been active in supporting the needs of women students. When Brown was not able to commit sufficient funds to provide women with dormitories, Anna Canada Swain, Class of 1911, and other alumnae organized a major capital drive to fund the construction of Andrews Hall.[75] Under the leadership of Doris Stapelton, Class of 1928, executive secretary of the Pembroke Alumnae Association, the association raised money for scholarships for women, offered continuing education programs in the 1960s, and developed a full-fledged alumnae magazine, the *Pembroke Alumna*.[76] Many alumnae were angry that they had not been consulted by the university about the merger and regretted that as a body they had had no formal input into the decision to merge the two administrations.

The Pembroke administration and alumnae had good cause to doubt Brown's avowals that it would meet the needs of its women students; throughout the 1960s and into the 1970s Brown continued to resist hiring women as faculty and electing women to the Brown Corporation. Many feared that without a separate institutions to look after the interests of women students and alumnae, equality for women at Brown would not be achieved. Alberta Brown, dean of admission, elaborated this view in her opposition to the merger:

> [G]iven the numerical imbalance of men and women at most levels of the university structure, the only hope I see for achieving our goal for the education of women with not too deliberate speed is to see that *there are women administrators, women faculty, women student leaders at all levels where policy is made and programs are launched.* We need this until that happy millennium comes when we shall not ask or care whether the candidate is man or woman any more than we shall ask or care whether he or she is black or white. Until that is achieved, I think parallelism, or a suitable equivalent, is necessary if we are to move fast enough toward our goal.[77]

The impact of the civil rights movement is evident again in Dean Brown's statement, particularly in her ironic use of the phrase "not too deliberate speed." She was demanding that the university do more in regard to sexual integration (and more quickly) than public schools were likely to do with regard to racial integration. But unlike the Supreme Court's assessment, in which separation was identified as intrinsic to racial inequality in public education, Dean Brown gave voice to a conviction, shared widely among alumnae, that sexual inequality was likely to persist, if not worsen, in the absence of separate, parallel educational structures for men and women.

At the recommendation of the Majority Report of November 1970, and following a vote of the Brown Corporation on June 4, 1971, Pembroke College ceased to exist as a separate administrative institution. In December 1970, when the prospect of a merger was a foregone conclusion, Rosemary Pierrel resigned from her post as dean of Pembroke and announced her intention to return to teaching full-time in the Psychology Department. Alberta Brown also resigned. Out of a total of approximately twenty-two women who comprised Pembroke's administration and physical education personnel, three deans and eight other administrators decided to stay on after the merger. Of the eleven women who moved over to Brown, six of them retained or improved on the title they had held at Pembroke, but only one, Leonore Pockman kept the directorship of her office when it merged. The other placement offices that combined with Pockman's – one at the men's college and one at the graduate school – were also directed by women. The women who joined the Brown administration after the merger received a significant increase in salaries, as the pay structure at Brown and Pembroke had been unequal and was now readjusted.[78]

Overall, financial considerations do not seem to have been a significant factor in Brown's decision to merge Pembroke into the Men's College, although there was a general perception among the Brown community that this decision was made in an attempt to save the university money during a period of fiscal crisis. However, President Hornig made it known that openings would be found for all Pembroke employees who wanted to work in Brown's administration and stated in the *Pembroke Alumna* that the "projected savings have nothing whatever to do with the decision." A financial study prepared in 1970 indicated that the projected savings were expected to be minimal: it was estimated that running a merged admission office would save Brown less than $30,000, while merging the placement offices would save roughly $19,000. No savings were projected for merging the two financial aid offices. According to one of the student members on the Pembroke Study Committee, cost considerations were not a major factor in the recommendation made by the committee: "it was a matter of saving $100,000, if that."[79]

In compliance with one of the Majority Report's recommendations to employ a high-ranking woman administrator, President Hornig hired Jacqueline Mattfeld to serve as dean of academic affairs and associate provost, the highest academic position held up to that time by a woman in the Ivy League.[80] Although Mattfeld was assigned the responsibility of addressing the special needs of female students, according to some associates she was never given the authority she needed to carry out this responsibility. As one colleague remarked after Mattfeld's resignation in 1975: "She was brought into the university . . . to be the spokesperson for all the things that the university didn't want to commit itself to." When Mattfeld left to assume the presidency of Barnard College, her post as associate provost was filled by Maurice Glicksman, who had previously served as dean of the Graduate School.[81]

Another woman, Karen Romer, was hired as a dean in 1972, and Mattfeld employed Kay Hall as her assistant in 1973. Mattfeld, Romer, and Hall worked together to create what eventually became known as the Working Group on the Status of Women, a group of roughly twenty-five women, including administrators, trustees, faculty, alumnae, and students.[82] Beverly Flather Edwards, an alumna of the Class of 1969, who worked in the chaplain's office at Brown counseling the women students who had just become the responsibility of the larger university, allowed her office to become the meeting place of this group. In 1974–75, when the Working Group on the Status of Women submitted a proposal to found the Sarah Doyle Women's Center, Edwards offered to act as coordinator of the center so that the center could get off the ground without a major financial commitment from the university. The women's center was given use of the Pembroke Alumnae Association's former building, which had been willed to Pembroke by a local resident. Under the direction of Edwards, the Women's Center came into existence in 1975, with the contribution of a few books, borrowed furniture, the volunteer efforts of alumnae and local residents and the help of a few students paid out of work study funds. The center established a library comprised of scholarship in women's studies and a gallery to exhibit the work of women artists, sponsored lectures and discussions for the Providence community and offered counseling services to students and alumnae. After the Women's Center proved its value to women in the community, the university came up with the money to make it possible to hire a full-time director. In 1977, Elizabeth Weed, a scholar and administrator, was appointed director of the center and later became the head of the women's studies program.[83]

Other recommendations in the Majority Report, such as increasing the proportion of women on the faculty at Brown, were not taken up until 1977–78 when Brown signed a consent decree to settle a class-action law suit brought by Professor Louise Lamphere. The suit put the university on the defensive concerning the hiring of women, and indirectly may have helped to raise money for an endowed chair for a female professor. This campaign was begun in 1960, initiated by Nancy Duke Lewis, who upon her death left the residue of her estate for this purpose. Alumnae and friends continued to contribute to the fund throughout the 1960s. Brown engaged visiting faculty to fill the chair temporarily, and in 1978–79, conducted a national search for a permanent faculty member. Professor Joan Scott was hired, and assumed her duties as a tenured member of the history faculty in the summer of 1980. With Scott's assistance, Ruth Harris Wolf, Class of 1941, led the fund-raising drive to completely fund the position. Within three years, the drive raised three quarters of a million dollars, and the Nancy Duke Lewis Chair was endowed permanently in 1983.[84]

In 1981, the Pembroke Center for Teaching and Research on Women was established. The idea for the center came, in part, out of the campaign drive for the Nancy Duke Lewis Chair, as the fund-raisers came to understand that an institutional structure was needed to ensure an ongoing commitment to the teaching of women's studies and to the pursuit of scholarship on women. A coalition of faculty, administrators, and alumnae realized that more visibility for the Pembroke legacy was needed: for alumnae because many still mourned the loss of their college; for students who had little sense of the history of women at Brown; and for the university community in general, which had little appreciation of the role women had played in Brown's past. Joan Scott and Elizabeth Weed drafted a document outlining the functions of the proposed center, the university agreed to create it, and the National Endowment for the Humanities and the Ford Foundation provided the initial funding.[85]

The Pembroke Center worked toward promoting attention to women's studies and established an undergraduate concentration in 1982. The center has funded twenty-five post-doctoral fellowships to women and two to men between 1982 and 1991 on topics ranging from depictions of women in cinema and the role of women in Moslem culture, to an analysis of the language of science and technology. One alumna, Christine Dunlap Farnham, Class of 1948, founded the Pembroke Center Associates, an alumnae organization devoted to supporting the Pembroke Center. She was serving as chair when she died in an automobile accident in 1984. After Farnham's death, as a tribute to her efforts and aspirations, the Christine Dunlap Farnham Archives was established.[86] These archives now document the history of women at Brown, and the experiences of Brown alumnae and women in Rhode Island.

As many among the Pembroke administration feared, the remaining all-female extracurricular activities disappeared soon after the merger, with the exception of women's sports, and the percentage of leadership positions held by women fell precipitously. Moreover, although the merged admission office at Brown continued to accept highly qualified women into the college – women who, as a group, received higher grades in high school and higher scores on standardized college tests than did the men who came to Brown[87] – a smaller proportion of these women than the men received A's in their college courses during their first year at Brown. This struck some people as a new and disturbing phenomenon. According to a survey completed in 1980,

> Freshman year seems to be a disorienting and disheartening experience for women students in academic matters. Their grades drop off sharply from high school, and in that year there occurs the greatest gap between men and women students' perceptions of their academic ability. Such a traumatic beginning may well lower academic expectations permanently.

Unsure about why these differentials appeared, the authors of the survey suggested that women at Brown were not receiving as much direct contact with and support from faculty as did male students.[88]

In retrospect, the adoption of coeducation at Brown may appear to have been inevitable, but many faculty, students, alumnae, and administrators at Pembroke supported a coordinate school as late as 1966 when Pembroke celebrated its seventy-fifth anniversary.[89] Throughout its history, Pembroke College provided resources and special services exclusively for women and organized separate women's activities and clubs, in which Pembroke students were able to participate without competition or interference from men. Yet many students in the 1960s experienced Pembroke's close supervision of dormitory life as an inexcusable invasion of their privacy. Associating academic freedom with Brown and social repressiveness with Pembroke, these students actively sought the introduction of coeducational housing and welcomed the dismantling of the Pembroke administration when it finally came to pass in 1971.

Thus have the debates over sexual equality in education at Brown moved back and forth between positions advocating separation or integration, and identical or different treatment. But none of these constructions proved satisfactory when the practices were assessed: at no point was there general agreement that sexual equality at Brown had ever been obtained. As the students who critiqued Brown's academic program in 1926 understood, it was not sufficient to teach women the same subjects in separate classrooms, not because of the separation, but because women were being taught subjects they found irrelevant and boring, by male faculty who seemed to them "contemptuous" and "insulting." Similarly, the problem with the separate Pembroke administration of the 1960s was not that it was a separate entity run by women, nor that it symbolized women's differences, but that this particular administration upheld and represented a social order and moral values that many students no longer respected and refused to accept.

This analysis of the history of Pembroke College points out the futility of moving back and forth along the axes of separation-coeducation and identity-difference in trying to assess and achieve sexual equality in higher education. Whether women are taught by men, taught without men, or taught like men are not the most important factors affecting the quality of women's education. Equality must be conceptualized in terms that are able to recognize discriminatory treatment by its effects: by low self-esteem, by anger and despair that women feel, or by the diminution of individual and collective power of women that accompany and are produced by inequality.

From today's perspective, we may wonder why some sort of compromise, short of merger, was not possible – why the university deans remained so resistant to altering the *in loco parentis* institutions. Part of the reason lies in widespread community support for the close supervision of college women. Many adults, whether parents of students, members of the Brown Corporation, faculty, administrators, or alumnae clearly hoped that this desire for "greater 'freedom' among young people... might be the end of a trend, and that the pendulum might soon swing back to a more conservative position."[90] But the pendulum did not swing back, and many Pembroke students grew ever more insistent that they be as unrestricted in social, as they were in academic, affairs.[91]

Unfortunately, immediately after dismantling the social system that women students judged to be sexist and repressive, the university at first neglected to preserve any part of the women's institutions or culture that had flourished less than a decade previously. Then, in the 1970s and 1980s, some of Brown's administrators labored to rectify this neglect. Still, it is troubling how little each generation of students knows of the history of the preceding generation, and how little use has been made of historical knowledge as each generation confronts its own questions concerning equality in education. For example, in 1973, just two years after the merger, a female student voiced the following concern:

> There is an urgent need for a center that women recognize as a place for their activities... a library and reading room, files and office space, meeting and practice rooms, special counseling facilities, a clearing house reference service, an exhibition gallery for women's work, and even a gym and a stage.[92]

And an alumna from the Class of 1955, well aware of the irony, wrote back: "We used to have something like that at Brown... practice rooms, gym, library, the whole works. We called it Pembroke College."[93]

NOTES

1. William H.P. Faunce, *Report of the President*, November 1928, p. 18. Unless otherwise noted, all documents cited in this chapter are available in the Christine Dunlap Farnham Archives of Brown University. Most are catalogued in Karen M. Lamoree, *Research Guide to the Christine Dunlap Farnham Archives* (Providence: Pembroke Center for Teaching and Research on Women and the University Library, Brown University, 1989).

2. Pembroke Study Committee, "Majority Report," 8 May 1970, p. 1.

3. *Announcement of Courses*, Women's College, 1901–1902.

4. These traditions included the Sophomore Masque, a play using Greek themes and costumes; Ivy Night; May Day, involving the crowning of a May Queen and a procession to celebrate the coming of spring; and in the 1950s, a Style Show, in which all the dormitories competed for awards for the "All-Campus Model" and the "Best Dressed Model."

5. *The Pembroke Manual*, 1953–54. In 1953, Brown and Pembroke students organized the Brown Outing Club to sponsor coeducational expeditions.

6. Pembrokers were themselves responsible for reporting and punishing their own violations through a student-run institution known as the Dormitory Council. See "Report of the Dormitory Council, Semester III," 1 March–1 July 1944, p. 3.

7. "Regulations Governing the Halls of Residence, Reports of the Dormitory Council," 1943–1950; *Students' Handbook of Pembroke College in Brown University*, 1938–39, 1940–41; *The Pembroke Manual*, 1953–54, 1955–56. Becky Krawiec's "Parietals and Pembroke: The Social System, 1962–69," Brown University, undergraduate seminar paper, 16 May 1988, provides an overview of the workings of the social system, including its evolution and eventual demise in the 1960s.

8. These quotations appear in the files of students who were enrolled in the college, so Pembroke did admit students who did not fit its ideal. Unfortunately, the records of students who were not admitted have not been kept, so it is not possible to make the comparisons that might elucidate how stringently Pembroke applied these criteria. The existing files are restricted, and the author was not granted access to them.

9. For further discussion of this issue, see Karen M. Lamoree, "Why Not a Jewish Girl?': The Jewish Experience at Pembroke College in Brown University," *Rhode Island Jewish Historical Notes* 10 (November 1988): 122–140.

10. The "Minutes of the Pembroke Advisory Committee" refer to an unofficial policy of accepting no more than one Black woman a year as late as 1960. Although all other women entering as freshmen and living on campus were housed in doubles, the sole Black woman roomed alone. These records also mention one instance of a white girl who expressed a desire to have a Black roommate, but her request was denied out of hand. See "Minutes of the Meeting of the Advisory Committee on Pembroke College," 14 March 1960, p. 3.

11. The perception of the superiority of Pembroke students continued throughout the 1940s and 1950s. Exhibiting his characteristically wry style, President Keeney in his report to the Advisory Committee on Pembroke College for 1957 wrote: "The Dean of Pembroke has an irritating habit of stating on every possible occasion that Pembrokers are superior to Brown men. Unfortunately, her assertions are borne out by elections to Phi Beta Kappa and Sigma Xi, which show that a much higher percentage of [Pembroke] students achieve the very highest academic level [than do Brown men]....This is particularly annoying to me because I have always asserted that young women, while more docile and dutiful than young men, do not achieve the highest level of distinction." *Report of the President, June 1, 1956*, p. 20, cited in Grace E. Hawk, *Pembroke College in Brown University* (Providence: Brown University Press, 1967), fn. 35, p. 301. See also, Charles Tillinghast's Address to the Pembroke Alumnae Dinner in 1969, as reported in "Pembroke: Sentiment for Change," *Brown Alumni Monthly* 70 (April 1970): 4.

12. Alice Gildin Silver, Class of 1932, Oral History, 16 April 1985; transcript, p. 3.

13. "Unfeminine Smokers," *Pembroke Record* 40 (22 April 1960): 2.

14. Julie Haig, "Pembroker Finds Too Many People Asking 'Why Go to College Anyway?" *Pembroke Record* 40 (December 1959): 2.

15. In the minutes kept from 1943 through 1960, there were only two instances when the council seemed concerned that its rules or punishments were not being taken seriously by the students, once in 1945 and once in 1946. "Dorm Council Report, November '45–February '46," pp. 1, 2; and "Report of Dormitory Council for Semester III, 1945," p. 3.

16. The exact wording of the Pembroke Honor Code was: "In order to provide for harmonious community living and to encourage the development of high standards of personal integrity, we, the students of Pembroke College do hereby establish an Honor Code . . . based upon the concept of a two-fold responsibility: first, the responsibility of the individual for her own standards and conduct, and second, the responsibility of the individual student for the standards and conduct of the college community of which she is a part. We willingly accept the privilege and the responsibility of self-government that the college administration has given us in a spirit of mutual trust and confidence." *The Pembroke Manual*, 1953–54, p. 1.

17. Ibid., p. v.

18. "The Report of the Senior Committee of the Women's College in Brown University," 1926, pp. 1–2.

19. Ibid., pp. 7–9.

20. Ibid., pp. 25–26.

21. The committee found fault with the lecture system, which was just beginning to supersede the recitation system. Lecturers, the report stated, "were free to talk as long as [they] desire with no interruptions" and had little personal contact with students. The committee recommended that the lecture system be modified so that only elementary courses whose goal was to lay out "facts essential to further study" should be taught with lectures; more advanced courses should be taught with discussions, or a combination of lectures and discussions. Professors were urged to stop using the "Missouri system" – i.e., grading on a bell curve – which the committee felt resulted in the passing of more students than ought to pass. See Ibid., pp. 17, 21–22, 32–33, 39–41, 72, 75.

22. Morriss, "The Affiliated College," 1928, p. 31.

23. Samuel Paul Capen, Luther Pfahler Eisenhart and Guy Stanton Ford, "Report of the Survey Committee on Brown University," September 1930, pp. 29, 30–31.

24. From roughly 1922 until 1931, Pembroke College operated a separate School of Education, in which students could earn a bachelor's degree in teaching. The program in home economics, introduced by President Faunce lasted only a few years before it was eliminated because of insufficient student interest.

25. Several times in the late 1940s and early 1950s, Dean Lewis assured members of the Pembroke Advisory Committee that the college was giving "all possible support" to the nursing program, but still "the mortality of those who enter is very high." President Wriston pointed out that Pembroke's nursing course was not accredited by any nursing association. In 1951, the nursing program was reorganized so that Pembroke students could get the Bachelor of Science degree in nursing with fewer science courses, but even this step did not attract sufficient numbers of students. The program was eventually discontinued in the early 1960s; students who entered in the Fall of 1959 were the last class to enroll in the program. See "Minutes of the Meeting of the Advisory Committee on Pembroke College," 14 December 1949, p. 1; 6 July 1951, pp. 4–5; and 5 October 1959, p. 2. Also see Lewis, "Report of the Dean of Pembroke College to the Advisory Committee on Pembroke College," 25 September 1958, pp. 2–3.

26. For the size of Pembroke College, see Hawk, *Pembroke College,* p. 198–99.

27. Morris, "Report on Pembroke College to the Advisory Committee," 7 April 1942, p. 2.

28. "Pembroke: Her Role Today," (n.d. circa January 1943) contained in "Pembroke/World War II." Also see Elizabeth Zwick, "The Pembroke Class of 1945: A Wartime Generation of College Women," Brown University, undergraduate thesis, May 1982, esp. pp. 27–28.

---

29. Morriss, "Report on Pembroke College to the Advisory Committee," 7 April 1942, pp. 3–5.

30. This analysis is based on information contained in Hawk, *Pembroke College,* fn. 27, p. 299. Studies of Pembroker's concentrations made in the early 1950s provide additional evidence for this argument. Dean Lewis found that during the period 1948–53, "the humanities continue to attract approximately half our students as concentrators, but ... the social studies have risen from 10% to 30% and the sciences have dropped from 30% to 20% with the Sc.B. group practically disappearing from the statistical table. This decrease in the sciences has come in spite of the fact that the Pembroke Admission Officers have emphasized our strength in this area when they have visited secondary schools, the Placement Office has constant calls for women so trained." Lewis, "Report of the Dean of Pembroke College to the Advisory Committee on Pembroke College," 4 October 1954, p. 9.

31. Cited in Hawk, *Pembroke College,* p. 187.

32. Deans Morriss and Lewis gave the results of these elections as well as statistics on how many Pembrokers graduated with honors in every one of their annual reports from 1930–1960. See also Footnote No. 11.

33. For male administrators' response, see Hawk, *Pembroke College,* p. 220.

34. Nineteen switched to a B.A. program, seven withdrew from college and two changed to another science. Lewis, "Report of the Dean of Pembroke College [to the] Advisory Committee on Pembroke College," 5 October 1959, appended to p. 4.

35. Lewis, "Report of the Dean of Pembroke College to the Advisory Committee on Pembroke College," 1 October 1956, p. 4.

36. Student Government Association, "Executive Minutes."

37. Judith Ginsberg, Class of 1968, Oral History, 30 March 1988; transcript. p. 6.

38. "Minutes of the Meeting of the Advisory Committee on Pembroke College," 5 October 1959, p. 3. Also see Lewis, "Report of the Dean of Pembroke College to the Advisory Committee on Pembroke College," 4 October 1954, p. 7.

39. Lewis, "Report of the Dean of Pembroke College [to] Advisory Committee on Pembroke College," 5 October 1959, p. 7.

40. Pembroke Cabinet of the U.C.A., "Coeducational Trends," [Letter to the Editor] *Pembroke Record* 40 (10 February 1960): 2.

41. Rosemary Pierrel, "Dean's Report [to the] Advisory Committee [of Pembroke College]," 17 November 1961, p. 7. The same sentiment is reiterated in the Dean's Report for 19 October 1967, p.8.

42. In this period, Brown University abolished distribution requirements in its implementation of the "New Curriculum" in 1969, another development that contributed to students seeing the Brown administration as more "liberal" than the Pembroke administration.

43. "Resident Study Applauds Robinson," *Pembroke Record* 42 (13 March 1962): 2.

44. Eileen Rudden, Class of 1972, *Brown Alumni Monthly* 72 (June 1972): 14. Also see oral histories of Eileen Rudden, Class of 1972, 22 March 1987; and Miriam Pichey, Class of 1971, 5 March 1988; Farnham Archives, as well as "P'brokers Attack Insobriety, Favor Parietal Rule Change," *Pembroke Record* 43 (7 December 1962): 5.

45. See oral histories of Susan Elizabeth Geary, Class of 1967; Pichey; and Rudden.

46. Pichey, oral history.

47. Ibid. Arlene Gorton, Class of 1952, remembers that "there was a lot of institutional racism at Brown both when I was a student and when I came back." Arlene Gorton, Class of 1952, oral history, 29 July 1988, Farnham Archives.

48. "Pembroke's 'Identity Crisis,'" [Editorial] *Pembroke Record* 47 (7 October 1966): 2.

49. "Minutes of the Meeting of the Pembroke Study Committee," 7 January 1970, p. 2.

50. This phrase was used by Jane M. Starkey in "Class of 1967 Supports Junior Lates, Considers 'Radical Changes,'" *Pembroke Record* 46 (12 October 1965): 1.

51. Ibid.; Candy Page, "Committee Concurs on Fines: Most Effective Punishment"

and "Pembroke: Reasonable or Restrictive?" *Pembroke Record* 46 (22 October 1965): 3.

52. Betsy Allen, Class of 1965; Nan Hoy, Class of 1965; and Judy Sims, Class of 1965, "Pembroke Opinions Vary About Recent Dismissals," *Pembroke Record* 43 (26 October 1962): 2.

53. Due to rule changes, students could have a friend sign them out and thus no longer had to plan their evenings in advance of 10 p.m. See "SGA Announces Changes in Social System Procedure," *Pembroke Record* 46 (19 November 1965): 3.

54. "Minutes of the Advisory Committee of Pembroke College," 16 April 1962, p. 2; "Administration Says 'No' to Senior Apts," *Pembroke Record* 43 (16 October 1962): 1.

55. Pierrel also changed the weekday curfew for freshmen. Instead of being allowed to stay out until midnight, freshmen now had to be back in the dorms by 11 p.m. Many regarded this move on the part of the deanery as "an hysterical message to the student body [–] that even though they might make an occasional concession the Deans still are in control of Pembroke Hall." "Who is to Blame?" [Editorial], *Pembroke Record* 47 (14 February 1967): 2; Gail Coyen, "SGA Ponders Social System," *Brown Daily Herald* 99 (23 September 1965): 1, 3.

56. See letter from Anne S. Dewart, dean of students, addressed to "Pembroke Parent," August 1966.

57. Rondi Erikson, "SGA Lollipop Poll Shows Extent of Rule Violation," *Pembroke Record* 47 (1 November 1966): 1, 4.

58. Kristin M. Fee, "Pembrokers Blast Dean's Procedures in Student Dismissal for Social Offense," *Pembroke Record* 47 (21 October 1966): 1.

59. Peter Magrath, professor of political science, chaired the nine-member committee, which included two additional faculty members, two undergraduates (the president of the Pembroke's Student Government Association and the president of Brown's Cammarian Club); a graduate student; and the heads of the three divisions of the university: Rosemary Pierrel, as dean of Pembroke; Robert Schulze, as dean of the College; and Michael Brennan, as dean of the Graduate School. "Heffner Names Nine-Man Group to Examine Social System," *Pembroke Record* 47 (15 November 1966): 1.

60. The official title of the Magrath Report was "Community and Partnership: Student Conduct at Brown University." It was released in May 1967 and was approved by the Brown Corporation on 3 June 1967. The *Pembroke Record* published it on 3 May 1967 under a huge headline which read, "Committee Blasts 'In Loco Parentis'; Asserts Need for Student Participation," 47 (3 May 1967): 1.

61. Quotations from "Community and Partnership," p. 35.

62. See Mary Tudor, "Social System Committee Study Shows Most Pembrokers Want Liberalization," *Pembroke Record* 46 (8 February 1966): 1.

63. Through the 1960s, the top administrators at Pembroke were: Rosemary Pierrel, dean; Charlotte Lowney, director of the Placement Office until 1967, then associate dean; Leonore Pockman, director of the Placement Office; Gretchen Tonks, assistant dean; Alberta F. Brown, dean of admission; Anne S. Dewart, assistant dean of students; and Bessie Rudd, director of the Physical Education Department.

64. In 1961, when Dean Lewis became ill and had to relinquish her duties, the Pembroke Advisory Committee discussed the qualifications they desired in Lewis' replacement. Although it was suggested that a married woman might bring more maturity to the position, the problem arose about "what to do with her husband." The Advisory Committee eventually agreed that "if the husband were in a profession not related to education and were or could be located in Rhode Island, he would not be considered a deterrent to her appointment." However, the question became moot when the position was offered to Rosemary Pierrel, who was unmarried at the time. See "Minutes of the Meeting of the Advisory Committee on Pembroke College," 7 March 1961, pp. 3–5.

65. Reporting to the Pembroke Advisory Committee on the events of the 1966–67 academic year, Pierrel wrote: "The difficult excitement [this year] was our brand of student

activities. The students have learned too well the techniques of the Civil Rights Movement, the non-violent riot. While I am convinced that to date we have experienced little if any hard-core activism, there is a significant minority whose adolescent rebellion, anti-establishmentarianism and anti-draft concerns are readily whipped up by a Paul Hoch or a *Brown Daily Herald*. For the past two years we had student leadership in Pembroke's SGA which tended to be either radical or ineffective....There has been a habit developing in recent years for SGA to ape and 'me too' the action of [the] Cam[marian] Club." Rosemary Pierrel, Dean's Report [to the Advisory Committee], 19 October 1967, p. 8.

66. Of this thirty-five, seventeen were enrolled in the freshman class, or 5.8 percent of the class. "Pembroke is Seeking Negro Girls," *Providence Evening Bulletin*, 24 September 1968, p. 30.

67. Leonore Pockman, director of the Pembroke Placement Office, explained to the Pembroke Study Committee that the "heart of the reason for having separate offices" was that a "special concentrated effort" was made on behalf of women. The Pembroke Placement Office, unlike Brown's, was actively involved in advising alumnae who had taken time off to raise families and wanted to return to the job market. It also made an effort to publicize part-time jobs suitable for women with families who could not work full-time. "Minutes of the Meeting of the Pembroke Study Committee," 11 March 1970, pp. 2–3. Also see Pierrel's marginal comments on "Revision of Subcommittee Draft of Report," p. 1 in the Pembroke Study Committee files.

68. See "Minutes of the Meeting of the Pembroke Study Committee," 11 February 1970, pp. 2, 3. It seems that many Pembroke students also felt ill-at-ease with the Pembroke counselors, whom they viewed as old-fashioned and out-of-touch with the social realities of the 1960s. See J.M. Hopkins, "Pembroke Lost," *Issues: The Brown Review* 8 (October 1977): 11. Laura Geller, Class of 1971, "Should Pembroke Go Co-ed? Yes!"; Laurel Leone, Class of 1972, "Should Pembroke Go Co-ed?" No!" and Paula Sich, Class of 1971, "Should Pembroke Go Co-ed? That's the wrong question," *Pembroke Alumna* 45 (April 1970): 14–16.

69. "Minutes of the Meeting of the Pembroke Study Committee," 11 March 1970, p. 3.

70. Peter Warren, "Broke dean quits black admissions," *Brown Daily Herald* 104 (3 December 1970): 1, 2. Donald F. Hornig, "Memo on Pembroke Admissions," 22 December 1970. Also see J.M. Hopkins, "Pembroke Lost."

71. In a recent interview, Rosemary Pierrel Sorrentino explained that she approached President Keeney in 1963 to discuss the possibility of ending the coordinate relationship, but Keeney, nearing retirement, told her to take it up with his successor. The presidency was unstable for a number of years. After Keeney's resignation in 1966, Ray Heffner served for three years, followed by Merton Stolz, who became acting president in the fall of 1969. Donald F. Hornig did not take over from Stolz until June 1970. See Rosemary Pierrel Sorrentino, oral history, December 1988, Farnham Archives.

72. Pembroke Study Committee, entitled document, n.d. [circa November 1969], pp. 2, 3.

73. Pembroke Study Committee, "Majority Report," 8 May 1970, pp. 1–4. Pockman left after one year. Gretchen Tonks, who had served Pembroke for nineteen years as an assistant dean in charge of financial aid, became a financial aid officer at Brown and left after one year. Charlotte Lowney [Tomas] left the dean's office to become director of the Extension Division until 1975 when it was phased out. She then became associate dean of the college, and continued to run the Resumed Education Program from 1973 until her retirement in 1990. Anne Dewart, dean of students at Pembroke, took a position in alumni affairs. Arlene Gorton, director of physical education at Pembroke, was made an assistant director and later associate director in the Athletics Department at Brown.

74. Pierrel, "Minutes of the Pembroke College Advisory Committee," 6 May 1970, contained in Stolz's file 149, "Pembroke College Advisory Committee." The same sentiment

is expressed by Rosemary Pierrel Sorrentino, oral history, and Sophie Schaffer Blistein, Class of 1941, oral history, Farnham Archives.

75. Swain's efforts were rewarded by President Wriston, who appointed her as the first woman trustee on the Brown Corporation in 1949.

76. In October 1957, the Pembroke Alumnae Association expanded its newsletter into a magazine, the *Pembroke Alumna,* appearing four times a year. The *Alumna* also served an outreach function, publishing articles by alumnae about their careers. Polly Welts Kaufman, Class of 1951, edited the *Pembroke Alumna* from 1957 to 1968, followed by Sallie Kappelman Riggs, Class of 1962, who continued as editor until the merger in 1971.

77. "Minutes of the Meeting of the Pembroke Study Committee," 11 March 1970, p. 6; author's emphasis.

78. See J.M. Hopkins, "Pembroke Lost."

79. Figures contained in "Summaries of 1970 Brown/Pembroke Studies," Pembroke College – Pembroke Alumna – Editor, files, 1968–1971 (Sallie Kappelman Riggs). Hornig is cited in "Corporation to Act on Brown-Pembroke Merger," *Pembroke Alumna* 45 (December 1970): 4.

80. News from Brown University, Press Release, 71/135/5/26/JC, 28 May 1971.

81. Based on interviews with Katherine Hall, 14 February 1990 and Karen Romer, 9 March 1990 by the author; audio tapes in possession of the author. Quotation is from J.M. Hopkins, "Pembroke Lost."

82. Based on interviews with Hall, 14 February 1990 and Romer, 9 March 1990.

83. "Sarah Doyle, Meet the Sarah Doyle Center," *Brown Alumni Monthly* 86 (September 1985): 16–18. Beverly Flather Edwards, Class of 1969, "Notes on the Formation of the Sarah Doyle Center," 24 April 1991, Farnham Archives. See also, "The Sarah Doyle Center," memo attached to Jacqueline Mattfeld's letter to Rosemary Sorrentino, 29 September 1975; contained in the Sophie P. Schaffer Blistein Papers, Farnham Archives.

84. Correspondence with Joan Scott, March 1990, in possession of the author.

85. Ibid.

86. See Polly Welts Kaufman, "Christine Dunlap Farnham (1926–1984)" in Lamoree, *Research Guide to the Christine Dunlap Farnham Archives,* pp. ix-x.

87. Office of Educational Measurement, "Changing Times at Brown University: A Comparison of the Classes of 1960 through 1970," April 1967, pp. 2–8.

88. Committee on the Status of Women at Brown, "Final Report," 30 May 1980; quotation appears on p. 8.

89. Numerous articles appeared in the *Pembroke Record* throughout the 1960s, discussing the advantages of maintaining Pembroke as a coordinate college. For example, see "Pembroke as Pembroke," 44 (2 May 1964): 2.

90. "Minutes of the Advisory Committee of Pembroke College," 16 April 1962, p. 2.

91. Pichey, oral history.

92. Susan Colwell, Class of 1973, "Center: For Women Only," *Issues* 3 (March 1973): 19–20.

93. Leslie Travis Wendel, Class of 1955, "We Called It Pembroke," [Letter to the Editor] *Brown Alumni Monthly* 73 (May 1973): 54.

From Equity to Equality: Women's Athletics at Brown

by CINDY HIMES

D URING THE 1963–1964 aca-
demic year, the Brown men's ice hockey coach, Jim Fullerton, decided to
teach his team a lesson after its 4–1 loss to Boston College. In doing so,
he called upon nineteen-year old Pembroke freshman Nancy Schieffelin,
an experienced ice hockey player. Disguised in a full team uniform,
Schieffelin participated in a practice warm-up and drill session with the
men's ice hockey team where she drove home Fullerton's intended message
that maybe it was time to start putting Pembrokers on the line. Despite
the implication behind the incident that men should be ashamed of being
equalled or bested by a woman, especially in such a male-dominated athletic domain, it spurred Schieffelin and a band of other Pembrokers to
form the first female collegiate ice hockey team in the United States.

The story of the Pembroke Pandas, as the team came to be known,
embodies many of the social tensions that came into play historically as
women at Brown, and in the larger society, laid claim to the traditionally
male sphere of sports and physical activity. Mothers worried that their
daughters would sport toothless smiles. Local sportswriters felt it necessary to reassure the public that several of the players were pretty and had
boyfriends. Players, too, worried that the opposite sex would be put off
by bruised shins. The paucity of women's teams forced a heated debate
on whether men and women should play against each other and, if so,
under what rules and conditions. And, finally, the recently retired Bessie
Rudd, an authoritative voice on all matters of women's sports at Brown

Pembroke Pandas, women's ice hockey team in the 1960s.

declared, "I see no reason for ice hockey for women...Let the women have their sports and the men have theirs."[1]

These concerns seem to have had little effect on the enthusiasm of a select group of Pembrokers, most of whom had never actually played ice hockey. With the support of Arlene Gorton and other members of the Physical Education Department, twenty women set about raising funds, learning the game, convincing Brown men to help coach them, and trying to find other women's teams to play.

In order to gain university and community support, players and their supporters in the Physical Education Department understood that they must move somewhat cautiously in the early years. Sarah Phillips, the team's official coach in the early years of its existence, told a *Providence Sunday Journal* reporter in 1964 that the women's ice hockey team would play by modified rules including shorter time periods and a restriction against any personal contact between players.

Aside from practice sessions with the Brown men's team, the team was forbidden to play against men. One exception to this rule took place in 1968 when the Pandas held a fund-raising game with the Brown Bruins junior varsity. The distaff side in this game held a considerable advantage, however, in that the men were armed only with brooms in their left hands (right hands if they were left-handed), were permitted only five sweepers on the ice, and were not allowed to move their defensemen over the red line. The game and the hoopla surrounding it apparently drew sufficient fan support to send the Pandas on their way to a game against the Golden Gals of Queen's University in Kingston, Ontario.

The establishment of ties with Canadian teams and the expanding number of women's teams in the United States eventually made competition against men a moot issue. Participation in Canadian tournaments also forced the abandonment of the rigid restrictions against body contact previously adhered to by Pembroke players.

Larger forces such as Title IX and the feminist movement also played a role in the evolution of women's ice hockey at Brown. Title IX of the Higher Education Act of 1972, by forbidding sex discrimination in the programs of federally-funded educational institutions, resulted in the creation and expansion of athletic opportunities, mostly interscholastic and intercollegiate in nature, for an increasingly interested and physically active young female public. In 1964, the Pembroke ice hockey team consisted primarily of freshman women, only one of whom had ever played ice hockey, and the team had great difficulty in finding other teams to play. By 1973, women's ice hockey had become an official varsity sport at Brown. In 1987, the team still relied heavily on freshman talent, but now the freshmen were seasoned veterans of high school and club programs throughout the country, were heavily recruited, and could expect to play a twenty-six game schedule. Pembroker Nancy Schieffelin had clearly helped to set a revolution in motion.[2]

It would be a mistake to think that women's ice hockey engendered the first, the last, or even the most controversial debate in the history of women's sports and physical education at Brown University. From the inception of higher education for women at Brown, students, faculty, and administrators have engaged in an ongoing and often heated discussion over what types, structures, and amounts of physical activity are appropriate for college women.

The Formative Years (1891–1930)

During the first forty years, physical training and sports became an integral part of the evolving student culture. In these years, sports, like other aspects of the Women's College experience, developed in an almost exclusively female setting. For those athletically inclined, participation in sports often served as an avenue to social status, self-esteem, and strong bonds of emotion and friendship with other women. By 1930, students, with the support of physical educators and college administrators, had built a shared value system through athletics emphasizing team, class and institutional loyalty, cooperation, the importance of good health, competitiveness tempered by good sportsmanship, leadership, and female solidarity.

When the Women's College Adjunct to Brown University opened in 1891, many models for organizing physical education and athletics at women's colleges were readily available. In answer to charges by Dr. Edward Clarke, a Harvard physician, that higher education would result in permanent physical, emotional, and sexual damage in women, the leading women's colleges had already instituted complex health maintenance systems. These programs generally included regular medical examinations, lectures on hygiene and physiology, two to four years of required physical education for all students, individualized prescriptive gymnastics programs, broad-based intramural athletic programs, and periods of required outdoor exercise or recreation.[3]

From the start, the Women's College was hampered in its efforts to establish a well-rounded program in physical culture by its urban surroundings and, hence, lack of wide-open spaces, and by a scarcity of funds for facilities and equipment. As early as 1892, President E. Benjamin Andrews had identified an exercise hall as one of the needs of the Women's College. During the 1892–93 academic year, women students were required to spend two hours weekly during the second term performing "Exercises with dumb bells and Indian clubs and in Swedish movements . . . ."[4]

In 1897, the Women's College established a Department of Physical Culture. From 1898–1901, the department was placed on firm footing with the hiring of Mabel Potter, Class of 1897, A.M., 1898, as its director. Under Potter, the assembly hall became the site of required classes in gymnastics for freshmen and sophomores, regular physical examinations, and periodic tests of skill. Gymnasium work for juniors and seniors was encouraged but elective and, therefore, rarely done. Potter urged all students to go beyond the required gymnastics and to take up sports and games such as tennis and basketball for recreation.[5]

Students showed greater enthusiasm for organized sports than they did for required gymnasium exercises. In an effort to bring more juniors and seniors into the gymnasium, a fencing class was offered in 1902 as an alternative to gymnastic drills. By 1905, the Department of Physical Culture allowed freshmen and sophomores to substitute instruction in outdoor sports (tennis, field hockey or baseball) for the regular gymnasium exercise.[6] Students did not, however, wait for faculty sanction to engage in organized athletics as demonstrated by the formation of a Tennis Association in 1900 and the Athletic Association in the spring of 1902.

As interest in all forms of physical activity grew, the inadequacy of athletic facilities at the Women's College became all the more apparent. In 1905, the college had only two tennis courts, both located behind Pembroke Hall. So that women students could opt for outdoor sports rather than gymnastics, the Department of Physical Culture first had to locate an available athletic field. Brown's President Faunce came to the rescue with permission to use an open field on Morris Avenue owned by the Botanical Gardens.[7]

The need for a gymnasium was a long-standing issue at the Women's College. In 1902, the Andrews Association pledged its help in securing better athletic facilities. In a 1902 *Sepiad* article, Senior Emma May Caufield summed up the problem when she referred to Pembroke Hall as "the chapel-gymnasium-study-philosophy-dance hall."[8] Another student declared, "No one who has seen the gymnastic classes slipping about in their effort to run on the waxed floor of the assembly hall, or the wild rush downstairs at the end of the hour in order to be first at the shower baths, can doubt that a gymnasium is one of Pembroke's pressing needs."[9]

Fund raising began in earnest in 1904 for the building of a new gymnasium. The Rhode Island Society for the Collegiate Education of Women put up $5,000 and a piece of land next to Pembroke Hall as its contribution. Plays, poetry readings, and other performances by students, faculty, and alumnae where admission was charged provided another source of funds. Stephen Metcalf and his sister Eliza Metcalf Radeke donated additional land to augment the building site and the surrounding campus area. And Frank Sayles capped off the fund-raising campaign with a $50,000 contribution toward the building that would bear his name, Sayles Gymnasium. The dedication ceremony took place in February, 1907.[10]

Sayles Gymnasium consisted of offices, a large hall with a gallery, a resting room, a hall for study, recitation rooms, and a basement with dressing rooms, bathrooms, lockers, and shower baths. In the spring of 1907, the alumnae contributed money for bowling alleys. Blanche Luella Smith attested to the "bowling madness" that had captured her peers:

> I will not admit that students have left in the middle of a lecture to secure an alley for the succeeding hour; I will not concede that professors have waited in vain for classes which were lingering about the magnet; I will merely say that gardens, containing thorn bushes, proving no barrier to the mad rush of students across the campus for the purpose of procuring an alley, wickets (extra size) have been introduced as a garden border to keep back the contestants.[11]

Another addition to the athletic facilities of the Women's College resulting from the acquisition of land adjacent to Sayles was the building of two new tennis courts. With the completion of the new gymnasium and the securing of athletic fields for outdoor sports, the place of physical education and sports in college life was cemented. These physical spaces and the activities that took place there played an integral role in shaping the rituals, customs, folklore, and language that constituted student culture at the Women's College.

As with all cultures, the creation of this common value system involved both conflict and resolution. Students, faculty, and administrators struggled to build consensus out of disagreement on a number of issues related to sports and physical education. Of course, there was never total agreement, but the end product of this process was an integrated system of physical culture based on a set of values many of which held fast until the early 1960s.

A more careful examination of the arenas of conflict concerning the physical aspect of education at the Women's College offers great insight into a variety of aspects of the female experience at Brown: student health, social life, intellectual pursuits, prevailing ideals of femininity, and relationships with male and female peers, to name a few.

Much of the debate over the appropriate structure for women's sports boiled down to how much and what kind of competition would benefit women. The Women's College at Brown was not alone in wrestling with the apparent contradictions between accepted feminine ideals and the growing competitiveness fostered in women by entry into such traditionally male spheres as higher education and athletics. Whether or not to encourage intercollegiate athletic competition was the burning issue in women's sports at most colleges in the early twentieth century.

The organizational scheme adopted by the Women's College for sports and physical education strongly resembled that found at other women's colleges. In 1916, the Women's College joined the ranks of those requiring four years of class work in physical education. This policy, which had apparently lapsed, was given official sanction by the faculty and President Faunce in 1922 as a result of a study indicating that many colleges across the country had a four-year requirement.[12]

As at other colleges, individual students became eligible for class teams in different sports if they displayed special aptitude for a particular sport in the outdoor component of required physical education classes. Student-run intramural athletic programs based on competition between class teams represented the highest level of competition available to students at many women's colleges. Here, the Women's College diverged somewhat from standard practice in providing regular, albeit limited, opportunities for its outstanding female athletes to test their skills against outside teams from area colleges, high schools, YWCAs, and churches.

In 1901, even before the Athletic Association was founded, a student suggested that the freshman and sophomore classes aid Janet Maria Auty, the instructor in physical culture, by forming their own basketball teams and making the arrangements for games with outside teams during the winter and spring terms. Another student, in 1908, expressed her strong "... hope for a long list of intercollegiate games during the second and part of the third term."[13] In 1916, the Athletic Association, polled its students on whether or not they believed in intercollegiate athletics for women. After a heated discussion, the students passed a motion in favor of intercollegiate athletics, but only by a bare majority.[14]

To the extent that Women's College teams actually participated in outside competition between 1910 and 1930, basketball was the main activity. The varsity, composed of the best players from each of the class teams, usually played four or five games with area teams. For instance, the 1922 schedule included five contests, one each with the alumnae, Lincoln School, St. Margaret's Church, Rhode Island State, and Wheaton.

An intercollegiate baseball game between Wheaton and the Women's College in 1928 drew reporters from three states, not to mention a crowd of small boys hoping to observe a girl fight. According to all accounts, the behavior of both teams was impeccable and the game was followed by ice cream for both teams in Miller Hall.[15]

In spite of forays into intercollegiate competition, most varsity teams at the Women's College were strictly "honorary" and never saw outside competition. In the years under discussion, varsity teams were regularly named in tennis, basketball, field hockey, fistball, apparatus, bowling and baseball. In a 1914 *Sepiad* article critical of the Athletic Association, one student asked, "What use is an 'Honorary Varsity?' Members of said 'Team' have their names brilliantly illuminated with red ink and posted on the athletic bulletin board. Said names also appear in the *Sepiad* and *Brun Mael*. What HONOR for college girls!" [16]

Athletic honors, then, were generally won in intramural rather than intercollegiate competition. The Athletic Association constructed an elaborate system of awards to recognize outstanding individual, team, and class efforts in the area of athletics. Exceptional individuals sported the "BW," (after 1929 the "P"), on their letter sweaters. Athletic standouts also received numerals for accomplishment in three sports, letters for making the first team in a sport, and circles to be placed around letters for making the varsity in that sport. Class shields prominently displayed in the gymnasium recorded the collective accomplishments of a class in all fields of athletic endeavor. Symbols of athletic achievement were everywhere. [17]

After the arrival of Elizabeth Bates in 1913, the Physical Education Department placed renewed emphasis on "proper body-posture, rational exercise and rest." [18] Hope Sisson, president of the Athletic Association in 1914, revealed a common belief that sports were the best antidote to hard study when she advised fellow students to take up tennis: "After that English theme or your History test, you can most satisfactorily vacuum clean your thoughts by a set." [19]

At its extreme, this attitude could and did lead to anti-intellectualism and the neglect of academic duties. In the 1906 *Sepiad,* a student lamented the situation:

> Most of us can discuss at length the prospects of our class basketball teams, the lunch counter, or the failings of the Student Government Executive Board, but very few of us can talk intelligently upon the Russian problem, the question of an East Side Approach, or about the reforms in Insurance management. [20]

There were many students, however, who would have dismissed this student with the popular term "greasy grind."

The 1917–1918 academic year witnessed a liberalization in the rules concerning academic eligibility for class teams. Prior to this, students with two or more failures were not permitted to participate in class contests. The new ruling stated that such students could not be captains of first teams (in some sports, classes had more than one team) but could play in the games. By 1922, the Athletic Association had once again reversed its policy and mandated the removal from all class teams of any student with two or more failures.[21]

While there were extremists on both sides of the question, "jocks" vs. "grinds," most students writing for college publications saw balance between intellectual and physical activity as the hallmark of the "ideal college woman."

The espousal of a physically active ideal of womanhood had its potential dangers in the context of early twentieth-century definitions of femininity. Athleticism, as a male domain, threatened to alter women's speech, mannerisms, dress, and self-presentation. To avoid the adoption of "masculine" characteristics and the loss of "feminine" attributes by athletic women, students, faculty, and administrators at the Women's College took a number of measures.

The Department of Physical Culture followed the standard practice of excusing students from required exercise and barring them from voluntary athletics during the first three or four days of the menstrual period, the time when medical opinion deemed young women's reproductive organs most vulnerable to damage. This restriction was listed along with "Training Rules" and "General Advice" in the 1927–1928 Student Handbook. Other warnings included no smoking, no late dancing, very little chocolate, and no water before, during, or after the game.[22]

Another concern involved the style of play adopted by participants. In 1905, Dean Lida Shaw King decided that boys' rules in basketball resulted in too rough a game.[23] But an article by Ethel L. Robinson in the 1907 *Sepiad* suggests that the ruling did not stick for long. Using the Irish Mr. Dooley as narrator, Robinson offered the following description of a junior-senior basketball game:

> There's tin in all, five on a side. Thin up runs a little man wid a swate smile an' a ball twice th' size iv a fut-ball an' throws it up between two iv thim. Thin th' rist all dove f'r th' ball an' pulled at whatever they got ther hands on. Sometimes 'twas th' ball an' sometimes 'twas a wad iv hair...Ivry onct in a while th' umpire, the little man wid th' swate smile, had to step in an' separate two iv them, f'r it ain't in th' rules f'r anny wan to be kilt outright.[24]

While students may have joked about the roughness of play in class games, they also criticized women who transgressed the limits of the feminine ideal. Scattered references to Amazons, brawny masculine types, and overboisterous or unladylike behavior in student publications attest to the existence of these negative stereotypes of athletes. In 1918, the Athletic Association replaced the insignia given to be worn on sweaters with armbands because of the "unpopularity of the mannish college sweater...."[25] Nonetheless, the most common attitude toward gender role transgressions seems to have been that they could be countenanced and corrected as long as they did not take place under the male gaze.

A case in point is the set of rules laid down by the Student Government Association governing the wearing of athletic garb. Sneakers, knickers, gymnasium bloomers, and athletic sweaters were not to be worn in classrooms, on the men's campus, or in the center of the city except on athletic outings.[26] Physical training for "overboisterous and unladylike Freshmen" could be most effective, according to Senior Anne Ottley, when "...safely confined to the precincts of the hygiene department."[27]

Historians of early higher education for women have identified a phenomenon called "smashing" at many all-female institutions. The term refers to intense emotional bonds between women, usually romantic in nature.[28] Student biographies in the *Brun Mael* suggest that this sort of bonding was perceived to be most common among female athletes. The 1914 edition contained a typically positive view of one such attachment:

> It would seem from her senior slip that her main interest in college life – yes, in life in general, – is Jenny Palmer. Her chief ambition in college has been to be with Jenny as much as possible and it was probably for this reason that she went out for basketball. Together they have played on the illustrious team of 1914, a fact which reflects honor upon themselves as well as upon the class.[29]

The absence of any stigma concerning such intense female bonding suggests that the gendered boundaries surrounding women's increasing athleticism prevented male criticism and interference even as they confirmed men's belief that women were not and could not be their athletic equals.

By 1930, physical activity was one of the strongest of many threads that, woven together, made up the fabric of student life at Pembroke. Participatory and communal in nature, annual athletic rituals such as Field Day, class championships in a variety of sports, the Athletic Association freshman picnic, and the Athletic Association awards ceremony in the chapel (attendance mandatory) were as much a part of the Women's College calendar as the Sophomore Masque, May Day, and Commencement.

Lest students forget the centrality of athletics in the mission of the Women's College in Brown University, Dean Margaret Morriss offered a strong reminder to the entering class in 1931:

> We are expecting great things of you – intellectual power, athletic prowess, and organizing ability; and we hope to give you of our best to develop all your talents and capacities.[30]

In the formative years of higher education for women at Brown, students, faculty, and administrators all played a part in the evolution of the value system championed by Dean Morriss, a value system that was forged in and helped to maintain an essentially separate female sphere within Brown University.

The Rudd Era

Throughout the 1930s, sports and physical education at Pembroke continued along the separatist path established in the formative years. As late as 1940, the Pembroke Athletic Association agreed that a coed recreation night would not generate enough interest among Pembroke women or Brown men to justify having one.[31] But this would soon change. The events of World War II and the post war era led to a strong cultural emphasis on the importance of dating, marriage, sexual compatibility and parenthood for young men and women.[32] Pembroke women and Brown men of this generation began to explore the possibilities for fun and romance between the sexes through coed recreational and athletic activities.

To the extent that physical education and athletics at Pembroke remained a separate female world between 1930 and 1961, the unquestioned matriarch of this world was Bessie Hunting Rudd. Although many unathletic students saw Rudd as a domineering and arbitrary woman, female athletes at Pembroke were drawn to her strength, good humor, independence, and unwavering belief in the capabilities of women.

Bessie Rudd arrived at Pembroke in 1930, having already acquired ten years of teaching experience in physical education at Radcliffe and a Certificate of Hygiene and Physical Education from the Wellesley College graduate program in physical education. Between 1922 and 1924, when Rudd attended Wellesley, Amy Morris Homans remained the most influential force in shaping the philosophy behind the physical education graduate program. Although retired, Homans continued to give lectures to new students regarding the role of women in the physical education profession and the importance of maintaining and cultivating standards of dress, manners, and behavior befitting " . . . a 'lady in the Wellesley tradition.' "[33] By 1930, Bessie Rudd was one of over 350 women in the physical education profession whose professional and personal values had been directly or indirectly molded by Homans.[34]

During the 1920s and 1930s, female physical educators founded and joined several policy-making organizations whose primary purpose was to avoid the perceived abuses rampant in male athletic programs. These organizations condemned commercialized and professionalized sports

Bessie H. Rudd, director of Pembroke Physical Education, 1930–61, in the doorway of Sayles Gymnasium.

programs as well as their underlying value system. Above all, female physical educators stressed the importance of female control of all aspects of women's athletic programs from administration and coaching to officiating.[35]

Throughout her career, Bessie Rudd held either elected office or membership in virtually every professional organization for women in physical education at the local, regional, or national level. At Pembroke, Rudd worked to implement the ideals concerning women's sports that she helped to shape in the national arena and attempted to instill in her students the same ideals. "A sport for every girl, and every girl in a sport" became an oft-cited motto and the fundamental principle behind the new sporting ideal for women. Bessie Rudd's unflagging commitment to the four-year requirement in physical education at Pembroke, despite strong and vocal student opposition, was rooted in her acceptance of this basic goal of her profession.

Students used a variety of arguments in their efforts to reduce the four-year requirement. They questioned the intellectual integrity of a college that " ... allowed the privilege of unlimited cuts in every class but gym."[36] A majority of 197 student respondents to a questionnaire administered by the *Pembroke Record* in 1938 favored only two years of compulsory gym and believed that juniors and seniors would participate voluntarily in some sports activity if they did not otherwise get enough exercise. Others defended their right to choose physical inactivity as a way of life.[37] In the late 1950s, four Pembrokers framed their protest as a matter of sexual equality: "We meet and follow the same scholastic program as Brown. Why then can't we follow their more reasonable gymnastic requirements of only a certain number of gyms for graduation which may be taken at the student's discretion?"[38]

What rebellious students failed to take into account was the impossibility of achieving in only two years the goals underlying Bessie Rudd's vision of physical education. Freshmen and sophomores were required to take one hour of gym three times a week, juniors and seniors one hour of gym two times a week. All entering students attended a mandatory series of lectures on hygiene and body mechanics once a week during their first semester. Each semester was divided into two terms. By the end of a student's junior year, she had to have taken two terms of rhythmic dancing. Two terms each of an individual sport and a team sport were to be completed during the four years. Students also underwent regular physical examinations and the taking of "posture pictures." And last, but certainly not least, each student had to pass a swimming test in order to graduate.[39]

Unathletic students were hard pressed to find the method in this madness. But it was there. The required program prevented specialization in a single sport, an evil that female physical educators associated with men's competitive athletics. It introduced students to dance, swimming, and individual sports, emphasizing athletic skills that could be used after graduation from college. Regular physical examinations identified any persistent physical problem in a student and became the basis for individualized gymnastics programs aimed at correcting the problem. The lectures on hygiene and body mechanics, which soon devolved into lessons on how to be a "lady," combined with posture training ensured the maintenance of a socially acceptable feminine demeanor in women who were exploring a previously male realm of activity.[40]

The long established student-run intramural sports program based on class teams continued to thrive throughout Rudd's tenure. As before, students who had taken or were currently taking required physical education classes in a particular sport or activity formed the pool of candidates for the class teams in a variety of sports. The introduction of several new sports into the physical education curriculum after 1930 expanded the intramural sports program as well. Among the innovations were field hockey, fencing, skiing, swimming, sailing, golf, and lacrosse.

One area of the physical education curriculum that took on increasing significance after 1930 was dance. Modern dance classes had been added to the available physical education courses as early as 1919. Students could also take folk, square, tap, athletic, and clog dancing. After the arrival of Flora Ricker in 1924, modern dance began to take center stage. The new instructor worked hard to change the image of the dance classes:

> I remember that I tried not to have any "cherry-picking," "dead birds" and "running through the waves" because I felt that this interpretation was one reason why the girls felt silly taking dance classes.... I tried to use large movements and not much pantomime.[41]

By 1934, a significant number of Pembroke students found Flora Ricker Hopkins' interpretation of modern dance compelling enough to join a dance group under her direction. Hopkins and her successor, Ann Coakley, played an important role in bringing such noted artists as Ted Shawn's Dance Group and Martha Graham's Dance Group to Providence for performances. Ted Shawn's visit was an Athletic Association sponsored fund raiser to complete Pembroke Field House.[42]

Steady growth in available athletic facilities made the expansion of physical education classes and intramural sports possible. Beginning in 1931, Brown permitted Pembroke students to use the Colgate-Hoyt pool on a regular basis. When Charles T. and Henry L. Aldrich left their house and its grounds to Pembroke, the college tore down the mansion and converted the grounds into Pembroke Field which was dedicated in 1936. This greatly improved the facilities for outdoor sports and provided the space for instruction and competition in field hockey, soccer, speedball, volleyball, archery, softball, golf, and lacrosse. The Aldrich property barn was also renovated and converted into the Pembroke Field House which opened in 1937. This building was used for lectures on rainy days, the camp counselor training course, Athletic Association functions, club meetings, and alumnae social gatherings.[43]

With the completion of Andrews Hall in 1947, the Metcalf Dining Room became an annex used for physical education classes in modern dance, body mechanics and fundamentals, fencing, and playground and camp work. The completion of Andrews Hall also resulted in the construction of four new tennis courts for the use of Pembrokers on Cushing Street next to Miller Hall. Despite increased access to both separate facilities and Brown athletic facilities, the Pembroke physical education and sports programs more than kept pace with new facilities.[44]

For many sports enthusiasts at Pembroke, gym class activities and intramural competition were not enough. As substitutes for intercollegiate competition, female physical educators in the 1930s developed forms of sport that downplayed competition and rivalry. Play days and telegraphic competitions were the outcome of this search for alternatives to the male model of college athletics.[45]

At a play day, a set number of representatives from three or four colleges traveled to the host campus. Once there, the participants were divided into teams consisting of representatives from each of the colleges. The teams usually engaged in round robin competition in a variety of sports followed by some sort of social gathering. For instance, when Pembroke students attended an archery play day at Connecticut State College in 1937, each participant took a gift and received one in return.[46] This type of ritual was intended to eliminate the institutional rivalry that characterized men's sports and to foster cooperation and friendship among women.

Students at Pembroke both hosted and attended play days. In 1934, twenty-five Pembrokers joined students from Mt. Holyoke and Bennington on the Mt. Holyoke campus for a day of tennis, field hockey, volleyball, speedball, and relays. Dorothy Lindsay, in her regular column entitled "Women in Sports" in the *Boston Herald,* declared that the event had " . . . all the excitement of an intercollegiate affair, without intercollegiate competition."[47] Just before dedicating Pembroke Field in 1936, students from Jackson, Wheaton, Radcliffe, and Pembroke inaugurated the field with play day activities that included field hockey, deck tennis, soccer, and fistball.[48]

Pembroke students also entered telegraphic competition at the national level in archery and duckpin bowling. In telegraphic competition, individuals or teams at different locations throughout the country, performed a standardized set of athletic events. Scores or times were recorded for each individual or team and then sent to a central tournament official who determined winners and relative rankings for all participants.[49]

Unlike many other women's colleges in the 1920s and 1930s, Pembroke did not discontinue its existing varsity intercollegiate athletic program. The structure of this program did, however, reflect an awareness and concern about some of the charges of corruption and exploitation levied against male intercollegiate athletics. Intercollegiate athletics at Pembroke did not involve long distance travel, extensive schedules, gate receipts, or a heavy emphasis on winning. Varsity teams rarely played more than five games with outside teams; in several sports, Pembroke had a standing arrangement with Radcliffe, Jackson, and Wheaton. Occasionally, this three-game schedule was supplemented by games with local club teams, YWCA teams, or even high school teams.[50]

The common assertion that women's intercollegiate athletics benefit-

Albina Osipowich, Class of 1933, winner of two gold medals in the 1928 Olympics.

ted only a few good athletes at the expense of the rest of the student body did not apply at Pembroke where the broad-based physical education and intramural sports programs provided ample opportunity for all students to engage in physical exercise and athletics. Bessie Rudd, in contrast with many of her colleagues in the physical education profession, believed that it was possible to engage in intercollegiate competition without losing sight of the " ... social benefits to be derived from friendly competition."[51]

The opportunities for athletic competition and regular physical training at Pembroke were extensive enough to attract and sustain the interest of a number of highly skilled female athletes. During the 1932–1933 academic year, two former Olympic gold medal winners and world record holders were enrolled at Pembroke. Albina Osipowich, Class of 1933, and Helen Johns, Class of 1936, had been champions in swimming at the 1928 and 1932 Olympics respectively.[52]

The daughter of Lithuanian immigrants, Osipowich won two gold medals in the 1928 Olympics, one for a world record-breaking performance in the 100 meters and one as a member of the 400-meter relay team, the event in which Helen Johns won her gold medal four years later.[53] When $4,000 was raised on her behalf by public subscription in Worcester, Massachusetts, she chose to apply it towards a four-year A.B. course at Pembroke, " ... partly because she could be near her family and partly because she could continue her swimming here."[54] Thus, athletics became the key to social mobility for Osipowich who became associate editor of the *Pembroke Record,* wrote articles for Lithuanian newspapers in the United States, served as Rhode Island director of women's activities for the National Youth Administration, and married Harrison Van Aken, Jr., Class of 1936.[55]

The presence of an Olympic swimmer at Pembroke apparently did not go unnoticed at Brown. In April 1930, Osipowich and four other Pembroke swimmers were invited to do exhibition swimming and diving during the Brown-Bowdoin water meet, marking the first time that women had been permitted to swim in the Colgate Hoyt pool.[56] Despite this initial concession, Pembroke women continued to do at least some of their recreational swimming by special arrangement at the Plantations Club.

This arrangement with the Plantations Club posed a problem for at least two African-American students at Pembroke in the 1930s since the Club had a "whites only" policy that Pembroke administrators chose not to challenge. Carolyn Minkins, Class of 1932, was turned away and told not to come back; her sister, Beatrice Minkins, Class of 1936, despite several invitations to go swimming from her classmate, Helen Johns, who probably did not know about the policy, simply avoided putting herself in an embarrassing and humiliating situation. This did not, however, imply her acceptance of the policy. Some fifty years later, Beatrice Minkins expressed resentment toward the club's policy and the college's lack of nerve: " 'I imagine the College would prefer to offend one person rather than risk losing the use of the pool. They didn't take a stand on it; they should have, but they didn't.' "[57]

Although Helen Johns and Beatrice Minkins were denied the simple pleasure of swimming together, their mutual interest in a wide variety of other sports at Pembroke brought them together frequently. They played on at least three teams together – class teams in baseball and basketball and varsity field hockey from their sophomore year on. In Helen Johns' case, athletic ability seems to have translated into high social status on campus as she held office in the Student Government Association for two of the four years that she served.[58] Jean Bauer, Class of 1933, a golf champion who played in both state and national women's tournaments, was elected president of her college class all four years.[59] Within the Pembroke community, the association between athletic prowess and high social status on campus remained a strong one even as the interest in coeducational recreation and sports emerged in the 1940s and 1950s.

Aside from their athletic peers, the most striking examples of athletic womanhood for Pembroke students must have been the members of the Physical Education Department which also attracted its share of prominent athletes. In the late 1930s, the department hired Hilda Boehm as an assistant. Boehm and her twin sister, Helen, who taught physical education at Wheaton, were national indoor tennis junior doubles champions in 1929 and Greater Boston doubles champions for five years running. In 1939, their former teacher and the "Mother of American Tennis," Hazel Hotchkiss Wightman, played exhibition matches with the Boehm sisters as part of the official opening of the new Cushing Street tennis courts.[60] In 1949, Ann Coakley joined the physical education staff as an instructor in lacrosse, softball, field hockey, and volleyball. Coakley held office in a number of regional and national lacrosse organizations and, in 1951, was named to the U.S. lacrosse touring team.[61]

The fact that so many high-caliber female athletes, both students and teachers, found Pembroke a comfortable home attests to Bessie Rudd's flexibility concerning highly competitive forms of sport for women. At many colleges, female physical educators would have forbidden or, at least, strongly discouraged students from participating in outside competitions. Where Bessie Rudd did draw the line, though, was at formal athletic competition between men and women.

As Pembroke women turned to Brown men for comradeship, coaching and the use of athletic facilities in sports such as sailing, fencing, and skiing, Bessie Rudd consistently warned Pembroke and Brown students that Pembroke students were not to enter any athletic competition at other colleges or universities that would pit them against male foes.[62] When *The Rhode Islander* carried a story about Sally Cunningham, Class of 1958, who in 1955 had helped the Brown rifle team defeat the University of Connecticut, Rudd expressed her disapproval and worried about what she considered to be negative publicity. In 1956, the Brown men declined Cunningham's services because " . . . it's awkward for one girl to travel with a team of boys and have to have special accommodations arranged for her."[63]

While Bessie Rudd did not approve of athletic competition between the sexes, she did support and encourage coeducational recreation featuring activities such as badminton, tennis, folk dancing, and swimming. During a six-month sabbatical in 1939, Rudd toured twenty-five colleges throughout the country to study and observe their physical education and athletic programs. She returned to Pembroke convinced that " . . . if college men and women in coeducational institutions may dance together, there is no reason why they can't play games together, too."[64] As Pembroke students began to explore the potential of coed sports, Rudd offered needed support, but cautioned her female charges against placing the power to shape the new coeducational athletic and recreational activities entirely in the hands of male peers.

The exigencies of World War II seem to have accelerated the interest among students and physical education faculty in establishing coeducational instruction and recreation. During the summer of 1942, Pembroke held its first summer session in the history of the college. Among the offerings were coed classes in physical education which resulted in a large "...number of men who are 'getting gym credit' at Pembroke."[65] On Tuesday and Friday evenings for two hours, the Colgate Hoyt pool became the site of mixed swimming parties, a new policy adopted in response to gasoline and rubber rationing which made it difficult for students to get away to beaches. Bessie Rudd attempted to get the use of the Brown Yacht Club facilities for Pembroke during the summer session, but the club held fast to its policy of only permitting individual Pembrokers occasional use if accompanied by a Brown man.[66]

The Outing Club and its offspring, the Yacht Club and the Ski Club, led the way in defining the new emphasis on coed athletics. The first references to coed recreation began to appear in the *Students' Handbook* during the war years. By the early 1950s, the *Freshman Handbook* promised the Pembroke freshman that she could improve her love life by joining the Yacht Club and that in the Ski Club, "...there is usually an advantageous ratio of Brown men to Pembrokers."[67] In the late 1950s, the *Freshman Handbook* repeatedly promoted athletics as a pleasant and effective means of keeping or acquiring a slim figure, presumably a prerequisite for success in attracting a male partner.[68] The Outing Club, the Yacht Club, and the Ski Club provided the atmosphere for athletic romance when they all merged with similar organizations of Brown men in the early 1950s.

Westcott Moulton, the dean of activities at Brown, made the connection between physical fitness and heterosexual romance explicit in a 1954 speech at the Pembroke Athletic Association banquet. "Sports learned here at Pembroke will mean much to you later on in life," said Dean Moulton. "In a happy successful marriage a bridge of common enjoyment is vital. Sports and their knowledge are important in this aspect."[69] Pembroke students received a similar message from the Physical Education Department in the form of the required freshman fundamentals course which taught students, under the rubric of physical education, "...how to walk in heels, how to lift a suitcase with a minimum of effort, and how to introduce your date to your grandmother."[70]

Assertions that female athletic participation could make a woman a more attractive mate for a man were, at least partially, a reaction against a widespread stereotype that emerged full force in the 1930s directly linking female athletic participation with lesbian tendencies. Although Pembroke faculty and administrators encouraged the increasingly common tendency among female students to see physical exercise as an opportunity for meeting and capturing the hearts of young men whom they might marry, students, nonetheless, must have perceived the message as mixed at best. Throughout the 1940s and 1950s, female physical education instructors who married, like other female faculty and administrators at Pembroke, almost invariably were forced to quit their jobs and left Pembroke to follow their husbands. The one exception was Flora Ricker Hopkins, the dance instructor who came to the Women's College in 1924, shortly thereafter married, and continued in her position at Pembroke until 1945. The most visible member of the department, Bessie Rudd, never married and along with her longtime housemate, Dean of Admission Eva Mooar, made up a duo known publicly as the "Ladies of Laurel Avenue."[71] In stressing the compatibility of female athleticism and heterosexuality, students, faculty, and administrators at Pembroke were assuring potential critics that the lesbian stereotype did not apply to the respectable ladies at Pembroke. In this context, female faculty and administrators, virtually all of whom were single, maintained their ability to serve as models for students of both feminine propriety and independence.

The growing dichotomy between the female recreational athlete and the committed competitive female athlete posed a difficult problem for the Athletic Association. As the number of activities for both types of athletes grew, the size and responsibilities of the Athletic Association burgeoned and its name was changed to reflect its new role; in 1959, it became the Athletic and Recreation Association (ARA). Marion "Barney" Welch, the president of the ARA during 1961–1962, summed up the organization's dilemma in a report on "The State of the A.R.A." While maintaining its role in organizing the all-female club and class sports, the ARA, Welch noted, would also need to expand further into coed recreation by sponsoring such events as coed ice-skating parties and Gate mixers.[72] In addition to these informal events, the evolving coed sports system produced opportunities for Pembrokers to participate in tournaments with women's club teams from other colleges. These tournaments were officially organized and officiated by male peers in coed athletic clubs.[73]

Although confusion may have been the end result of such a dizzying array of athletic options, Bessie Rudd and her vision of athletics served as an anchor for those students who found themselves adrift. She guaranteed the continuation of the "tried and true rituals" of the separate women's sports program at Pembroke. Through attendance at Athletic Association meetings, she constantly reminded Pembroke athletes that they were part of a national and regional network of women's sports organizations grappling with common problems and she saw to it that AA members attended the meetings of such organizations as student delegates. Athletic Association members continued to enjoy Bessie Rudd and Eva Mooar's hospitality at the annual AA Christmas party held in their home. This party was always characterized by a gift exchange, an appearance by Santa Claus, and an exchange of short original poems to accompany the gifts.[74] This central component of Pembroke athletics involved little interaction with Brown men and, therefore, remained a relatively autonomous women's sphere within the University.

Rudd also played a crucial role in helping Pembroke students to avoid cooptation by their male peers as they formed coed organizations. As a result of her watchful eye, the constitution adopted by the Yacht Club when the Pembroke and Brown Yacht Clubs merged in 1953 stated that Pembroke students could be nominated for and elected to office in the club under the same rules as Brown men. Although this fell short of Rudd's suggestion that the women ask for a guarantee of female representation on the Executive Board, it was a considerable improvement over the 1952 ruling that two Pembroke representatives could attend Executive Board meetings but not be members of the board.[75]

When Bessie Rudd retired in June 1961, the foundations of her carefully constructed empire were already beginning to crack from both internal and external pressures. The growing emphasis in American society in the 1940s and 1950s on the importance of heterosocial leisure activities as a prelude to companionate marriage rendered highly competitive female athletes, separate women's sports programs, and compulsory physical activity suspect and increasingly unpopular among Pembroke and Brown students. Such programs and their participants were alternatively ignored or attacked as relics of an unenlightened era.

Still, Bessie Rudd left an indelible imprint on women's sports at Brown. Upon her retirement, women students immediately set up an annual award in her name to go to the Pembroke student who had contributed the most to the ARA, later to the female student who had done the most to advance women's athletics during her undergraduate years. Throughout her career, and even afterwards, Rudd was instrumental in gaining recognition for women's sports at Brown. In 1952, she became the first female full professor at the university. She accomplished another "first" in 1975, when she was the first woman to be named to the Brown University Athletic Hall of Fame. In 1976, the women's crew team christened its new shell the "Bessie Rudd" in her honor.[76]

Bessie Rudd's most lasting and influential legacy to women's sports at Brown, however, may well be a former student, Arlene Gorton, Class of 1952, who assumed the directorship of the Pembroke Physical Education Department in September, 1961. As a student leader in athletics during the early 1950s, Gorton straddled the line that often separated the casual weekend athlete from the varsity competitor. She demonstrated a commitment to providing programs for both types of athletes and herself participated in the whole array of athletic options available to Pembrokers.[77] As a result, Arlene Gorton was uniquely qualified, when she returned to Pembroke in 1961, to meet the challenges facing the women's physical education and sports programs at Pembroke/Brown in the ensuing years.

The Era of Equality

The Pembroke that Arlene Gorton returned to in 1961 differed markedly from the one she remembered from her days as a student.[78] Nowhere was this change more apparent than in the arena of sports and physical education. As the decade wore on, students became more and more involved in the social and political issues that confronted a changing America in the 1960s: civil rights, the anti-war movement, anti-poverty campaigns, the sexual revolution, and feminism. Against this backdrop, athletic programs figured less prominently in student life and often came under critical scrutiny by both students and faculty who labelled them part of the "establishment."

Students found growing support among faculty and administrators for the elimination of the four-year physical education requirement, the cornerstone of women's sports and physical education at Pembroke. Even Bessie Rudd had compromised in 1957 by eliminating the senior year physical education requirement for those students who had not overcut in previous years. In 1963, the students' appeal for equality with Brown men no longer fell on deaf ears; the physical education requirement at Pembroke was reduced to one year to bring it into line with the Brown requirement. An article in the *Pembroke Record* in 1963 equated compulsory gym with other conservative practices at women's colleges such as curfews and sign-outs, hence linking it to common sexual and social restrictions on women students.[79] When the largely male faculty voted to eliminate the physical education requirement altogether in 1970, the debate focused on faculty memories of militaristic physical education programs and instructors in their college days.[80] In this context, the Pembroke physical education faculty and staff found it difficult to address what they considered to be the central issue, the health and well-being of the female college student.

In 1963, the Physical Education Department found itself embroiled

Arlene Gorton, Class of
1952, director of Pembroke
Physical Education,
1961–71, assistant and
associate director of
athletics, 1971–continuing.

in a controversy over the issue of civil rights. At the invitation of the United
States Field Hockey Association, the South African women's field hockey
team was part of a nationwide exhibition tour involving teams from
twenty countries and was scheduled to play several games at Brown.[81]
Despite protests from the *Brown Daily Herald* and the Rhode Island
NAACP, Arlene Gorton, in consultation with President Barnaby C.
Keeney,[82] had decided that Pembroke and Brown had a commitment that
must be kept to host the South African team (though she had not been
involved in the arrangements) and that this was an issue of open athletic
competition, not a political issue.[83] Gorton's perspective has shifted over
the years, partially because of the events of the turbulent 1960s. Currently
teaching a course on Sport in American Society at Brown, Gorton now
encourages students to see the connections between organized sports and
the larger society. Under her aegis, the Athletic Department has run educational workshops in recent years for Brown athletes addressing issues
such as racism, sexism, homophobia, and drugs in sports.[84]

One of the most troubling issues to come out of the political turmoil
of the 1960s and 1970s was how to define and achieve equality for women,
not only in athletics, but in many arenas of American society. As elsewhere,
at Pembroke and at Brown this process engendered a great deal of conflict
and required sometimes painful, sometimes exhilarating transformations

at the personal, institutional, and societal levels. In the area of athletics, women in the early 1960s had a long journey ahead of them if they were to reach equality with men at Brown or anywhere else.

The institution of the one-year requirement in physical education in 1963 required a restructuring of both physical education and athletics at Pembroke. Arlene Gorton, early on, took steps to include Brown men in Pembroke physical education classes, since Brown had no instructional program. Another outgrowth of the reduction in the requirement was the creation of voluntary recreation programs and classes to serve the whole university community. Faculty spouses (mostly wives, of course) were the first group to take advantage of this innovation in large numbers, though they eventually recruited husbands and children into the new programs.[85]

The Pembroke intramural sports program declined, though did not disappear, throughout the 1960s. The elimination of required physical education classes that fed into the intramural program combined with a general demise in student interest in athletics were the contributing factors. Outside of physical education in the freshman year, most Pembrokers who participated in sports did it through a number of clubs in dance, field hockey, basketball, tennis, synchronized swimming, skiing, sailing, and, of course, the newest addition, ice hockey. All of these clubs sponsored limited intercollegiate competition.

The lack of separate women's facilities for swimming and ice hockey posed a special problem for these clubs. Ice hockey and synchronized swimming enthusiasts often had to practice very early in the morning or late at night, as men's varsity, club, and intramural teams took precedence. The synchronized swimming team faced the additional problem that male students and faculty swam nude during the hours designated for recreational swimming. Although this practice went unquestioned for several years, in the late 1960s, Arlene Gorton announced that women students would be swimming during these hours. Male students and faculty alike objected to putting on suits, but gave in when they realized that Gorton and her students did not intend to back out.[86]

Not surprisingly, the lack of university funding for women's sports in the 1960s also created severe problems. Season schedules, of necessity, were short and equipment was inferior, makeshift, or nonexistent. What funding women's club teams were able to secure often depended on their own initiative and sales skills. The women's ice hockey team, for instance, sold rulebooks for women's ice hockey, "Panda Power" buttons, and chocolate bars in their efforts to finance trips to play Canadian teams.[87]

Another problem that plagued women's sports at Brown throughout the 1960s and 1970s was the lack of publicity, especially in the *Brown*

Daily Herald. Lynn Plant and Linda Fox, two members of the Panda ice hockey team, made satire of this issue in a letter to the editor of the *Herald* in 1966. Claiming to be somewhat uneasy about their growing notoriety in the *Boston Globe* and the Associated Press and the resulting expectations that might accompany such notoriety, they feigned total paralysis when the *Herald* gave them significant coverage: "But now, to have been placed in the spotlight of a *Brown Daily Herald* editorial – well, it brings to our collective guts a jelly-like sensation that not even a good slapshot can equal and only a Sharpe Refectory cranberry can understand."[88]

Coed sports and recreation continued to have strong appeal in the 1960s. Despite this fact, athletic women still battled negative stereotypes, but in the process, rarely questioned the assumptions underlying the stereotypes. A 1966 article in the *Pembroke Record* about Wendy Hanford of the Brown-Pembroke Outing Club clearly demonstrates this: "Wendy Hanford, recently elected head of all collegiate Outing clubs in the nation, is fighting to 'avoid the outing-club image.' A petite Pembroke junior from Interlaken, New York, Miss Hanford jokingly confided to the *Record* that she is trying to stamp out the image of the 'brutal and hairy-chested' outing club female."[89] Such statements questioned the validity of stereotypes but left intact the assumption that large women with muscles who excelled too noticeably in sports deserved to be ridiculed.

Whereas romance and companionship had been the anticipated rewards of coed sports in the 1950s, coed sports in the 1960s seemed to hold out promises of playful sexuality. While Steve Shabika, dive master of the coed skin diving club in 1967 stated that the presence of women "'makes the guys act like gentlemen,'" Emily Paynter, Class of 1968, a member of the club declared, "'The boys pinch me and make me go faster.'" In 1968, the Pembroke Dance Club was one of five from other women's colleges invited to perform at Yale. According to an article in the *Yale Daily News,* the male crowd anticipated a "sexual extravaganza." A member of the Pembroke Club pointed out that they "were not there to do a striptease," but the article continued by discussing the buxomness of the Vassar ballet dancers. While these attitudes reflected a somewhat more open approach to sexuality in the 1960s, they ultimately served to denigrate female athletes by turning them into sexual objects.[90]

Despite the numerous barriers placed in their way, Pembroke women in the 1960s, with the assistance of the Physical Education Department, steadily built their own opportunities for athletic participation through the expanding club structure. From 1961 on, the Pembroke Sailing Organization attended regattas at other New England colleges and universities that belonged to the Women's Intercollegiate Sailing Association. This umbrella group for women's sailing associations formed because men in coed sailing clubs were increasingly sponsoring varsity competition from which women were barred. Pembroke's ski team belonged to a similar organization called the Women's Intercollegiate Ski Conference. In 1968, the team had five races scheduled against other women's colleges, even though some team members raced "doing the snow plow all the way down."[91] In 1967, the newly formed basketball team, under the coaching of Sarah Phillips, played a five-game schedule and a round robin tournament at Wellesley College. The synchronized swim team, under the direction of Arlene Gorton, put on annual shows at Pembroke beginning in 1962, competed in AAU meets, and traveled occasionally to other colleges to perform. While a few students complained that the Athletic Association focused too exclusively on organizing competitive contests for these club teams, it was the club athlete who kept the women's sports program alive at Pembroke in an era of widespread disinterest in athletics.[92]

A serious critique of the sexism that pervaded the 1960s awaited the emergence of the feminist movement in the late 1960s and early 1970s. At Pembroke in the early 1970s, the merger with Brown, the growth of feminist sentiment among women faculty and students, and the passage of Title IX of the Higher Education Act of 1972 converged to initiate yet another significant transformation in the women's sports program.

One of the first casualties of the merger was the physical education requirement in all of its aspects: the freshman fundamentals course, the swimming test, the motor skills tests, posture pictures, and activities classes. With the elimination of the physical education requirement, the faculty and staff once again had to rethink the structure of the program.[93] In many ways, the elimination of the requirement simply accelerated trends that had developed out of the reduction of the requirement in 1963. The voluntary instructional program increasingly offered coed classes and recreation programs for children, faculty, and their spouses.

In the context of the merger, the elimination of the requirement also forced discussion on the role of female physical education faculty and staff in the new order of things. Janet Lutz, an instructor at Pembroke since 1958, suggested the creation of four divisions in the new athletic department (intercollegiate, instructional, intramurals, and recreation) and expressed her concern at a departmental meeting in 1971 that a woman be included in "a top administrative position such as Assistant Director of Athletics and a woman should also head one of the divisions."[94] For Arlene Gorton who eventually became the assistant director of athletics, but was repeatedly denied the position of director of athletics, the merger meant a loss of position and authority.[95]

For women students, the effects of the merger were more positive. As men's and women's sports came under one administration, the inequities in funding, promotion, and institutional support became all the more apparent and easy to document.[96] The passage of Title IX in 1972 encouraged educational institutions to examine athletic programs with an eye toward correcting sexual discrimination, though the publication of Title IX guidelines was delayed for two years. At Brown, as at many other institutions, Title IX reinforced a growing emphasis on intercollegiate sports for women, at the expense of intramural and recreational programs.[97]

By 1980, Brown supported thirteen teams in the women's intercollegiate athletic program. Over the course of the 1970s, many of the previous club teams were promoted to varsity status. New sports such as cross country, track and field, soccer, lacrosse, and softball entered the picture as intercollegiate sports in the 1970s. Many club teams sought the prestige and funding that came with varsity status. In 1981, one student complained about the ascendancy of intercollegiate athletics from her perspective as a club sport participant: "Club sports at Brown rarely receive recognition for their efforts.... Some are just as demanding as varsity sports but simply do not hold varsity status."[98] The article went on to describe the variety of club sports available to Brown women, including skiing, indoor track, sailing, rugby, and riding.

While intercollegiate athletics captured the lion's share of attention and funding in the 1970s, athletes and coaches still had grievances concerning sexual inequality. Many of these were discussed at the women's coaches' meetings which were stopped in 1978 at the request of the athletic director who argued that they were inappropriate since women's athletics did not have a separate administrative structure at Brown. Probably more to the point were the issues being raised at these meetings: differentials in men's and women's coaches' salaries, the poor condition of women's playing fields, the lack of coverage of women's sports by the Sports Information Office, differential access to facilities, and the absence of full-time trainers for women's sports teams.[99] Although the status of women's athletics had improved considerably from the 1960s, the women were still playing catch-up with the men.

The appearance of the *Sportswoman at Brown Newsletter* in 1977 heralded the growing awareness on the part of Brown female athletes concerning national debates on women's sports, their own place within the Brown athletic system, and the history of women's athletics at Brown. The *Newsletter* staff did interviews with Pembroke alumnae and former physical education faculty members. One interviewee was Marjorie Brown Smith who had served as head of the Physical Education Department in the early 1920s. She and her husband Stan Smith were strong supporters of women's intercollegiate athletics in the 1970s and 1980s. Marjorie Smith was one of only two donors who contributed more than $500 to the Brown women's discretionary fund for athletics in 1980–1981. Brown female athletes showed their appreciation for such support by naming a shell after Marjorie Smith while she was still alive and by creating the Marjorie Smith Award for the outstanding Brown woman athlete of the year after Smith's death in 1981.[100] By the end of the 1970s, Brown women athletes had taken the problem of lack of recognition into their own hands.

Throughout the 1970s, the Brown women's intercollegiate athletic program adhered to the standards of two outside governing bodies – the Ivy League and the Association of Intercollegiate Athletics for Women (AIAW). The AIAW was founded in 1970 by female physical educators and coaches who wished to prevent women's athletic programs from engaging in what they deemed to be exploitative practices characteristic of men's intercollegiate athletics such as high-pressure recruiting, athletic scholarships, commercialized athletics, and disregard for the academic responsibilities of student athletes. Because of a lawsuit brought by female student athletes who saw the refusal to give athletic scholarships as a sex discrimination issue, the AIAW was forced to back down on that issue, but the organization continued to uphold a much tighter set of restrictions against recruiting abuses than its male counterpart, the NCAA.[101] The liberalization of AIAW policy concerning athletic scholarships had no effect on women athletes at Brown since Ivy League policy forbids the practice.

In 1981, the NCAA, in a bid for control over the increasingly profitable domain of women's athletics, proposed to offer national championships in a variety of sports during the 1981–1982 academic year. This move forced women's athletic programs to choose between competing in the existing AIAW championships or in the NCAA championships for which much greater amounts of travel funding were available. The end result of the protracted struggle that took place at many colleges and universities over this issue was the demise of the AIAW and the takeover of women's college athletics by the NCAA.[102]

At Brown, Arlene Gorton, who had been present at the founding meeting of the AIAW, opposed the NCAA bid for control. Her position in the matter was not a popular one. Not only was she rejected as a Brown representative to subsequent NCAA meetings, but she was also instructed by the athletic director and by President Swearer not to attend the meetings in any capacity for two years. Thus the impact of the NCAA takeover at Brown reflected the situation across the country; the vast majority of representatives to the major governing body in women's athletics were men, many of whom were hostile to the AIAW philosophy.[103] One of the ironies of the 1970s and 1980s, a period when the participation rates of women students in athletics soared, is that women increasingly lost control over women's athletics at the administrative level and within the coaching ranks.[104]

In many respects, Brown women athletes have achieved the much sought-after equality of the early 1970s. In 1988, Brown fielded the same number of intercollegiate athletic teams for women as it did for men, fifteen each. While inequities in recruiting still exist, the women's athletic recruiting budget makes the annual total budgets for women's athletics in the 1960s look like pocket change. Brown women athletes have also gained tremendously in the area of publicity and visibility at the local, regional, and national levels.

The fruits of this movement toward equality are obvious: greater opportunities for highly competitive female athletes, growing respect for the athletic accomplishments of women, an almost constant upgrading of women's athletic skills levels, public recognition for Brown University, and opportunities for women to develop confidence and self-esteem through keen competition. One only need scan the student press and university publications in the 1980s to identify a number of all-Americans and obvious successes like the women's soccer team's claim to nine out of ten Ivy championships in the 1980s. All can support the achievements of Teri Smith, Class of 1991, an African-American who was the first Brown woman to earn All-American honors in track and field. These honors represent real progress for women in sports at Brown.[105]

Looking toward the future, some important issues confront Brown women in sports. Arlene Gorton points to the continuing underrepresentation of women of color as athletes, and of all women as coaches and sports administrators as a problem that must be addressed in an aggressive and persistent manner. She also believes that "it is time to put to rest once and for all the issue of the sexuality of women and athletics. Obviously there are lesbian women in athletics," she stated. "There is no need to deny their presence, and we rejoice in their contributions. In fact, it is time to open women's athletics to all, regardless of race, sexual orientation, age, or ableism."[106] As intercollegiate teams receive a larger and larger portion of the money and recognition given to women's sports at Brown, the creation and maintenance of more inclusionary athletic and recreational programs will pose a major challenge for the future of Brown women's athletics.

In an era of shrinking budgets at colleges and universities throughout the country, it is likely that both recruiting programs and intercollegiate athletic programs will face some tough and unpopular decisions in the future. At an academic institution like Brown, another issue is the extent to which student athletes can fulfill academic responsibilities and get a decent education as intercollegiate athletic schedules begin to cover a larger and larger portion of the year.[107]

Looking back at the history of women's sports at Brown, some troubling questions remain. What have been the costs of the hard-won equality of the 1980s? It is hard not to glorify those days when women athletes and physical educators struggled against an indifferent, sometimes even hostile, public to define a place for women in physical education and athletics. While few people would lament the demise of the invisibility of female athletes, forced physical activity, traditional notions of femininity, or class-based elitism – all aspects of Brown women's athletic history, the loss of that relatively autonomous women's sphere has been one of the casualties of equality. The abandonment of a philosophy of sport that emphasized mass participation, good health, non-exploitation of student athletes, instruction in sports suitable for lifetime participation, and the development of skills in a variety of sports is another significant loss. Only time will tell if Brown women athletes and their counterparts elsewhere have won the battle but lost the war by adopting what an earlier genera-tion of physical educators and athletes would have identified as a male athletic model. If history offers any clues, Brown women athletes will not settle for anything less than total victory.

NOTES

1. "Bessie Rudd Dies," *Providence Journal,* 12 January 1978, Bessie Hunting Rudd Biographical File, Christine Dunlap Farnham Archives, John Hay Library, Brown University. All files referred to in subsequent notes for this chapter are in the Christine Dunlap Farnham Archives collection.

2. The history of women's ice hockey at Pembroke and then Brown can be traced in the following sources: "Girls Develop Hockey Team at Pembroke," *Brown Daily Herald,* 4 March 1964; File 1 Z–P, Pembroke College – Athletic and Recreation Association, Execu-tive Board Records, Folder 7, 1963–1964; Physical Education Department Files, Spring 1963–Spring, 1966 Department Scrapbook and Fall, 1966–1972 Department Scrapbook. An insightful analysis of the impact of Title IX appears in Mary A. Boutilier and Lucinda SanGiovanni, *The Sporting Woman* (Champaign, Illinois: Human Kinetics Publishers, 1983), pp. 170–181.

3. See Carroll Smith-Rosenberg and Charles Rosenberg, "The Female Animal: Medical and Biological Views of Woman and Her Role in Nineteenth-Century America," *Journal of American History* 60 (September 1973): 340–343.

4. File 1-ZP, "Women's College Adjunct to Brown University," 1892–1893.

5. File 1-ZP, "Women's College in Brown University: Annual Announcement," 1898–1899, pp. 24–25.

6. "Editorials," *Sepiad* 6 (December 1905): 42.

7. Ibid.

8. Emma May Caufield, "Miss Curious Visits Pembroke," *Sepiad* 3 (June 1902): 96.

9. "Free Press," *Sepiad* 3 (December 1902): 159.

10. Grace E. Hawk, *Pembroke College in Brown University: The First Seventy-five Years 1891–1966* (Providence, R.I.: Brown University Press, 1967), p. 56.

11. Blanche Luella Smith, "Address of Welcome," *Sepiad* 7 (June 1907): 6.

12. Hawk, *Pembroke College*, 129–130; Also File 1-P, "A Bit of Brown Tradition: An Interview with Marjorie B. Smith," *Sportswomen at Brown Newsletter*, June 1981.

13. Quote from "Athletics," *Sepiad* 9 (December 1908): 38. See also "Free Press," *Sepiad* 2 (November 1901): 21.

14. "Athletic Association," *Sepiad* 16 (April 1916): 35.

15. Physical Education Department Files, Newspaper Clippings from *Providence Sunday Journal* and *New York World* in Baseball Folder.

16. "A Few Points for the Athletic Association," *Sepiad* 14 (February 1914): 31.

17. M.T. Jones, "A.A.," *Brun Mael*, 1918, p. 87. A more serious explanation of the athletic awards system can be found in *Student's Handbook of the Women's College in Brown University*, 1927–1928, p. 29.

18. M. Elizabeth Bates, "Hygiene and Physical Education," *Catalogue of Brown University*, 1913–1914, p. 228.

19. *Students' Handbook of the Women's College in Brown University*, 1913–1914, p. 20.

20. "Free Press," *Sepiad* 6 (February 1906): 37.

21. "Student Government Association," *Sepiad* 17 (April 1917): 16–17; Also file 1-ZP, Pembroke College – Athletic Association, Executive Board Records, 14 February 1922, p. 101.

22. *Students' Handbook of the Women's College in Brown University*, 1927–1928, pp. 30–31.

23. Hawk, *Pembroke College*, p. 54.

24. Ethel Robinson, "On Basket-Ball," *Sepiad* 7 (February 1907): 9–10.

25. Elsa Metzger, "Athletic Association," *Sepiad* 18 (June 1918): 31.

26. Student Government Association Constitution, 1924, p. 13.

27. Anne Ottley, "Address to the Undergraduates," *Sepiad* 13 (June 1913): 11.

28. Nancy Sahli, "Smashing: Women's Relationships Before the Fall," *Chrysalis* 8 (1979): 22; Helen Horowitz, *Alma Mater: Design and Experience in the Women's Colleges From Their Nineteenth-Century Beginnings to the 1930s* (New York: Alfred Knopf, 1984), pp. 65–68.

29. *Brun Mael*, 1914, p. 51.

30. *Students' Handbook of the Women's College in Brown University*, 1927–1928, p. 8.

31. File 1-ZP, Pembroke College – Athletic Association, Executive Board Records, January 1940, p. 285.

32. Elaine Tyler May, *Homeward Bound: American Families in the Cold War Era* (New York: Basic Books, 1988) explores the origins and the impact of these trends in post-war America.

33. Betty Spears, *Leading the Way: Amy Morris Homans and the Beginnings of Professional Education for Women* (New York: Greenwood Press, 1986), p. 127.

34. Ibid., p. 143.

35. Joan S. Hult, "The Governance of Athletics for Girls and Women: Leadership by Women Physical Educators, 1899–1949," *Research Quarterly for Exercise and Sport*, Centennial Issue (1985): 64–77; Nancy Theriot, "Towards a New Sporting Ideal: The Women's Division of the National Amateur Athletic Federation," *Frontiers* 3 (1978): 3–4.

36. Physical Education Department Files, "Gym Again," *Pembroke Record*, 6 March 1935, in 1934–1935 Department Scrapbook.

37. Physical Education Department Files, "Students Vote Against Four Years of Gym," 28 May 1938 and "Gym Aftermath," *Pembroke Record,* 19 October 1937, in 1933–1939 Department Scrapbook.

38. Physical Education Department Files, "Students Question Gym Need," in 1956–1959 Department Scrapbook.

39. File 1-ZP, *Catalogue of Pembroke College in Brown University, 1937–1938,* p. 131.

40. Physical Education Department Files, "Avoid That Drudgery Curve," *Providence Sunday Journal,* 24 October 1943, in 1942–1945 Department Scrapbook.

41. Quoted in Susan Puretz, "Pembroke's Dance Tradition," *Pembroke Alumna* 40 (July 1965): 14.

42. Physical Education Department Files, "Ted Shawn's Dance Group Comes to Pembroke on Friday, January 29," in 1933–1939 Department Scrapbook; "Martha Graham and Dance Group to Appear at School of Design Auditorium," in 1948–1952 Department Scrapbook. Under the direction of Julie Strandberg, dance became part of the Department of Theatre, Speech, and Dance in the late 1970s. See Vicki Sanders, "The Insistent Muse," *Brown Alumni Monthly* 91 (February 1991): 22–27.

43. Bessie H. Rudd, "Beginning of Dexter Property Development," *Pembroke Alumna* 24 (October 1959): 16.

44. Ibid., 16–17.

45. Ethel M. Bowers, "Play Days and Festivals," *American Physical Education Review* (October 1929): 471–473; Mabel Lee, "The Case For and Against Intercollegiate Athletics for Women and the Situation as it Stands Today," *American Physical Education Review* 29 (January 1924): 16.

46. Physical Education Department Files, "The Tumbler," *Pembroke Record,* 28 October 1937, in 1933–1939 Department Scrapbook.

47. Physical Education Department Files, Dorothy Lindsay, "Women in Sports," *Boston Herald,* 29 October 1934, in 1933–1939 Department Scrapbook.

48. Physical Education Department Files, "Pembroke Field, Aldrich's Gift, Was Formally Opened October 24," *Pembroke Record,* in 1933–1939 Department Scrapbook.

49. Physical Education Department Files, Dorothy Lindsay, "Women in Sports," *Boston Herald,* May 1935, in 1933–1939 Department Scrapbook; "Pembrokers Participate in Duck Pin Bowling Tournament," *Pembroke Record,* 27 February 1951, in 1948–1952 Department Scrapbook.

50. Physical Education Department Files, "They're Giving the Men Back Their Athletic Sports," *Providence Journal,* 13 June 1937, in 1933–1939 Department Scrapbook.

51. Ibid.

52. Brown Hall of Fame Program, November, 1984, in Albina Osipowich Biographical File.

53. "That She May Bear Her Name to the Crest of Athletic Fame," in Albina Osipowich Biographical File.

54. "Pembroke Girl Olympic Champion," *Providence Sunday Journal,* 6 April 1930, in Albina Osipowich Biographical File.

55. "Albina Osipowich, Olympic Champion in '28, Betrothed," 28 September 1936, in Albina Osipowich Biographical File.

56. "Pembroke Girl Olympic Champion."

57. Katherine Hinds, "The Minkins Sisters," *Brown Alumni Monthly* 82 (April 1982): 41.

58. *Brun Mael,* 1936, 42.

59. Physical Education Department Files, "Rhode Island's Babe Didrikson," in 1933–1939 Department Scrapbook.

60. Physical Education Department Files, "Mrs. Wightman to Open Courts," and "Pembroke Tennis Courts Opened," in 1933–1939 Department Scrapbook.

61. Physical Education Department Files, "Miss Coakley, Pembroke Gym Instructor Named to U. S. Lacrosse Touring Team," *Pembroke Record,* 27 February 1951, in 1948–1952 Department Scrapbook.

62. Physical Education Department Files, Charles Ill, Commodore, Brown University Yacht Club to Bessie Rudd, 3 April 1949 in Sailing Folder; Bessie Rudd to Saul Moskowitz, 22 December 1955, in Fencing Folder.

63. Physical Education Department Files, "This Year, The Boys Can't Ask Her to Go," *The Rhode Islander,* 22 January 1956, in 1948–1952 Department Scrapbook.

64. Physical Education Department Files, "Miss Rudd Sees How 25 Colleges Run Their Games," *Providence Evening Bulletin,* 29 September 1939, in 1933–1939 Department Scrapbook.

65. Physical Education Department Files, Clipping, *Pembroke Record,* 9 July 1942, in 1942–1945 Department Scrapbook.

66. Physical Education Department Files, "Mixed Swimming," *Providence Bulletin,* 8 July 1942, in 1942–1945 Department Scrapbook; Bessie Rudd to A. Chester Snow, 21 April 1942, and A. Chester Snow to Bessie Rudd, 8 May 1942, in Sailing Folder.

67. *Students' Handbook of Pembroke College in Brown University,* 1940–1941, p. 42; 1942–1943, p. 19; and 1944–1945, p. 17. *Freshman Handbook – Pembroke College in Brown University,* 1953–1954, p. 49; 1954–1955, p. 54.

68. *Freshman Handbook – Pembroke College in Brown University,* 1956–1957, p. 22; and 1957–1958, p. 40.

69. Physical Education Department Files, "Dean Moulton Speaks Favorably of Physical Education at Banquet," 14 May 1954, in 1952–1956 Department Scrapbook.

70. *Freshman Handbook – Pembroke College in Brown University,* 1962–1963, p. 31.

71. On the emergence of the lesbian stereotype in women's sports, see Susan Cahn, "Coming on Strong: Gender and Sexuality in Women's Sport, 1900–1960," (Ph.D. Dissertation, University of Minnesota, 1990).

72. File 1-ZP, Pembroke College – Athletic and Recreation Association, Executive Board Records, Folder 5, Barney Welch, "The State of the A. R. A.," September, 1961.

73. Physical Education Department Files, Robert Grasson, Fencing coach at Yale, to Director of Athletics at Pembroke, 16 February 1947, in Fencing Folder; Charles Ill to Bessie Rudd, 3 April 1949, and Ann White, "Report on Tufts Regatta," 1950, both in Sailing Folder.

74. File 1-ZP, Pembroke College – Athletic and Recreation Association, Executive Board Records, Folder 1, A. A. Meeting Minutes, 8 November 1949 and 25 April 1950; also Folder 3, A. A. Meeting Minutes, 9 December 1957 and 17 February 1958.

75. Physical Education Department Files, Bessie Rudd to Celia Richmond, n.d., and "Proposals Made By the Executive Committee of the Brown Yacht Club for a Tentative Agreement to Lease Our Facilities to a Pembroke Sailing Organization," in Sailing Folder; "Pembroke Yacht Club is Merged With Brown's Club," in 1952–1956 Department Scrapbook.

76. "At 80, Bessie Will Join Select Company in Brown Hall of Fame;" Physical Education Department Files, Brown University, Women's Coaches meeting Minutes, 24 September 1976.

77. Arlene Gorton, interview by Cindy Himes, 29 July 1988, Christine Dunlap Farnham Archives, Oral History Collection; also File 1-ZP, Pembroke College – Athletic Association, Executive Board Records, Folder 1, 15 March 1950, 2 May 1950, 26 April 1951, and 17 February 1952.

78. Arlene Gorton, interview by Cindy Himes.

79. File 1-ZP, Pembroke College – Athletic and Recreation Association, Executive Board Records, Folder 7, "Corporation Set to Vote Concerning Liberalized Gym Proposal," *Pembroke Record,* 15 March 1963.

80. Arlene Gorton, interview by Cindy Himes.

81. File 1-ZP, Pembroke College – Athletic and Recreation Association, Executive Board Records, Folder 7, "University to Host White Hockey Team Here From Segregationist

South Africa," *Brown Daily Herald*, 20 September 1963.

82. File 1-zp, Pembroke College – Athletic and Recreation Association, Executive Board Records, Folder 7, "South African Team Wins at Hockey; Causes Controversy Over Apartheid," *Pembroke Record*, n.d.

83. "University to Host White Hockey Team."

84. Arlene Gorton, interview by Cindy Himes.

85. Ibid.

86. Ibid.

87. Ibid. Also Physical Education Department Files, "Hockey Captivates Folks on the Hill," *Providence Evening Bulletin*, 27 February 1964, and "Pandas Prepare for Game with Ontario's Golden Gals," *Pembroke Record*, 12 January 1968 in Fall, 1966–1972 Department Scrapbook.

88. Physical Education Department Files, "Letter to the Editor," *Brown Daily Herald*, 10 March 1966, in Spring 1963–Spring 1966 Department Scrapbook.

89. Physical Education Department Files, "BPOC'er Makes Good," *Pembroke Record* 7 May 1966, in Spring 1963–Spring 1966 Department Scrapbook.

90. Physical Education Department Files, "Notes From Underwater: Skin Diving," *Pembroke Record*, 21 April 1967, and "Davenport Hosts Dancing Lovelies," *Yale Daily News*, 29 February 1968, in Fall 1966–1972 Department Scrapbook.

91. Physical Education Department Files, "Penny Jocks Have 'Jolly Time' With Hockey, Skiing, Lacrosse," *Pembroke Record*, 7 November 1967, in Fall 1966–1972 Department Scrapbook.

92. Physical Education Department Files, "New Hoopsters Win Wellesley Tourney," 28 February 1967, and "Dartmouth to Host Champion Divers," *The Reporter*, 8 February 1966, in Fall 1966–1972 Department Scrapbook; "Sports News," in Spring 1963–Spring 1966 Department Scrapbook.

93. Physical Education Department Files, Pembroke College, Minutes of Department Meetings, 1968–1972, Minutes for 14 May 1970.

94. Physical Education Department Files, Pembroke College, Minutes of Department Meetings, 1968–1972, Minutes for 26 January 1971.

95. Arlene Gorton, interview by Cindy Himes.

96. Ibid.

97. Boutilier and SanGiovanni, pp. 173, 176. In reassessing priorities during the merger, the Physical Education Department agreed in May, 1979 that "high priority should be given to club activities and highly skilled groups, both in staff time and facilities." Physical Education Department Files, Pembroke College, Minutes of Department Meetings, 1968–1972, Minutes for 14 May 1970.

98. File 1-P, "Club Sport Competition," *Sportswomen at Brown Newsletter*, March 1981.

99. Brown University – Physical Education Department File, Women's Coaches Meetings, 1975–1977, Minutes for 8 September 1975, and 22 April 1977.

100. File 1-P, *Sportswomen at Brown Newsletter*, June 1981, Winter 1982, and Fall 1982.

101. Boutilier and San Giovanni, pp. 177–178.

102. Ibid., p. 177.

103. Arlene Gorton, interview by Cindy Himes.

104. Boutilier and San Giovanni, pp. 176–177.

105. James Reinbold, "Sports: Women's Soccer Gains Eighth Straight Ivy Title," *Brown Alumni Monthly* 89 (December 1989): 20; James Reinbold, "Sports: Names," *Brown Alumni Monthly* 89 (April 1989): 19.

106. Arlene Gorton, letter to Cindy Himes, 17 March 1991.

107. Arlene Gorton, interview by Cindy Himes.

Ph.D.s Earned by Women, Brown University, 1971–1990

Year	Total Ph.D.s Earned	Number of Ph.D.s Earned by Women	Percent of Ph.D.s Earned by Women	National Percent of Ph.D.s Earned by Women
1971	not available	15	not available	
1972	162	15	9	16
1973	148	17	11	
1974	162	26	16	
1975	142	30	21	
1976	139	36	26	
1977	148	35	24	
1978	127	33	26	
1979	133	41	31	
1980	150	40	27	30
1981	126	24	19	
1982	137	44	32	
1983	112	38	34	
1984	119	37	31	
1985	139	31	22	
1986	121	38	31	35
1987	145	45	31	
1988	156	54	35	
1989	147	48	33	36.5
1990	130	52	40	
TOTAL	2643	699		

Brown statistics compiled from data provided by Brown University Graduate School, November 1990 and January 1991. National statistics from National Research Council, cited in Mariam K. Chamberlain, ed., *Women in Academe: Progress and Prospects* (New York: Russell Sage, 1988), p. 257; "Summary Report 1989," National Research Council quoted in *Chronicle of Higher Education*, 6 March 1991, p. A13.

CHAPTER 5

The Costs of Partial Support: One Hundred Years of Brown Graduate Women

by LINDA EISENMANN

W HEN ROSEMARY PIERREL finished her Ph.D. in psychology in 1953 and embarked on a college teaching career, she wished to stay on at Brown, where she had earned her doctorate with Professor Walter S. Hunter. Pierrel taught introductory psychology and a senior seminar for two years, after which time her department sought to promote her to assistant professor. Her chairman received his answer directly from the university's president, Henry M. Wriston:

> Mr. Wriston told him that, words to the effect that, they were very happy [with me], that the Psychology Department liked me and would like to promote me, but that I must understand that Brown was primarily a men's institution, and that I would be the nicest white-haired assistant professor Brown ever had.[1]

Pierrel left for Barnard College and Columbia University before she returned to Brown as dean of Pembroke College in 1961 under a different president with a different philosophy. Not until the merger of Pembroke and Brown in 1971 did she become a full professor.

As Pierrel reflected later on Wriston's comment, she explained that the president was being "conscientious" about the situation at Brown: "The way he saw it, there was no future for women on this faculty."[2] In fact, because of its longstanding resistance to hiring women faculty in full-time tenure slots, Brown limited the possibilities for its women graduate students to build academic and research careers. In the early years, Brown did hire some of its female graduates to teach courses specific to

Graduate student Patricia Rose at a Pembroke Center round-table in 1988.

women, such as hygiene, biology, and physiology; a male professor for these courses was considered inappropriate. The university also hired some of its women graduate students as assistants. All of these positions, however, were few in number and low in authority.[3] Since the other Ivy League schools which offered graduate degrees to women also took this halfway approach to supporting women professionals, these women lost the chance for careers at the type of school where they had received training. Only in the most recent years have Brown's women Ph.D.s begun to share in the full range of academic employment, with a few securing positions at Brown and other Ivy League institutions.

Many costs – to women, to Brown, and to society – are associated with Brown's past decisions to train academic women but not to employ them and to offer them only tepid assistance in finding positions through established academic networks. Many of the issues center on the lack of opportunity to develop a locus for professional women's activity at the university. Without women professors, female students had no role models who might help them envision their own commitment to graduate-level scholarship. The women who did complete graduate work had to find jobs in institutions all over the country, preventing the development of a critical mass of women academics at Brown or similar institutions. Although some women did build strength at women's colleges like Mount Holyoke or Wellesley, these schools were without the resources to provide widespread graduate training. Thus there was little opportunity for women to develop "progeny," as this method of training and nurturing academic protegees has been described.[4] The scatter-shot nature of women's employment outside the women's colleges provided female academics little chance to shape departments by applying the press of numbers. In addition, because the diffusion of women's employment was coupled with the notable lack of promotion for women, their chance of exerting leadership in their fields was sorely weakened.

Faced with such resistance to their advancement, graduate women developed strategies over the decades to combat the antipathy and indifference which often surrounded their decisions to pursue careers. Historian Margaret Rossiter divides these strategies into two types: an "idealistic" goal of full equality, and a "less strident" strategy of acknowledging sexual stereotypes but working to exploit every possibility for advancement.[5] Historians Penina Migdal Glazer and Miriam Slater expand these approaches into four specific strategies that women followed to enhance their participation in the professions: *superperformance, subordination, separatism,* and *innovation.*[6]

At the Brown Graduate School,[7] women preparing for the professions faced the obstacles and employed the strategies cited by Rossiter, Glazer, and Slater. Brown *superperformers*, for example, include Elizabeth Leduc (Ph.D. 1948) and Helen Butts Correll (A.M. 1929) who made different personal choices as they pursued academic and research careers: Leduc, who never married, became Brown's first tenured woman professor who was not also a dean; Correll combined marriage and motherhood with a series of full- and part-time teaching and research positions, some shared with her husband, in her long career as a botanist.

Other graduates played a *subordinate* role in male-dominated fields, although the term "subordination" should not connote women's lesser talent or effort. Frances Wright (A.M. 1920), for example, had a tremendous influence on the students to whom she taught celestial navigation. But much of her career was spent as an assistant under other astronomers at the Harvard College Observatory. It was not until 1958 that she returned to graduate school to earn a Ph.D.

Following the strategy of *separatism*, many of Brown's graduate women built their careers in separate female institutions: women like Isabel Ross Abbott (A.B. 1922, A.M. 1923) who had a long career at Rockford College, and Mary Emma Woolley (A.B. 1894, A.M. 1895) who served a lengthy presidency at Mount Holyoke College. More recently, Helen Johnson Loschky (A.B. 1955, A.M. 1965, Ph.D. 1970 in English) pursued a career in a different type of "separate" institution, the historically African-American Lincoln University.

The last strategy, *innovation*, has proven to be one of the hardiest over time. An early Brown innovator is engineer Lillian Moller Gilbreth (Ph.D. 1915) who, after working alongside her husband Frank, developed an entirely new field by applying the principles of industrial efficiency to the home. Carmen Huber (Ph.D. in physics, 1983) and Mary Wilson Carpenter (Ph.D. in English, 1983) both used innovative approaches in their job searches, as they worked to solve dual career issues.

Highlighting the costs of Brown's academic policy may seem like a negative way to discuss the contributions of graduate women when, in fact, Brown produced hundreds of women Ph.D.s and master's graduates from the 1890s to 1991. Most of those women valued highly their opportunity to train at Brown and pursued interesting, even illustrious, careers in various professions. But turning a lens on the special issues that women professionals faced reminds us that women were forced to develop alternate paths and strategies when they were given some, but not all, of their share of benefits. Just as the undergraduate coordinate relationship between Brown and Pembroke had disadvantages, so did the university's partial commitment to the advancement of women scholars.

This chapter will explore the history of Brown's graduate women, discussing both their status at Brown and their relation to the wider academic women's community. The first part of the chapter will consider three eras, focusing on the general situation for academic women and then the particular circumstances for women at Brown in: 1) the early years of graduate education, prior to the 1930s, when women established their claim; 2) the 1930s to 1970, when women found increased competition from men and lost some of their earlier gains, reclaiming some strength only in the 1960s; and 3) 1970–1991, when both the women's movement and specific changes at Brown boosted the number of women earning graduate degrees and finding suitable academic employment.[8]

The second part of the chapter will examine some representative career histories of Brown women who faced obstacles and chose different strategies to accommodate themselves to the situation around them, concluding with a look at the present and at the long-term costs to women's professional advancement incurred by earlier decisions.

Women in Graduate Education Before 1930

Graduate education became commonplace in the United States only in the last quarter of the nineteenth century. Before then, the master's degree was usually awarded pro forma three years or so after a bachelor's degree; there was little expectation of additional formal scholarship. The Ph.D. itself was imported from German universities, where the research tradition was thriving. The first American Ph.D. was earned by a man in 1862; the first woman followed only fifteen years later.[9]

The apparent rapidity with which women followed men into graduate work belies a decades-long push for women's opportunities, a process which Rossiter calls "a kind of educational 'guerrilla warfare'" against universities both in Europe and the United States.[10] Yet in some institutions, women were welcomed more easily or equally into advanced coursework than they were into traditional undergraduate programs. At Brown and Columbia, for example, graduate women were admitted into coeducational programs while undergraduate women entered separate, "coordinate" colleges. At Yale and Pennsylvania, women were accepted into the graduate schools but not at all in undergraduate work. Perhaps the existence of a few exceptional women at the graduate level created less concern than the mass of women who were eager to pursue bachelor's degree training. Women were admitted into graduate work at Brown in 1891, and within a year they were eligible for graduate degrees.

Much of the plan to move women into the university was conceived and administered by President E. Benjamin Andrews (1889–1899), with the steadfast support and strategizing by the local women of the Rhode Island Society for the Collegiate Education of Women. Andrews envisioned a larger Brown University filled with women and graduate students – both new populations for Brown. Although his predecessor, Ezekiel Robinson, had actually started the fledgling graduate program at the university, Andrews doubled the size of Brown's faculty in the 1890s and mounted a huge fund-raising drive to benefit the faculty and their research. By 1898 the president had increased the number of graduate students to 101, or 8.5 percent of the total enrollment at Brown. Thirty-nine of those graduate students were women. Only the financial difficulties of the 1890s hindered Andrews in his ambitious plans for university expansion.[11]

When William H.P. Faunce succeeded Andrews to the Brown presidency in 1899, he brought a different vision of the university, one that focused strongly on the undergraduate men's college as Brown's center. Eschewing the fragmented programs and curriculum that were likely to develop with a growing graduate effort, he wanted advanced study to remain in the background. Faunce preferred the liberal training offered to master's candidates over research-oriented doctoral work.

To carry out his vision, Faunce selected Carl Barus as dean of the graduate department, a role which the physicist pursued for a quarter century (1901–1926). During that time, general master's students outnumbered Ph.D.s and Master of Science candidates by three to one, and the graduate enrollment remained at approximately 10 percent of Brown's total enrollment. In those twenty-five years, the school awarded 884 A.M. degrees and 102 Ph.D.s. Of that total, women earned 34 percent of the master's degrees, but only 10 percent of the doctorates. Over the era, women's annual share of all advanced degrees ranged from a low of 21 percent to a high of 47 percent.[12] Although twelve departments awarded doctorates, fully two-thirds of the Ph.D.s from Brown were earned in biology and chemistry; biology was especially hospitable to women. Foreign languages, English, and history accounted for most of the rest.[13] By 1924, 312 women had earned graduate degrees at the university; all but eleven of those were master's degrees.

Seven of the women who received the first eleven Brown doctorates were already Brown alumnae: Martha Tarbell was the first woman to earn a doctorate from Brown (A.M. 1894, Ph.D. 1897); Hermione Dealey earned a Brown A.B. in 1914, then studied at Clark for her A.M. in 1915 before returning to Brown; Marion Dodge Weston (Ph.D. 1917) came to Brown for the master's and doctorate, following her bachelor's degree at Mount Holyoke; Edna May Round (Ph.D. 1920) earned a Brown A.B.

and A.M. before the turn of the century and then returned for her doctorate two decades later; and Norah Eloise Dowell (Ph.D. 1916), Margaret B. Church (Ph.D. 1918), and Elsie May Flint (Ph.D. 1922) each earned three degrees from Brown.

Four of the women Ph.D.s had not studied at Brown prior to the doctorate: Gertrude E. Hall (Ph.D. 1907) received her A.B. from Cornell in 1897; Lillian Moller Gilbreth (Ph.D. 1915) received her undergraduate and master's degrees from the University of California-Berkeley in 1900 and 1902; Grace E. Bird (Ph.D. 1918) earned her A.B. from the University of Chicago in 1897, then waited until 1916 to attend Columbia for the A.M.; and Marjorie W. Cook (Ph.D. 1919) attended Mount Holyoke for her 1911 A.B., and earned her Ph.D. without a master's.[14]

Two other unusual graduate school women from that era went on to earn doctoral degrees at other institutions: Grace Emma Cooley, a botanist, who earned her master's at Brown in 1893, followed some of the female pioneers of her day to Europe where she earned the Ph.D. from Zurich in 1894;[15] and physician Ellen Appleton Stone, a Radcliffe A.B. (1895) and Brown A.M. (1896) went on to the Johns Hopkins Medical School, earning her M.D. in 1900.

By 1934, another eight women who had earned their master's degrees at Brown went on to earn Ph.D.s at other institutions, including another Hopkins physician, two women at Yale (both in science), two at Pennsylvania, and one each at Chicago, Cornell, and the University of Missouri (the latter two in science).[16] The sciences, especially the natural and physical sciences, served Brown women well in the early years.

In the larger group of 301 women who earned master's degrees before 1924, only about one-third (108) received their bachelor's degree from a school other than Brown. Many of those non-Brown candidates came in the earliest years of Brown's program, before the undergraduate school had produced a strong pool of its own female candidates. At least in the earliest decades, staying on to do a master's at one's own institution was commonplace and perhaps even necessary, given the preponderance of local women who attended Brown.[17]

This figure does provide an opportunity to examine which other institutions were providing women graduates to Brown's master's program. Data from the 1934 catalog shows fifty different institutions, many of them women's colleges, which granted A. B. degrees to women who came to Brown for their master's. The most frequently mentioned colleges were the well-established women's colleges in the northeast later known as the Seven Sisters. Before 1934, Wellesley College provided more women students (thirty-one) to Brown than any other. Mount Holyoke and Smith were not far behind, with twenty-five and twenty-one students, respectively.[18]

Few surprises exist in the job figures for the graduates listed in the historical catalogs. Of the fifty-four women (master's and Ph.D.s) who provided job information, forty were working in education – a percentage that matches most studies of women's early career choices. Of those forty, twenty-three women were high school teachers and eleven were teaching in higher education.[19] The remainder were writers, laboratory technicians, librarians, and students.

Women gradually pushed their way into the professions and into academic life by 1930, feeling that these were places where talent could carry them, regardless of their gender, and where they could offer professional service to the community.[20] Armed with this belief in the twin qualities of merit and service, women made some professional progress. By 1930, women had reached a peak in their share of Ph.D.s awarded: nationally that year, 18 percent of all doctorates were won by women, and women held 27 percent of all faculty positions.[21] At Brown, women fared this well only at the master's level. Although 36 percent of the A.M. degrees were earned by women (twenty-four of sixty-six), only one of twelve Ph.D.s that year was earned by a woman (Hope Frances Kane).

A thorough profile of academic women was provided in 1928 by Barnard economist Emilie J. Hutchinson who conducted a national study of 1,025 women who had earned the doctorate between 1877 and 1924. Hutchinson found that the fields of study undertaken by these women were evenly divided: one-third in languages, literature, and the arts; one-third in natural sciences and mathematics; one-third in the social sciences. Generally the graduates advised younger women to go on with doctoral work if they intended to pursue collegiate teaching and research.[22] Their own career choices attested to this advice: a full 58 percent of the graduates were teaching, as compared to 74 percent of Brown's graduate women (including Brown Ph.D.s and master's recipients). Five-sixths of the teachers in Hutchinson's sample taught in colleges and universities. At Brown, comparable information is scanty; job information is available on only five women Ph.D.s, three of whom taught in colleges.[23] However, of the forty Brown women Ph.D.s and master's who worked in education, twenty-three taught in high schools (58 percent). Many of Hutchinson's other doctorates worked in administrative or executive positions, most in social work or educational institutions. Less than 10 percent (and most of those were the scientists) worked in research. At Brown, the non-teaching jobs included writer, laboratory technician, librarian, and student.

Although only 10 percent of the women surveyed by Hutchinson flatly advised younger women against pursuing the Ph.D., and although most found "definite economic value" to the degree, they also revealed some of the difficulties and costs of life as a professional woman in the 1920s. Three-quarters of the women were unmarried, a figure attesting to the commitment required by a scholarly lifestyle. In addition, the women unleashed "a torrent of complaint" about the sex bias they had encountered in the supposedly merit-based professional world. Those in academe felt especially strongly about the bias they found in promotions, pay, research assistantships, and fellowships.[24]

Occupational segregation and lack of promotion seemed to operate especially strongly in women's academic employment. For example, the figure behind the overall sum of women holding 27 percent of faculty positions revealed that most of those positions were in women's colleges or normal schools, a situation common to Brown's graduate women. At seventy research universities, for example – schools most like Brown – only 9 percent of the faculty were women; of full professors, only 1.3 percent.[25]

Nancy Cott notes a surprising realization about women's stalled movement into the professions in the early twentieth century. She explains that "the expectation of the nineteenth-century women who pioneered women's entry into the professions – that the more women entered, the easier it would be for their successors – was not fulfilled." The timing may have differed for the various fields, but Cott finds a sameness which characterizes the pattern of professional development: early advance within women's institutions; gradual opening of male institutions; rising expectations by women, which are eventually dashed by barriers, quotas, and marginalization.[26]

At Brown, little of this apparent advancement for women occurred, given the university's continuing refusal to employ female academics. Women students did share in the overall growth of the university during the 1920s, but their opportunities for academic employment were not enhanced. In fact, the entire presidency of William Faunce, which ended in 1929, was marked by a continuing focus on the male undergraduate college, a fact that was symbolized in 1928 by the name change of the Women's College to Pembroke College.[27]

The 1930s to 1970: The "Great Withdrawal"?

On the national scene, the decades between 1930 and 1970 witnessed enormous fluctuations in both educational and occupational opportunities. Depression followed by war and then prosperity drew a range of responses from women and men as they prepared for the job market. Unfortunately for academic women, however, the increases in professional opportunities tended not to benefit women as well as they did men.

At Brown, although academic opportunities grew with the prosperous times, the inclusion of women into professional positions did not change markedly. By the 1960s, more women Ph.D. graduates worked in college-level teaching and research compared to earlier female doctorates who had worked in secondary schools. But although women doctorates held a more secure place in higher education than they had in earlier decades, they still had not been welcomed into the full range of postsecondary institutions. Notably, neither Brown nor its Ivy League peers had made major efforts to increase women's roles on the faculty.

Many historians of education have characterized the decades between 1930 and 1960 as a "great withdrawal" for women in academic employment, finding in these years an actual decline in women's proportion, if not in numbers, of earned doctorates and academic employment.[28] At Brown, that story is confounded by the changing position of the Graduate School vis-a-vis the undergraduate college.

Dean Carl Barus's retirement from the Brown Graduate Department in 1926 opened the graduate deanship to a new person and a new approach, although the opportunities for women did not change noticeably. Roland G.D. Richardson took over the dean's job in 1926, and during the next twenty-two years oversaw considerable growth in the size and reach of the Brown Graduate School (upgraded from a program in 1927). He expanded programs in mathematics, physics, philosophy, psychology, chemistry, economics, history, and foreign languages, and also added more stipends and assistantships. Just as the undergraduate programs were growing, the graduate enrollment jumped from 246 in 1927–28 to 333 in the early Depression year of 1932–33. Also similar to the bachelor's candidates, graduate students came from a more diverse background: unlike the earlier years when the majority of graduate students were Brown alumni, after 1927 only about one-third had Brown bachelor's degrees.[29]

By 1933, however, the Depression hit most programs hard. Although Brown was buoyed by a 1933 invitation to join the prestigious Association of American Universities – a sure sign that its graduate program was attracting attention – it also witnessed the waning of much of the fellowship money used to attract doctoral candidates. The Graduate School held its own throughout the Depression, then suffered a drop to 132 students during World War II.

Predictably, the Graduate School shared in the resurgence of enrollment with the war's end. Interestingly, however, women students seem to have played a less significant role in maintaining the graduate program through its fluctuations than they did on the undergraduate level. Only 20 to 25 women per year received advanced degrees in the 1930s and 1940s, despite wide variations in the total number of graduate degrees awarded. For example, at the close of the war years in 1945, only fifteen women received advanced degrees out of a total of thirty-six. Those numbers suggest that the university preferred to have dwindling graduate enrollments rather than to keep up the size of those programs by admitting more women.[30] In the graduate Class of 1949, twenty-eight men and only five women earned the Ph.D. With those five women, the sciences predominated: three were biologists, one a chemist, and one a psychologist.[31]

By the mid-1960s, college enrollments had grown tremendously, and the growth in sheer numbers was accompanied by changes in the populations entering higher education. But, unfortunately for women, this change brought an increased proportion of men who entered college and graduate school with the boost of the G.I. Bill following World War II. Women academics and professionals faced increased competition from male graduates in an era when their own foothold had not been especially strong.

Thus, even in a time of general prosperity, the overall job picture for Brown's graduate women did not change remarkably, although an expansion in types of jobs held by women did occur. A sample of 369 of the more than 1400 women who received graduate degrees from Brown by 1964 (both Ph.D.s and master's recipients) shows the continued attraction of education as a field for academic women. Fully 65 percent of the women who listed their employment were pursuing careers in education.[32] Forty years earlier, almost three-quarters of the jobs Brown women held had been in education.

Isolating just the Ph.D. recipients in this sample does reveal one strong and obvious difference from the master's women: doctoral recipients pursued teaching, but they did so in higher education. Although job information is available for only one-third of the 112 women who had earned a Brown Ph.D. by 1964, a full 70 percent of those women were working in collegiate institutions.[33] Although women may not have reached parity at the premier research universities, they did win academic jobs across a range of postsecondary institutions that had burgeoned during the 1950s and 1960s. Women in the 1964 sample also displayed a wider range of jobs that used their academic training. A full 10 percent of the jobs listed were in research; additional graduates were scattered among jobs in libraries, museums, government, business, social services, laboratories, and publishing. The passing decades had clearly brought some advances.

Economist Susan Carter found that women's overall share of academic employment remained steady between 1930 and 1960, even with shifts in student populations, because of the willingness of the land-grant universities to hire women as professors after the 1930s. As more female students came to the land-grant programs, female professors were imported to instruct them.[34] Carter concludes, however, that "powerful forces of tradition operated in large sectors of the higher education system."[35] Only slow changes occurred in the willingness of certain schools, particularly the Ivy League, to employ female faculty.[36] With the exception of its women deans and graduate assistants, Brown continued its tradition of producing but not employing talented women academics.

1970 to 1990: Slow Changes

In addition to huge shifts in women's status encouraged by the women's movement over the past twenty years, those decades also brought two particular changes to women's place at Brown University: the 1971 merger of Pembroke and Brown, and the 1977 consent decree established through the discrimination suit of Professor Louise Lamphere. Although it is not possible to show a causal effect on graduate enrollment by these events, enrollment figures at Brown's graduate school over these years do show increases in both absolute numbers and proportions of Ph.D.s earned by women. Presumably, the combination of these changes has helped produce a climate that supports women's career advancement at Brown.

As the table on page 154 shows, women began to earn more Brown Ph.D.s in the mid-1970s. For the first three years of the decade, fewer than twenty women completed their doctorates each year. Beginning in 1974, however, a jump in numbers occurred that sustained itself for a dozen years, growing again in the last few years. Generally, since the mid-1970s, at least thirty women have completed their Ph.D.s at Brown each year. Nearly 700 women have earned their doctorates in the past twenty years, and their proportion has increased from less than 10 percent to 40 percent.[37] From 1972 to 1990, the number of men earning doctorates at Brown has declined as the number of women increased. This matches national figures, which show a rise in women's share of all doctorates from 16 percent in 1972, to 30 percent in 1980, to 36.5 percent in 1989.[38]

The data also suggests that women are participating in all academic areas of the graduate curriculum. As the accompanying graph shows, the humanities have produced more women Ph.D.s than any other area, a figure that matches national data. However, the physical sciences – often said to be less inclusive of women – have provided the second largest group of women Ph.D.s, with 19 percent. In fact, next to English, chemistry has

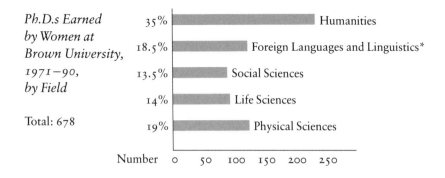

Ph.D.s Earned by Women at Brown University, 1971–90, by Field

Total: 678

35%	Humanities
18.5%	Foreign Languages and Linguistics*
13.5%	Social Sciences
14%	Life Sciences
19%	Physical Sciences

Number   0   50   100   150   200   250

* Including Classics and Area Studies
SOURCE: Data Provided by the Brown University
Graduate School, November 1990

produced more women Ph.D.s than any other field.[39] Nationally, women earned only 16.1 percent of all doctorates in the physical sciences in 1986.[40] Biology has the third largest number of women Ph.D.s, continuing a tradition at Brown that dates from the era of J. Walter Wilson and Herbert Walter.

Brown's recent women Ph.D.s have also managed to find work suitable to their training. A sample of 400 of 696 women Ph.D.s (from 1971 to 1990) reveals that 170 (54 percent) are pursuing teaching positions in collegiate institutions, a figure similar to Emilie Hutchinson's data in the 1920s, a "boom time" for academic women. Unlike earlier groups of Brown women, however, only 2.5 percent of these recent graduate women are working in secondary schools (eight women). To that figure of 54 percent must be added the groups of women Ph.D.s who work as research associates (45), hold postdoctoral appointments (34), and work as higher education administrators (5), most in colleges and universities. In total, 80 percent of the women Ph.D.s who listed employment are working in academic positions that match their training.

Despite the advancement for women suggested by these figures, a closer look at the types of institutions which employ Brown's academic graduates shows that Brown women have not yet entered the Ivy League institutions as professors in significant numbers. Of the women employed as professors and researchers, a few are employed at Brown and only a handful work at the other Ivy League universities. The 1990 data shows only one woman with a Brown Ph.D. each at Harvard, Princeton, Dartmouth, Pennsylvania, and Cornell.[41]

Otherwise, Brown's women Ph.D.s work at a range of collegiate institutions. Several have continued to find positions in the women's colleges, with Smith, Mount Holyoke, Barnard, Wheaton, and Wellesley colleges among the employers. Brown's recent Ph.D. women also work at selective liberal arts colleges such as Kenyon, Carleton, and Connecticut colleges; they work at large research universities such as Pittsburgh, Michigan, and Chicago; they work in teaching-oriented institutions such as Bridgewater State and Salem State (both in Massachusetts); and they work in defense-related institutions such as the Naval Weapons Center, the Naval Academy at Annapolis, and at the Defense Language Institute.

For a combination of reasons – some outside the university and some within – women have pursued their graduate degrees at Brown in increasing numbers over the last twenty years and have managed to secure strong professional employment as well. However, more than these aggregate numbers are necessary to tell the story of women's status in the academic world at Brown and after Brown. How have women coped with the challenges of graduate work, employment, and life choices?

The Academic Women of Brown: Individual Strategies for Achievement

While aggregate data on graduate women indicate the scope of Brown's program and suggest patterns in women's employment, the experiences of individual women and how they negotiate the academic and career issues around them provide additional insights.[42] Their stories suggest that they often match the strategies described by historians Glazer and Slater in their study of professional women: *superperformance, subordination, separatism,* and *innovation,* and that innovation seems most suited to recent graduates.

Superperformance

Two Brown women almost a generation apart provide complementary examples of what Glazer and Slater call academic "superperformers" – those women who, despite the odds, made extraordinary efforts to advance in their careers. Many of these women, like their counterparts at the turn of the century, never married because of the press of a professional commitment. Other superperformers who did pursue a family life worked their own career ambitions into home demands, again with an unusual variety of strategies. Elizabeth Leduc (Brown Ph.D. 1948) and Helen Butts Correll (Brown A.B. 1928, A.M. 1929; Ph.D. Duke University, 1934) exemplify these approaches.

Elizabeth Leduc combined her own intellectual abilities, hard work, and her facility to learn from other people into an impressive academic career that included earning tenure as Brown's first woman professor who was not also a dean. Born in Rockland, Maine, Leduc expected to follow many of her female colleagues into high school teaching. It was the influence of her college professors at the University of Vermont that turned her toward a career in university teaching and research. Having decided to pursue an advanced science degree, Leduc realized that she needed a knowledge of German, so she earned a master's at Wellesley College in 1945 while she studied the language.

Two academic women at Wellesley, one of whom had earned a Brown Ph.D.,[43] encouraged Leduc to go to Brown to study with J. Walter Wilson, professor of biology, a man known for his encouragement of women and minority students. Leduc arrived just as World War II was ending and remembers only a few students in her department: two or three were men, and two or three were women, as she recalls. But Leduc also remembers Wilson's even-handed treatment and encouragement of the graduate women. In fact, she feels that men helped her career at every stage: "I owe my elevation through the academic realm," she recalled in an interview, "to the fact that I was always supported by men who were broad-minded and supported women."

Leduc had set her sights on an academic career, but learned that Brown did not hire its own graduates onto the faculty. She notes that this policy, at least in the Biology Department, was not a male/female issue; rather, "I was told well before I graduated that I could not stay at Brown, because they never kept their own graduates." She recalled Professor Wilson's advice that "you have to go elsewhere and prove yourself. Then we will decide whether we want you to come back."[44]

Leduc did just that, working for four years at Harvard Medical School before she returned to Brown. At Harvard she once again found the academic prejudice against one's own scholars; she explained that she left Harvard because of its policy of not promoting people into tenure, but instead choosing "outsiders" for senior-level positions.

By Leduc's own account, she was utterly devoted to her work. She reported, "I had my nose plunged into research, morning, noon, and night," regularly working at the lab until midnight and rarely involving herself in activities beyond her own department and students. This focus on her work apparently made her "oblivious" to some of the difficulties other academic women faced in their research and teaching opportunities. Leduc recalls her surprise at receiving letters from women all around the country congratulating her when she earned tenure at Brown, an Ivy League university. These were women she had never met, but who were thrilled that a woman had been recognized on the basis of merit. "That's when I began to realize how lucky I was, in taking all these things for granted," Leduc remembers. She had never realized she was unusual in her steady series of promotions, and was in fact, "surprised" to see "how much more difficult some women found their experiences."[45]

Helen Butts Correll, another scientist, took a different approach from Elizabeth Leduc's, but in some ways was also oblivious to the extraordinary nature of her accomplishments. Correll, who received an A.M. in biology in 1929, sounds much like a 1990s "superwoman." She met her husband while in graduate school, took time off from teaching to have four children, and then worked part-time until the children were grown, including a lengthy collaboration and co-authorship with her husband on their botanical research. Yet, in true superperformer fashion, she was surprised to realize at the age of seventy-six that she had managed to combine career and family successfully for forty-five years.

Having always planned on a career, Correll had followed her friend Gladys Holmes (who also eventually earned a Ph.D., in 1929) into the Biology Department at Brown where she earned an A.B. and a master's under Herbert Walter. Correll spoke highly of the encouragement she received at Brown, both from Walter and from Dean Margaret Morriss. Correll won her initial teaching position through Professor Walter's sponsorship: he recommended her for a job teaching mammalian anatomy and physiology at Smith College. Correll also indicated the close cooperation between academic departments: "They [Smith] depended on this department [Brown] to produce ... someone they would admire." Interestingly, this strong women's college apparently regularly turned to Brown for its supply of women professors – a hint of the workings of the academic job market. Realizing that a solid college teaching career would require a Ph.D., Correll went to Duke where, in 1934, she became the first woman to earn a doctorate in zoology and where she met her husband, a graduate student in the same department.

From then on, Correll's career became a balancing act that she hardly acknowledged at the time. She taught at Wellesley College while her husband pursued additional graduate work at Harvard. Then came the four children, and a short respite from academic work. When the youngest child was in kindergarten, Correll enlisted her sister for child care and worked part-time, including sharing a botanical lab with her husband. She took over after her husband's death the management of his botanical research project in Florida. An interview in her seventies gave Correll the occasion to step back, as did Elizabeth Leduc, and see how her own accomplishments stood out among other women's. "Lately I've been thinking about it," she mused, "and I've had a career and a family and a wonderful husband for forty-five years." But she never realized how hard she had worked to make the pieces fit: "I hadn't thought about it all these years," she explained with surprise.[46]

Subordination

Many other women did not experience the success or support that Elizabeth Leduc and Helen Correll found in their careers. In fact, many Brown graduates may have had skills equal to the "superperformers," but found, as Leduc noted, that "experience was more difficult" for them. The type of strategy that Glazer and Slater call subordination, termed idealism by Margaret Rossiter, found many talented, ambitious women fighting outright prejudice or lack of opportunity in traditional fields and making accommodations to the reality of their situations. Frances Wright (A.B. 1919, A.M. 1920) achieved success as an astronomer specializing in celestial navigation. After completing her master's degree at Brown, Wright taught astronomy and mathematics at Elmira College for eight years before leaving for the Harvard Observatory and a fifty-year career as a researcher and teacher. Yet much of that time was spent assisting other famous astronomers at Harvard; she worked as an assistant first to Cecilia Payne-Gaposchkin, then to Harlow Shapley and Fred Whipple. Eventually, Wright also pursued doctoral studies, and, nearly forty years after earning her master's degree at Brown, Wright completed her Ph.D. in 1958 from Radcliffe College. The next year, she joined the staff at the Harvard College Observatory, from which she retired in 1971. Although Frances Wright ultimately won her share of professional success, one wonders how much sooner she might have advanced in a different milieu and with greater support.[47]

Two of Brown's women deans who held graduate degrees from the university, Lida Shaw King and Rosemary Pierrel, exemplify another route that moved many academic women into the faculty, a route that fits the "subordinate" strategy. The "dean of women" position evolved at most coeducational institutions to meet the disciplinary and social demands created by having a group of women in the midst of an otherwise male institution. What differentiated the dean of women role from the earlier positions was the eventual award of faculty status to these women. Women like Anne Crosby Emery, the first female dean of the Women's College, brought strong scholarly credentials (in Emery's case, a Ph.D. from Bryn Mawr) along with their ability to manage the female students. Since these women were already prepared to teach, they were often given part-time faculty status as part of the dean's package. This situation represents yet another case where women lacked power commensurate with their skills.

Geraldine Clifford has called this accommodation to women deans "academic employment by transfer," or a "subfaculty" status, because the women were brought in primarily to watch over the students and only secondarily because of their academic credentials. However, over time, the faculty status of the deans of women solidified. By 1928, 93 percent of institutions which enrolled women had a dean of women; three-quarters of those deans held faculty status, even if they did not teach full-time and did not progress at the same rate through the faculty ranks.[48]

When Lida Shaw King took over as dean after Emery's marriage to Brown Classics professor Francis G. Allinson, she continued the scholarly tradition: King, also a classics scholar, had received her master's degree from Brown. Although King and Emery did teach some of the women, they were known, remembered, and judged for their work as deans.

Rosemary Pierrel assumed the Pembroke deanship in a later era and with a different career history behind her decision, although her story speaks to the continuing issues for women deans. After Pierrel had left Brown for faculty work at Barnard and Columbia, she was lured back in 1961 through the personal intervention of President Barnaby Keeney, who came to Pierrel with a "very persuasive" offer. But Keeney's persuasion required a good deal of effort; Pierrel recalls being quite satisfied with her faculty status in New York: "I was doing exactly what I wanted to do, with graduate students and research." Eventually, Pierrel was drawn by Keeney's suggestion that she could affect the curriculum and academic life of Brown's women through the deanship, and at the same time continue her research and scholarship in the Psychology Department.

Over the years Pierrel continued to teach and conduct research, but lamented how little time she could actually spend on her faculty role. As she explained, it was hard to "turn off the other concerns of the job" while she was in the classroom.[49] Like the many women deans before her, and after, she found that the faculty status of a dean was frequently subordinated to the administrative demands of the job.

Separatism

Although some Brown graduates pursued their careers within male institutions, many others followed the strategy Glazer and Slater describe as separatist. That is, by choice or happenstance, these women professionals worked in "separate" institutions, most notably the women's colleges. Brown's graduate records abound with examples of academic women who taught in women's institutions, scholars like Evelyn P. Wiggin (A.M. 1924) who taught mathematics at Randolph-Macon Women's College, Clara Wilm (A.M. 1930) who taught at Colorado Women's College, Dorothy L. Bernstein (Ph.D. 1939) who taught mathematics at Goucher. Others taught at normal schools/teachers colleges – schools that were not women's colleges but which served a majority of women students, and at least one committed her career to a historically African-American institution.[50]

Helen Johnson Loschky (A.B. 1955, A.M. 1965, Ph.D. in English, 1970) intended to work at Lincoln University, an African-American institution, "just for a few years," but found that the school became the center of her professional life. Scholarships helped her through Brown, and she terms her decision to enter graduate school "one of the three major turning points" in her life. She explains that

> Brown has had an inordinate influence on my life. My graduate work there in the exciting 1960s made up for the 1950s complacency. I am persuaded that my lifetime commitment to minority (Black women's) education is a direct result of my Brown University education.

Lincoln University provided a focus for Loschky's work, enabling her to create the school's first Honors Program and to be the first woman in Missouri to teach behind the walls of a maximum security prison.[51]

Another strong example of long-term dedication to a separate institution is Isabel Ross Abbott (A.B. 1922, A.M. 1923), who earned a Ph.D. in history at Bryn Mawr in 1937. Abbott taught at all-female Rockford College in Illinois for thirty years, as well as administering the summer school. She then served as academic dean at Western College for Women in Ohio. Not ready to retire, she taught part-time for another three years at Westminster College in Missouri.

While in college Abbott had planned, like so many of her classmates, on a secondary school teaching career, earning her master's immediately so that she could teach in the Providence high schools. But very quickly she discovered that she "enjoyed teaching," but "hated discipline." That realization eventually sent Abbott to pursue her doctorate, and she found college teaching much more to her liking.

Abbott was aware of the difficulties for a woman pursuing a professional career, although she did not fully articulate these issues until her time at Bryn Mawr. In an oral history interview, she explained her early feelings and her determination:

> I felt that the world was a man's world, that it was made by men convenient for men, and it was difficult for a woman to make her way. But I was determined to go on and do graduate work and hoped to get a doctorate in spite

of all that. I didn't know that I knew fully how difficult it would be, in a field like history where there was a great resistance on the college and university level for a woman in the history department.

She further explained why she pursued a career in a woman's institution: "No university would have a woman in the history department. Of course, men's colleges weren't about to have a woman anyway."

However, Abbott was also aware of certain benefits to the all-female setting. Reflecting on her reaction to the Women's College at Brown, she explained:

> I think there were great advantages for girls at that age having a chance to run things themselves. I think it gives you a lot of self-confidence....The class president was a *girl*, the head of student government was a *girl*. We ran our own thing.[52]

Providing the opportunity for women to "run things themselves" is the hallmark of another Brown graduate who pursued her career in a woman's institution. Mary Emma Woolley (A.B. 1894, A.M. 1895) became one of Brown's most famous female graduates, serving as the president of Mount Holyoke College from 1901 to 1937, during which time she became a nationally-known leader in higher education. But Woolley was more than a participant in a separatist institution; she actively fostered female leadership and scholarship among the faculty and students of Mount Holyoke.

Woolley had an expanded vision of what an academic woman should be, a vision based on the importance of scholarship. Although she possessed only the master's degree from Brown, Woolley quickly insisted on the doctorate from any teacher who wished to advance through the faculty ranks at Mount Holyoke. And along with that insistence on advanced graduate work came the importance of continued research and scholarship, which Woolley encouraged through a new system of sabbaticals and other means of faculty development.[53]

Such emphases were not only new at Holyoke, but they were on the cutting edge of ideas about collegiate faculty generally. Large universities like Harvard, Chicago, Stanford, and others were professionalizing their faculties in the same way as Woolley envisioned. But the difference at Mount Holyoke was the overwhelming proportion of women on the faculty. Here was an institution, as Glazer and Slater observe, that was "the mirror image of faculty gender relations elsewhere": men were the minority faculty members who moved more slowly through academic ranks, and who were often ignored when they tried to speak at faculty meetings.[54]

Had women's colleges like Holyoke also been able to support their own female doctoral students, perhaps an approach like Woolley's faculty model would have succeeded, producing successive generations of female professionals and academics, nourished by the same sort of support and encouragement provided to generations of male graduates. However, the lack of resources available to the women's institutions did not permit them to build such strength or to generate "progeny." Although Holyoke was somewhat successful in building "daughter colleges" by placing several of its graduates into professorships or presidencies at certain women's schools, its influence was hindered by the limits on its resources.[55]

Glazer and Slater see the ouster of Mary Woolley at Mount Holyoke in 1937, and her replacement by a less ambitious, married male professor from Yale, as the turn to a new approach in the academic profession. A decade later, many women's colleges would begin to hire more male faculty, and even male presidents, believing that hiring well-trained men was a sign of commitment to higher standards. No longer would there be such special, separate institutions to foster women's academic training and advancement. As Margaret Rossiter has explained in her study of the development of women in the scientific professions, getting women admitted to schools and then awarding them the degrees appropriate to their efforts were only the first two steps in the fight for professional equality; women then needed to be hired as faculty and promoted.

Although separate women's institutions had grown in the nineteenth and early twentieth centuries to provide education and jobs when male institutions offered neither, these places were waning in influence by the time women needed these next steps in their collective professional advancement. In an academic hierarchy ruled by research universities, small, teaching-oriented colleges like Mount Holyoke could not compete for academic leadership. On the other hand, a school like Brown with its strong undergraduate program and a graduate school that was ready to move to the forefront in the 1930s was a much more likely source of faculty leaders.

Innovation

Some women faced the barriers of the academic job market with their own creative approaches, discovering innovative ways to put their training to use. Of the four strategies described by Glazer and Slater, innovation seems the one most useful to recent women graduates who face an era of high hopes but a continuing lack of institutional support for their expectations. This strategy was also useful in the past, however, most notably by one of Brown's most illustrious innovators, Lillian Moller Gilbreth.

Gilbreth was clearly a 1920s role model. In oral histories and even in the student newspapers of the era, Gilbreth, mother of the *Cheaper By the Dozen* family and Brown Ph.D. (1915), was cited time and again (including by Helen Butts Correll) as an example of what could be achieved by a devoted and efficient career woman.[56] Although certainly a "superperformer" by anyone's standards, Gilbreth stands out as an example of the innovator career strategy. Building on the experience she acquired as a partner in her husband's management consulting firm, after his death Gilbreth developed a new specialty in the application of industrial efficiency techniques to the household. Yet her career was not without some particular gender-related difficulties.

Gilbreth had planned an academic career for herself before she met her husband Frank. She began a doctorate after earning her bachelor's and master's degrees in literature from the University of California, but married Frank Gilbreth in 1904, settled in New York City, and became his partner in the study of managerial and technological ideas for faster building methods. Twelve children followed.[57]

Gilbreth continued to work while her family was growing. The adventures of the huge family are detailed humorously in *Cheaper By the Dozen,* a well-known book by two of the children.[58] With help from her own mother and from numerous servants (as well as the application of some of her professional efficiency ideas), Lillian Gilbreth earned a doctorate in psychology from Brown, served as a partner in the engineering firm, and published her own and edited her husband's books.

After Frank died, Lillian found several clients unwilling to accept her as head of the firm. Nonetheless, she persevered in the engineering work, earning enough money to put all eleven of her surviving children through college. After 1924, Gilbreth extended her influence into the academic world, first taking over her husband's part-time teaching job at Purdue University. Working from this slender footing, she went on to become a full professor of management at Purdue and to earn twenty honorary degrees and professional medals, including the highest award from the Society of Women Engineers.[59]

Gilbreth eventually became known for her novel application of industrial techniques to household economics, certainly an area of special concern to women. Yet her success was achieved not solely because she focused on a woman's field, but rather because she discovered innovative ways to use traditional skills and ideas in a new application.

Two Brown graduates of the 1980s demonstrate the continuing importance of innovation to academic women who face today's tightly constrained job market. Carmen Huber (Ph.D. in physics, 1983) felt two aspects of her situation working against her ability to find an academic job in physics: she was foreign-born (Argentina), and she was married to a fellow physicist who would need a job in the same locale. Even with these inherent difficulties, Huber found little outward discrimination against her during her graduate years at Brown; in fact, she found the department "small and friendly." Nonetheless, Huber believed she and her husband needed a non-traditional approach in order to find good academic positions.

Seeking a location where they both could teach and pursue research, Huber and her husband found jobs at the University of Puerto Rico, an institution eager to shift towards research and happy to hire two well-trained academic physicists. Even though the jobs were good matches, Huber noted that she and her husband found the positions "mostly on their own." Established academic networks offered only conventional paths not well-suited to their situation. They were well aware of the unwritten rule that academics must prove themselves first before they might move into an established research institution, and their circumstances required an innovative approach to earn those credentials.[60]

Mary Wilson Carpenter (Ph.D. in English, 1983) studied in a field where women students were much more common than in Huber's Physics Department. Whereas Huber recalled "only six or so women students out of sixty" in her department, Carpenter found many supportive women colleagues. Carpenter also found good encouragement for her feminist interests in literature and in her personal life. In fact, she felt that her term as a graduate fellow in the 1981–82 Pembroke Center seminar greatly sharpened her skills in feminist literary criticism. Generally, she found the women and men of the department "very mutually supportive" of each other's work and interests.

For Carpenter, however, the complication was as a woman earning her Ph.D. at the age of forty-five. The job market seemed to prefer men, and most women who secured good jobs were young, she noted. As Carpenter explained, "It was generally assumed that I would have a lot of trouble finding a job." At one point, even though she was the only job seeker who had published an article and made a presentation at the Modern Language Association, Carpenter had more trouble than her male colleagues in securing a position. She determined that "the job market didn't have anything to do with your qualifications."

Carpenter decided that she would have to be creative to find a suitable academic position and planned to interview for jobs around the country even though her family was based in the Boston area. She and her husband agreed that, since their children were grown, Carpenter could commute or even live away during the week for the right academic position. Unfortunately, she noted, few of her professors ever asked her about her willingness to travel. They assumed she needed to stay in the local area: "They took it for granted," she explained, "that I would prefer a non-tenure-track job – even part-time – in Boston to a tenure-track position that required commuting." Carpenter continued to seek jobs equal to her talents, however, and eventually accepted a position in the English Department at Queens University in Canada. She commutes to her home in Massachusetts once or twice monthly.

Looking back, Carpenter wishes that, although her advisors were very supportive, they had considered more options for older women students like herself. Only a woman professor, Barbara Kiefer Lewalski, seemed to accept fully Carpenter's desire for a tenure-track job, even with commuting costs. Carpenter notes the high costs to women of such an approach in today's tight job market, explaining that women limit both their immediate and their ultimate career possibilities if they are unwilling to move.[61] When the market works against them, women academics and their advisors need to consider a range of innovative possibilities if women are to reach their potential.

The Effects of Brown's Policies

It is unfair, of course, to suggest that Brown never hired women faculty or never supported its own female graduate students. Through the testimony of graduates like Elizabeth Leduc, Rosemary Pierrel, and others, we know that over the years many women in graduate programs held teaching assistantships and that several stayed on in instructorships for a few years after their graduation. In recent years, Brown has hired more of its own graduates onto the faculty.[62]

Brown was not alone in its approach to hiring women; comparable schools in the Ivy League and around the country took the same stand. Brown's preference not to hire its own graduates onto the faculty would not, in itself, discriminate against women if indeed females could leave Brown and secure employment at a comparable school. However, many doors to the research universities and the Ivy League were open only to male Brown graduates, a situation that has not dramatically improved even with the most recent graduates. Without the opportunity to maintain a succession of female academics at Brown or in comparable institutions, women professors moved around the country to different types of institutions. The well-established women's colleges were excellent sources of employment; as we have seen, however, they were not able to sustain research support in the early eras when such work was growing in importance.

The early policies at Brown's Graduate School and similar institutions inhibited women from developing a critical mass of female scholars who could exert leadership in their fields or shape departments in new ways. Such an approach encouraged women to identify most closely with an individual faculty mentor, who was, most often, a man. On the other hand, the shift in the academic profession over this century has been for professors to identify less with their institutions and more with their disciplines.

The ability of women to exercise leadership earlier either at an institutional or a national level could have encouraged the quicker advancement of academic women. By scattering themselves around the country, often in institutions that were hesitant to promote them, women had a longer road to positions of authority and influence. At a school like Brown, where the commitment to training women for the professions is a century old, the concomitant effort to promote them or to help women find positions in comparable institutions was slow to develop.

The graduate women of Brown, like their colleagues elsewhere, did devise and pursue a number of strategies that enabled them to achieve marked success in the professions. And the most recent increases in numbers and proportion of women earning Ph.D.s at the University are quite encouraging. Yet, with greater – and timelier – support from institutions like Brown, the energies these women expended in holding their own in the academic world might have been more profitably spent in their challenging, leading, and redirecting those same professions. Perhaps the next twenty years will witness an increasing advance by women academics into equal participation and leadership.

NOTES

1. Rosemary Pierrel (Sorrentino) interview, December 1988, Christine Dunlap Farnham Archives, Brown University.

2. Ibid.

3. See Chapter 6 of this volume for more information about these early faculty positions.

4. See Penina Midgal Glazer and Miriam Slater, *Unequal Colleagues: The Entrance of Women into the Professions, 1890–1940* (New Brunswick, NJ: Rutgers University Press, 1987), and Patricia A. Palmieri, "Here was Fellowship: A Social Portrait of Academic Women at Wellesley College, 1880–1920," *History of Education Quarterly* 23 (Summer 1983): 195–214.

5. Margaret Rossiter, *Women Scientists in America: Struggles and Strategies to 1940* (Baltimore: Johns Hopkins University Press, 1982), pp. xvii-xviii.

6. See Glazer and Slater, *Unequal Colleagues*, pp. 211–227.

7. The graduate program at Brown was known as a department until 1927, when it

became the Graduate School under R.G.D. Richardson's deanship. The longstanding status as a department reflected the university's focus on the undergraduate college.

8. Most of the available information on Brown's graduate women comes from the brief career sketches in the university's *Historical Catalogues,* published in 1914, 1924, 1934, 1950, 1964, and 1979. The 1914, 1924, and 1934 volumes are good sources for studying the first women to earn Brown graduate degrees. Unfortunately, the data provided in the catalog iterations differs. For example, the 1934 and 1950 volumes note where a graduate student earned her undergraduate degree, allowing for an interesting comparison of Brown and non-Brown graduates. But this information disappears in the 1964 catalog. That 1964 edition, however, offers a new advantage: it categorizes graduates' jobs into thirty-five areas. Unfortunately, the 1964 book lists only the most current job. Data on recent graduates (1970–1990) has been provided by the Brown University Graduate School. Because of these differences in the sources as well as the large number of Brown master's students by the 1970s, it is difficult to present comprehensive information.

9. This woman was Helen Magill, an A.B. graduate of Swarthmore, who earned the Ph.D. at Boston University in 1877.

10. Margaret Rossiter, "Doctorates for American Women, 1868–1907," *History of Education Quarterly* 22 (Summer 1982): 159–183. The quotation is on p. 161.

11. Brown Professor John Shroeder suggests that only finances halted Andrews. See his "Jubilee Chapters in the History of Graduate Education at Brown University," *Books at Brown* 27 (1979): pp. 7–35. The figures on enrollments are on p. 21.

12. In 1901, when the graduate program was new, women earned 44 percent of all degrees (fourteen of twenty-nine). They did not reach a similar proportion until 1925 when twenty-two of forty-seven degrees granted were to women (47 percent). Other figures include: 1910, 28 percent; 1915, 26 percent; 1920, 36 percent. Compiled from 1924 and 1934 *Historical Catalogues.*

13. Ibid., p. 23.

14. Data collected from the 1924 and 1934 *Historical Catalogues.*

15. Although Brown has no record of the year Cooley earned her Zurich degree, alumnae records of Wellesley College (where Cooley earned her B.A.) give the date of her Ph.D. as 1894.

16. The eight were: Eleanor Stuart Upton (Ph.D. 1930, University of Chicago), who worked as a librarian at Brown and at Yale; Elizabeth C. Hickson (Ph.D. 1931, University of Pennsylvania), who became an associate professor of English at Beaver College; Margaret F. Upton (Ph.D. 1925, Yale University), who worked at St. Luke's Hospital, New York, as a laboratory technician; Alice Dimick (Ph.D. 1925, Yale University), who worked at Yale as an assistant in pharmacology; Charlotte Haywood (Ph.D. 1927, University of Pennsylvania), who worked as an assistant professor of physiology at Mount Holyoke and at Vassar; Madelaine R. Brown (M.D. 1927, Johns Hopkins University), who became a graduate assistant at Massachusetts General Hospital; Ella C. Rogers (Ph.D. 1928, University of Missouri), who became an assistant professor of chemistry at Connecticut State College; and Katherine Degnan (M.D., Cornell University, 1915), whose later career is not listed. Data is collected from the 1924 and 1934 *Historical Catalogues,* Degnan from 1950 *Catalog).*

17. See Chapter 2 in this volume for more information on the geographic distribution of Brown University's women students. Generally speaking, even by 1925, only 5 percent of the women came to Brown from outside New England; a full 66 percent came from within twenty-five miles of Providence. For a fuller discussion of the student body, including comparisons of the "city girls" and "dorm girls" at Brown, see the author's "Women at Brown, 1891–1930: 'Academically Identical, But Socially Quite Distinct'" (Ed.D. Dissertation, Harvard University, 1987), pp. 144–184.

18. Boston University, which granted the nation's first Ph.D. to a woman, provided ten students to Brown's graduate program, and Vassar College provided seven. The other Seven Sister schools did not send many graduates on to Brown, perhaps because they had graduate

programs in their own or in their affiliated universities: Radcliffe, Barnard, and Bryn Mawr sent only four students for Brown degrees by 1934. However, a few of the Catholic colleges did use Brown as a source for graduate training. Trinity College in Washington, D.C., and the College of St. Elizabeth sent fourteen and five students to Brown, respectively, and schools like the College of the Sacred Heart, Mount St. Vincent, Emmanuel, and Ursinus also began to provide candidates. Data collected from 1934 *Historical Catalogue*.

19. Although the Ph.D. was becoming a desirable credential for professors by 1920 or 1930, women and men were easily able to secure a college teaching position with only a master's degree.

20. Nancy Cott offers a good discussion of women's movement into the professions in *The Grounding of Modern Feminism* (New Haven: Yale University Press, 1987), p. 216. See especially Chapter 7, "Professionalism and Feminism."

21. Barbara Miller Solomon, "Table 6: Trends in Academic Degrees and Faculty Employment, 1870–1980," *In the Company of Educated Women: A History of Women and Higher Education in America* (New Haven: Yale University Press, 1985), p. 133.

22. Emilie J. Hutchinson, *Women and the Ph.D.*, Institute of Women's Professional Relations, Bulletin No. 2 (Greensboro, NC: North Carolina College for Women, 1929).

23. Of the five, Gertrude Hall became a high school principal, and Lillian Gilbreth worked as a consulting engineer. The three who worked in collegiate positions were Grace Bird, a professor of educational psychology at Rhode Island College of Education; Marion Weston, a professor of botany at the same college; and Marjorie Cook, who became a professor of bacteriology and physiology at the Constantinople College for Women in Greece.

24. Discussion of Hutchinson's study in Cott, *Grounding of Modern Feminism*, p. 227.

25. Ibid., p. 227. Susan B. Carter finds that 70 percent of women faculty were in normal schools or women's colleges in 1900; by 1940, the percentage was still 43 percent. See her "Academic Women Revisited: An Empirical Study of Changing Patterns in Women's Employment as College and University Faculty, 1890–1963," *Journal of Social History* 14 (Summer 1981): 675–699.

26. Cott also reminds us of two important points when assessing women's participation in a professional field. First, the declining proportion of women in any field relates to the behavior of men in that field. That is, the actual *number* of women earning a law degree might increase, but their *percentage* of participation might drop if more men begin to pursue law. Second, the declining proportion of women in any field might hide an increase in the percentage of all women who choose that work. That is, women may be a lower percentage of all lawyers, but the percentage of women professionals who choose the law might be on the rise. Cott, *Grounding of Modern Feminism*, pp. 223–224.

27. See Chapter 2 for an explanation of how the name change exemplified a distancing of the women from the mainstream life of the university.

28. See Carter, "Academic Women Revisited," pp. 675–677. Solomon explains that although actual numbers increased for women earning Ph.D.s, their proportion declined over this era. See Solomon, *In the Company*, p. 191.

29. R. Bruce Lindsay, "Roland George Dwight Richardson and the Creation of the Brown University Graduate School, 1927–1948," *Books at Brown* 28 (1981): pp. 58–74.

30. Lindsay assesses the situation in a most matter-of-fact way, saying, "It is not evident that Dean Richardson made any particular attempt to encourage by special efforts the enrollment of women as such, through he was thoroughly hospitable to their presence in the School." Ibid., p. 71.

31. Data from 1950 *Historical Catalogue*.

32. That is, seventy-eight of the 120 jobs listed.

33. Unfortunately, the 1964 catalog lists only those Brown graduates who were still liv-

ing at the time of the survey. I have added the names of the women Ph.D. recipients who were listed in earlier catalogs to the list in 1964, for a total of 112 earned Ph.D.s.

34. Carter, "Academic Women Revisited," pp. 681–684.

35. Ibid., p. 690.

36. See "Tomorrow's Professors Are Here Today," *Brown Alumni Monthly* 89 (December 1989): 22–29 for a discussion of the academic job market.

37. Compiled from computer listing of graduate degrees earned by women at Brown University, 1971–1990, Brown University Graduate School.

38. Mariam K. Chamberlain, ed., *Women in Academe: Progress and Prospects* (New York: Russell Sage, 1988), p. 257; *Chronicle of Higher Education,* 6 March 1991, p. A 13.

39. The top ten fields in number of Ph.D.s earned by women (1971–1990) are: English, 108; chemistry, 63; biology, 56; sociology, 45; psychology, 35; linguistics, 29; art history, 28; American civilization, 27; anthropology, 24; and history, 24. Compiled from data on graduate degrees earned by women provided by Brown University Graduate School, 1990.

40. Chamberlain, *Women in Academe,* p. 258.

41. Compiled from Graduate School data, 1971–1990.

42. One good source for information about individual women comes from the ongoing effort by Brown's Christine Dunlap Farnham Archives and the Pembroke Center to solicit oral history interviews of Brown women graduates from the 1910s to the present.

43. Unfortunately, Leduc does not provide the name of this woman.

44. Elizabeth Leduc interview, December 1988, Farnham Archives.

45. Ibid.

46. Helen Butts (Correll) interview (no date), Farnham Archives.

47. Astronomy was a field that did bring acclaim to some women, at the same time as it hindered the careers of others. Cecilia Payne-Gaposchkin, for instance, herself complained early on about the lack of recognition available to women at Harvard. See Rossiter, *Women Scientists in America,* pp. 210–212. Data on Frances Wright from her obituary in *The Boston Globe,* 31 July 1989, p. 9.

48. Geraldine Joncich Clifford, *Lone Voyagers: Academic Women in Coeducational Institutions, 1870–1937* (New York: The Feminist Press, 1989), p. 13.

49. Pierrel interview.

50. For example, Marion Dodge Weston (Ph.D. 1917) and Clara E. Bird (Ph.D. 1918) both taught for many years at Rhode Island College of Education.

51. Survey questionnaire by Helen J. Loschky, April 9, 1990, in Farnham Archives.

52. Isabel Ross Abbott interview (no date), Farnham Archives.

53. Glazer and Slater provide a good discussion of Woolley's term at Mount Holyoke in *Unequal Colleagues,* pp. 25–68.

54. Ibid., p. 36.

55. Ibid., p. 51.

56. In addition to various references in the student newspaper, Lillian Gilbreth is also mentioned in oral history interviews with Sarah Mazick (Saklad) and Kathe Liedke (Beyer), both Class of 1928.

57. Biographical information from entry on Gilbreth by Ruth Cowan, in *Notable American Women: The Modern Period,* eds. Barbara Sicherman and Carol Hurd Green (Cambridge, MA: Harvard University Press, 1980), pp. 271–273, hereafter cited as *NAW.*

58. Frank Gilbreth, Jr., and Ernestine Gilbreth Carey, *Cheaper By the Dozen* (New York: Thomas Y. Crowell Co., 1948).

59. "Gilbreth," *NAW,* pp. 272–273.

60. Carmen Huber, interview with author, 6 December 1990.

61. Mary Wilson Carpenter, interview with author, 12 December 1990.

62. One example is Anne Fausto-Sterling, Brown Ph.D. 1970, current professor of biology at Brown.

CHAPTER 6

"A Place for a Good Woman": The Development of Women Faculty at Brown

by LYDE CULLEN SIZER

THE FIRST WOMAN faculty member to teach women at Brown slipped in quietly, with only a brief mention in Dean Louis F. Snow's Report to the President in June, 1897. "Under the personal charge of Professor H.C. Bumpus," Snow wrote, "instruction in Biology and Hygiene has been given by Miss Ada G. Wing, A.B. Wellesley 1887, A.M. Brown 1896." Under her tutelage assembled "enthusiastic students of all classes." Later in his report Snow solidified Wing's position by adding: "I respectfully request that she be made Instructor in Hygiene and Domestic Science in the Women's College for this period."[1] The following year Mabel Potter was added in order to develop a Department of Physical Culture.

Both the manner in which these women were introduced and the positions they filled are significant. Ada Wing eased into teaching life after earning a master's from Brown, chosen by and under the "personal charge" of a noted male professional. Her tenure seemed uncertain; she had no long-term contract, but was hired year by year. Mabel Potter was hired to create a department specific to the needs of women. Biology and physical education were the only two academic faculty positions available for women until well into the twentieth century. Certain issues of biology were deemed too delicate to be taught to women by a man; physical edu-

At the blackboard with chalk in hand is Louise Lamphere, at the time a Brown assistant professor of anthropology. Her successful class action suit in 1977 led to an increase in the number of tenured women faculty at Brown.

cation for women was considered necessary to offset the rigors of an intellectual life. The women instructors charged with these duties never taught men at Brown.

Over the years a gap widened between the increasing numbers of young women studying at the university, and the numbers of women teaching there. Only in the areas of physical education and biological science were women consistently represented in the faculty until 1939. And while women deans, beginning with Anne Crosby Emery in 1900, served as role models for the women students at Brown, they also served to remind those students of the limits to the progress of their academic careers. The early women with long-term professional status at Brown had positions primarily as administrators, not as scholars.

From the beginning, women professionals on campus sought to inculcate Brown's women students with a sense of their own ability and promise. What this meant in terms of their future prospects changed over time, as did the degree to which the deans were willing to push the university to hire and tenure women as faculty members. Despite the work of successive deans, particularly Nancy Duke Lewis, their efforts met with little success. Not until a class action suit led by anthropology professor Louise Lamphere was settled out of court in 1977 were significant changes made in the makeup of the faculty at Brown, although a trend toward the hiring of greater numbers of women had begun tentatively in the late 1960s. In 1976, 2.5 percent of the tenured faculty were women and 8.5 percent of the untenured faculty; by July 1991, 16 percent of the tenured faculty were women, and 43 percent of the junior faculty.[2] The efforts of successive deans and women professors to define and expand their place at Brown University, as well as their subsequent struggle for equity in hiring and tenure decisions form the focus of this chapter.

"The Role Model of Role Models": Early Women Deans

The story of women faculty at Brown can be broken into three rough time periods, signifying shifts in both national and university beliefs about the role of women faculty in coeducational universities. The first period, spanning from 1897 to 1938, is primarily a record of the progress and presence of deans of the women's college. These women, among the first generation of college and university graduates, were academics in their own right but accrued power and status almost entirely through their administrative positions. They were to lead the women at Brown to the achievement of personal as well as academic goals, and to serve as examples of a top level of deportment and achievement.

The early narrative of women faculty at Brown necessarily focuses on the decisions and personalities of these early deans. Only briefly did the numbers of other women faculty grow. From 1920 until 1927 women were a slightly greater presence on campus, although congregated in low status positions and hired to teach only women students. Turnover among them was very high. Most of the handful of instructors teaching physical education, biology, elocution, and other subjects in the humanities and social sciences, stayed for only two years. In 1925, the year in this period of the greatest numbers of women, there were four women faculty at Brown. Of those four, three were instructors and one, the dean, was an associate professor. In 1928 through 1938 the numbers dropped to one.[3]

Anne Crosby Emery, the first woman Ph.D. hired at Brown, took Dean Louis F. Snow's place as dean of the Women's College at Brown University. Brought in by the newly appointed President William Faunce in 1900, Emery was to play a maternal, or "womanly" role Snow could not fulfill. It was a position five women would successively fill until the merger seventy-one years later. The deans of the women students were the most visible and most powerful women in the college, and their policies shaped the lives of the students they served. Each was, as a student in the seventies termed them, "the role model of all role models." President Donald Hornig of the merger years claimed that the dean was "the focus of the attention of all the Pembroke women and the Pembroke graduates. Even if she had no duties at all," he added, "she had this very important role as a figurehead."[4]

If Hornig focused on the dean of Pembroke's status as "figurehead," however, that should not underrepresent the very real "duties" of the dean of the Women's College and later, of Pembroke. The dean that Hornig worked with, Dean Rosemary Pierrel, or the last dean of Pembroke, is a case in point. Pierrel's position was far more than merely a "figurehead": she was a tenured faculty member who continued researching and teaching (unlike earlier deans). In addition, Pierrel was an important senior administrator, voting on appointments of senior faculty, and introducing those new senior faculty to Brown history and tradition.[5]

Yet at the same time, however, Pierrel was seen – according to Hornig – as fulfilling an important function as a role model for women. It is important to note that what a role model was supposed to be and the messages such a leader was to send to the women at Brown changed over time and with the disparate personalities of the women acting in that position. And yet that serving as a role model was *the* essential reason for having a woman as dean never seemed in question.

If Dean Anne Crosby Emery ultimately was viewed warmly and

exuberantly, initially it was with some suspicion that the young women of Brown greeted her, an alumna recalled twenty years later. Dean Snow left, she remembered, and the women students learned

> that the next Dean was to be a woman, and that our somewhat too efferves-
> cent minds and manners were to be made refined and gentle by her influence.
> I, for one, hated the thought. Was this to be a young ladies' finishing school?
> She came – and within a month groups of us were lingering around the office
> door, wishing – oh, so much – that we could find some pretext to enter and
> enjoy one of those little talks which, even now, we remember as one of the
> finest influences in all our college life.[6]

Despite the initial resistance of this student to the notion of a woman as role model – there was less prestige attached to women – Emery's inspirational and buoyant style won this student over. In a speech to the departing class of 1901, the senior class president described the women at Brown as not only proud of their new dean but "vainglorious" to have acquired a dean of such academic credentials. Emery was a graduate of Bryn Mawr, and came to Brown from a professorship and the position of dean of women at Wisconsin. She came also with a doctorate in the field of Greek and Latin literature and language, although her position at Brown did not include teaching.[7]

Emery was committed to the traditional – and previously male – intellectual aspect of college life, was wary of changes that would mute it for her female students, yet was expected to bend to notions of what women students should be learning. Reluctantly at first, Emery in 1902 helped develop what turned out to be a short-lived Department of House-hold Economics designed specifically for women.[8] Emery had doubts about the usefulness of vocational courses at Brown, but pledged to the president that the courses for women "shall represent not only their immediate purpose, but also the conviction that knowledge must precede the application of knowledge."[9] In 1904 Marion L. Shorey, a recent graduate of Brown, was hired as an instructor in this department. "It is hoped," Emery recorded, "that through her concentrated work and influence a large number, if not all, of the students will be led to elect as an essential part of their college curriculum courses which will give them an appreciation of the fundamental importance of the home." Emery continued, "Such an appreciation will only quicken and inspire their intellectual activities along other lines."[10]

Yet what Dean Emery often was remembered for were her "universe meetings," biweekly informal gatherings she sponsored at her house. At these meetings there was no set topic, although they often began with one. In a laudatory editorial, one student described those evenings: "Wildest excitement – when everyone wants to talk at once – reigns one minute and the most awestruck silence the next. Freshmen propound questions which the Seniors are strangely reluctant to answer, and before which even the Dean stands appalled." In the student newspaper, *The Sepiad,* the editor praised Emery's meetings for inspiring thought. She wrote: "Each gains new ideas or strengthens her own opinions, improves her power of expression, develops her insight, acquires self-reliance – in short, the meeting wakes us up spiritually and mentally, a clear proof of the fact that 'culture and morals' are not incompatible."[11]

Emery also guided her students' thoughts during chapel ceremonies through inspirational speeches. Some of her "cardinal teachings," Barbara Louise Clark, Class of 1905, recalled, advocated "an absolute sincerity in seeking truth, and fearlessness in speaking it; honesty and courage of character; and withal, no prudish solemnity, but a gaiety that shall make life richer for oneself and happier for others." The students felt "rich," Clark professed, "in having before them, day by day, the embodiment of the ideal that the truest college culture produces."[12]

Anne Crosby Emery was not long in her job; in 1905 she left to marry Professor Francis G. Allinson of the Classics Department.[13] Married women, by custom, if not explicitly by policy, did not teach at Brown. Marriage was considered – for women – to be its own career. In a parting speech by the senior class president, Emery's action was presented as a new challenge rather than a retreat from public life.[14] It was seen as a natural fulfillment of her work at Brown for Emery to marry and be supported by her husband.

Yet Anne Emery Allinson did not retreat from Brown altogether. For years thereafter she continued to hold her "universe" meetings. She collaborated with her husband on several academic works. In addition, she wrote on a variety of topics, both on classical literature and, for *The Providence Journal,* on practical advice. Her visibility to Brown students offered the prospect of an alternative career to full-time homemaking or full-time professional life.

Lida Shaw King succeeded Anne Emery as dean of the Women's College. Her interpretation of the deanship was quite different from Emery's. Seemingly not as warm, and certainly not as beloved, King directed her attention towards expanding the college both in terms of enrollment and of buildings and grounds. King's advanced degree in Latin, Greek, and archaeology, her M.A. from Brown, and her family connections to Brown (her father was on the Board of Trustees) made her an attractive candidate.

Rather than gathering the women students into her home to muse on philosophy, Dean King did a great deal of traveling to advertise the

Women's College. Her tenure at Brown was described by the students as one of "realism" and "scholarliness" rather than Emery's "pure sunshine."[15] Her reception and memory by students is characterized by respectful acknowledgement of authority, but some sense also of resistance to her recommendations for them.

King did not have the same tone in addressing the women students at Brown that Emery did. She maintained a professional distance from her students, rather than adopting Emery's more maternal style. While these differences can be attributed to distinct personal styles, King was also at Brown far longer than Emery, and during a time period characterized by a growing dissatisfaction among the young with previously accepted Victorian restraint. King's lectures seem more critical than inspirational, and stress the students' failure to obey. In a speech to departing seniors in 1912, for example, King chided the college graduates, for the "weak points" in their "preparation" for life. The graduate, King said, is not through with her education. She should continue reading, among other things, biographies "which show how the really big people of the world do things."[16]

In 1909, the *Sepiad* reported that King turned down a prestigious job offer with a "well-known Eastern women's college." The students showed their approval by pledging "more loyal service to our Alma Mater and . . . a more earnest effort to help in furthering the plans of our Dean," in response to King's "unselfish interest in our college."[17] Even here the tone belies strong gratitude; the students cheer King's decision, but there is no sense of a shared affection, rather a shared commitment to the school.

In 1920 King took a leave of absence due to mental stress. Mention made of her illness was couched in carefully neutral terms in the minutes of the Executive Committee of the Women's College, which expressed "sincere regret and sympathy." In the spring of 1921, however, when King had improved and was to return from her leave, the Executive Committee voted that "since the ill health was due in part to certain questions of administrative policy, the Committee desires to have in the Dean's own interest a frank discussion of such problems before work is resumed." It was further noted that the committee wished "to simplify rules and regulations, to develop personal contact between students and administrative officers and to promote in every way a free, spontaneous type of student life."[18] This message suggests that King was hindering this "free, spontaneous" student life the Executive Committee envisioned, and failing to develop the "personal contact" that would further King's influence. Without the support of the women at Brown, she could not function as a role model. King resigned at the end of 1922. Anne Emery Allinson filled in as acting dean in 1920 to 21, and then again in early 1923 for a semester.

Before the new dean was selected, President William Faunce clarified the position of the Women's College in Brown University. In so doing he also made explicit the policy of the university concerning any female additions to the faculty:

> It was informally agreed that the best interests of the Women's College demanded that its students have practically identical instruction with the men. The obvious exceptions would continue to be the Dean, and a woman instructor in Biology, in order to cover personal hygiene. No vote was taken, but President Faunce stated that he should, in the future, appoint men rather than women, in increasing the number of classes in the Women's College.[19]

Because women did not have the same kind of prestige as men, the "best interest" of the college was to continue hiring men except for those positions that demanded the personal attention of a woman.

The fact that the faculty teaching at the Women's College were predominantly men was celebrated by some students. In an oral interview, Charlotte Ferguson Roads, Class of 1924, asserted that this aspect of college life was more than acceptable. "I like men," she said. "I thought that was the biggest thing about it, that we didn't have to have women."[20] Men conferred a standing, a perceived intellectual rigor that women did not, a social view shared and furthered by the school.

Margaret Shove Morriss: A New Model of Educator

At chapel services, on February 7, 1923, Margaret Shove Morriss was introduced to the college as the new dean. She never had an inauguration, picking up the reins, as she did, midyear. "And from then on," an alumna remembered, "nothing was the same on campus." A "new model of educator," she recalled, "radiating beauty and grace in unaffected dignity," Morriss was influential from the first, "with an impact that deepened through the decades."[21] Like Emery, Morriss had a great deal of influence on her students, and expected a great deal from them. Yet unlike Emery, Morriss projected a more forceful and commanding persona, compared to Emery's more nurturant and benevolent one.

Morris, who held a Ph.D. from Bryn Mawr in American history, entered as an associate professor. In 1932 she became the second woman full professor at Brown, following Dean King. Like King, this position was largely cosmetic, since most of their time was spent in the administration. Morriss, however, was felt as an intellectual presence, one that extended to the greater community as well. From 1937 to 1941 she filled the presidency of the American Association of University Women. She also served as president for the New England Association of Colleges and Secondary Schools, and first vice president of the National Association of Deans of Women.

Morriss encouraged her students to go on with their academic lives after college. Unlike King, she did not mean for her students to read the biographies of "big people" but perhaps to write them. Her vision for the women at Brown was an ambitious one. "She kindled in many a new awareness that, by becoming educated, women could become leaders in new fields in a changing world," one graduate recalled.[22] Among the students who enjoyed a great deal of support from Morriss was Sarah M. Saklad, Class of 1928. She later became a physician through Morriss's help and connections and felt that she owed her "a tremendous amount."[23]

Margaret Shove Morriss had confidence in women's ability to achieve in the professions. She wasn't afraid to call herself a feminist, even in the post-suffrage climate in the late 1920s. While lauding the quality of the faculty at Brown, she stressed that this quality arose from the scholars involved, rather than their gender. "Of course, the outstanding advantage that leaps to mind at once is the University Faculty," she wrote in the 1927–1928 *Alumnae Record*. But, she added:

> As a good feminist, I rather resent the fact that students say, oh yes, they come to Brown because they want men to teach them. I think that fundamentally it is not because the faculty of a great University is made up almost entirely of men that it is a better Faculty than that of a women's college. It is because the Faculty of a great University is made up of well-known scholars that it is significant and important.[24]

The handful of other women teaching at Brown during the 1920s were also mentioned in student reminiscences, but many graduates did not remember any contact with women faculty. Others recalled only Mabel Wilder, a biology instructor hired in 1922, memorable primarily for her uneasiness discussing sex. Yet for some, the few relationships that they made with women faculty stood out. Doris Hopkins Stapleton, a 1928 graduate, recalled Grace Maurer, the first woman instructor in the History Department:

> She was the closest to a woman scholar that we knew. She was a charming woman, and we used to go to her apartment and carry on conversations that were on a completely different level from what we had with other instructors or professors.... She probably of all the women I knew at Brown, had more of an impact on students, women students.[25]

"I don't think I'll ever forget the Renaissance," another 1928 graduate asserted, "because she made it come alive... She really was the kind of person that you felt could inspire you to pursue things on your own."[26] Maurer taught for five years as an instructor after earning her M. A. from Brown in 1921.

In 1926 the paucity of women professors – four in that year – was noted by the Pembroke College Curriculum Committee, a group of juniors chosen by the administration to study and report on the college to the administration in their senior year. Committee members were quite critical of the teaching style of many of the male professors, although they did not seem to question that a quality faculty would be primarily male. Some older men treated their students, they recorded, with "contemptuous paternalism," while the youngest members of the faculty often lectured in a "caustic fashion." According to this group of students, only a few middle-aged professors achieved a balance of diplomacy and equality when advising and lecturing to their women students.[27]

The 1930 minutes of the Executive Committee shed further light on efforts made on behalf of women faculty. In all likelihood these efforts were joined by Morriss, if not instigated by her. It is recorded that "the perennial subject of the appointment of women on the Faculty to give instruction at Pembroke College" had again come up. The Executive Committee decided "that for the present women shall be appointed to the teaching staff of the University for Pembroke College only in such fields as Physical Education and Spoken English." The only temporary exception to this rule was appointments of "outstanding women scholars to lectureships."[28] There was no explanation of this policy. It was clear that the university was not willing to make a long-term commitment to women professors, however outstanding.

Lois Wolpert Graboys, Class of 1959, M.A.T. 1973, in a 1972 study of the position of women on the faculty at Pembroke and Brown, found that the few women employed at Brown had little chance at advancement. Biology professor Magel Wilder, hired first in 1922 with a M.A. for five years, and then again after she had earned her Ph.D. in 1939, rose only as high as an assistant professor, a position she held until her death in 1947. "This inability to visualize women as a vital part of the faculty," Graboys concluded, "was the residual effect of a conservative history at Brown, reinforced by a national reluctance to alter the traditional male-female roles."[29]

A Target in a Period of Transition

Unlike national trends, which record that the percentage of women in college teaching positions grew, sustained a peak from 1920 to 1946, and then declined, women faculty grew in numbers at Brown starting in 1939, subsiding again only in the late 1950s and growing slowly after that until the early 1970s.[30] Despite the growth in the period from 1939 to the merger of Pembroke with Brown in 1971, women were still grouped almost exclusively in nontenured positions. Furthermore, few stayed very long, leaving for better opportunities, or because the road to advancement at Brown was so difficult, or perhaps to get married. Yet the women who did come to Brown worked more vociferously in this period than previously on opening opportunities at Brown for their compatriots. The Pembroke deans came to see the paucity of women on the faculty as a problem to be solved and looked to the university to solve it.

Hiring in elite institutions since the turn of the century had generally been controlled by specific departments. The market was an "internal" one, historian Geraldine Clifford explains. Yet, she argues, "unlike most internal markets, where selection criteria were quite explicit, the academic market operated with vague rules and unsystematic procedures that derive from custom." This, she finds, made it particularly difficult for certain groups. While "the formal criteria of competence in teaching and research might qualify women, the informal criteria of 'collegiality' and 'fitting in' could exclude them." Once established in the field, professors could draw in younger colleagues whose work they approved of, their own students, or the students recommended to them by other colleagues.[31]

A few early women with Brown master's degrees taught at the Women's College. In biology, Ada Wing, the first woman to teach at Brown, came straight from graduate study at the university, as did Mabel Potter.[32] Marion Shorey, in home economics, and Grace Maurer, in history, were both Brown graduates. Magel Wilder earned her master's at Brown in the 1920s. These women may have had an easier time fitting into a department they joined initially as students and subordinates. Their competence would also have been well established.

Quoting a study done in the 1960s, Clifford further explains the persisting paucity of women in academia. "Women," she says, "tend to be discriminated against in the academic profession, not because they have low prestige but because they are outside the prestige system entirely and for this reason are of no use to a department in further recruiting."[33] This may help explain the resistance of Brown departments in the years between 1939 and 1971 to make significant changes in the compositions of their departments despite the rising chorus of voices – from individual teachers, committees including students, and, particularly, women deans.

Penelope Hartland Thunberg, hired in 1946 by President Henry Wriston as an instructor of economics over the objections of the department chairman, resisted the discrimination she found in her new position. A graduate of Brown in 1940, with a Ph.D. in economics from Radcliffe, Thunberg had taught at Wells and Mount Holyoke Colleges and published several articles. Shortly thereafter she discovered that there was a significant disparity between her salary and that of her recently hired Harvard colleagues – who were less qualified than she was. When she approached the department chairman on the issue, he told her: "I don't have to pay you what I pay men. You have no bargaining power."[34]

Thunberg came to have significant bargaining power. Discovering from a friend that a job had opened up at Carnegie Tech, she applied and was offered the job. The salary was, she recalled, a 50 percent raise over what she was earning at Brown. The department chairman met Carnegie's terms, and Thunberg was promoted to an assistant professor. The next year Thunberg was offered a one-year job at a think tank for the National Bureau of Economic Research; the following year she was hired by the Council of Economic Advisers for the White House, another year-long project. After two years on leave, her department chairman advised her to take the next attractive job offer elsewhere. President Wriston, he said, would block her further advancement at Brown.

It was, however, even more difficult for an outsider with no department to "fit in" or enjoy University "collegiality." Margaret Burnham Stillwell was appointed as a "research" professor of bibliography in 1948 when the Annmary Brown Memorial became part of Brown.[35] Her experience, unusual as it is, corroborates Graboy's and Clifford's findings. Like the two women who preceded her to the status of full professor – King and Morriss – Stillwell did not teach the men at Brown despite her knowledge of the collections now available to them and her willingness to do so. Stillwell was a 1909 Brown graduate who also received a master's from Brown in 1925.

Stillwell's memoirs, published in 1973, reveal the difficulties and inequities attendant upon her position as a woman in a faculty of men. The Brown Corporation, she stated, was "incensed at the appointment of a woman to a full professorship on the Faculty." Brown refused to raise her salary to match her rank, and in later years did not offer her the same raises others received.[36] Stillwell recognized that this attitude towards her was "indicative of the times, the sort of thing a woman in the academic world had to expect (and accept) in the middle of our century."[37]

As a "lone target in an ugly period of transition," Stillwell recalled dealing with the rancor not only of the corporation, but also of certain of her colleagues. Some were quite supportive. Vice president Bruce Bigelow, Stillwell recalls, "knew the intensity of the opposition" to her, and

Margaret B. Stillwell, Class of 1909, who was appointed research professor of bibliography in 1948, was the first woman to be a full professor at Brown who was not also a dean.

attempted to shield her from it, a realization she came to after his death.

Using the faculty club became an ordeal if none of her special friends were there, Stillwell recalled. At the first meeting of a group of professors who called themselves the "Renaissance Group," she offered to make the resources at the memorial and her own expertise available to the students. One professor, she remembered, "announced in pompous tones that he felt nothing Miss Stillwell would have to say to his students would be of any value." On Commencement Day one year Stillwell was subjected to a further indignity when the young English professor assigned to walk beside her slipped away to another part of the procession and left her standing alone. "Worst of all," she records, "was the unpalatable fact that I, a woman, had invaded a world they had pre-empted for themselves. In some instances, this antagonism was subtle and hidden like a snake in the grass. In others, it was blatant and rude."[38] Despite her difficulty in gaining acceptance from several faculty and corporation members, Brown recognized her work by awarding her an honorary doctorate in 1942.

"A Place for a Good Woman": Nancy Duke Lewis

Another recent arrival to the university shared Stillwell's concerns. Nancy Duke Lewis, an instructor with a master's in mathematics and the Pembroke social director starting in 1943, was appointed dean in 1950 after the resignation of Margaret Morriss. Lewis was acutely aware of the dearth of women faculty and of a greater discrimination that hindered their efforts in the academic world. It was her efforts, perhaps more than anyone else's, that inspired the increased awareness of the issue during this period. In speeches at the University of Alabama in 1954 and Randolph Macon College in 1958 she discussed the low numbers of women professors and the prejudice they met.

The paucity was particularly acute in the field of mathematics, Lewis asserted. This, combined with insensitive comments by male colleagues, often made it very difficult for women professors. "How many of us," she asked, "who have ventured into this field have had our masculine friends and acquaintances say to us, 'But you do not look like a mathematician!', a statement which we are supposed to accept as a compliment."[39]

Lewis's concern for this issue extended to the young women she served. In her report to the corporation's Advisory Committee for Pembroke College in 1952 Lewis included a letter from a particularly talented alumna. "I want to teach, of course," the letter began,

> and am really most interested in the college level. However, I don't really know how women can get into the teaching side of higher education. If I do not want to live my life on a woman's college campus, am I foolish to think of teaching? Is it impossible to get a job elsewhere? Are woman professors rare and unusual things or is it because I went to Pembroke and never saw one?

Dean Lewis's only reply was "No Comment!"[40]

Lewis's wry irony on this subject was reinforced by her continued efforts on behalf of women at Brown. Scarcely a year went by without a reference in Lewis's report to the Advisory Committee on the need for more women professors. At the end of her long essay to the committee in 1953, Lewis discussed the reasons that helped explain "why Pembroke should rank low in the area of the production of scholars." One reason was that "our academic prestige does not equal our academic standing," due, Lewis argued, to the fact that "all normal academic and scholarly publicity bears the name of Brown." Women's achievements needed to be proclaimed under Pembroke's name as well. Finally, she added, "I could suggest that an all male faculty is not so apt to inspire or encourage undergraduate women to continue their studies into graduate school."[41]

In a sexually stratified society, Lewis argued, role models need to represent more than one gender. In order to envision themselves as scholars, she implied, young women had to see older women well established in academic arenas. In 1954 Lewis again made reference to the need for more women faculty, this time with regard to developing a more extensive education department to answer the forthcoming teacher shortage resulting from the "baby boom." "This could very well be," she reminded the Advisory Committee, "a place in which a good woman could be appointed!"[42] Later in the report she became more explicit. "There are still few women of any rank permanently appointed on the Brown faculty ... " She continued, "The lack of contact with women scholars still continues to play a subtle role of influence upon the attitudes of Pembroke women toward themselves as scholars."[43]

In the 1957 report, Lewis addressed the issue of married women working as professors, both at Brown and elsewhere. Lewis suggested that effort was not always expended for women graduates because "so few continue in the profession," and that many married women continue to work in positions that do not reflect their educational accomplishments. This could be remedied "if society could come to accept for women an interrupted career and could find a way to offer part-time employment at a higher level. A college faculty might offer solutions to both of these problems," she added. "I wonder how many faculty wives could assist most ably in solving the coming faculty shortage."[44]

In 1958 Lewis could report progress. "A number of young women appointed quietly to the faculty of the University are continuing here in their teaching and are being steadily advanced," she wrote. She also mentioned the beginning of a funding effort, initiated by the Class of 1933, to establish an endowed chair to be occupied by a woman professor. Although the effort was only recently begun, Lewis added, "We have optimism that the seed thus planted will soon begin to grow."[45] This initiative came to bear her name. In 1960 illness forced Lewis to retire, and she died soon afterwards of cancer.

Nancy Duke Lewis's passion fueled further efforts by women and men on the Brown campus on behalf of women faculty. In tribute to her, fund raising for an endowed chair designed for a distinguished woman scholar was publicized in a special issue of the *Pembroke Alumna* published in 1962. The issue focused on woman professors, both at Brown and elsewhere in American academia, with a short essay by Professor Frances Clayton and a series of sketches of women professors introduced by Brown's President Barnaby C. Keeney. The issue, the editor wrote, was dedicated to Lewis's memory:

Deeply concerned about the fulfillment of the intellectual life of her students and all women with college educations, she particularly hoped for greater numbers of women on college and university faculties. By directing that the balance of her estate be eventually applied to the establishment of a chair for a woman professor at Brown, Dean Lewis hoped to provide a notable example of a woman in academic life for Pembroke women.[46]

Unfortunately, despite the attention given it in this issue of the *Alumna,* the chair was not fully endowed by outside sources or the university for twenty years.

In her article, "A Source for College Faculties," Frances Clayton, an associate professor of psychology, chronicled a disturbing story. Even in the institutions most likely to hire women – the women's colleges – there had been a decline in the percentage of women faculty members in the early 1960s. She blamed this trend on two factors besides the "usual anti-feminine-prejudice reason" which she felt was not applicable to women's colleges. First, the combination of the upgrading of qualifications for work as a professor with the graduation of a smaller proportion of women Ph.D.'s to men had produced this negative situation, Clayton found. Yet she did not altogether discount the second factor, prejudice. "Large enrollment universities themselves may indicate that where a large faculty is needed and money is limited, women must be hired," Clayton wrote, "but where more money is available and the university may be more discriminating, they prefer to discriminate against women."[47]

The numbers of women will grow, Clayton asserted, but not until both men and women change. The department policies she encountered outside of Brown had been discriminatory about both hiring and promotion. As the need for college faculty grew, Clayton suggested, departments would have to hire women. Social circumstances would then produce the changes that ideological or administrative pressure did not. "Once departments have women on the staff and discover they aren't necessarily scatterbrains or vamps, or too competitive, and that the ivied walls don't crumble," Clayton prophesied, "much of the prejudice will disappear."

Women were holding themselves back too, Clayton surmised. Social convention hampered their autonomy and dictated many of their choices. Often they left school altogether when they got married. If they continued on after marriage, "the traditional primary responsibility (and enjoyment) of a woman is supposed to be her home and husband; this may make her a poor scholar." Yet despite these factors, Clayton stated, women often did not make the scholarly contributions necessary to achieving and maintaining their position in the academic world. While confessing that she was "going out on a limb," she speculated that this was the result of the cultural notion many women had that "to make scholarly contributions is to be unfeminine." Again, Clayton felt change would happen over time, that "the problem may solve itself" with an increasing number of women represented on campus.[48]

President Barnaby C. Keeney, the author of the introduction to a section in the *Alumna* featuring the few women then teaching at Brown, was equally optimistic about the force of slow change. "All things being equal," he proclaimed, "fifty per cent of the professors in the total of colleges and universities ought to be women." To this end, and in celebration of Lewis's contribution and concern for this issue, Keeney applauded the fund for a "distinguished professorship." "By placing one and eventually many women in positions of great distinction on our faculty, we would present to the students at Pembroke a living example of the possibilities that lie before women in academic life," he concluded.[49] With unintended irony, Keeney proposed that hiring one woman professor at Brown implied a significant commitment to equitable treatment of women.

In 1961 the university turned again to the search for a suitable role model for women at Pembroke in the person of a new dean. The Advisory Committee minutes, in a session of rare candor, allowed remarkable insight into the qualifications necessary for Lewis' successor. By extension, they also were commenting on the role women were to play at Brown generally.

It was crucial, the committee decided, that the dean be scholarly, "although eminence in scholarship was not essential but that the 'habit of scholarship' was important." Further qualifications included "femininity, grace, charm, poise, warmth and vision, presence and speaking ability." "Emphasis was placed," the minutes continued, "on an attractive appearance and personality and the 'scholarly aspect' in view of the Dean's responsibility for public projection of the college, maintenance of the integrity of Pembroke, and development of the intellectual life of the students." A role model for Pembroke women, it can be inferred, must first be presentable, and then be scholarly enough to get by.[50]

A Teaching Professor for Dean: Rosemary Pierrel

Rosemary Pierrel, the eventual choice, never went through a formal interview process. Following the pattern of networking earlier described, Pierrel was chosen through her earlier associations with the university. She was well known at Brown, where she had earned a doctorate in experimental psychology in 1954. She had worked as an instructor for the period 1953–1955, and at the time of her appointment, she had reached the position of associate professor at Barnard College. President Keeney showed up at Barnard one day looking for her, she recalled in an oral interview later. He persuaded her to consider the position.

When in Providence in the spring of 1961, Pierrel was invited to a tea by the alumnae corporation members. "I suppose they had some non-academic qualifications in mind," she correctly surmised, "though no one ever mentioned them. Probably being able to use the 'proper fork' and possessing an appropriate hat and gloves were among them."[51] The job, she further recalled, had no description of duties outlined. When she asked Keeney just exactly what she was going to do, he replied ambiguously: "You can do anything I don't want to do."[52]

Teaching was a top priority for Pierrel, who had told Keeney when he came to Barnard that if she returned to Providence, "it would NOT be in the role of administrator (but maybe as a professor)."[53] During her term as dean, Pierrel continued to teach and to run a lab in the Psychology Department. The importance of sustaining that side of her career was clear to Pierrel. She felt, later, that this had given her needed credibility with the faculty, for "I not only *had* 'been there,' I *was* 'there now.' "[54] For Pierrel being a visible role model for women at Brown meant continuing to practice her scholarship.

Pierrel found in her position as dean that she had little interaction with the students. She met them as freshmen, again as they graduated, if they were in difficulties, or if they were among the notably outstanding scholars. Even some of these tasks were eliminated with the addition in 1964, of a dean of students who "freed" Pierrel "from certain responsibilities [she] found most onerous."[55] These responsibilities, like meeting students personally, were no longer central to the position of dean. Pierrel's commitment to her work as a scholar, it seemed, was the example she wished to set for her students.

Clearly, the role of the dean had changed from the days of inspirational speeches in chapel and close associations particularly common with deans such as Lewis and Emery. Pierrel noticed a change just in her ten years as dean. She progressively felt a distance between her and the students of Pembroke. This was not due entirely to her interpretation of the meaning of the deanship. When problems surfaced in the "Old Pembroke," Pierrel remembered, "it was almost always possible to resolve them through discussion with student leaders and an appeal to commonly-shared values." In later years this was no longer true. "By 1966 the body of shared values was beginning to become much smaller, and had shrunk almost to invisibility by the 1970s."[56] The numbers of women faculty at Brown fluctuated significantly during this period. From six women in

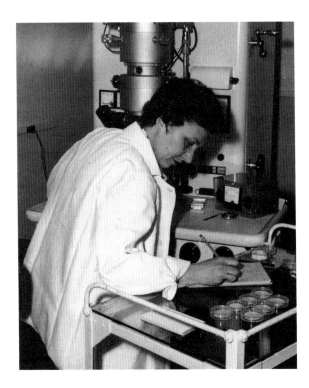

Elizabeth Leduc, professor of biology, who, in 1953, became the first woman full professor to hold an academic position at Brown.

1939, or two percent of the total faculty, the numbers grew to a relatively astounding fifteen in 1947, or five percent of the total faculty, almost certainly because of World War II. In 1958, when Lewis recorded that women were being hired and advancing, there were twelve instructors, five assistant professors, three associate professors, one full professor and one visiting professor, a total of twenty-two, or six percent of the faculty. The following year, unaccountably, the women on the faculty grew to twenty-four. A decade later there were thirty-six women teaching at Brown, but they had slipped to under five percent of the total faculty.[57]

A few women were reaching the higher echelons of faculty rank. Brown awarded tenure to Elizabeth Leduc in 1964, a biology professor who had earned her Ph.D. at Brown before working for some years at the Harvard Medical School. Her advisor invited her back to Brown to the Biomedical Department in 1953, where she worked on cancer-related research and taught biology.

Professor Leduc did not realize the difficulties other women were having with tenure and promotion. When she was promoted, Leduc recalled in an oral interview, she received letters from women all across the country congratulating her on her achievement. She was shocked to be told that she was only the third woman to be a full professor at Brown.[58] More significantly, perhaps, Leduc was the first woman promoted to full professor for an academic position.

Like Leduc, Dean Pierrel became increasing aware of the problems faced by women both aspiring to be faculty, and aspiring to rise in the ranks of the faculty at Brown. By 1970, when Pierrel resigned as dean, and as Pembroke hovered on the brink of merger, she joined a rising chorus of voices reinforcing Dean Lewis's lone voice of the early fifties. These women were concerned not only that there were too few women as faculty, but those hired had less opportunity for advancement into tenured faculty positions than men of the same rank and experience.

Pierrel would not completely associate herself with feminists now visible on the campus (unlike Morriss' frank avowal of feminism forty-four years earlier), and yet she agreed with their stance on this issue. "Though I am not a card-carrying member of a Women's Lib Cell," Pierrel announced at convocation in 1970, "I share with the Lib the concern that special effort must continue to be made to hasten equal opportunity for women in careers and in equal pay for equal work." Brown University, she asserted, "can encourage this by seeing to it that highly qualified women exist in larger numbers in the student body and at all levels of the faculty and administration."[59]

A Rising Chorus

This rising chorus cannot be attributed only to a context of increased vigilance regarding discrimination in American society, although that should not be ignored. In the seven years since Clayton's article in the *Pembroke Alumna*, the "problem had not solved itself."[60] Funding for the Nancy Duke Lewis Chair, although growing each year, did not seem to be a priority of the administration. Recommendations for the hiring and promoting of women in the university submitted in both the majority and minority reports of the Pembroke Study Committee (PSC), appointed in the fall of 1969 to consider the merger of Pembroke College with Brown, apparently did not appear in the final report.[61] Members of the committee were drawn from all different constituencies: the faculty, the administration, the corporation, students, and alumnae. The committee's chair was Elizabeth Leduc.

The study committee's majority report recommended immediate merger, "that a woman be appointed to a high-level position, such as Associate Provostship," and that "the number of women on the faculty be substantially increased."[62] These women were necessary to act as role models for both graduate and undergraduate women. "It is illogical," the report continued, "for Brown to assure its women undergraduates and graduate students that their academic aspirations are valid and then to hesitate to hire similarly qualified women as professors."[63] The minority report, representing four of the twelve members, also recommended an increase in the numbers of women "in significant faculty and administrative positions."[64]

The Pembroke Study Committee's report, however, was never taken as a blueprint for change. It was, President Hornig said, "*a* committee's ideas as to what should transpire [and it was] important in that respect," but it "was certainly never taken by us as a detailed prescription." A different proposal from that of the PSC was made to the Advisory and Executive Committee of the Brown Corporation. It, the student news magazine *Issues,* stated, "was not greeted with as much enthusiasm by the students as the original report of the PSC. It left out the committee's recommendations... [regarding] 'substantially' increasing the number of the women on the faculty."[65] The recommendation concerning an appointment of a woman "to a high-level administrative position, such as Associate Provostship" was retained, however.[66]

The merger was made final in June 1971 by a vote of the corporation without reference to the need for further women faculty. An administrative appointment was made, however, and offered to Jacquelyn Mattfeld. Her appointment to dean of faculty affairs and associate provost was made public in 1971. Described as the "conscience of the university," Mattfeld was expected to be a role model for Brown women. Yet the parameters of Mattfeld's positions were not clear. Mattfeld was one of two associate provosts, working in conjunction with the university provost.[67]

Mattfeld shared the concerns of many of her colleagues about the hiring of women professionals at Brown. In a speech in 1972 to the American Council on Education she asserted that

> The popular view that academic excellence and prestige of an institution are directly proportional to the number of men in it and to the prevalence of their values, interests and concerns in all areas of its endeavors is pervasive in American higher education. But nowhere is it more obvious than in the Ivy League.[68]

Those concerns were made obvious in response to a report submitted to the faculty from the American Association of University Professor's Committee on the Employment and Status of Women Faculty and Graduate Students at Brown. The report stated baldly that "Brown does not have enough women faculty members, particularly in the upper ranks.... Women seeking full-time teaching jobs are likely to encounter discrimination."[69]

Meanwhile, Clayton's earlier optimism about the necessary pace of change had left her by 1971. "Those of us who came in years ago," she reported, "were trying very hard to act like the men faculty. Unless we succeeded in de-emphasizing our differences, we didn't stand a chance of staying. My head has opened up a lot since then." Recent comments in her department had exacerbated her sense of alienation. Her colleagues' assertions that "women just don't like to work as hard as men," and "women can't make decisions" are irritating but, she added, "I hear 'present company excepted' so much that sometimes I feel invisible."[70]

Pressure towards solving the problem of the lack of women faculty came from the scrutiny Brown was then under from the Department of Health, Education and Welfare (HEW) concerning discrimination in employment practices. HEW administrators suspected that discrimination was often more pervasive in one department than another on university campuses. One HEW staff member commented that "Brown University has a commitment, so if one department is out of compliance, that throws the whole university out of compliance. If certain departments need poking, well, they'll be poked."[71]

The entire issue of the hiring of faculty women was complicated by the administration's announced faculty cutbacks in a three-year retrenchment program in 1974. In a reorganization of the university, Mattfeld's position was clarified. She was given a new title – Dean of Faculty and Academic Affairs – and assigned responsibility for all academic departments, hiring and budgets.[72] This, unfortunately, put her in the middle of the retrenchment program. Mattfeld, then – the one top woman administrator at Brown – became the messenger of bad news to the faculty, whose job security was left hanging in the balance. In the fall of 1975 Jacquelyn Mattfeld was offered and accepted the presidency of Barnard.[73]

That year the *Brown Daily Herald* reported that a group called the Committee of Women Faculty "found the university's affirmative action program to hire female professors 'insufficient.'" "According to the report," the article continued, "the outside filling of tenured positions helps to keep the total number of women at its current low level and closes off promotion opportunities to those women who have been hired at the junior level ... stated in other terms, twelve women were hired last year, but eight others were asked to leave."[74] This form of discrimination was called a "revolving-door policy," meaning that a number of women were hired in non-tenured positions for short terms, but only a token few received tenure, regardless of their performance. Affirmative action in hiring alone was deemed a failure in sparking change, the committee felt. Without "affirmative action in promotion, the status will remain quo."[75]

The retrenchment program, while hard on all untenured faculty, was particularly devastating for those eager to see women attain positions of status in the community. "We are defeated before we begin," Mary Yaeger, an assistant professor in the History Department, told a *Herald* reporter. "It's a serious situation, and I don't know what recourse there is, or what the alternatives are."[76] In an article in the *Brown Alumni Monthly*, Sandra Reeves reported that on campus women believed

> Brown did increase its total number of women faculty during the early seventies, they acknowledge, but if the increases have been realized almost entirely in dead-end positions, then the University's approach to affirmative action amounts to little more than window dressing.[77]

Amid these pressures, the university finally faced a legal challenge that would force the pace of change on behalf of women considerably. A class action suit brought against Brown for sexual discrimination was pending when Reeves wrote her article. The suit had been initiated by Professor Louise Lamphere, a member of the Anthropology Department denied tenure in Spring 1974.

Legal Challenge

The tenure decision of Louise Lamphere was unusual from the start. She was notified of the decision by her department thirteen days after the departmental recommendation had been sent to the provost rather than immediately, which was the practice, and which she had specifically requested. It was then too late to initiate grievance procedures. She did so the following fall, and her grievance was heard by an ad hoc committee, the Faculty Policy Grievance Subcommittee, headed by Arlene Gorton, Class of 1952, a tenured associate professor and assistant director of athletics.

The Gorton committee reported that due process had been denied Louise Lamphere because of the late date of her receiving notice of the tenure decision, and "because of serious procedural violation, we can therefore have no confidence that the correct decision has been made by the university in this case."[78] Lamphere declined to have the case reviewed again by the department, feeling that the review would not reverse the original decision; instead she filed a complaint in federal district court. The committee, however, required that the department reconsider the decision before submitting it to the Academic Council, the final arbiter of hiring and tenure decisions. The department again denied Lamphere tenure, and the Academic Council, four months after the Gorton Committee had finished its report, reviewed and approved the tenure denial.[79]

Lamphere filed her complaint as a class action alleging there was a pattern of discrimination at Brown regarding women faculty in hiring, promotion, contract renewal, and other conditions of employment. Her suit was certified "class action" in July 1976. Joining her were Pat Russian from the German Department, Claude Carey from Slavic languages and literature, and Helen Cserr from the Division of Biology and Medical Science. Lamphere claimed that the department had undervalued her scholarship on women, that she was as qualified or more so than the last person in her department to receive tenure, and that she was considered for tenure with standards stricter than those she was led to expect when she was hired.

The discovery process in the trial – which allowed both sides equal access to files pertinent to the case – involved oral testimonies of university officials and faculty, requests for specific information called "interrogatories," and the production of departmental and administrative files. This was the focus of a great deal of concern on campus, as professors were asked to supply the plaintiffs with personal files. These files, testimonies, and interrogatories would, in the event of a trial, have been made part of the public domain.[80]

In one instance, letters between the chairman of the Anthropology Department, Philip Leis, and another member of the department, George Hicks, were supplied with substantial portions deleted. Lamphere's lawyers charged the two with contempt of court. Federal Judge Raymond J.

*Percentage of Men
and Women Faculty*

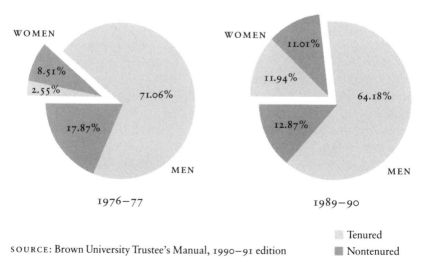

WOMEN

8.51%
2.55%
71.06%
17.87%

MEN

1976–77

WOMEN

11.01%
11.94%
64.18%
12.87%

MEN

1989–90

Tenured
Nontenured

SOURCE: Brown University Trustee's Manual, 1990–91 edition

Pettine decided to defer the contempt charges until after the trial, but awarded Lamphere's lawyers close to $8,000 in fees to pay for their efforts in recovering the documents. Later, it was suggested by the plaintiffs that these letters were of particular significance. "Most faculty and administrators who had access to part of this evidence," Carey, Cserr, and Russian wrote in an article in the *Brown Alumni Monthly,* "concluded it was in the interest of individual faculty defendants and the entire institution to try to reach an out-of-court settlement."[81]

The case did not go to trial. President Howard Swearer, new to Brown in January 1977, decided that it was in the best interest of the university to settle out of court. Through five months of negotiation the plaintiffs and the university constructed a plan to minimize discrimination on campus and implement the increase of women faculty at Brown. Lamphere, Cserr, and Carey, who had been up for tenure, were reviewed by other academics in their fields outside the university. All were recommended for tenure by their reviewers; all were ultimately granted tenure by the university. Russian, who had not been in a tenure track position, was awarded damages.

The consent decree, or the Lamphere decision, as it is often called, was agreed upon in the fall of 1977, and represented a major milestone in the struggle of the university community to better represent women in the ranks of its faculty. Yet the process of change was painful and costly in terms of effort, time, and money. The Brown campus became charged with the anger, disappointment, and differing views of all involved. University publications were crowded with opinions that assessed the situation, concerning not only the end the plaintiffs sought, but the means ultimately settled upon.

The university, while it did not admit to having discriminated against women, agreed in the decree to "correct previous injustices, if any, and to achieve on behalf of women full representativeness with respect to faculty employment at Brown University." The decree required that each department establish and publish their criteria for evaluation, that tenured faculty review untenured faculty annually, and that a review procedure for all tenure decisions be established. In the instance of a non-minority male being hired over a woman, the department must defend the decision to an Affirmative Action Monitoring Committee set up by the decree. Faculty members were to have access to salary data within their respective departments. The basic goal was to achieve a proportion of faculty women in each department that reflected the proportion of women nationally holding doctorates in each discipline.

The Monitoring Committee was to consist of five members: two chosen by the plaintiffs, two by the faculty, and one agreed upon by both. Goals and timetables for the hiring of women were agreed to be reviewed again in 1987.[82] The maximum liability for the class part of the suit was set at $400,000; claims by members of the class (which included all women hired by Brown since 1972) had to be submitted within six months after the decree was approved.[83] These claims were heard by a faculty hearing committee, and at least one appeal against a decision by that committee was subsequently brought to court, which upheld the decision.[84]

Judge Pettine called the consent decree "fair, reasonable, and adequate," and on March 6, 1978, gave final approval to the decision. Gorton and Wessen's assessment was "that ultimately both male and female, tenured and nontenured faculty will benefit from better employment procedures."[85] "Of greatest importance to us," Swearer said later, "is to put this case to rest, for the morale of the University and so that we can get along with our primary functions of teaching and scholarship."[86]

Tensions concerning the class action suit, and the later application of the consent decree, triggered an ongoing dialogue on the subject by faculty, students and alumni. Arguments in Brown publications, particularly the *Brown Alumni Monthly,* flew back and forth between those who saw the decree as a fair measure long awaited, and those who considered it an insidious form of "reverse discrimination."[87] Philip Bray, a Brown physics professor, candidly faced the possible problems on campus when he wrote before the settlement in March 1977,

> If there is injustice that must be set straight, I hope that we will all see ourselves as sharing the responsibility, and not turn quickly in harsh judgement against our colleagues who may more candidly – and in recoverable ways – have revealed the fruits of prejudice whose seeds lie in all of us.[88]

Philip Leis, a defendant in the case, saw the issues differently. In a later article to the *Brown Alumni Monthly* titled "It is clear the University 'lost' the case," Leis asserted that the University lost money, autonomy, academic freedom, and credibility when it settled out of court. He concluded that "there may be much lost to the University as a result of the decree and little gained, apart from satisfying the personal claims of those who 'won' the case."[89] Others saw it as a personal victory for Louise Lamphere, and a boon to the university. A 1975 graduate, Marina Capelletto, who termed Lamphere a "superior" teacher, wrote that

> A very important part of my educational experience at Brown was the opportunity to have professional women such as Louise Lamphere as a role model. I do not wish to see this opportunity taken away from any young woman presently studying at Brown.[90]

The landscape at Brown changed considerably after the consent decree was put in place. The accompanying graph demonstrates the sharp rise in numbers of women faculty. The total numbers of professors soared in the eighties.[91] Women undergraduates are now unlikely to leave Brown without being taught by a woman professor.

Growing Numbers of Faculty Women

The women faculty at Brown have achieved a great deal in the past two decades of growth. In 1972 the Nancy Duke Lewis Chair was first filled despite the fact that the chair was still underfunded as a permanent position.[92] Rosalie Colie, already on the Brown faculty and chair of the Comparative Literature Department, was the first recipient. Colie saw her purpose at Brown in significantly different terms from those of the early deans. Although the press release describing her rise to department chair remarks that she "could well be considered a 'role model,' it is a phrase, the author admits, that Colie herself 'hates'." Professor Colie agreed that there was "something to that concept" but denies that it is bounded by shared gender. "I've had marvelously good woman scholars as teachers and it was very important to me," she recalled. "But of course I've had lots of role models who were men, too."[93] Later that year Colie drowned in a boating accident.

The Lewis chair went unfilled for five years. With faculty pressure, the university agreed to bring annual distinguished visiting scholars to fill it as a way of testing the response to a field in women's studies.[94] The chair was filled in 1977 by Helen Astin, a distinguished visiting professor from the University of California at Los Angeles. At Brown she held a joint appointment in the departments of sociology and psychology. Ann Seidman, who held the chair in 1978, was an economist with a degree from the University of Wisconsin who joined the Department of Sociology.

The following year the chair was offered for the first time as a tenured position to a professor outside the Brown faculty. Joan Scott, a labor and women's historian, came to Brown in 1980. After she arrived, Scott became the founding director of the Pembroke Center for Teaching and Research on Women. In 1985 Scott resigned when the Institute for Advanced Study at Princeton invited her to join their small permanent faculty. The fifth holder of the Nancy Duke Lewis chair, Professor Naomi Schor, taught in the Department of French Studies. Schor came to Brown as an associate professor from Columbia in 1978, and was offered the Nancy Duke Lewis chair in 1984. In 1990 Schor resigned to take a post at Duke University.

In mid-1991, a search for her replacement was underway.[95]

Although it is impossible to list all the achievements won by the women faculty at Brown in the last decade, their record taken together is nothing short of outstanding. Since 1980, ten faculty women have won John Simon Guggenheim fellowships.[96] Persons winning this nationally renowned award are chosen on the basis of "demonstrated accomplishment in the past and strong promise for the future."[97] Women faculty have also been well represented among the award winners on campus. Henry M. Wriston fellowships and grants, given to junior faculty of exceptional promise, were given to ten women during the same period of time.[98] In 1990, a thirty year veteran at Brown, associate athletic director and professor Arlene Gorton of the Physical Education Department, was awarded the Katherine Ley Award by the Eastern Collegiate Athletic Conference for outstanding leadership as a woman athletic administrator, and for providing a strong role model to other women in athletics. In June 1991, professor and women's historian, Mari Jo Buhle, was named a MacArthur fellow, awarded "to exceptionally creative individuals," and consisting of an unrestricted grant over a period of five years.[99]

In the late 1980s, the results of the consent decree were assessed on campus. In a report released by the Affirmative Action Monitoring Committee in 1988, the year following the review stipulated in the decree, the results of several questionnaires sent to both men and women faculty were analyzed. The committee found that "there are good reasons for taking heart, though not for becoming complacent."[100] The purpose of the report was to alert the university to "deep-seated attitudes and cultural constructions" that perpetuate sexism. The committee also noted that "women's often unwilling complicity in sexual stereotyping has served to compound the problem, and the hesitancy of many women to report incidents of sexual harassment has helped to perpetuate it."[101]

Among the responses recorded were those of faculty and staff women, the committee found, who still expressed unease about the few numbers of women in positions of authority within the university. Others discovered to their dismay that they were frequently not given their proper titles, were subjected to sexist jokes, or were expected to fulfill stereotypically nurturing roles. The report ended on an optimistic note. A male senior faculty member, the committee wrote, offered "perhaps the most eloquent concluding statement" when he said "...the 'consent decree' should be regarded as a blessing rather than a burden."[102]

Conflict between some of the faculty and administration policy re-emerged over the university's request that Judge Pettine terminate the consent decree. In October 1987, faculty met to discuss the possible end to the decree. Then, and in the following spring, strong opposition was voiced by those at the meeting to changing the decree until an alternative affirmative action mechanism was set up.

In October 1988, the university asked the court to allow it to vacate the consent decree immediately, or to set a date of June 1990 and advise the university of the terms necessary to end the decree. Lawyers for the university argued that the original 1987 goals had been met, and that they had set in motion efforts to establish a system to monitor affirmative action. Even though there were not the required number of tenured women by that date, the university argued that unanticipated attrition, not intention, was the cause for the disparity.

In open and closed sessions Judge Pettine counseled the university and the women faculty to reach a compromise solution, and to set up an internal strategy for insuring hiring equity. An ad hoc committee was established made up of three class representatives, two members of the Affirmative Action Monitoring Committee, three administration representatives, and two faculty Executive Committee members. Finally, he requested all briefs on the matter to be filed December 2, 1988.[103]

On February 9, 1989, Pettine issued a court order retaining major portions of the decree, and setting a goal that Brown grant tenure to an additional thirteen women by 1991 in order to vacate the decree. Pettine lifted guidelines for the hiring of non-tenured women faculty. The court denied the university's request that it be freed from the consent decree's stipulation that the "burden of proof" lies with the university in sex discrimination cases.[104] The university then filed a "Motion for Reconsideration," arguing that Pettine did not take attrition into account in determining his number, nor did he consider that the number of sixty-seven had been decided upon after consultation between the university and the Affirmative Action Monitoring Committee.[105]

On May 12, 1989, Judge Pettine for the U.S. District Court lowered the goal for Brown to sixty-seven from seventy tenured women faculty. Awards of tenure to sixty-seven women by 1991, Judge Pettine allowed, would be "substantial compliance" and 90 percent of "full representativeness" of the number of women faculty Brown would have had if it fully reflected the availability of women Ph.D.'s from 1954 to 1985.[106] He implied, thereby, that if Brown reached or surpassed that goal it could then vacate the consent decree. In July 1991 the Brown faculty included sixty-five tenured women.

In May 1991 the faculty voted to accept an internal mechanism for monitoring the advancement of women faculty designed by the ad hoc committee appointed in 1988. The women faculty voted to join the university in asking the court to vacate the consent decree, conditional on the Brown Corporation's acceptance of the mechanism designed by the ad hoc committee.[107]

The Legacy of the Lamphere Decision

Responses to a questionnaire sent to the women faculty at Brown in the spring of 1989 indicate complex and differing responses to the legacy of the Lamphere decision.[108] The majority suggested in their responses that the decree had a positive effect on Brown. One respondent recalled that the timetable demanded by the processes of the consent decree – the monitoring committee reviews all hiring decisions, which takes time – "almost prevented me from coming to Brown, since I needed to get an offer before deadlines for other job offers. But," she added, "I wouldn't have it any other way – it has been a tremendous boon to the community in general, and has made everyone more conscious of the issues."[109]

Another respondent expressed concern that tenure decisions may be misconstrued, or underappreciated, as a result of the decision. "There are women who have proved themselves to be extraordinary researchers, teachers & friends to students who should be recognized," she said. "I would not like to have their contribution 'cheapened' by a quota. They deserve tenure on their own merits." Another wrote that the consent decree was "one reason I came to Brown. I've seen so many tenure cases where the deck was stacked against women that I wanted to go somewhere where I could get a break."[110]

Yet some of the respondents to the questionnaire expressed reservations about their treatment as women. One wrote that women in her department are "expected to take on many more of the nurturing activities – seeing students, 'hostessing' at functions, taking on extra administrative tasks, etc." Another felt that: "Women are expected by colleagues and students to be better teachers than male faculty, while at the same time given less respect, a helpful component in teaching effectiveness." And so, she added, "we have to work harder and generally do."[111] Another respondent disagreed. She wrote: "My colleagues are *all*, male or female, giving to students in various ways."[112]

Another concern, voiced in several questionnaires, was that women do not have the same access to mentoring that men do and thus miss out on an important way of receiving support and information beneficial to their teaching and research.[113] At issue was the way that colleagues talked to each other. One professor felt that the language used in her department effectively made her invisible.[114]

Disparity in situations across departments was noted. Certain departments had a long tradition of hiring women and a sense of gender difference may not be as acute. One respondent saw the department tenure decisions as a particular problem. She explained that a perceived disparity in opportunity for women

> is because of departmental autonomy, the way in which tenured members have most power and the fact that they are all men in many departments. Women do not have mentors (in my dept) which is important to understand in evaluating success. In sum, the *teams* (her emphasis) decide who they want to play with.[115]

Other women faculty were very positive about the conditions for women at Brown, and the prospects for positive change. One respondent remarked that "The administration is a refreshing change from most Ivies – [Dean] Sheila Blumstein is a great asset, & Gregorian will spot & highlight female and minority talent."[116] Another calls Brown "much better than most places."[117] Another echoes that thought, saying "Brown is considerably better (in terms of sexual discrimination) than other places I've taught."[118] And yet, one respondent cautions that "until the presence of women *at all levels* [her emphasis] at Brown has become routine, the power of sexist thinking in society and our own heads means that risks remain."[119]

When the commitment of Brown University to women in 1991 is compared with that of the university one hundred years earlier, the change can only be deemed positive. Yet the changes in the university faculty were very recently won despite years of determined and vocal persistence by the few women professors at Brown and the Pembroke deans. With the deans the major exceptions, men were seen as fundamentally more superior, and more prestigious teachers for women in intellectual endeavors. Deans were to present the women at Brown with a polished, presentable model for their achievement, a model, that, while embued with administrative power, did not include an academic career.

The numbers of women at Brown in positions that denoted status and achievement in the academic community – tenure and promotion to full professor – clearly grew after the university agreed to the consent decree in 1977. From 10 percent in 1978, the percentage of women faculty jumped to 19 percent in 1988 and 23 percent in 1991.[120] The issue of promotion, as good as the comparison looks, still concerns women professors at Brown.[121] National statistics, however, locate Brown within an average range for 1985. At that time the percent of tenured women professors to total tenured professors nationwide was 17 percent. As noted

Percentage of Faculty, by Field,
who are Women, 1989–90

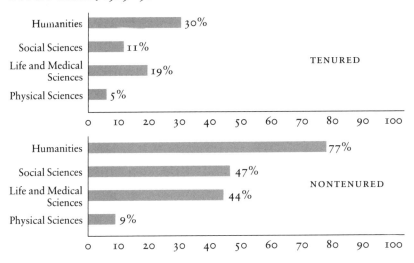

SOURCE: Brown University Trustee's Manual, 1990–91 Edition

earlier, by July 1991 at Brown, the percentage of tenured women faculty to tenured male faculty had risen to 16 percent.[122]

By mid 1991, when this book goes to the press, the consent decree which changed the landscape of Brown may be in the process of being dismantled. Its legacy, if perceived in different ways within the Brown community, has insured the presence of significant numbers of outstanding scholars on campus, carefully and methodically chosen. Women in places of prestige and achievement are visible and active at Brown, if they are not, as yet, fully represented.

The Lamphere case has also made an impact nationally. When Elizabeth Kirk, English Department chair, entered the department, she was one of two women. Now the department has the same number of women as men. Kirk cites the "national impact" of the Lamphere case. "It is the most important piece of voluntary social change I've ever seen," she said. "I think people will be writing textbooks about what happened at Brown. This is not a mark of shame."[123]

NOTES

1. Louis Franklin Snow. *Report of the Dean of the Women's College,* 17 June 1897, p. 62.

2. The Brown University Trustee's Manual, 1990–91; Office of the Dean of the Faculty, July 1991.

3. The numbers quoted are from a graph devised from data gathered from university catalog listings by Karen Lamoree, Christine Dunlap Farnham Archivist at Brown University until spring, 1990. See "Development of Women Faculty" graph, Farnham Archives.

4. *The Sepiad* 1 (June 1901): 72; J.M. Hopkins, *Issues* 8 (October 1977): 9 (Hornig quoted by Hopkins).

5. Maurice Glicksman, memorandum to Robert Reichley, 26 March 1991, p. 3, in author's possession.

6. Jessie Wheeler Freeman, Class of 1901, letter to *The Sepiad* 1 (June 1901): 25–26.

7. Speech reprinted in *The Sepiad* 1 (June 1901): 72. See also Grace E. Hawk, *Pembroke College in Brown University* (Providence, R.I.: Brown University Press, 1967) for information on Anne Crosby Emery.

8. Hawk, *Pembroke College in Brown University,* p. 47.

9. Emery, *Report,* September 1902, p. 28. For the failure of the home economics experiment, see Chapter 2.

10. Emery, Report, September 1904, p. 30.

11. Editorial in *The Sepiad* 1 (May 1901): 60–61.

12. Bertha Louise Clark, Class of 1905, *The Sepiad* 5 (June 1905): 126.

13. Ada Wing also left her position to marry a Brown professor in her department. See Linda M. Eisenmann's: "Women at Brown, 1891–1930: 'Academically identical but socially quite distinct,' " (Ed.D. dissertation, Harvard University, 1987), pp. 85–86.

14. Winifred Florence Chase, Class of 1906, *The Sepiad* 6 (June 1906): 8.

15. Student Government Association resolution printed in *The Sepiad* 9 (June 1909): 35.

16. Student rendering of King's talk, printed in *The Sepiad* 12 (June 1912): 64.

17. *The Sepiad* 9 (June 1909): 35.

18. Minutes of the Executive Committee, June 1920, p. 111; Minutes, 1921, p. 113.

19. Minutes, 1923, p. 121.

20. Oral interview with Charlotte Ferguson Roads, Class of 1924, Christine Dunlap Farnham Archives, Brown University; also cited by Eisenmann, pp. 64–65. Wellesley's faculty was all women at this time; see Patricia A. Palmieri, "Here was Fellowship: A Social Portrait of Academic Women at Wellesley College, 1880–1920," *History of Education Quarterly* 23 (Summer 1983): 195–214.

21. "An Alumna Remembers," *Pembroke Center Associates Newsletter* 1 (Spring 1985): 5.

22. Oral interview with Alice Gilpin Silver, Class of 1932, p. 2, Farnham Archives.

23. Oral interview with Dr. Sarah M. Saklad, Class of 1928, pp. 15–17, Farnham Archives.

24. Margaret S. Morriss, "The Affiliated College," *Alumnae Record,* 1927–28, unpaginated; cited by Eisenmann, p. 63.

25. Oral interview with Doris Hopkins Stapelton, Class of 1928, p. 18, Farnham Archives.

26. Oral interview with Alice Chmielewski, Class of 1928, pp. 7–8, Farnham Archives.

27. "The Report of the Senior Committee of the Women's College in Brown University," 1926, Farnham Archives, pp. 8–9.

28. Minutes of the Executive Committee of the Women's College, 2 April 1930.

29. Louise Graboys, "The Conservative University – Action or Reaction?" Honors Thesis, 1972, Farnham Archives. Graboys suggests that Wilder had been teaching for Brown between 1927 and 1939, an assertion not confirmed by Karen Lamoree's data from university catalogs.

30. Geraldine Joncich Clifford, ed., *Lone Voyagers: Academic Women in Coeducational Universities, 1870–1937* (New York: The Feminist Press, 1989), p. 1. For data on Brown, see graph accompanying this article and "Development of Women Faculty" graph,

Farnham Archives.

31. Clifford, *Lone Voyagers,* p. 7.

32. The university catalog records them as being hired in the same year.

33. Clifford, *Lone Voyagers,* p. 7. Clifford quotes Theodore Caplow and Reece J. McGee, *The Academic Marketplace* (New York: Science editions, 1961), p. 111.

34. Interview by author with Penelope Hartland Thunberg, 31 January 1991.

35. She also became the head librarian of Annmary Brown Memorial.

36. Margaret Bingham Stillwell, *Librarians are Human* (Boston: Colonial Society of Massachusetts, 1973), p. 276.

37. Ibid., p. 276.

38. Ibid., pp. 277, 279–80, 284–85.

39. From Nancy Duke Lewis, Speeches, Farnham Archives, 3 May 1958.

40. "Report of the Dean of Pembroke College to the Advisory Committee on Pembroke College," 24 November 1952, pp. 4–5.

41. "Report of the Dean of Pembroke College to the Advisory Committee on Pembroke College," 6 April 1953, p. 4.

42. "Report," 4 October 1954, p. 10.

43. Ibid., p. 13.

44. Ibid., p. 10.

45. Minutes of the Executive Committee, 6 October 1958, pp. 7–8.

46. *Pembroke Alumna* 38 (October 1962): 2. Polly Welts Kaufman, Class of 1951, was the editor.

47. Ibid., p. 6. Barbara Solomon notes, however, that although the percentage of women earning Ph.D.'s declined, absolute numbers rose. See *In the Company of Educated Women* (New Haven: Yale University Press, 1985), p. 191.

48. *Pembroke Alumna* 38 (October 1962): 7.

49. Ibid., pp. 8, 9.

50. There was also concern about hiring a married woman because of "what to do with her husband," who might "face the possibility of becoming an appendage." Advisory Committee Minutes, March 6, 1961, pp. 3–4.

51. Oral interview with Rosemary Pierrel Sorrentino, 7 December 1988, p. 1, Farnham Archives.

52. Ibid., p. 2.

53. Ibid., p. 1.

54. Ibid., p. 2 [Her emphasis]

55. Ibid., p. 2.

56. Ibid., p. 7.

57. These percentages were derived from total numbers of faculty listed in the university catalogs: 2.34 percent for 1938–39; 4.83 percent, 1947–48; 6.45 percent, 1957–58; 4.62 percent, 1966–68. See "Development of Women Faculty" graph, Farnham Archives.

58. "Notes from an interview with Elizabeth Leduc," 6 January 1988 by Karen Lamoree. The university catalog data would make her fourth after Dean King, Margaret Stillwell, and Dean Morriss. Professor Bessie Rudd, the director of physical education at Pembroke, became the first woman to be a non-administrative full professor at Brown in 1952. See Chapter 4.

59. Rosemary Pierrel, Convocation Speech, Farnham Archives, 23 November 1970, p. 2.

60. "Present Company Excepted," *Brown Alumni Monthly* 71 (January 1971): 23; hereafter referred to as BAM.

61. J.M. Hopkins, "Pembroke Lost," *Issues* 8 (October 1977): 10. The university's final recommendations to the corporation referred to here, reports on the Committees on the Status of Women, and the minutes of the AAMC during the time that Professor Mari Jo Buhle administered it were "restricted" in the university archives and thus not available. The

information that informs the following section was gleaned from BAM articles, *Brown Daily Herald* articles, the *George Street Journal,* Brown University Press releases, a published report of the AAMC, interviews with General Counsel Beverly Ledbetter and Professor Louise Lamphere and the author's questionnaire to women faculty.

62. Majority Report of the Pembroke Study Committee, 8 May 1970, pp. 3, 5.

63. Ibid., p. 5.

64. Minority Report of the Pembroke Study Committee, 8 May 1970, p. 4.

65. Hopkins, *Issues,* p. 10. This proposal was "restricted."

66. Ibid.

67. Ibid., pp. 12–13. See the *Issues* article itself for further elaboration of this point.

68. Jacquelyn Mattfeld, "Women in Administration," panelist, American Council on Education, 6 October 1972, p. 4, Farnham Archives.

69. "Present Company Excepted," BAM 71 (January 1971): 19. This report was also restricted. All quotations are gleaned from the article.

70. Ibid., p. 22.

71. Ibid., p. 23.

72. Apparently she, herself, chose this title. Glicksman, memorandum, p. 6.

73. Hopkins, *Issues,* p. 13.

74. "Faculty Group Doubts Commitment to Women," *Brown Daily Herald* 59 (October 1975): 1. This report was also restricted.

75. Ibid., pp. 1, 3.

76. *Brown Daily Herald* 59 (October 1975): 1.

77. Sandra Reeves, "Is Brown guilty of discrimination against women faculty?" BAM 77 (April 1977): 29.

78. Information gathered from "The Looking Glass," *Issues* 7 (March 1977): 4.

79. Ibid., pp. 3–4, 33–36.

80. The material thus "discovered" was protected from public disclosure during this process by the judge. After the consent decree this prohibition, of course, continued. Maurice Glicksman adds in his memorandum: "Individuals were hence barred from discussion of them; some did not refrain from so doing, and, in fact, one such document was later given into circulation anonymously." p. 6.

81. Claude Carey, Helen Cserr, Pat Russian, "The Lamphere Settlement: The Plaintiffs reply to Professor Leis," BAM 78 (May/June 1978): 43–46.

82. Arlene Gorton and Albert Wessen, "The Lamphere Settlement: A Faculty View," BAM 78 (November 1977): 26.

83. The maximum liability of $400,000 was not reached with subsequent claims. Glicksman memorandum, p. 6.

84. Ibid.

85. Ibid., p. 7.

86. BAM 80 (February 1980): 13.

87. See the BAM "Carrying the Mail" section for this dialogue, as well as the BDH and *Issues* magazine from spring 1977 to fall 1978. For the issue of "reverse discrimination" see particularly "Carrying the Mail," BAM 78, (Jan/Feb 1978): 46–47.

88. Philip Bray, "Confidentiality and the Courts," *Issues* 7 (March 1977): 5.

89. Philip Leis, "It is clear the University 'Lost' the Case," BAM 78 (March 1978): 27–29.

90. Letter to BAM, Marina A. Capelletto, Class of 1975, 78 (April 1978): 46.

91. See accompanying pie graphs.

92. Glicksman, memorandum, p. 7.

93. News Release, Office of Public Information, Brown University, Farnham Archives; 28 March 1972, #72/089.

94. Details of this policy supplied by Professor Joan Scott.

95. Other women in endowed chairs at Brown include Professor Annette Coleman of

the Biology Department who was appointed in 1987 the Stephen T. Olney Professor of Natural History.

96. They include: Barbara Lewalski, Renaissance studies; Barbara Anderson, sociology; Dagmar Barnouw, German and comparative literature; Annette Coleman, biology; Naomi Baron, linguistics; Kathlyn Parker, chemistry; c.d. Wright, poet and English; Naomi Lamoreaux, history; Mary Ann Doane, modern culture and media; Karen Newman, comparative literature and English; Naomi Schor, French.

97. *George Street Journal* 7 (1980): 4.

98. They included: Karen Newman; Mary Ann Doane; Martha Schaffer; Alison Elliott; Carol Poore; Joan Richards; Anne Fausto-Sterling; Carole Beane; Sheila Bonde; Meera Viswanathan.

99. *Providence Journal-Bulletin,* 27 June 1990; *Boston Globe,* 18 June 1991.

100. "A Report on Sexism at Brown University by the Committee on the Status of Women," issued by the Affirmative Action Monitoring Committee, October 1988, p. 1, Farnham Archives.

101. Ibid., p. 2.

102. Ibid., pp. 3 – 13. The final quote was longer in the report than is included here.

103. The following section is based on articles in the *Brown Daily Herald,* 6 September 1939, pp. 1, 6; BAM 89 (April 1989), p. 12; *Chronicle of Higher Education,* 22 February 1989.

104. BAM 89 (April 1989), p. 12.

105. The university also questioned the notion of "grievous wrong." Under the decree the university had to prove that no discrimination had taken place, rather than the faculty member proving it had taken place. The court had denied the university's request to be freed from this stipulation.

106. All the numbers cited here as goals to be reached have been quoted by the university's general counsel, Beverly Ledbetter. The press sources otherwise cited were often incorrect in the numbers they provided. *Brown Daily Herald* 124 (6 September 1989): 1.

107. Interview with Elizabeth Kirk, 23 July 1991.

108. Direct quotes from the questionnaire devised by the author and sent to regular (i.e., not visiting) women faculty on campus at Brown in the spring of 1989.

109. The AAMC can only delay hiring timetables for forty-eight hours. [Glicksman, memorandum, p. 8]. Gleaned from questionnaire labelled "D."

110. From questionnaires labelled "C," and "F", respectively.

111. From questionnaire labelled "B."

112. From questionnaire labelled "C." [Emphasis hers]

113. Mentioned in questionnaires labelled "B," "N," "M" and "H."

114. From questionnaire labelled "G."

115. From questionnaire labelled "N."

116. From questionnaire labelled "D."

117. From questionnaire labelled "O."

118. From questionnaire labelled "E."

119. From questionnaire labelled "B."

120. Percentages derived from listings of instructors in the Brown university catalogs for 1977 – 79 and 1987 – 89; Brown University Trustee's Manual, 1990 – 91. Final percentage from the Office of the Dean of the Faculty, July 1991.

121. A chart listed in the *Boston Globe* listed the percentage of tenured women to men at Brown for the academic year, 1987 – 88, as 13.7 to 86.3 percent. Phyllis Coons, "Women Try To Turn the Tide on Tenure," *The Boston Globe,* 2 October, 1988.

122. Derived from numbers listed in Table 191, *Digest of Education Statistics,* (U.S. Department of Education, Office of Educational Research and Improvement, 25th edition, 1989), p. 212. Final Brown figure from Office of the Dean of the Faculty, July 1991.

123. "The Lamphere Case: an Update," BAM 90 (May 1990): 15.

Finding a Voice:
Women on the Brown Corporation

by J EAN E. H OWARD

IN *EYES ON THE PRIZE*, the docu-
mentary of the civil rights struggle in the United States in the 1950s and
1960s, members of the movement frequently recall being urged to wait,
to moderate their demands until the time was "right." The problem, of
course, was that the "right" time constituted an ever-receding horizon.

On a much smaller scale, women's pursuit of seats on the Brown
Corporation was a similarly protracted undertaking repeatedly impeded
by arguments about the untimeliness of requests for inclusion. Perhaps
the most notorious example occurred in June of 1927 when the Alumnae
Association of Brown University presented to the corporation a petition
requesting the right to nominate women graduates of Brown for positions
as trustees. At the time, Arnold Buffum Chace was chancellor of the university, William H. P. Faunce serving as university president. The petition for-
warded by the women is striking for its reasonable tone and its attention
to fact. It enumerates, respectively, the male and female graduates of
Brown; describes how seats are allotted on the Board of Trustees; notes
that alumni nominate twelve of the thirty-six denominational trustees
and two of the non-denominational trustees; and requests that alumnae
have the same right of nomination. The argument is one of equity. Women
graduates of Brown should have the same opportunity to serve on the
governing board of the university as male graduates, the Women's College

Anna Canada Swain, Class of 1911, the first woman Brown trustee, stands
with other members of the 1951 Brown Corporation, including: Chancellor
Henry Dexter Sharpe, Brown President Henry M. Wriston, first row, left;
Rhode Island Senator Theodore Francis Green, third row, sixth from left,
and other prominent business, educational, and political leaders.

in Brown University having "such an important place in the life and activities of the University."[1]

In October of the same year the corporation replied to this petition. The reply, signed by H. C. Bumpus, secretary of the corporation, and addressed to Louise Gamwell Cobb, Class of 1901, president of the Alumnae Association, is striking for its brevity and its refusal to account for the action taken or to reply to the arguments advanced in the women's petition. In its entirety the letter read:

> The petition from the Alumnae Association of Brown University, which was addressed to the Corporation on June 11th, 1927, has received the careful attention of both the Corporation and the Advisory and Executive Committee.
>
> It seems to be quite generally felt that the *time has not arrived for the election of a woman to membership in the Corporation* and at the recent meeting of the Corporation formal action was taken to that effect [author's emphasis].[2]

One might well ask: *for whom* was the time not yet right? The women petitioners most certainly felt ready to assume the duties of trustee. Those who found the request untimely were those for whom the status quo was comfortable. Astonishingly, the corporation made no attempt to justify, with arguments, its decision that nothing should change. As it turned out, it was twenty-two more years before a woman would take up a seat on the Brown Corporation, the body which in the largest sense is responsible for oversight of the university's affairs, particularly its financial well-being, as well as the appointment of its chief executive officer, the president.

In a 1988 essay entitled "Women as Trustees," Mariam K. Chamberlain argues that university boards, especially at elite institutions, are conservative in nature, having little impulse to espouse diversity. She documents that the majority of university trustees are white men in their late fifties who tend to vote Republican and are affiliated, at least nominally, with Protestant churches. Collectively, such men are deeply enmeshed in the traditional structures of political and economic power in this culture. As she writes, "in spite of some attention paid to the need for more diverse representation on boards, the numbers of women and minority trustees have increased insignificantly, even in the last decade, and periodic efforts to raise issues of women in higher education to the board level, including the special concerns of women's own roles on boards, have met with little success."[3] In the context of Brown in the 1980s and 1990s, Chamberlain's conclusions appear too pessimistic. Nonetheless, as this chapter will demonstrate, the full inclusion of women into the highest governing body of the university has involved the unceasing efforts of several generations of women and is an achievement even now not fully realized.

At Brown the corporation is a bicameral entity, with the Board of Trustees (numbering thirty-six until 1926 and forty-two thereafter) having slightly different duties from the Board of Fellows (numbering twelve), but with each body regularly meeting together and approving all actions jointly. The exception is the conferring of degrees, a task solely entrusted to the Board of Fellows, which bears special responsibility for the academic well-being of the university. Together the Board of Trustees and the Board of Fellows, jointly comprising the entity known as the Brown Corporation, oversee such matters as the approval of budgets, the management of fund-raising activities, the oversight of the university's endowment, the authorization of new buildings, and the selection of the university president. In nearly all aspects of university life the corporation serves to advise the president on policy decisions in matters ranging from student life issues to collection-building strategies for the university's libraries. In short, its power is immense.

From the beginning of the establishment of the Women's College in 1891, women's role in the governance structures of the university had been a point of repeated contestation. In 1901 the first alumnae association for the Women's College was formed under the name of the Andrews Association. This group asked for places for alumnae on the Advisory Council for the Women's College that had been established in 1895. In 1905, the request was granted and five alumnae were named to the council. There was also, however, an Executive Committee of the Women's College established in 1903 whose members were appointed by the Brown Corporation. It had no alumnae on it.

In the period 1927–28, the issue of alumnae participation on the Executive Committee of the Women's College became entwined with the issue of alumnae participation on the corporation. When the corporation rebuffed the Alumnae Association's petition for alumnae seats on the Board of Trustees, it was endangering its relationship with a constituency whose help and support it needed. The impetus for the request for corporation seats had come in part from the Alumnae Association's success in raising money for the construction of Alumnae Hall. And the woman whom the association had recommended for an immediate place on the board had been the distinguished alumna, Mary E. Woolley, Class of 1894, president of Mount Holyoke College and holder of ten honorary degrees, including one from Brown. By their refusal, the corporation was in danger of giving serious offence to those alumnae who were supporting the institution in vital ways, including financially, and who found in the achievements of such women as Mary Woolley a strong argument for the inclusion of women in every aspect of university governance.

All through the winter of 1927–28, in the wake of the corporation's denial of the Alumnae Association's petition, negotiations continued to secure at least one or more seats for alumnae members on the Executive Committee of the Women's College. Apparently, the corporation felt it needed to give some positive response to the alumnae, for in the spring of 1928 it granted the addition of an alumna to the Executive Committee. The Alumnae Association selected its president, Nettie Goodale Murdock, Class of 1895. In her annual message to the association, Murdock said the vote was "a graceful recognition of the strength and importance of the alumnae body," but she later added, as Grace Hawk, Pembroke College historian, reported: "that it felt very odd to be a member of a Corporation committee without being a member of the Corporation." Disappointed at the failure to get alumnae onto the corporation, Dean Margaret S. Morriss nonetheless chose to be optimistic, saying that alumnae member-ship on the Executive Committee was a distinct step toward that end.[4]

Things, however, moved slowly. In 1935 the Alumnae Association, under the leadership of Alice Manchester Chase, Class of 1905, petitioned the Executive Committee of the Women's College to urge alumnae repre-sentation on the Board of Trustees. This step clearly was considered a politically risky one by many women who in principle supported the request. Marion Shirley Cole, Class of 1907, had been elected to the Execu-tive Committee for the term 1933–38. In June of 1935 the petition from the Alumnae Association reached the Executive Committee and, in a report written by Cole in that very month, she said that the petition came first to the Executive Committee because "any business concerning Pembroke College which comes before the Corporation comes with much more effectiveness if first endorsed by the Executive Committee." She went on to say that "The granting of this request would be a forward step of which every alumna would be justly proud."[5]

A year later, in June 1936, she again reported, in a much less exuberant tone: "after discussion by members of the Committee, particularly Miss Cole and Miss Morriss, with Mrs. Murdock and Mrs. Williams and other informed and influential people, after long deliberation informally and more formally, it was decided that it was not expedient at this time to continue the work toward the representation by women on the governing body of Brown University – that is, the Corporation. The connection between the College and the University is now close; agitation of a question more for the future good than for the present need is perhaps not wise in a world as chaotic as this, for change in and of itself is not advancement."[6]

Change, however, was thrust upon Brown University in the form of World War II, an event that at least temporarily changed the place of women in institutions of higher education, not just at Brown, but across the nation. As Barbara Solomon demonstrates in her book, *In the Company of Educated Women,* opportunities for women both in the work force and in education expanded enormously as young men were mobilized for war. Suddenly women were needed in jobs previously closed to them, and colleges needed women to fill the classrooms left newly empty as men departed for the war. One consequence was that some women found places in academic fields from which they had previously been effectively excluded. The early 1940s, for example, saw the number of women majoring in the sciences expand markedly; and institutions such as Harvard admitted the first twelve women to Medical School in 1945, including Shirley Gallup, Class of 1945.[7] Gains in many areas were not permanent; when the G.I.s returned, women were often moved out of the jobs and positions they had just acquired and back into the newly idealized realm of the nuclear family. It was not possible, however, simply to erase the legacy of women's increased access to certain forms of cultural power. Especially within the professions, women continued to exploit the opportunities that the early forties had opened up for them, though it was not until the late 1960s and early 1970s that a revitalized woman's movement began again to agitate for equity for women in every sphere of national life.

At Brown the war catapulted the women of Pembroke into a central position in university life. At certain points in the early forties there were only about 250 male students on campus, most of them seventeen-year-olds waiting to be drafted. Women in many ways held the institution

Women Who Have Served on the Corporation of Brown University

Board of Fellows
Doris Brown Reed '27, 1969–75
Ruth Burt Ekstrom '53, 1977–88
  (*Secretary of the Corporation,*
  1982–88)
Nancy Lillian Buc '65, 1980–
Eleanor H. McMahon, M.A. '54,
  1988–99

Christine Dunlap Farnham, Class of 1948, alumnae trustee from 1976 to 1981, receiving a Brown Bear award for service to Brown. An archive of materials about women at Brown and in Rhode Island was named to honor her memory. INSET: Doris Brown Reed, Class of 1927, on left, who became the first woman fellow on the Brown Corporation in 1969, examines the model for Verney and Woolley Halls with Dean Nancy Duke Lewis and President Barnaby C. Keeney.

Board of Trustees	(T) Term
Anna Canada Swain '11, 1949–56 (T)	(A) Alumnae

Virginia Piggot Verney '28, 1951–58 (T)
Sarah Morse Beardsley '18, 1956–63 (T)
Doris Brown Reed '27, 1956–62; 1963–69 (T)
Pauline Barrows Hughes '21, 1960–67 (T)
Elizabeth Goodale Kenyon '39, 1965–70 (A)
Penelope Hartland Thunberg '40, 1966–71 (A)
Frances Weeden Gibson '45, 1967–72 (T)
Vera Matteson Sundquist '29, 1967–72 (A)
Sophie Trent Stevens '39, 1968–73 (A)
Barbara Susan Mosbacher '45, 1969–74; 1981–87 (T)
Bette Lipkin Brown '46, 1970–75 (A)
Sophie Schaffer Blistein '41, 1971–76 (A)
Ruth Burt Ekstrom '53, 1972–77 (T)
Ruth Harris Wolf '41, 1972–77 (A)
Nancy Lillian Buc '65, 1973–78 (A)
Elizabeth Jackson Phillips '45, 1973–78 (T)
Ann Francis Farish, 1974–79 (T)
Jean Elizabeth Howard [Baker] '70, 1974–81 (T)
Isabelle Russek Leeds, 1974–79 (T)
Joyce Wetherald Fairchild '47, 1975–80 (A)
Angela Brown Fischer, 1975–80 (T)
Helen Howard Nowlis '34, 1975–80 (T)
Christine Dunlap Farnham '48, 1976–81 (A)
Ann Ruth Leven '62, 1976–81 (A)
Rita Caslowitz Michaelson '50, 1977–82 (A)
Judith Cameron Whittaker '59, 1977–82 (T)
Carol Schwartz Greenwald '65, 1978–83 (A)
Julianne Heller Prager '46, 1978–83 (T)
Sally Hill Cooper '52, 1979–84 (A)
Beth Becker Pollock '51, 1979–84 (T)
Martha Sharp Joukowsky '58, 1980–85 (T)
Marie Jean Langlois '64, 1980–85; 1988–94
  (A/T) *(Treasurer of the University, 1988–91)*
Margaret Conant Michael '51, 1981–86 (A)
Nancy Gidwitz '70, 1982–88 (T)
Barbara Martin Leonard '46, 1982–87 (A)
Sheryl Grooms Brissett Chapman '71, 1983–89 (T)
Victoria Santopietro Lederberg '59, 1983–89 (A)
Jean Macphail Weber '54, 1983–88 (A)
Barbara Landis Chase '67, 1984–90 (A)
Sally Leung, 1984–90 (T)
Helena-Hope Gammell '48, 1985–91 (T)
Susan Adler Kaplan '58, 1986–92 (A)
Martha Clark Briley '71, 1987–93 (T)
Donna Constance Erickson Williamson '74, 1987–93 (A)
Gail Caslowitz Levine '63, 1988–94 (A)
Norma Caslowitz Munves '54, 1988–94 (T)
Phyllis Van Horn Tillinghast '51, 1989–95 (A)
Agnes Gund [Shapiro], 1990–96 (T)
Wendy Jo Strothman [Metzger] '72, 1990–96 (A)
Marcia D. Lloyd '68, 1991–97 (T)
Jane Lamson Peppard '67, 1991–97 (A)

225

together during the war years, and it was in the 1940s that another drive was mounted to get women on the Brown Corporation. But again, this quest was frustrated, although indirect progress was made when, in 1942, alumnae were for the first time allowed to vote for alumni representatives to the corporation. Ironically, while not themselves considered fit to serve on the board, women were accorded the privilege of voting for the men who *would* serve. In order to make the most of this new "privilege," the Alumnae Association, again under the leadership of Alice Chase, sent out a letter urging the alumnae to vote to show their interest in the administration of the university. In 1945, more women voted in the trustee elections than did men.

The main prize, however, the actual election or appointment of an alumna to the corporation, had not yet been achieved. Finally, in 1949, after a history of nearly fifty years of women's repeated efforts to join the governing bodies of the institution, President Henry Wriston made the long awaited move. He appointed Anna Canada Swain, Class of 1911, as a term trustee. In doing so, he acknowledged the importance of women to the effort of maintaining the fabric of the university during the war years, and he was, of course, paying tribute to the distinguished record of accomplishment the alumnae had maintained during the long period since the founding of the Women's College in 1895.[8]

Anna Canada Swain exemplified such accomplishment. She was a national leader in Baptist missionary activities, and Brown University had been traditionally affiliated with the Baptist denomination. She was also a member of the Executive Committee of the World Council of Churches, and she was a past president of the Rhode Island branch of the American Association of University Women. She had also been active in serving Brown, particularly as chairperson of the Gift Committee that had raised money for the building of Andrews Hall. Interestingly, the women of the Pembroke Alumnae Association who had been urging the election of women to the board were not consulted about Swain's appointment. Doris Hopkins Stapelton, Class of 1928, who was soon to become president of the Alumnae Association, recalls how surprised she was when President Wriston announced Swain's appointment at the annual Alumnae Association dinner. She reports that while the women present were very happy with Swain's appointment and very proud of her accomplishments, many felt they were being asked to accept as a gift, as an act of largesse, what equity suggests they should have obtained by right and through the direct exercise of the vote.[9] It was yet another fifteen years before women graduates of Brown University could cast ballots for women trustees. In the immediately intervening decade, however, four more women – Virginia Piggot Verney, Class of 1928; Doris Brown Reed, Class of 1927; Sarah Morse Beardsley, Class of 1918; and Pauline Barrows Hughes, Class of 1921 – were appointed to terms on the Board of Trustees. With the appointment of Hughes in 1960, three women (Reed and Beardsley were the other two) were simultaneously serving on the board. Notably, the first women trustees shared a common characteristic: they were married, generally to prominent men, but had no children, a pattern different from that of the male trustees.

The irony remained, however, that even in the 1950s the time was not deemed "right" for the alumnae actually to elect their own representatives. That concession, requested on multiple occasions since the famous petition of 1927, only was granted by the corporation in the mid-1960s. When President Henry M. Wriston wrote in retrospect about the appointment of Anna Canada Swain to the corporation in 1949, he implied that resistance to this move had come, not from him, but from within the corporation itself. He commented: "It is extraordinary how slowly the position of women has been recognized in boards of trustees, especially in the East.... Brown, despite the fact that Pembroke College had been part of the University for half a century, had never elected a woman.... it required twelve years of patient effort before the first woman trustee was appointed. After that election, further nominations occasioned no resistance, indeed no remark."[10] This account is interesting for several reasons. First, Wriston implies that from at least 1937 on, the university president was in favor of the appointment of a woman trustee. Second, his statement somewhat blurs the significant difference between the appointment by the corporation and the election by the alumnae/i of women trustees. While a few women did continue to be appointed to positions as term trustees through the 1950s and early 1960s, women were not elected by the graduates of Brown University until another significant initiative was undertaken, this time spearheaded by Elizabeth Goodale Kenyon, Class of 1939, president of the Pembroke Alumnae Association in 1964 and after her by Vera Matteson Sundquist, Class of 1929, president in 1965.

Sophie Schaffer Blistein, Class of 1941, was an integral part of this last phase of the long campaign to get women trustees elected to the corporation. She recalls that at an Alumnae Association banquet on May 31, 1963, President Barnaby Keeney had seemed to suggest that the time was right to elect women to the corporation.[11] Impishly, he had said that "To put an alumna on the ballot, all you need is 150 signatures on a petition."[12] The grounds for this claim, apparently, were that in university documents referring to alumni and their rights to elect trustees, *alumni* could be construed as a generic term covering both men and women. In actuality, of course, electing women to the corporation was much more difficult than merely getting 150 names on a petition and asserting that the word *alumni* meant members of both sexes. Keeney's remarks were taken as a sanction for renewed efforts, and in April of 1964 an extremely important meeting occurred at the Faculty Club between representatives of the Associated Alumni and representatives of the Pembroke Alumnae Association with Rosemary Pierrel, dean of Pembroke College, and Doris Reed and Pauline Hughes, alumnae then serving as term trustees, also in attendance. At that time Earl Harrington, Jr. was president of the Associated Alumni, and Elizabeth Kenyon of the Pembroke Alumnae Association. The meeting was crucial because the maximum number of alumni/ae trustee positions on the corporation was fixed at fourteen, and by an agreement between the corporation and the Associated Alumni first forged in 1942 and then modified in 1954, all of these seats were to go to alumni. The corporation was not willing to expand the number of positions allotted to alumni/ae representatives, so the Associated Alumni would, in effect, have to cede some of its places to alumnae. Those present agreed that this was the desired outcome, and that it was preferable that the two associations establish a committee to work out details of such an arrangement than that the corporation appoint an ad hoc committee to devise such a plan.[13]

The business went forward with dispatch. Sophie Blistein chaired the committee charged with working out the details of the agreement. On January 12, 1965, an agreement between the corporation and the Associated Alumni and the Pembroke Alumnae Association was formally signed. It mandated that the term for alumni/ae trustees be reduced from seven to five years, and it proposed that at the end of five years, four of the fourteen seats reserved for alumni/ae be occupied by women, ten by men. This would be accomplished by electing two alumni trustees each year and one alumna in four out of every five years. These numbers were to reflect the relative proportion of men and women in the total alumni/ alumnae body. In 1965 Elizabeth Kenyon became the first elected alumnae trustee. Fittingly, Kenyon was the niece of Nettie Goodale Murdock, the first alumna to be appointed to the Executive Committee of the Women's College. Murdock died in 1964, just one year before her niece assumed a seat on the governing body of the institution in which she had pioneered as one of the first women students nearly seventy-three years before. Blistein stressed that without the support of the Associated Alumni president, Earl Harrington, and of its executive secretary, Paul Mackesey, the agreement would never have been worked out so easily and quickly. In September of 1978, a second agreement increased the number of alumnae trustees to five; in October 1981 a third agreement increased the number to six.

In 1966 Penelope Hartlund Thunberg, Class of 1940, became the second elected woman trustee. Among the women who followed was Elizabeth Jackson Phillips, Class of 1945, the first African-American woman to serve on the corporation. Gradually, the number of women who served as term trustees increased also, though never, even to this day, approaching parity with the number of men so appointed. In 1991, thirty-one men serve as trustees, as do eleven women, six elected by the alumnae/i and five appointed by the president on the recommendation of the corporation, in comparison to eight men elected by the alumnae/i and twenty-three men appointed by the corporation. In short, while the number of women trustees still lags considerably behind the number of men serving in the same posts, enormous gains have been made since the petition of 1927 when the then all-male corporation had determined the time not yet right for women's inclusion in its midst. Not until alumnae were elected as trustees did women with a variety of life-styles, including women with children, join the corporation.

The inclusion of women on the Board of Fellows, in effect the senate of the corporation, requires a separate account. Only after the election of women trustees had been accomplished in 1965 did the time seem right to appoint a woman to this body. In 1969, Doris Reed, who had already served two influential terms as an appointed trustee, was made the first woman member of the Brown University Board of Fellows. Ray Heffner was then president, and in a gesture of far-reaching symbolic significance, he appointed the first African-American fellow, J. Saunders Redding, Class of 1928, and the first Jewish fellow, Alfred Joslin, Class of 1935, at the same time as he appointed Doris Reed, the first woman fellow. She was followed in 1977 by Ruth Burt Ekstrom, Class of 1953, in 1980 by Nancy L. Buc, Class of 1965, and in 1988 by Eleanor H. McMahon, M.A. 1954. Those who served with Reed on the corporation, both men and women, speak of the enormous influence she quietly exerted during her terms both as trustee and as fellow. As Sophie Blistein reports, "whenever women needed support, Doris was there."[14] Blistein recalls that when she herself was asked to stand for election to the corporation, she wondered aloud whether she had enough of the three qualities – wealth, wisdom, and work – Henry Wriston had delineated as the requisites for a successful trustee. She recalls Reed telling her that what she lacked in any of these categories she more than compensated for by her long memory of the institution and of women's struggles within it.

The 1980s saw other important breakthroughs in regard to women's position on the governing board. In 1982, Ruth Ekstrom, then a fellow and formerly a trustee, was appointed to serve as the first woman secretary of the corporation. As secretary, she wielded considerable power, sitting on the Advisory and Executive Committee and on the crucial Committee on the Senior Administration, a committee charged with the task of reviewing the performance of the most senior members of the university's administrative staff. She also automatically became chair of the Committee on Consultation between the corporation and the faculty. Besides the actual power Ekstrom held by virtue of this office, there was also important visual symbolism involved in her appointment as secretary. When the corporation meets, the fellows sit on one side of the room, trustees on the other; at the table at the front of the room sit the university president, who officially chairs the Board of Fellows; the university chancellor, who officially chairs the Board of Trustees; and the corporation secretary. As Nancy L. Buc, a trustee and now a fellow, remarked, "it made a tremendous difference the first time a woman sat at that table. There was a woman right at the symbolic, and literal, center of power."[15]

In another crucial move, the 1980s saw the appointment of Marie J. Langlois, Class of 1964, then a term trustee, as the first woman treasurer of the university. The treasurer serves as the link between all the corporation committees dealing with financial matters, helping to coordinate all aspects of Brown's fiscal policy. In 1991, as treasurer, Langlois serves on the following corporation committees: Budget and Finance, Investments, Advisory and Executive, Development and Audit. She offers policy advice about such matters as whether immediate capital needs should be met by borrowing or by taking money from the endowment and helps to decide what percent of the interest earned by the endowment should be available to support university operating expenses in any given year. An experienced investment banker and twice head of the Brown Fund, Langlois was appointed treasurer because of her skills and experience. But, once again, the symbolic resonance of her appointment was also very important. Overarching fiscal responsibility for Brown University was for the first time officially lodged in female hands. While a woman has not yet served as chancellor of the university, that is, as the chief executive officer of the corporation, the time may some day soon also be right for that honor and responsibility to fall to a woman.

The Changing Position of Women on the Corporation

Obviously, the role women *could* play on the corporation has varied from the time Anna Canada Swain was appointed as the first woman trustee in 1949. For at least two decades the number of women on the corporation remained so small that women remained a token presence on the board. In the view of some of the women appointed or elected to the corporation in the sixties, choice committee assignments often eluded them. Budget and Finance, Development, the Advisory and Executive Committee – these powerful committees were less often peopled by women than committees having to do with student life, the libraries, or faculty relations. Traditional expectations about the expertise, respectively, of men and women seem to some extent to have governed committee assignments, with men planning capital campaigns, overseeing investment portfolios, and deciding when new buildings would be built, and women attending to quality of life issues.[16] It must be said, however, that such assignments could be exciting and important ones. Elizabeth Kenyon was appointed to the Student Life Committee during her five-year term as trustee from 1965 to 1970. This was the period when student activism was at its height and Brown was attempting to cope with anti-war protests, demands for coeducation, demands for institution of the "new curriculum," and demands for the end of parietals. As Kenyon recalled, when speaking to the Pembroke Center Associates in 1984: "Need I tell you that our meetings of the Committee on Student Life were lively and long? We often had dinner meetings that lasted until around midnight. A hot topic among many we considered was the curriculum; Elliot Maxwell and Ira Magaziner were both student representatives on our committee. Brown's 'New Curriculum' [authored by Maxwell and Magaziner] was born a few years later."[17]

In other areas, progress was slower. Even when women had achieved some quite remarkable success in the world of finance beyond the university, that expertise was not always tapped until the women themselves pushed for utilization of their talents. Penelope Hartland Thunberg, the second woman elected to the Board of Trustees, took office in 1966. When elected, she had already been active in university governance matters as a member of the Pembroke Advisory Committee. The holder of a Ph.D. in economics and at an earlier point a faculty member in the Brown Economics Department, at the time of her election as a Brown trustee Thunberg had recently been appointed by President Lyndon Johnson to a seat on the U.S. Tariff Commission (now known as the U.S. International Trade Commission). Thunberg reports that, being eager to serve the university well as a trustee, after several meetings she decided to tell the officers of the corporation where she felt her expertise would be most useful. Approaching Patrick J. James, then treasurer of the corporation, she told him that as a Washington-based economist she felt she would be most helpful on committees where her knowledge of policy developments in Washington might have a bearing on the university's investment strategies.

She reports being greeted with a look of incredulity. James slapped his forehead, stepped backward, and exclaimed that he had "been looking for someone from Washington to serve on the Investments Committee, but had never thought . . . ," Thunberg reported. "What he meant, but was too polite to say," she added, "is that he didn't expect to find that someone wearing a skirt."[18] Happily, she was eventually appointed both to the Investment Committee and to the Advisory and Executive Committee.

Nancy L. Buc, also a former trustee and now a fellow, concurs that numbers matter. She argues that in the early days of women on the corporation, just having women there was an important fact in itself, but their talents were often underutilized, and they were too frequently positioned as *the* representative of the female point of view.[19] She argued, however, that women have increasingly been used in ways central to the life of the corporation. She herself is a good example. Elected as an alumnae trustee in 1973 and appointed a fellow in 1980, she has served on a number of crucial corporation committees. These include several terms on the Advisory and Executive Committee, two Presidential Search Committees (those which led to the appointment of Howard Swearer and of Vartan Gregorian), the Legal and Governmental Affairs Committee, the Committee on the Structure and Function of the Corporation, the Biomedical Affairs Committee, and others. In 1991 she is chair of the Budget and Finance Committee. In fact, in 1991, five of the twenty-two corporation committees are chaired by women. Victoria Santopietro Lederberg, Class of 1959, chairs the Committee on Legal and Government Affairs; Nancy L. Buc, the very powerful Budget and Finance Committee; Barbara Landis Chase, Class of 1967, the Committee on Admissions and Financial Aid; Marie Langlois, the Committee on Proxy Issues; and Eleanor McMahon, the Committee on Graduate Education and Research. Commenting on this development, Corporation Treasurer Langlois, who is serving her second term as trustee, says that in her view women hold these positions because they are perceived as capable and not because the corporation feels it must give women token representation.[20]

Looking back over nearly twenty years of involvement with the Brown Corporation, Ruth Ekstrom, former fellow and former trustee, makes the point that when there were relatively few women on the board, each woman was asked to "represent" the entire sex. "What do the women think?" is a question she remember being asked frequently, and one which she never felt comfortable answering, arguing that women, like men, think differently from one another on any number of issues. The assumption that there is *a* woman's point of view erases differences among women and allows institutions to be content with appointing token women to positions of power since one stands for all, an assumption that would never be made about men. That is why, Ekstrom argues, when she was appointed to the Board of Fellows she pressed vigorously for the appointment of other women, so that no one would be forced into the position of token spokesperson.[21]

Part of the problem of full utilization of women's talents on the corporation, especially in the early years of their inclusion, also stemmed from the position of women in society at large. Many but not all of the first women appointed or elected to the corporation were of the age of their male counterparts, but did not have their experience in business or finance or the professions. Instead, they had often been active in volunteer organizations. In the next wave of trustees, more individuals with experience in business, the professions, and academe appeared. But because of the earlier exclusion of the majority of women from these realms, many of them were relatively young when appointed to the corporation. The author of this essay, for example, was appointed when she was twenty-six and finishing her Ph.D. at Yale. Such women were in some ways at a disadvantage vis-a-vis their male counterparts on the corporation in that they were younger and lacking in the kinds of experience a fifty-year-old chief executive officer takes for granted. Optimistically, it will take several decades of further social transformation before the effects of generations of gender inequality will cease to be visible in such institutions as boards of trustees.

Given this fact, it remains a question exactly how women on the corporation should position themselves vis-a-vis their status *as* women. On the one hand lies the Scylla of assimilation and on the other the Charybdis of narrow, special interest politics. Many women who have served on the Brown Corporation feel that, like all other trustees, their job is to consider the welfare of the entire university and the needs of all its constituencies, not just the needs of women. They resent being called upon only when someone must speak "for women." They want both the plurality of women and the diversity of their own interests and areas of expertise acknowledged; and they argue that there should be no difference in the treatment and utilization of men and women members of the board. This is an attractive position in many ways, but there is always the danger that to gain acceptance as a mainstream member of the board, women will implicitly have to adapt themselves to conventions of behavior and thought developed in situations and institutional settings traditionally dominated by men. In such cases, equity, defined as treating women and men the same way, may actually mean rewarding those women who successfully, if unconsciously, conform to masculine definitions of what constitutes competence and good sense. This is the assimilationist nightmare of a world where there is no friction between genders because one has been entirely co-opted.

On the other hand, many of the women who have served on the Brown Corporation feel themselves part of a tradition of feminist activism founded on the assumption that in a social world in which gender inequality exists, women who ascend to positions of power must use that power to speak for values and needs ignored by the dominant culture. They argue that in the long run the welfare of an entire institution depends upon acknowledging the realities of social difference, whether those are differences of race, gender, or social class, and changing institutions to accommodate the needs of different groups, rather than changing the groups to fit a normative institutional or social model. Women trustees who identify with this position see their jobs, at least in part, as being in some way advocates for the needs of women, though most would deny that women form a homogeneous group or that as trustees they should focus *only* on women's issues, since to do so would be extremely limiting and would quickly devolve into parochial special interest politics.

The history of women on the Brown Corporation suggests a canny ability on the part of most women trustees to move skillfully between their roles as advocates for women's needs and their roles as caretakers of the entire institution. Ruth Ekstrom, former trustee and former fellow, argues that to be effective as a woman trustee requires knowing when to resist the temptation to raise feminist concerns, as well as when to push full steam ahead; when to work behind the scenes and when to "go public."[22] This is a theme sounded repeatedly by women who have served on the board. Legitimacy depends on not being perceived as too strident, too militant, too focused on one set of issues. But working for women's needs sometimes requires speaking out in ways that can lead to marginalization. The women trustee or the woman fellow performs a difficult balancing act.

A History of Achievement

Certainly the women on the corporation, collectively and singly, have managed, through intelligence and tact, to be effective advocates for women's concerns even while playing other roles in their capacities as trustees and fellows. A good example is afforded by the role of women trustees in establishing the first university chair designated specifically for an exceptional woman member of the faculty. When the university launched a capital campaign in the mid-1970s, several women trustees, including Ruth Harris Wolf, Class of 1941, argued that some part of the campaign should target the needs of women. Specifically, she suggested that the university raise an endowment to complete the funding for a university chair in honor of Dean Nancy Duke Lewis, former dean of Pembroke College. At her death Lewis had left the balance of her estate to Brown to be applied toward establishing a chair for a woman professor. By the mid-70s, with the addition of occasional gifts by alumnae, the Nancy Duke Lewis fund totalled about two hundred and fifty thousand dollars. However, endowing a chair required at least one million dollars. Luckily, Wolf had had some experience with fund raising, and she took it as her task, with the help of the Development Office, to raise three quarters of a million dollars.

In many ways it was fitting that Wolf should work to raise the money to establish a chair honoring Dean Nancy Duke Lewis. In 1953 Wolf had collaborated with Doris Stapelton, then the president of the Pembroke Alumnae Association, in establishing the first Pembroke College fund. Before that time, there had been little focus on raising funds specifically from women graduates to support the needs of Pembroke College. It was Dean Nancy Duke Lewis who had encouraged Stapelton and Wolf in their endeavors, since it was Lewis' belief that Pembroke College had to establish a distinctive identity for itself and not be overshadowed by the men's college. Consequently, she encouraged Stapelton and Wolf as they worked to establish a separate mailing list of Pembroke graduates and to solicit funds from them. Since the university provided very little in the way of material support for this initiative, much of the sorting, mailing, and opening of envelopes was done by alumnae working on a volunteer basis. As Wolf says, "It was definitely a shoe box affair."[23]

At the end-of-the-year alumnae dinner, however, Wolf was able to announce that the first annual Pembroke College Fund had raised twenty-five thousand dollars. This fund-raising effort was so successful that the university continued it in subsequent years and increased staff support for it. In 1955 Stapelton was appointed executive secretary of the Pembroke Alumnae Association and used that position to encourage the work of Pembroke clubs across the country and to promote the growth of the Pembroke College Fund.[24]

When twenty years later, Wolf accepted the challenge to raise money to endow a chair in the name of Nancy Duke Lewis, she certainly did so with some sense of how daunting such an undertaking would be, but also with profound respect for the dean who had so ably promoted the identity of Pembroke in the 1950s and who had supported Wolf in her earlier fund-raising ventures. Early in the campaign, crucial support was given by a fellow trustee, H. Anthony Ittleson, Class of 1960, in the form of a quarter-million dollar gift to match the quarter million dollars already in the Lewis fund. In one stroke the fund doubled in size, leaving "only" another half million to be raised. Eventually, thanks to the efforts of many hands, the goal was reached. A plaque in the Crystal Room of Alumnae Hall bears the names of all those who gave $1,000 or more to this important campaign.

In 1980 historian Joan Scott was appointed the first Nancy Duke Lewis Professor to come as a tenured professor from the outside. She served until 1985 when she was appointed professor of social science at the Institute for Advanced Study in Princeton. Scott was followed by a critic of French literature, Naomi Schor. Like Scott, Schor makes a consideration of women's role in culture a central aspect of her work. Both holders of the chair have been women of exceptional intellectual ability with a profound commitment to enhancing the status of women and of women's studies within the institution. In this case, initiatives taken by women on the corporation have had a direct impact on the academic possibilities open to university students of both genders.

Women corporation members have also had a role to play in establishing and supporting the Pembroke Center for Teaching and Research on Women. After the merger of Pembroke and Brown in 1971, many people were concerned that the name and the history of Pembroke College would be lost to memory, along with the specific institutional emphasis on the needs of women that had been almost automatically afforded by the coordinate college structure. Prompted by women faculty, administrators, and trustees alike, President Howard Swearer established the Pembroke Center with Nancy Duke Lewis Professor Joan Scott as the first director. Scott worked to obtain research funding from the Ford Foundation, the National Endowment for the Humanities, and the Rockefeller Foundation to begin an ongoing faculty and post-doctoral research program which still continues. The Pembroke Center bears the name of the women's college, and part of its function is preservative: to make sure the history of women at Brown is never forgotten. Another function is generative: to insure that new paradigms of feminist knowledge are being constructed by men and women at Brown in conversation with feminist scholars across the globe.

Women of the corporation have, from the first, been active on the Advisory Board of the center and active on its committees. Christine Dunlap Farnham, Class of 1948 and alumnae trustee from 1976–81, worked with enormous persistence to set up the Pembroke Center Associates, an alumnae support group, to begin fund-raising efforts, and to establish an archive of materials in the John Hay Library relating to the history of Pembroke College and of women in Rhode Island. Jean Howard, Class of 1970 and term trustee from 1974 to 1981, followed Farnham as president of the Advisory Board after Farnham's untimely death in 1984. The archives, established largely at Farnham's initiative, now bear her name. Corporation members Ruth Ekstrom, Nancy L. Buc, Sophie Blistein, and Marie Langlois have served, officially and unofficially, as advisors to the center's academic and financial initiatives. As part of the events that in 1991–92 celebrate the centennial of women's participation in the academic life of Brown University, a new fund-raising effort is in progress to provide the Pembroke Center with a three million dollar endowment of its own. Marie Langlois, trustee and university treasurer, is spearheading this campaign with the help of the center's director, Professor Karen Newman, and the Brown Development Office. As with the funding of the Nancy Duke Lewis Chair, women trustees and women faculty are working together to secure an academic resource that will be of lasting benefit, not just to women students, but to all members of the university community.

Both of these initiatives, the establishment of the Nancy Duke Lewis Chair and the establishment of the Pembroke Center, occurred in the wake of the merger of Brown and Pembroke in 1971. This complicated event seemed to many, especially to the students who worked to bring it about, to signal the end of "ladies' education" at Brown and to promise the full integration of women into every facet of the university's life. To many others, especially alumnae who had worked to secure Pembroke College as a place where women's needs would receive special attention, the merger seemed to signal the loss of valuable traditions and women-centered institutional structures. Among the various university constituencies concerned with the consequences of the merger, the corporation had its own worries about and investments in this decision. What would happen to alumnae loyalty to the institution once Pembroke College no longer existed as a separate entity? Would alumnae stop giving money to Brown? How would full coeducation affect the recruitment of students? Would SAT scores rise or fall? Would the number of applicants plummet or surge? And since the absolute number of women students would rise considerably with the merger and eventually reach parity with the number of men, would the university be able to offer them appropriate support services (academic services, health services, placement services) within the merged entity?

Women corporation members had their own versions of these concerns. Above all, they were worried that the special needs of women would be overlooked in an institution in which the faculty was still predominantly male and in which many of the separate organizations such as the Pembroke Student Government Association and the Pembroke student newspaper were in one stroke being abolished, along with the separate administrative services until then offered through Pembroke Hall. Moreover, women on the corporation were by the mid-1970s present in much greater numbers than had been the case earlier. By 1975 women could be said to be more than token presences on the board, and in that year, four years after the merger, the corporation moved to establish an ad hoc Committee on the Status of Women at Brown. In part, the charge to the Committee read:

> The Committee shall assess the consequences of coeducation at Brown five years after the merger of Pembroke College with The College and shall make recommendations for further improvements in the educational opportunities offered to women. It shall have the responsibility of formulating and recommending to the Corporation goals for the University with respect to the education of women students, and the role which women are to play at Brown, including teaching and administrative functions. As part of its task the Committee shall assess the role which women presently play in the life of the Brown community and shall recommend ways in which the talents of women may be more fully utilized and their needs more fully met.[25]

The goals were a greater institutional awareness of how coeducation had affected the lives of everyone, but especially women, at Brown and a concerted commitment to improve the model in ways beneficial to women on the campus.

In my second year as a term trustee, I was appointed to head this corporation committee which also included corporation members Ruth Wolf, Arthur Taylor, Penelope Hartland Thunberg, Elizabeth Phillips, Paul Johnson, Knight Edwards, and Jay Fidler, and was given administrative support through the office of Dean of the Graduate School Maurice Glicksman. The committee decided that to avoid bias or the potential whitewashing of problem areas, it should secure some outside aid in carrying out its charge. The Ford Foundation and the Rockefeller Family Fund, with the assistance of their program officers, Mariam Chamberlain and Marilyn Levy, provided grants to conduct a wide-ranging study of the impact of coeducation at Brown, and educational sociologist Carole Leland was hired to head the research team.

The study focused on such aspects of women's life at Brown as: how the institution affected women's academic self-esteem, preparedness for graduate school, career choices, and preparation for life inside or outside families. Questionnaires were distributed to cohorts of undergraduates in each class, and in-depth interviews were conducted with about sixty of them. Some data was collected from other institutions (Wellesley, Princeton, Stony Brook, Barnard, and Dartmouth) so that comparisons could be made with students in other educational settings. In addition, material was systematically collected concerning SAT scores and high school class standings of men and women before and after the merger, student satisfaction with the ratio of 50 percent men and 50 percent women on the campus after the merger, alumnae/i attitudes to the merger, and women students' participation in leadership positions before and after the merger.

What emerged from this complicated study was a mixed picture of coeducation's effects on the institution and on women students, in particular. The good news was that the move to coeducation had not harmed the quality of the student body as measured by class standing in high school and SAT scores; moreover, the even ratio of men to women in the student body and the coeducational structure of Brown seemed to be major sources of student satisfaction with Brown once they were admitted. In addition, though there were pockets of resistance to the merger among the alumnae, most had come to accept it as a positive good.

On the other hand, the study unearthed a number of problems, some expected and some quite unanticipated. For example, while the recruitment of women faculty had become a university priority, many fields, and especially but not exclusively the sciences, still contained few women professors. This seemed to be one, but not the only reason, for the unanticipated drop in women's academic self-confidence during their years at Brown. While women entered Brown with higher grades and college board scores than men, both their grades and their intellectual self-esteem fell below that of men during their college years. This was, in some ways, the most disturbing finding in the report; and it cannot be explained by any one cause. The relative paucity of female faculty in some fields seemed to be part of the explanation; unconscious bias in the classroom seemed to be another part; lack of mentoring relationships between faculty and women students seemed to be a contributing factor in other cases. While workshops to call attention to unconscious sexism in pedagogical situations are a partial solution, the continuing of affirmative action initiatives in the hiring of female faculty remains a crucial component of any long-term solution.

Another disturbing finding was that the number of women students in campus leadership positions fell markedly in the period immediately following the merger. When a number of student organizations run by and for Pembroke students disappeared with the merger, women did not – at least for the years in the 1970s when data was collected – assume one half of leadership positions in merged campus organizations. This suggested to the corporation committee the need, at the very least, to offer leadership training programs targeted to women students.

A third area of concern emerged in relation to men's and women's expectations concerning family life and work. At the time of the study, most Brown undergraduates, both men and women, wanted to combine careers and families. But they differed considerably in their responses to questions about whether and how long mothers should stay home with young children. Men in general felt women should stay home for longer periods than women themselves felt they should, and neither group articulated a very complex awareness of what "stopping out" for a number of years would mean for the eventual career aspirations of women who did so. In general, with the continuing pressure being exerted on traditional family structures in American culture and with the ongoing transformations of sex and gender ideology affecting college students in the 1980s, it seems reasonable to suppose that students need all the skilled institutional support they can get in planning for equitable arrangements of work and reproductive lives.

The funding of the Nancy Duke Lewis Chair, the establishment of the Pembroke Center, the research into coeducation's effects conducted by the Corporation Committee on the Status of Women – these are just a few of the instances of the educational impact of women's long-delayed inclusion on the university's highest governing board. Only the efforts of several generations of women made that inclusion a reality. They were women such as Nettie Goodale Murdock, Alice Manchester Chase, and Margaret Shove Morriss who would not accept the bland pronouncement that "the time has not arrived." As Marie Langlois has noted, women now serve in nearly every capacity on the board from which they were excluded, holding positions from university treasurer to chair of the Budget and Finance Committee to chair of the Committee on Admission and Financial Aid. No longer token presences, women are now central players in the corporation's life. But in doing the work of the corporation, women have in many instances quietly and sometimes not so quietly redefined that work to include a concern for the university's treatment of women, minorities, and others whose backgrounds make them embodiments of cultural difference. In the tough balancing act of striving for equity for all while remembering the reality and value of difference, the woman corporation member finds her difficult place and voice.

NOTES

1. The petition, dated 11 June 1927, also asks that until such time as arrangements for the election of alumnae to the corporation can be arranged, the corporation should appoint a representative alumna to a vacant undenominational trusteeship. As we shall see, having a woman appointed by the corporation to such a trusteeship would itself be a protracted struggle, though not so protracted as the campaign to attain the direct election of alumnae members of the corporation.

2. In writing the history of women's struggles to gain access to seats on the corporation I am indebted, among other accounts, to Doris Stapelton's narrative of these events as

recorded in the essay, "Women and the Brown Corporation," *Pembroke Associates Newsletter* (Spring 1984): 2–4.

3. Mariam K. Chamberlain, "Women as Trustees," in *Women in Academe: Progress and Prospects* (New York: Russell Sage Foundation, 1988), pp. 333–56.

4. Grace E. Hawk, *Pembroke College in Brown University: The First Seventy-Five Years 1891–1966* (Providence: Brown University Press, 1967), p. 146.

5. Marion Shirley Cole, Report on the Meeting of the Executive Committee of the Women's College, June, 1935, p. 16, Christine Dunlap Farnham Archives, Brown University.

6. Marion Shirley Cole, Report on the Meeting of the Executive Committee of the Women's College, June, 1936, p. 14, Farnham Archives.

7. Barbara Miller Solomon, *In the Company of Educated Women* (New Haven: Yale University Press, 1985), p. 188. A picture of Shirley Gallup with the other eleven women entering Harvard Medical School in September of 1945 is included among the photos preceding p. 115 in Solomon's book.

8. Excerpts from the minutes of the corporation meeting of 18 June 1949 indicate that Anna Canada Swain was nominated by the Committee on Trustee Vacancies for confirmation as a trustee on that date. President Wriston spoke in favor of her nomination, and the trustees and fellows each concurred unanimously in endorsing the nomination.

9. Doris Stapelton interview with the author, 11 April 1991.

10. Henry Wriston, *Academic Procession: Reflections of a College President* (New York: Columbia University Press, 1959), p. 73.

11. Sophie Blistein interview with the author, 21 April 1991.

12. Barnaby Keeney's address to the Pembroke Alumnae Association dinner, 31 May 1963, p. 4. Farnham Archives.

13. This meeting occurred on 24 April 1964. Those in attendance were Earl Harrington, Jr., president of the Associated Alumni; Stanley Mathes, immediate past president; two alumni trustees, Foster B. Davis and John Chafee; Paul Mackesey, executive officer of the Associated Alumni; Rosemary Pierrel, dean of Pembroke College; Elizabeth Kenyon, president of the Pembroke Alumnae Association; Vera Sundquist, president-elect; two alumnae term trustees, Doris Reed and Pauline Hughes; and Doris Stapelton, executive secretary of the Pembroke Alumnae Association.

14. Sophie Blistein interview with the author, 21 April 1991.

15. Nancy L. Buc interview with the author, 18 February 1991.

16. In many ways the experience of the first women on the Brown Corporation paralleled the experience of women who entered male-dominated business organizations. In the business world, according to Rosabeth Moss Kanter, the pioneering women were often treated as if they resembled women on the average, with little regard for their individual skills and abilities. When there are few women in an organization, says Kanter, men often ascribe sex-stereotyped roles to them, such as "mother," "sex object," "pet," (group mascot), or "iron maiden" (militant and unapproachable). See M. Milman and R. M. Kanter, *Another Voice: Female Perspectives on Social Life and Social Science* (New York: Anchor Press, 1975).

17. Elizabeth Goodale Kenyon's address to the Pembroke Center Associates, 25 May 1984, p. 2.

18. Penelope Hartland Thunberg interview with the author, 23 February 1991.

19. Nancy L. Buc interview with the author, 18 February 1991.

20. Marie Langlois interview with the author, 23 February 1991.

21. Ruth Ekstrom interview with the author, 24 February 1991.

22. Ibid.

23. Ruth Wolf interview with the author, 11 April 1991.

24. Doris Stapelton interview with the author, 11 April 1991.

25. The charge to the corporation committee is included in the final report of the research project, *Men and Women Learning Together: A Study of Coeducation in the Late 70's* (Providence: Brown University, 1980), p. 256.

The Challenge of Diversity: Undergraduate Women at Brown in the 1980s

by SHELLEY MAINS and SANDY MARTIN
with MARTHA GARDNER

W OMEN   AT   BROWN   develop
knowledge of the world around them – and their role in it – not only
through their books, but through all their experiences at college. For this
reason this chapter explores the lives of eighties undergraduates in several
areas: academics, extracurricular organizations, residential and social life,
politics, and community outreach.[1] With the 1980s barely over, it seems
too early to present any neat theories about why particular events happened, or what their meanings were. We therefore present anecdotal docu-
mentation of the eighties, with the hope that in another few decades, it
will be helpful to others who have the distance to analyze the lives of
undergraduate women at Brown during this decade.

For many students, life at Brown represents a challenge in dealing
with diversity while establishing one's own identity. Students of different
races, socio-economic classes, political persuasions, sexual orientations,
religions, and cultural backgrounds make up the Brown community. Such
diversity can foster tension, and the eighties were years of increasing debate
about pluralism, diversity, and tolerance. Unlike many other schools which
clung to integrationist models despite student protest, the Brown administration embraced the concept of diversity and undertook efforts to promote acceptance of differences. Since the early 1980s, the entire entering
class has been required to attend a presentation during orientation week,
opened by the president and the provost, on Brown's commitment to

Toby Simon, director of health education, and son at the
Women's Speak Out in 1985.

pluralism. This is followed by mandatory workshops in residential units, facilitated by teams of faculty, administrators, and seniors. While many other colleges introduced workshops on diversity during the decade, few if any others incorporated this as a required component of students' orientation to their new campus. By the end of the decade, the administration had also developed an anti-harassment policy that prohibits the "subjection of another person, group, or class of persons, to inappropriate, abusive, threatening, or demeaning actions, based on race, religion, gender, handicap, ethnicity, national origin, or sexual orientation."[2]

As the eighties drew to a close, a *Brown Alumni Monthly* (BAM) article discussed how at Brown:

> The notion of a color-blind society has been indefinitely postponed and has been replaced by one of a pluralistic society in which groups maintain their differences. There is some talk of color-blind equality, but for the most part today's dominant ideal among minority students embraces ethnic difference, and emphasizes the importance of ethnicity in defining who you are.[3]

The terms "minority" and "ethnic" could easily be replaced by, or combined with, "female" and "gender" in this quote. Indeed, many parallels can be drawn between the experiences of students of color and those of women at the college. With their unique perspective on diversity, women of color at Brown (as elsewhere in the United States during the eighties) were often in the forefront of movements demanding more concrete support to reinforce the university's stated commitment to diversity.

Women's lives at Brown in the eighties must be examined against this backdrop of diversity and pluralism, assimilation and separatism. Some of the decade's reforms – like the acceptance of women into several fraternities – were championed in the interest of bringing women's experience at Brown up to par with men's. At the same time, other efforts – like women-only programs at the Sarah Doyle Women's Center – were advocated not as attempts to equalize men's and women's lives, but to illuminate the differences, to value women's unique perspectives and experiences, and to empower them to improve their lot at Brown – and in society.

As undergraduate women, often on their own for the first time, face the challenge of living with diversity, they often endeavor to find a "home" at Brown where they feel supported by others with whom they share an aspect of identity. This can be particularly important for those women who feel especially marginalized at Brown, such as women in predominantly male academic fields, women of color, lesbians, women from poor or working class backgrounds, and of course, women for whom these identities overlap. This chapter highlights a variety of areas where women at

Brown find safe haven, often with other women – in living situations, religious groups, political organizations, and academic programs.

The Core of the University: Academics

While academics do not encompass the whole of a university, they are the core around which all other aspects of life are built. Everything else fits around the schedule of classes and exams; virtually nothing takes precedence over study, or at least not when it comes to finals week. Hence, it is critical to examine women's lives at Brown by looking first at how they fare in the classroom.

While the 1971 merger of Brown and Pembroke might have signalled an end to questioning the costs and benefits of coeducation, instead it precipitated new examination of the status of women. The questions about coeducation which were highlighted by the merger prompted the Brown Corporation to create a Committee on the Status of Women and then to convene The Brown Project, a group of educators and researchers who wrote *Men and Women Learning Together: A Study of College Students in the Late 70s,* commonly referred to as the Coed Report. Published in April 1980 after two years of study, the Coed Report clearly documented the ways in which men and women did not fare equally within academe in general and ended with a number of recommendations about how to improve the status of women at Brown. These recommendations included: increasing the number of women faculty and administrators; continuing study of women's lower academic self-confidence and achievement; sensitizing faculty to the needs of women students; examining unconscious sex bias in the classroom; creating programs to help women address math anxiety and inadequate preparation; enhancing women's self-esteem overall; addressing the problems of men students in developing interpersonal skills and emotional maturity; attention to differing values for men and women regarding premarital sex and dual career families through counseling and health services; and establishment of a mechanism for implementation of these recommendations, including periodic self-review of the status of women at Brown.[4]

One critical finding of the Coed Report was that while women entered Brown with higher grades and self-confidence than their male counterparts, they left Brown with lower grades, lower self-esteem, and lower educational goals. Just eight years later, a study of the Class of 1988 as freshmen and again as seniors showed an impressive change with respect to grades: women continued to enter Brown with higher average grades and academic standing than the men, and, after three years at Brown, their grade point averages were still better than the men's. The advantage that the women had upon entering Brown did slip during these years, however, leaving the women much more closely matched to the men than they had been when they entered. And, fewer women than men in the Class of 1988 reported feeling that they had "much stronger abilities and skills" in any particular field after three years at Brown than they did upon entering (62.5 percent of men, 54.3 percent of women).[5]

Using data collected by the Admission Office and the Registrar's Office, women's expected fields of study upon application to Brown can be compared with their concentrations upon graduation. While many individuals change their minds several times during their four years, the percentage of entering students planning to concentrate in any given area is generally a good predictor of the number of students who will eventually graduate with that concentration. Significant shifts, however, can be seen between the time of application and graduation in the percentages of women who expect to concentrate in the traditionally male disciplines.

The Mathematics Department sees the largest shift in this area, and physical sciences and engineering also see significant shifts, though much smaller than that in math. Over a six-year period in the mid-1980s, 16.1 percent fewer women graduated in math than planned on concentrating in math upon entering Brown. During the same years, the physical sciences saw an average decrease of 5.6 percent of women, and engineering saw a decrease of 4.4 percent.[6] The study of the Class of 1988 also shows that while there is very little gender differential in satisfaction with courses in the humanities, there is a distinct difference between women's and men's satisfaction with math and science courses (83.2 percent of men, 68.5 percent of women).[7]

There are, no doubt, distinctions between departments that this somewhat gross data (incorporating twelve departments into the physical sciences and seventeen departments into the social sciences) misses. At least one early 1980s woman graduate of the Computer Science Department suggested that the newness of that field enabled her to ignore the fact that computer science was dominated by men.

The types of problems women may face in male-dominated fields is illustrated by the following incident. One Japanese-American woman reported that, during her first semester at Brown, an exam question asked about the Celtics, a Boston-based basketball team, of whom she had never heard. This question (which the male professor no doubt meant to be an easy point for students) infuriated the woman, causing her to write an angry answer on the exam. The professor's response was to refer her to psychological services. The student eventually switched from her intended major in the professor's department, to an interdisciplinary field, enabling her to avoid taking as many courses in traditionally male departments.[8]

Organizations which are not officially part of the curriculum in any department, yet are more closely related to academics, can be seen as somewhat reflective of the position of women within those fields. The Society of Women Engineers (SWE), a national organization, has a Brown chapter advised by the only woman faculty member in the Engineering Department, with about forty women involved in 1990. SWE attempts to minimize the attrition rate of women in engineering by offering support and a big sister program where upperclass women offer tutoring and advice to first and second year women. Undergraduate members also give talks at local elementary and high schools to present role models to the students. The organization also provides women engineering students with professional connections to women engineers for internships and employment.[9]

Women students in Brown's Program in Medicine have organized Women in Medicine, while the Program in Liberal Medical Education (PLME) sponsors both a Women in Medicine Mentor Program and a Medicine in Action program, which links pre-med undergraduates with doctors in their specialty area, giving some attention to pairing women students with women doctors. The Biology Department, on the other hand, where 50 percent of the undergraduate concentrators are women, represents the integration approach with no special attention given to the needs of women students.

Women and men share equally the Undergraduate Teaching and Research Assistantships which pair students with faculty members. This program introduces undergraduates to scholarly research, to curriculum development, and to the nature of college teaching. Women and men who are Odyssey Fellows work with faculty to revise courses to include material on racial or ethnic minorities; three quarters of these have been minority students. Since the mid 1980s, women have comprised 60 percent of the writing fellows who serve as writing advisors to undergraduates in specially designated courses.[10]

Academic awards are another indicator of how women are currently faring at Brown. Women earn slightly more than their share of honors in their fields of concentration, but slightly less than their share of degrees awarded magna cum laude, an award made to the top 20 percent of the graduating class.[11] Women at Brown receive more awards which require breadth of interest and achievement and fewer of the more narrowly defined science and engineering awards. Women earn slightly more than their share of Phi Beta Kappa awards, an average of 51.7 percent. In Sigma Xi, for excellence in science, women receive 41.5 percent of the member-

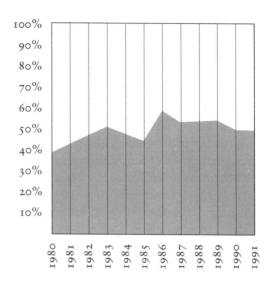

Percentage of
Phi Beta Kappa
Graduates
who are Women,
1980–1991,
Brown University

100%
90%
80%
70%
60%
50%
40%
30%
20%
10%

1980 1981 1982 1983 1984 1985 1986 1987 1988 1989 1990 1991

ships even though only 38.8 percent of science majors are women.[12] Women do less well in engineering where they comprise 22.7 percent of the concentrators but receive only 19.2 percent of the memberships to Tau Beta Phi, the honor society for engineering students. In each year since 1985, graduating women have been awarded two of the three Arnold Fellowships for independent exploration.[13]

More women than men experiment with the array of options provided by the New Curriculum. One particularly challenging option in the New Curriculum is designing one's own concentration. Women accounted for more than half of independent concentrators in five of seven years between 1982 and 1989, with the proportion of independent concentrators who are women going well above 60 percent in two of these years.[14] While these numbers are striking, their meaning remains unclear. Possible explanations include: (1) women at Brown are more independent and creative than the men, supported by the fact that women rate "achieving in a performing art," "writing original works," and "creating artistic work" as more important than men do; (2) women are less career-oriented and therefore more willing to take risks; or (3) women are less satisfied with the regular offerings at Brown and therefore compelled to initiate their own courses of study. Women's participation in New Curriculum options would be a valuable topic for a reassessment of the gender, race, and class differences within the Brown student body.

Data on undergraduates who take time off from Brown during their four years show consistently more women than men choosing this option.[15] Most students, both women and men, took time off to "reconsider goals and interests" or because they "wanted practical experience." However, there are some reasons for taking time off which reveal significant statistical differences between women and men. For larger percentages of the men than women, being "bored with course work," not "doing well academically," and being "tired of being a student" are also reasons to take time off. For women, inability to "afford college," wanting to be "closer to home," and wanting "wider course selection" are important reasons which are not even mentioned by men.[16]

While men and women reported similar financial backgrounds, none of the men in the study responded that they couldn't afford college while 14.6 percent of the women responded that way. A larger number of women than men in the study were dissatisfied with financial aid services at Brown. Between 1975 and 1980, for example, women accounted for just under 50 percent of the undergraduate population, but received only 35–40 percent of the financial aid given to Brown students from both the university and outside sources. In the late 1980s, women received 42 percent of the funds awarded in university scholarships. Not surprisingly, then, larger numbers of women than men worked part time, and women averaged more hours per week.[17]

A common indicator of quality education for women and people of color is the availability of appropriate role models and mentors. In the early 1970s, the newly merged Brown and Pembroke had only eight tenured women in a tenured faculty of well over 300. Thanks in part to the 1977 consent decree, women students now have more opportunities to study with women professors and to seek out women as advisors and mentors. This distribution of women faculty is still very uneven, however, with far fewer women in the traditionally male fields than in other areas and with few faculty women of color.[18]

The formation of a number of new interdisciplinary centers at Brown in the 1980s has had an effect on women's choices of concentrations and eventual careers. Most obviously connected to women's education is the Pembroke Center for Teaching and Research on Women. In addition, the Program in Community Health, the Center for the Study of Race and Ethnicity in America, the Center for Public Policy and American Institutions, and the Center for Environmental Studies all offer students opportunities to pursue interdisciplinary studies. Many of these interdisciplinary programs offer women the chance to explore courses in traditionally male fields without locking them into a full course load in such a department. As one woman of the Class of 1981 said, "Too many of my courses were male-taught and [male-]dominated science courses which left me feeling intellectually incompetent. It has taken me the almost ten years since then to get that sense of intellectual competence back and to begin connecting my academic interests with my personal agenda as a woman."[19] Interdisciplinary programs and centers often provide women students the opportunity to connect their academic interests to their personal ones.

The founding of the Pembroke Center in 1981 sparked an increase in women's studies courses as well as in the numbers of students enrolled in existing courses. In the late 1970s, course brochures compiled by the Sarah Doyle Women's Center listed ten to twelve courses per semester focused on issues of gender; students who wanted to major in women's studies had to design an independent concentration. In 1983, the first regular concentrators in women's studies graduated and, by 1990, a total of sixty-seven students had graduated as women's studies concentrators. In the Class of 1990, 49.3 percent of women took a women's studies course.[20] By 1989, while only a few more women's studies courses were available each semester than in 1981, there was also a yearly offering of numerous courses of related interest. A coalition of Third World women is currently working for the addition of women's studies courses presented from a multi-cultural point of view.

Women's comments on their experiences in women's studies courses point to discrepancies between their experiences in those courses and in other courses:

> Women's studies classes I experienced during Brown altered my way of thinking. The impact was enormous. When I refer to alteration – I mean just that – after taking Women's Studies courses I approached almost everything in my life in a different way ... My experience in these classes was made different by the students – most of the time we were all women and this was a big change from a very male cognitive science department. The competition was not as fierce and the minds more open.[21]

> [One women's studies course was] incredibly challenging and forced me to develop analytic skills. I think that was one of the only courses that truly taught me to be a more critical thinker....[22]

> [Women's Studies courses] changed my academic priorities/focus, as well as my life, dramatically, opened up a whole perspective of social history, studying *ourselves,* as women, studying marginalized populations ... My experience in these courses was far more exciting, relevant and egalitarian than in other courses.[23]

Centers such as the Pembroke Center or the more recent Center for the Study of Race and Ethnicity in America provide a much needed physical and intellectual home for a particular area of study. Of equal importance is the focus they provide for an entire community, in this case the whole college, for issues and individuals related to the goals of the center.[24]

Brown is a residential college; that is, students (with the exception of Resumed Education students, married students, and commuters) are "required to live in University residences unless excused by the Director of Residential Life."[25] This policy is built on the assumption that Brown is more than a school, it's a community, and much learning goes on outside the classrooms and library. This concept of the importance of social life is confirmed by the students themselves: in a 1987 survey of Brown undergraduates, a full third of respondents stated that they "place intimate relationships above academics."[26] Life at the college not only offers an academic opportunity, but a heady challenge in establishing identity, experimenting with social independence, building intimate relationships, and exploring sexuality. Many women undergraduates find themselves for the first time negotiating the contradictory pulls of traditional gender roles and seemingly unlimited academic, social, and career opportunities.

The sense of community at Brown is encouraged by the administration, which recognizes that this is one of the college's major strengths. At the same time, the administration recognizes that while the college years may be an exciting time of personal growth for undergraduates, they may also be fraught with turmoil. Just as Brown boasts a range of academic support services, it also offers an impressive network of psychological and social support services. And pressure from students – primarily women – led to an expansion of these services in the eighties, when issues like date rape, alcohol abuse, eating disorders, AIDS, racism, and homophobia burst on the scene at Brown and other campuses in the United States.

A student's choice of where to live both shapes and reflects her sense of identity and her social and academic interests. A student's father captured the essence of residential life when he wrote in the *Brown Alumni Monthly* of his daughter's accommodations in a coed Brown residence created for students interested in environmental issues:

> Now, 111 Brown [St.] isn't a dormitory as such. Rather it is a turn-of-century house converted to student living quarters where fourteen men and women eat, drink, sleep, bathe, brush their teeth, play music, smoke dope, have food fights, study, make love, write, yell, and endure.[27]

One way Brown recognizes and promotes diversity in undergraduate life is by offering a range of student living options. First-year students are assigned rooms in "freshman dorms," but after their first year, students may petition to live off campus, and about 20 percent of students do so each year. Students who opt to stay on campus can choose among a variety of living situations, including a special sophomore dorm, on-campus apartments, social halls, single-sex hallways in coed dorms, cooperative houses, and language/cultural/special interest houses. As of 1988–89, there were twelve residential fraternities and two residential sororities on campus as well.[28]

Brown has a strong program of peer advisors serving in first-year dorms as resident counselors. Since 1989 more than half have been women. These students are elected in a competitive process and the positions are important leadership positions on campus involving considerable training. Two additional programs are based in residence halls (serving more than only first-year students): the Woman Peer Counselors (WPC) and the Minority Peer Counselors. During the 1980s the numbers of women of color increased steadily in the WPC program; by 1991 they represented half the Women Peer Counselors.[29]

When Brown and Pembroke merged in 1971, a faculty member recalls, the administration looked favorably on coed life as a means of bringing women into the previously all-male Brown residential community to act as a "civilizing influence."[30] While it's safe to say that few Brown women choose mixed-gender living arrangements with this benevolent notion in mind, women do choose to live in coed dorms to fulfill a variety of social and personal needs. First year women students often choose mixed dorms as a way of plunging into whatever they imagine college life to be, and simply as a way of making friends with men. As one undergraduate wrote, though she found the lack of privacy in her first-year dorm difficult,

> I am glad that I had the experience. Living with males was a good experience for me, especially after coming from an all-female high school. . . .[31]

Yet women at Brown often find their experiences of coed dorm life, particularly life in large freshman dorms, to fall short of their hopes and expectations. One woman said, "Although I requested to live in West Quad, I quickly learned that I much prefer smaller, more intimate situations."[32] Another expressed her misery at large coed dorm life more bluntly, summing up her first year living situation as "a *disaster.*"[33]

The atmosphere of first year dorms, and students' behavior in them, cannot be attributed solely to gender issues. One undergraduate pondered: "was first year louder because we were first-year students or because there were men around?"[34]

While coed living is the norm at Brown, particularly for first-year students, many women still opt for all-women settings for reasons ranging from a sense of safety to a feeling of like-mindedness with one's neighbors. As one woman summed it up, "while it was 'fun' living in a mixed-gender setting, it felt 'safer' and more 'nurturing' in a female house."[35] Another woman chose to live with women in her later years at Brown as "my politics and personal identification as a woman developed and became more dominant for me."[36]

While the issue of mixed-gender versus single-sex housing influences women's sense of comfort in their living situations, women describe other factors that emerge as important during their years at Brown. As women students mature and develop a sense of identity and solid friendship networks, they discover that other factors emerge as important in making a "home" at Brown. A Latina student wrote:

> I found large dorm life to be awful because of everyone's lack of respect of others, regardless of gender. When I lived in the Romance Languages House during my sophomore year I enjoyed sharing common interests with my neighbors, the ability to speak Spanish a lot, and the solitude of a small dorm.[37]

Another woman recalled:

> I don't think the differences in my housing experiences were due to gender situations – they were attributed to the difference between on-campus/off-campus living. Living off-campus was important for gaining further skills of independent living/growing up, etc. The other housing dynamic that was important to me was 'group' living versus 'roommate' living. Sharing a home with 3–4 people was a positive developmental experience for me, and a 'growth' experience after living with one woman.[38]

While not as widespread at Brown as on many other campuses, fraternities have nonetheless served an important function for many undergraduate men at the college by providing them with a sense of group identity and belonging, as well as academic support, a built-in social life, and automatic access to prime housing. Despite the fact that there are now two residential sororities at Brown, female undergraduates lack a similar, extensive network of residential/social institutions designed to shepherd them into life at Brown. Women at Brown during the eighties have responded to the very existence of the fraternity system on campus, as well as their disproportionate access to its benefits in two fundamental ways: by fighting the fraternities and by joining them.

Wriston Quad, where most residential fraternities are located, has long been the focal point of complaints about sexual harassment at Brown. Allegations of fraternity members' sexual exploitation of women abound on campuses across the country, and Brown is no exception. As a result, fraternities at Brown have increasingly come under attack by individual women and feminist organizations.

Brown women's challenges to the fraternities coincided with increasing reports of racist incidents at the fraternities and mounting concerns about dangerous hazing practices. At the same time, a housing shortage at Brown prompted the administration and students to reassess the fraternities' hold on desirable campus housing. While these challenges have not eliminated fraternities at Brown, they have helped transform the relationship of the fraternity system to social life at the university. Some of these changes were mandated by the administration. In 1985, one of the fraternities considered "most offensive" to women had its charter revoked and another had its housing rights withdrawn.[39]

Other fraternities, facing pressure from students and administration, changed from within. The eighties witnessed the transformation of the all-male fraternity Zeta Psi into the coed fraternity Zeta Delta Xi. Female member Tracey L. Scronic, Class of 1992, documented this evolution.[40] During the 70s, Zeta Psi ("Zete") had many female "friends of the house" who enjoyed some privileges but were excluded from certain decision-making powers. At the time, some members of the fraternity supported becoming coed, but this wasn't considered seriously until the eighties, in the face of deteriorating ties with the national organization, a dwindling and apathetic membership, and pressure from the university on the fraternity to increase its membership to avoid losing its choice housing. The brothers resented what they saw as external pressure to become coed. Rather cynically, the voting members in 1983 agreed to "become coed only in the eyes of the administration while remaining all-male and in good standing with the national. . . . " But as the local chapter's relationship with the national chapter continued to deteriorate, the house moved toward becoming coed "in almost all respects."

By 1986, the local chapter of Zeta Psi had seceded from the national, leaving it to the house members to create a new fraternity, to be named Zeta Delta Xi. Ironically, writes Scronic, this "drastic change" at Zete managed to alienate some women because the fraternity changed from "a mellow house of eclectic individuals into a 'hot fraternity' of enthusiastic revolutionaries." At the same time, many past brothers "tend to be rather bitter and upset by the demise of their frat." But however painful the change, the evolving history of Zete reflects how even the fraternities – those most traditional of social institutions at Brown – have responded to internal and external pressures, and are changing and adapting in relation to women.

In a more recent instance of the shifting social norms at Brown's fraternities, the March 1990 *Brown Alumni Monthly* ran an article about the "first Brown fraternity to abolish pledging," Psi Upsilon. This change happened during the presidency of a woman, Suong Hyunh, Class of

1991. According to the *BAM* article, "any student willing to commit to the spirit and comradeship of Psi U need only submit his or her bid card to become an associate brother (sic)." This creates a varied membership, according to Huynh. As she puts it:

> We don't recruit from a certain crowd. We have people who work for the BDH, others who work for WBRU, people who volunteer for Safewalk, people who escort at Planned Parenthood. It's very diverse. I know "diversity" is Brown's key word, but it's true here at Psi U.[41]

Women Seeking Identities: Social, Extra-Curricular, and Religious Life

Brown and Providence offer a wealth of organizations and opportunities to help students develop all of their varied selves: social, artistic, political, and emotional. These opportunities exist on and off campus, and are both coed and single-sex. Women are involved in virtually every one of the organizations on campus and support a large number of women-only organizations as well. The Society of Women Engineers; the Lesbian/Bisexual Collective; the Chattertocks and the Ursa Minors, both women's a cappella singing groups; Zeta Phi Beta, a Black women's sorority; Building Bridges – Asian Women Together; and the women's fencing team are just a few of the diverse women's organizations on campus.

The decade of the 1980s has been characterized by the dwindling of "issue politics," focused on such issues as the environment and peace, and the growth of "identity politics." Within the context of identity politics, individuals often seek a "home" of sorts in the political organizations to which they belong. This trend has been a national one, and Brown has reflected the trend. Identifying with a subgroup of the Brown community can help students develop a sense of self and negotiate their independence. For women students in particular – pushed and pulled in a variety of directions by conventional social expectations of women, demands for academic excellence, racial and ethnic identifications, mixed messages regarding sexuality – finding like-minded others to provide support and act as role models is crucial.

The Sarah Doyle Women's Center (SDWC) functions as one of the important umbrellas on campus for organizations which provide support and "homes" for women students and feminist organizations. At the start of the 1980s, SDWC worked to provide women with both an academic and a social/political home within the college. With the 1981 founding of the Pembroke Center, the Sarah Doyle Women's Center gave over the strictly academic portion of its mission in order to focus on issues of gender in the world outside the classroom. The SDWC and the Pembroke Center remain integrally connected.

Throughout the 1980s, the SDWC organized and sponsored an array of programs for women at Brown. Friday Forums, begun in 1975, are the center's oldest lecture series, bringing a wide range of women scholars and activists to speak to the Brown community. Students in the center initiate an array of support groups each year on such topics as sexuality, eating disorders and body image, political activism, and violence against women. Students may join such ongoing committees and organizations as the Women's Political Task Force, Third World Women as Friends, the Library Committee, the Gallery Committee, and the Lesbian/Bisexual Collective. During the early 1980s, the Women's Center was managed by two administrators and a host of interested women students. The students staffed the reception desk of SDWC, ran a variety of programs and support groups, bought and organized books for the women's studies library, coordinated shows in the art gallery, and held weekly staff meetings where they used consensus to make decisions on the running of the SDWC.

Throughout the decade, both at the SDWC and within the feminist movement nationally, there has been a shift away from a global focus (and issues which might traditionally be considered "political") and towards more personal and introspective issues. As a campus-based women's center, some issues have remained constant at SDWC despite off-campus trends. Concern about date rape and eating disorders, both issues which have a disproportionate effect on adolescent women, have been two such constants in the support groups and political organizations at the women's center.

During the mid-1980s, women involved at the SDWC undertook major structural changes in an attempt to create and protect racial diversity among the students who used the center. Abandoning a collective decision-making process in which all women were welcome to participate as often or as seldom as they pleased, the new organizational structure attempted to institutionalize diversity, ensuring that decisions were made by women who represented the broad array of women at Brown. Those students hired as the paid coordinators of the various programs and organizations sponsored by the center also became the decision-making body, each as the representative of their particular group.[42]

The committees meeting at the SDWC had always represented the diversity of Brown women. Yet before the restructuring these groups had operated autonomously and the women who chose to participate in the decision-making collective had tended to be an unrepresentative subset of those women, a homogeneous group of women who sought out SDWC as their "home." During the reorganization there was extensive discussion about the concept of "home" versus the idea of "coalition" or "community," and, while it was acknowledged that most women wanted a "home," it seemed that not all women at Brown could make a "home" in the same place. Like many of the other political discussions at Brown, this "home" versus "coalition" discussion has been a prominent one in politically radical circles nationally during the decade.[43] The restructuring plan attempted to support the diverse groups who use SDWC by providing opportunities for the exploration of identity and unique experiences of "home" for each group. And it planned to turn the center itself into a true umbrella, a coalition-building space.

The Third World Center (TWC), another umbrella organization at Brown, underwent major expansion during the 1980s. With the 1989 establishment of the Center for the Study of Race and Ethnicity in America, the TWC gained an academic counterpart to help complement its mission, in much the same way that the Pembroke Center does for the Sarah Doyle Women's Center. At the end of the decade, there were two groups housed at the TWC specifically for women: Building Bridges – Asian Women Together, and Third World Women As Friends. Latinas, poorly represented in the early 1980s simply by their small numbers, became a strong force within the TWC in the closing years of the decade. While Latinas did not create their own women's organization during the 1980s, they began the 1990s with a conference for Latina activists from area colleges.[44]

The proliferation of organizations based on racial and ethnic identity housed at the TWC reflects the shifting racial politics of the minority communities in the country during the 1980s. Complementing the separate identity-based groups, the TWC hosts the annual Third World Transition Program (TWTP). This annual summer program is open to all Third World students who are entering Brown, offering them an opportunity to begin building a community with each other and learn about the resources available to them before being thrown into the frenzy of courses and "the blizzard" of white students.[45]

The TWTP is a community-building program which begins before Third World students even decide to matriculate at Brown. This program cements the TWC's image as "home" for many students before they've sampled the array of other identities possible for them on campus, a controversial issue despite the commitment to pluralism espoused by the administration.

The TWC organizations, with their different cultural traditions, each provide different opportunities for women. In the early 1980s, women's issues were given low priority by those organizing at the TWC. In 1981, one African-American woman student who had been involved in the

Entering women students celebrate during a
Third World Transition Week in the 1980s.

SDWC took it upon herself to organize a major conference for Third World women. This conference, highlighted with a concert by Sweet Honey In the Rock, an a cappella African-American women's group, helped both the TWC and the SDWC progress toward their parallel struggles of the 1980s: for the TWC to incorporate gender awareness and for the SDWC to incorporate race awareness. In 1982, a group of Third World women inspired, in part, by the conference, produced "Watch Us Rise: An Anthology For and By Third World Women," a journal including poetry, prose, and art, much of it dealing with the women's multiple identities – as women and as members of the Third World community.[46]

Throughout the 1980s, the TWC and SDWC jointly sponsored Third World Women As Friends. This group is the only ongoing joint project of the two centers, but the centers frequently turn to each other for joint sponsorship of programs and events, and the Sarah Doyle Women's Center has a Third World Affairs Committee to provide a link between the centers and to help both organizations focus on issues of importance to Third World women.

This growing autonomy of Third World women within the Third World community at Brown seems to have helped some women escape a common dilemma for Third World women, that of choosing a primary identity and "home" for activism and social life. As is true for Third World women elsewhere in the United States, the 1980s have seen growing acceptance both within the Third World community of all-women's groups and projects and within the women's community of Third World women-only efforts. This acceptance has been won through hard work and struggle by many women who refused to settle into one "home" or the other, but insisted on maintaining two "homes" and/or doing coalition work. The 1980s saw a burgeoning of widely available Third World women's literature, theory, music, health centers, and organizations. The 1981 conference and the formation of organization of women of color mirror the national trend toward multiple identities and acceptance in a variety of communities. While much progress has been made towards resolving this tension, the dilemma still remains. Even though there has been more acceptance within the TWC and SDWC communities, many Third World women still feel more "at home" in one place than in the other. Members in Third World Women As Friends, a group which meets alternately in the SDWC and the TWC, say that they actually feel more "at home" at the TWC. Their other involvements are more often with the TWC than with the SDWC. And, certainly, some women do not find their "home" in either of these places, but find it in some other identity.

Along with the SDWC and the TWC, women seek their identities in many other student organizations on campus. In 1986, the heads of over fifteen student organizations were women, including the *Brown Daily Herald,* the Undergraduate Council of Students (the student government, UCS), Brown Community Outreach, Brown Student Agencies, University Food Services, Keep Brown Beautiful, the debate union, *Issues* magazine, Organization of United African Peoples (OUAP), and three other Third World organizations, among others. While this was an exceptional year, it is clear that women have made a place for themselves in virtually every organization on campus.

Although women and men report spending comparable amounts of time in campus clubs and organizations, gender often influences their positions in these groups. One woman who was involved with the campus radio station, WBRU, felt that during her years there women and men had very different roles at the station – men had the more high-profile glamorous jobs, primarily as disc jockeys, while women held the low-profile yet more powerful positions, such as station manager and music director. These roles shifted during the late 1980s, with men taking more of the behind-the-scenes jobs as well as the on-the-air ones. *Issues* magazine had a woman editor in 1986; in 1990 women hold only three of nine titled positions although they make up the entire production staff – both low-profile and low-power positions. In 1989, the *Brown Daily Herald,* on the other hand, had four women on the editorial staff of eight, with women in the top two positions.[47]

Women at Brown often choose to explore their identity through the arts. Many performances initiated by women in the Theater Arts Department focused on this exploration. Such performances included a three-woman play that pieced together writings of Calamity Jane with contemporary questions and issues, a play exploring the implications of reproductive technologies, and one confronting the issues of consent and power during a sexual assault. In the late 1980s, students and faculty formed Awareness Theater for exploring issues of identity including eating concerns and body image.[48]

Religion is another area of activity which many women are drawn to for reasons of identity and a sense of "home." At the close of the decade, four of Brown's nine chaplains – the university chaplain, the associate chaplain for minority concerns, one of the Catholic chaplains, and the associate chaplain for women's concerns – were women. Since three of these positions cross denominational lines, the effect is broader than it might be if students in each denomination were in contact only with one chaplain.

The chaplain for women's concerns began an experimental women's spirituality group, called WEB, in the fall of 1984. WEB "seeks to create a space in which women can explore spirituality outside of specific faith traditions."[49] WEB participants include undergraduates, graduate students, and some staff members. Some women participate both in WEB and in a traditional religious practice; others find WEB an alternative to traditions they are no longer satisfied with; while still others are new to religious practice altogether. WEB is the oldest all-women's religious group at Brown, but in the past few years, it has been joined by Kolisha, a Jewish feminist group convened by a former WEB member, a Catholic women's group, and, at the end of the decade, there was also talk of a Muslim women's group.

In a study of alumnae, Jewish and Episcopalian women report higher rates of involvement in organized religion after graduation than do women from other religions. For Jewish women, this may in part be due to having women in key positions within Hillel and the Brown Jewish community since the mid 1970s. During the late 1970s, Jewish women also formed a women's Rosh Hodesh group, which designed feminist liturgy. As with many of the other trends visible at Brown during the 1980s, this self-conscious women's identification with Judaism paralleled the national trend towards identity politics which included more and more progressive Jews, and especially Jewish feminists, identifying themselves as such and making explicit connections between their political commitments and Judaism.[50]

In the United States, the eighties have also seen radical changes within organized Christianity, primarily through the growth in numbers and in power of Christian fundamentalists. The emphasis on traditional values and family certainly have powerful implications for the lives of women. Brown has not yet been visibly affected by this trend, probably because Brown has such a strong tradition of liberalism, suggesting that high school students from strongly Christian right and fundamentalist families would not consider Brown an acceptable school for matriculation. Brown does have a Brown for Life group and a Campus Crusade for Christ. However, one chaplain observed that these groups are smaller, less powerful, and less conservative than are their counterparts at other universities.

Sexual Identities and Relationships

Along with establishing group identities, Brown students' social experimentation often includes their exploration of sexuality. While many at Brown feel that "fellow students are unwilling to get involved, that an intimate relationship is like a 5th course," students are nonetheless fascinated with the issue of sexuality. By the late eighties, workshops on sexuality at Brown included "How to Be a Better Lover," "The Fine Art of Sexual Communication," "Surviving a Long-Distance Relationship," and "Are You Ready for Sex?" A Psychology Department course on human sexuality became a firm fixture in the academic curriculum. Brown also offers several peer counseling groups – Women Peer Counselors, Resident Counselors, Student-to-Student Counselors, and Student Life Resident Advisors – who are trained in sexuality education and counseling.

In 1984 the Office of Health Education at Brown conducted a sex survey on campus, which was repeated in 1987. The study found that males and females differ in sexual experience: men at Brown are less likely to be virgins than their female counterparts. As the report summary suggests, some of the gap might be accounted for by over/underreporting, but the statistics probably reflect a reality among students who have been raised in a culture which condones the sexual activity of young males far more than that of young females. Interestingly, the gap between men's and women's experience seems to be narrowing:

> In 1984 we found that 51% of the women and 17% of the men reported they were virgins. There may be a tendency for men to overreport sexual activity

and possibly for women to underreport; such reporting phenomena reflect societal expectations of sexual behavior and things like the "good girl syndrome." In 1987, 32% of the men had not had intercourse, a sizable increase over 1984. . . . It is possible that the pressure on men to be sexually active or to boast about their experience has lessened, and maybe that the AIDS scare has had an effect on men's behavior. Interestingly, there were fewer virgin women in the 1987 survey.[51]

In spite of gender differences in sexual experience, it seems at first glance that male and female Brown students espouse similarly liberal attitudes about sex roles and norms. Over 80 percent of both men and women each year agreed that premarital sex "is acceptable to me," and a full 93 percent of males and females *disagreed* with the statement that in a heterosexual relationship "women should not initiate sex."[52]

However, it appears that men and women at Brown do differ in their expectations of sex and relationships. These differences suggest that traditional sex roles and expectations indeed die hard. Of respondents who answered "yes" to the question "Are you satisfied with your sexual experience at Brown?," 61 percent were women and only 39 percent were men. And while only 15 percent of students "strongly agreed" that they "would like to be more sexually active," a majority (61 percent) of these responses were from men. This raises the question of whether there is a discrepancy between the sexes in expectations from relationships, with men more interested in sex and women concerned with other aspects such as romance. The survey found that of the 38 percent who agreed that "most men are primarily looking for sex from women," 57 percent were women and only 43 percent were men, and of the 41 percent of students who agreed that "most women are primarily looking for romance from men," the divergence was even greater: 64 percent women, 36 percent men. Along similar lines, of the 44 percent of the students who answered "no" to the question "Can you have sex without intimacy?," 63 percent of the students were women and only 37 percent men.[53]

These dramatic differences in Brown men's and women's expectations about sex illustrate the tenacity of traditional sexual norms, even at a school with the socially liberal reputation Brown had in the eighties. In the absence of radical shifts in power and attitudes regarding sex and gender in our culture, it falls to the individual parties in a relationship to communicate and negotiate about conflicting needs, expectations, and limits in the areas of intimacy and sex. Given the likelihood that a man and woman may enter a relationship – or go on a date – with very different desired outcomes, the possibility is great for miscommunication and even sexual abuse, particularly in the form of date rape.

Indeed, in 1987 a striking 42 percent of men and 26 percent of women agreed with the statement "Even if someone says no to sex, you can't always tell if they want to have sex or not." In 1987, although 15 percent of the women answered "yes" to "Have you ever had sex without your consent or against your will?," only 6 percent considered themselves "a victim/survivor of rape." The researchers concluded that the discrepancy indicated "an unwillingness or inability to recognize an encounter which is without consent as 'rape.'"[54]

Recognizing that date rape is a serious problem on college campuses, Brown's Office of Health Education established programs to teach students the necessary skills to communicate about sex. Student activism called for an examination of rape within the context of power imbalances between women and men at Brown and in society, and pressed for the initiation of both student- and university-run programs. As a result, a number of programs and groups were developed and expanded in the eighties. These included the Women on Call Hotline, Health Education Program workshops, Women Peer Counselors, a night-time escort service run by women, courses in self-defense, Men Against Rape, Brown Against Rape and Sexism (a mixed-gender group), and the Survivors of Sexual Assault and Incest support group.

The 1980s have also been characterized by public discussions on other "dangerous" aspects of sexuality. While concerns about unwanted pregnancy and sexually-transmitted diseases have long been common among sexually active college students, the specter of AIDS has raised the level of concern. While Brown students have relatively easy access to health and sexuality education, as well as medical care and birth control methods, they do not always protect themselves against unwanted pregnancy and sexually-transmitted diseases. The 1987 Brown Sex Survey found that seven percent of women said they had experienced an unplanned pregnancy, but more than a quarter of the women and a third of the men reported "unprotected intercourse."[55]

The AIDS epidemic has challenged traditional notions of responsibility in a sexual encounter, and has forced Brown students and administrators alike to publicly discuss sexuality and protection. The Student AIDS Task Force (SATF), formed in 1987, trained students as AIDS peer educators to provide educational programs in residential halls. Since 1986–87, the campus has celebrated National Condom Week with t-shirt sales and workshops on AIDS, safer sex, condom use, and the politics of AIDS.[56]

While many students negotiate the intricacies of heterosexual romance at Brown, others find that college is where they first explore their sexual orientation; many gay, lesbian, and bisexual alumni/ae of Brown recall "coming out" at college. According to the Sex Survey, 11 percent of students in 1984 and 9 percent in 1987 experienced at least "some homosexual orientation."[57]

Coming out while at college can be a pivotal experience for lesbians like this Brown student:

> . . . the whole revelation of sexuality is amazing to me. I see it in terms of, say, a painting hanging on a gallery wall, except that people who have never considered homosexuality as an option have obstructed their view of the landscape with a heavy metal frame.[58]

On the personal level, lesbians at Brown must confront the questions of whether to "come out" publicly, how to meet other lesbians, and how to deal with other students' attitudes about homosexuality. As this woman wrote:

> The very idea of coming to Brown and having to find a new group of friends who would accept my lesbianism was frightening. In addition, I'd have to deal with a roommate who might not accept me, try to find some social activities in which I would feel comfortable, and participate in some activities where I wouldn't have to hide my lesbianism.[59]

Many lesbians find Brown to be a relatively safe environment in which to explore their sexuality:

> I've been lucky to find at Brown not only an atmosphere conducive to coming out as a gay woman, but also a network of women friends (along with a few good men) that has helped make my choice of sexuality a positive one. Except for the few inevitable bigots, Brown is fairly tolerant of homosexuality – I feel that I've found the time here to think, gather strength, and face the world that lies beyond Prospect Street.[60]

Other lesbian students find the college as homophobic as the larger society. As a student painfully related:

> There are the other things you have to live with: the queer jokes, sexist comments from professors, and people automatically assuming that you're straight. Being a lesbian at Brown means being afraid that your roommate who has a boyfriend back home will find out, that you'll tell the wrong person about your sexuality, or that you'll wake up to find more slurs scrawled on your message board. . . . [61]

While many lesbians find "home" in informal friendship networks and never join formal gay or lesbian groups, others find support in organizations of lesbian, gay, and bisexual students. In the 1980s there has been an increasingly visible presence of gay, lesbian, and bisexual students at Brown and an increased awareness of homophobia. During the eighties, the two most visible student groups doing lesbian and gay organizing at

Brown were the Lesbian, Gay and Bisexual Association (LGBA), which had its roots in an organization primarily of gay men, and the Lesbian/ Bisexual Collective (LBC), which was based at the Sarah Doyle Women's Center. Much of the work of the lesbian and gay organizations in the decade focused on increasing lesbian and gay visibility and pride at Brown and on protecting lesbian and gay students from harassment and discrimination. Through a project called "OUTReach," lesbian and gay students give presentations in dorms and for student organizations, giving students an opportunity to ask questions and openly discuss homosexuality. The Ad Hoc Committee on Homosexuality in the Curriculum is working for inclusion of lesbian and gay issues in the curriculum. Lesbian Gay Awareness Week was launched in 1983; the annual event includes speakers, live entertainment, lesbian and gay films, and workshops on sexuality. In 1983 during Gay Awareness Week, a large pink triangle (a symbol of lesbian and gay pride) outside of Faunce House was destroyed by arson; another year the pink triangle was stolen. In response, lesbian and gay students have built ever larger and sturdier triangles, and have even organized round-the-clock vigils to guard the triangle, insisting that Brown's tolerance of diversity include lesbians and gay men.[62]

In the 1980s, students organized to extend the protections of Brown's antidiscrimination policy to include lesbians and gay men. Although over half the student body signed a petition for inclusion of a clause on sexual orientation in 1983, the corporation declined to vote for it until 1988. One organizer felt a barrier to inclusion of the anti-discrimination clause was the pervasive belief that Brown's liberal attitudes were sufficient and that institutionalized protection was unnecessary to creating a safe environment for lesbians and gay men.[63]

Political Activism

Throughout the 1980s, activist students at Brown have tackled a variety of issues, as well as creating a few of their own. Despite the media stereotyping of the 1970s as the "me generation" and 1980s students as apathetic, Brown has had a solid core of politically active students throughout. In early 1985, the *Brown Alumni Monthly* wrote,

> Although many college campuses report the death of activism, student dissent is alive and thriving at Brown. This fall saw the creative "suicide pill" poll that brought hordes of media to College Hill and focused attention on the proliferation of nuclear arms. Every Thursday at noon, a group of students joins hands on the Green in a "Circle of Solidarity" to protest United States intervention in Central America. And now sixty-five students are facing charges of disruption for halting an information session held by CIA recruiters.[64]

One national study of four year universities, done in 1976, showed 54.8 percent of entering Brown students describing themselves as "liberal" or "far left," compared to only 28.4 percent nationally who described themselves in this way. Brown women were more radical than the men, with 59 percent of women describing themselves as "liberal" or "far left" and only 51.5 percent of men doing so. Women's political activity continues once they arrive on campus: in the Class of 1988 survey, a full 60.4 percent of women reported having been involved in campus protests and demonstrations, compared to 46.5 percent of men.[65]

Throughout the 1980s, Brown has held mandatory diversity and pluralism training for entering freshwomen and freshmen. Fortunately, eighteen to twenty-two year olds are fairly literal minded, which means that many have taken the diversity trainings seriously. And these students, especially the women, have forced the university to take themselves literally as well. Every few years during the eighties, a few women students have become outraged at the gap between the stated goals and the actions of the college. And they've acted in creative and dramatic ways to force other students, the administration, and the entire Brown community to address their concerns. Some of the most dramatic gains have been the results of these actions: a safety shuttle, mandatory workshops on sexual assault and harassment, and an ombudswoman for women students.[66]

Throughout the 1980s, CIA recruiters who came to campus to interview students sparked political controversies. Students repeatedly attempted citizens' arrests of CIA recruiters; in the largest of these protests, in November 1984, at least two of the main organizers were women. Their activism was fueled by their feminist analysis of the military and its role in society. The mid-1980s also saw renewed debate on campus about bringing ROTC to Brown, ongoing protests demanding Brown's divestment from corporations doing business in South Africa, the early sparks of student protest against financial aid cutbacks and policies, controversy over whether or not to add "sexual preference" to the university's non-discrimination policy, and renewed activism by Third World students, commemorating the 1975 takeover of University Hall by African-American students. Asian and Asian-American students protested discrimination on campus, especially within the admission process.

In the late 1980s, SOFA, Students on Financial Aid, became the center of political debate on campus. SOFA attempted to call attention to the classism inherent in such elite institutions as Ivy League universities, and the ways it works in conjunction with racism and sexism. SOFA members were primarily white students and, to some extent, these students were taking up classism as another form of diversity at Brown, a form which they claim had been ignored amidst trainings and seminars on diversity and pluralism. Some of the women in SOFA have had concerns with the sexism of men in SOFA echoing the experiences of women in earlier activist efforts. While this concern is not unique for women in political groups, the presence of sexism among the most progressive students at Brown led the women in SOFA to shift their activism toward gender issues.[67]

Since 1983 women students have been continually speaking out publicly against rape and sexual assault, creating change in themselves, other students, and the university. In 1983 FIRE, Feminists Involved in Reaching Equality, began another campus wide debate by spray painting sidewalks around campus with the words "1 in 3 women are raped: fight back." Their actions and the ensuing controversy sparked articles in the *New York Times* and in *Ms.* magazine. Their actions led to a new women's peer-counseling program, a night-time escort service run by women, courses in self-defense, a series of educational forums and films on rape, and the organization of Brown Against Rape and Sexism, which wrote a booklet about rape distributed to all Brown students. After the incident, one dean said, "Although I don't excuse the graffiti incident, it had the effect of moving along the entire university community toward programmatic development in the area of women and their needs."[68]

In May 1985, women students organized a speak-out held in Wriston Quad, home of the fraternities on campus. The statement of purpose, read at the beginning of the speak-out, said,

> We are women of Brown University and we are breaking the silence.... In solidarity with women who have suffered rape, harassment, intimidation and fear, we all agree: something is wrong here. We agree on the problem, but not on the solution. We come to listen to white and Third World women, to straight and lesbian women. It is important for us to remember that the violence affects each of us differently.... By comparing notes, we learn that the problem is not ours individually, but ours collectively. As such, it demands a cooperative response.[69]

While the event was planned to last an hour, over 120 women chose to speak-out about their own experiences, filling five hours with women's stories, and displaying an awareness by the women of the connections between racist, sexist, and homophobic violence. The university agreed to all but one of the demands put forth by the women who organized the speak-out. (The demand not met was for the inclusion of "sexual preference" in the non-discrimination clause, noted above.) Some fraternities did not respond positively – some jeered the women during the speak-out, and one fraternity later hung a sexually mutilated effigy of the Women's Political Task Force coordinator out their window.

After the speak-out, and despite the backlash from some quarters, women at Brown made new connections – women who had never been involved politically became so, women who had never seen their own experiences as sexual harassment were suddenly aware of the political content of their experiences, women who were active made new personal contacts with other activists and made new political connections between issues of racism, sexism, and homophobia. This political energy was reflected in the longitudinal survey of the Class of 1988: the most significant change in the personal goals was an increase in women listing "participate in community action" and "promote racial understanding." At the same time, the men – who entered Brown already less liberal and radical than the women – reported a decrease in their valuing of these same items.[70]

The 1990s have begun with no less tenaciousness on the part of Brown women. One controversy of the academic year 1990–91, which became an issue for college women all over the country, surrounds date rape. In reaction to the lists kept by fraternity men of women who they alleged were sexually active, a group of Brown women kept lists of male students who they claimed sexually assaulted female students. These lists were available to all women – on the walls of the women's bathrooms in the main campus library. The women reasoned that public lists of men accused of such attacks would help other women take precautions and share information. The Brown administration responded to the activists' concerns, by reallocating some of the responsibilities for women's issues among administrators, naming an assistant dean of student life responsible for women's concerns, designating an ombudswoman for students, and creating a new mandatory seminar for entering students on sexual assault and harassment.[71]

Community Outreach

Along with helping to change conditions on the Brown campus, many women students reach beyond Van Wickle Gates to work for broader change in the surrounding Rhode Island community. Many feel a limit to the kinds of learning that can occur within a college environment and want to expand their own education through community involvement. Even with all their diversity, one thing women students at Brown have in common is just that: they are all students, and as students, they bring their resources, time, and thought into the larger community and return with tangible experiences and knowledge that enrich both their lives and Brown as a whole.

The history of Sojourner House, a shelter and hotline for battered women, provides a prime illustration of women students reaching out into the community to create change for women. In the mid-1970s, students in a socialist/feminist study group started to become aware of domestic violence as a widespread problem for women. One member of the group worked at Rhode Island Legal Services and witnessed many women coming there to request restraining orders against their husbands. Women in the study group began to wonder how prevalent domestic violence was and decided to research the issue in Providence; they wanted to test the analysis they had developed in a tangible realm. Women from the group went to police stations, hospitals, and church groups inquiring about incidents of battery; the responses they received were significant. From this beginning, the students decided to go beyond research to community action. They organized an initial meeting attended by both Brown students and women from the surrounding community and formed the Rhode Island Task Force on Domestic Violence. They eventually raised funds and instituted a hotline and a shelter called Sojourner House.[72]

Thanks in large part to Brown students, Sojourner House continues to be an active agency that supports and serves as an advocate for many battered women in the state. Throughout the 1980s Brown students were instrumental in keeping the agency going. One alumna recalled how difficult it was to staff the hotline while students were away for winter vacation, so integral was their continued involvement.[73]

Brown students are a significant component of many other feminist organizations in Rhode Island. Students have been active as both hotline volunteers and interns at the Rape Crisis Center, working at its speakers bureau and in the Child Assault Prevention (CAP) project that visits Rhode Island elementary schools.[74] The Coalition Against Domestic Violence, which is the umbrella group for all the shelters concerned with domestic violence in Rhode Island, also has benefited from Brown student participation. Recently, one student took on the project of writing a training manual for them.[75] Other feminist groups in which Brown women participate include Dorcas Place, which provides literacy training for women, the Rhode Island Feminist Chorus, and the Women's Center, another shelter serving battered women in Rhode Island.

On an electoral level, many Brown women were active in a statewide campaign in 1986 when there was an anti-choice proposition on the state ballot. Women students organized voter registration drives on campus and got a great number of students to the polls. The proposition was defeated by a ratio of two to one, partly because of student participation. Women students have continued to be involved in the abortion issue in

Rhode Island; they were instrumental in organizing to "escort" clients to local abortion clinics, often besieged by anti-abortion demonstrations. In the 1990s, a group called Brown Students for Choice is active on campus, and it stays in touch with Rhode Island's pro-choice groups.

Another place where women students have actively pursued community service projects at Brown is in the Black sororities. Delta Sigma Theta, for instance, has a strong belief in the value of promoting community. Central tenets of the sorority are service to the underserved and the support of personal identity. Black women join Delta Sigma Theta to be able to place their identity as Black women at the forefront, and with that sense of identity strengthened and supported by the sorority, the women contribute to the community. They tutor high school students in Providence, serve as mentors to teen parents in a program organized through the Providence Urban League, and teach sex education to teen women.[76]

Among the institutional avenues facilitating community work at

Brown women students marching for "Choice" in the 1986 March for Women's Rights in Washington, D.C.

Brown is the Resource Center. Begun in 1976 by students, the Resource Center's explicit concerns are to promote "student initiated learning projects and involvement with the larger Rhode Island community."[77] This focus has particularly appealed to women students, and the Resource Scholars program is a good example, with more than half of the participants women. Begun in the 1985–86 school year, the program "is designed to integrate the theoretical and practical approaches for study of a particular topic."[78] Projects over the years have included a study of language-minority students in Rhode Island schools, an examination of women nursing home residents, and a look at the implications of instituting an HIV testing law. After doing all the planning and research, the student presents a final project at a forum attended by the professor(s) who sponsored the project and members of the Rhode Island community involved in the issue, giving everyone a chance to interact and learn from each other.[79]

The Urban Environmental Lab (UEL) is another place on campus where university-community relations are well developed. In existence since 1978, the Urban Environmental Lab is the home of the environmental studies concentration, and its concepts and goals are well grounded in the Rhode Island community. Through UEL, students and professors research and implement environmental programs in Rhode Island. Throughout the eighties women consistently formed the majority of environmental studies majors.[80]

Finally, women students continue to be very active in the more traditional volunteer programs. Brown Community Outreach (BCO), the umbrella group and volunteer clearinghouse at Brown, gives students access to volunteer opportunities in 120–140 community organizations providing a range of services from tutoring to child care and gardening. Each year there is a "BCO Day" where community groups set up tables with information and students come to sign up to help the organizations that appeal to them. Women have always been leaders in BCO and its president has consistently been a woman student.[81]

Brown's support for community involvement continues to be strong. In 1987, the Center for Public Service officially opened its doors, providing a place for both the local and national coordination of volunteer students services. The Sarah Doyle Women's Center has for the first time included a paid student position of community outreach coordinator for the 1991–92 school year. The coordinator's express purpose is to build connections with the Rhode Island community and to encourage and support student involvement.[82]

Looking for ways to expand academically and politically, women students throughout the 1980s enhanced their Brown experience by expanding beyond its parameters. They sought out and benefited from the "real world" outside the university and in the process contributed to the community around them.

The Challenges of Diversity

From the perspective of many at Brown, the 1980s could be characterized by the concepts of diversity and pluralism. Brown has worked to promote a campus environment of tolerance, understanding and recognition of difference. Yet there are many holes in this fabric of diversity – some of which have appeared as racist graffiti in dorms, sexual harassment of women, and other holes which are more subtle, like the imbalance in the gender of financial aid recipients and the slow growth of the minority faculty. Brown works hard on issues of diversity – the important question still to be answered is whether the hard work is resulting in a truly changed environment for women students.

Brown does not pretend to be color-blind or uniformly non-sexist. It has chosen to address color, gender, and other differences head on and it attempts to define diversity as a value rather than a deficit. At the same time, Brown's attempt to celebrate diversity has left space for a wide divergence of opinions on these matters.

Whether faculty, administration, students, or fraternity members are really listening to the diversity training and experiencing the diverse community at Brown is unclear. Some women students, however, are clearly listening and taking the ideas seriously. In the survey of the Class of 1988, more women than men reported cultural diversity as essential (31 percent of men, 44.1 percent of women).[83] As one woman at the 1985 Speakout said, " . . . we think we can make changes. We want to make this school a less homophobic, sexist, racist and less Eurocentric place. By working together and raising our voices, we will all be more culturally affluent."[84]

NOTES

The section, "Community Outreach," was written by Martha Gardner.
    1. Special Thanks to Beth Zwick, Class of 1982 and coordinator 1985–89, Sarah Doyle Women's Center, who began this project; and to Kate Garrett and Jane Hitti, authors of *Piecework*, an excellent reference on women at Brown in the early 1980s. We'd also like to thank all the people we, or Beth, spoke with and who helped find necessary documents and information: Debra Abeshaus, student affairs officer, PLME; John Andrews, Office of Curricular Research, registrar; Victoria Ball; Julia Bengochea; Janet Blume, assistant professor, engineering; Carol Cohen, Class of 1982, assistant dean; Rabbi Sharon Cohen, Class of 1982; Gigi DiBello, coordinator, Sarah Doyle Women's Center; Martha Gardner, Class of 1988; Mark Gloria, Office of Curricular Research, registrar; Katherine T. Hall, registrar; Julia Jooyun Hyun, Class of 1991; Flora Keshgegian, associate chaplain for women's con-

cerns; Elizabeth Kirk, English Department; Karen McLaurin, associate director, Alumni Relations; Lois Monteiro, professor of community health; Margaret Moser, Class of 1981; Louise Newman; Kris Onishi, Class of 1991; Lori Pope, Class of 1988, minority peer counselor coordinator; Karen Romer, associate dean for academic affairs; Robin Rose, Psychological Services; Edee Saar, Class of 1992; Robert Shaw, associate dean; Toby Simon, director of health education; Jeanne Smith, coordinator, Third World Center; Barbara Tannenbaum, Department of Theatre, Speech and Dance; Charlotte Tomas, associate dean; Marjorie Thompson, assistant dean, biology; Elizabeth Weed, associate director, Pembroke Center for Teaching and Research on Women; Shirley Wright, director of financial aid; and others who wish to remain anonymous or who we've neglected to mention.

2. As of this writing, Brown is engaged in a controversy over its expulsion of a male student for violating this policy as well as those "against alcohol abuse and disruptive behavior." "The Evolution of Brown's Anti-Harassment Clause," *Brown Alumni Monthly* 91 (March 1991): 44; "Brown U. Expels Student Who Yelled Racial Epithets," *Chronicle of Higher Education* 20 (February 1991); "Robin Rose to Coordinate Women's Concerns," *Brown Alumni Monthly* 91 (February 1991): 11–12.

3. David Temkin, "Times of Tension," *Brown Alumni Monthly* 89 (June/July 1989): 26.

4. *Men and Women Learning Together: a Study of College Students in the Late 70s,* Report of *The Brown Project,* Brown University, April 1980.

5. Cooperative Institutional Research Program – Conducted jointly by the American Council on Education and the University of California, Los Angeles, Fall 1986, files from Bob Shaw. This study compares Brown students to their peers at other schools and covers everything from parents' income to attitudes on nuclear weapons to scholastic achievement.

Two later studies which asked some of the same questions raised in the Coed Report failed to include an analysis by gender or race. The Yankelovich Survey in 1987 questioned 12,000 graduates of 1973 to 1985 on their assessments of Brown's "New Curriculum," and a report in 1990 by the Dean of the College examined the concentrations chosen by Brown students and their choices of post-college careers and graduate studies. By not including gender and race breakdowns in these studies, the university missed the opportunity to discover and address variations by gender and race in the success and happiness of Brown students.

6. These percentages were tabulated by the authors using: Table 4a-d, "Total Completed Concentrations, June 1984 through June 1989, Humanities, Life Sciences, Physical Sciences, Social Sciences", 17 July 1989; curricular research from the registrar and "Academic Interests as Declared upon Application, 1982 through 1991." Note that these statistics are kept by two separate departments, and each office breaks down the categories in different ways, making some comparisons impossible. The Admission Office, for instance, does not separate the physical sciences into its twelve components. It would be valuable to be able to compare smaller categories and thereby discern if the pattern is different for, say, geology than it is for physics or computer science.

7. 1986 Follow-up of 1984 Freshmen Institutional Summary; *Cooperative Institutional Research Program,* pp. 2, 8.

8. Anonymous interview with author, December 1990.

9. Neither the Math Department nor the Computer Science Department have women's student groups.

10. Statistics on the programs supplied by Dean Karen T. Romer.

11. Women received an average of 51.45 percent of Honors awards over six years, while comprising slightly less than 50 percent of each class. Women earned 47.2 percent of the magna cum laude degrees. Registrar, Table 1, "Undergraduate Awards of Magna cum laude, Honors in Concentration, and Honor Society by Gender, June 1984 through June 1989," 17 July 1989; Curricular Research.

12. Phi Beta Kappa is awarded "primarily upon scholastic standings as shown by offi-

cial college records" but at least 40 percent of the student's course work must be in the humanities and social sciences and must show a breadth of disciplines. Sigma Xi awards are for the "encouragement of original investigation in science, pure and applied" and "nominations are made by representatives of the various science departments." Brown, *Catalogue of the University*, 1977–79, p. 376.

13. Tau Beta Pi is the national engineering honor society, both students and alumni are eligible, and membership is based upon scholarship and "integrity, breadth of interest both inside and outside of engineering, adaptability, and unselfish activity." Brown, *Catalogue of the University*, 1977–79, p. 377.

14. Yearly lists of "Independent Concentrators by Name, Concentration Title, Faculty Sponsor and Graduation Year," kept by the Office of Dean Karen Romer; 1986 Follow-up of 1984 Freshmen; *Cooperative Institutional Research Program.*

15. Registrar, Table 2, "Undergraduate Separations by Gender: 1983 through 1988," Curricular Research, 17 July 1989.

16. The actual figures are: "reconsider goals and interests," 69.6 percent men, 63.4 percent women; "wanted practical experience," 39.1 percent men, 39 percent women; "bored with coursework," 13 percent men, 4.9 percent women; not "doing well academically," 17.4 percent men, 12.2 percent women; and being "tired of being a student," 43.5 percent men, 24.4 percent women; inability to "afford college," 0 percent men, 14.6 percent women; wanting to be "closer to home," 0 percent men, 7.3 percent women; and wanting "wider course selection," 0 percent men, 7.5 percent women. 1986 Follow-up of 1984 Freshmen; *Cooperative Institutional Research Program.*

17. The numbers are: "satisfied with financial aid": 54.5 percent men, 45.4 percent women. 1986 Follow-up of 1985 Freshmen; *Cooperative Institutional Research Program.* Kate Garrett and Jane Hitti, *Piecework: Women's Lives at Brown*, Sarah Doyle Women's Center, 1982, p. 69. Reporting part-time work was 40.4 percent of men and 51.6 percent of women. 1986 Follow-up of 1984 Freshmen; *Cooperative Institutional Research Program;* late 1980s financial aid figures supplied by the Financial Aid Office.

18. Trustee's Reports, Data on Faculty Composition, 1989–90. One woman professor in science told us that her department makes a conscious effort to have women teach some of the large introductory courses in order to emphasize the women as role models for both men and women students. The positive aspects of this for students are, to some extent, countered by the negative effect this may have on women faculty who need to focus on publishing to secure tenure.

19. Elizabeth Zwick, Anonymous survey of women students and alumnae, 1989, hereafter cited as Zwick survey.

20. Registrar, Table 6, "Undergraduate Women Ever Enrolled in a Women's Studies Course By Entry Year, 1983 through 1988," Curricular Research; 17 July 1989; Elizabeth Weed, 12 April 1991.

21. Zwick Survey, anonymous student, Class of 1989.

22. Zwick Survey, anonymous student, Class of 1985.

23. Zwick Survey, anonymous student, Class of 1983.

24. The founding proposal for the Center for the Study of Race and Ethnicity in America stated that "It is assumed that the study of non-European minorities in America will enlarge and deepen our appreciation of the varieties of the American experience and that our understanding of American society will thereby become more realistic, more sophisticated and more complete." Members of the Brown Faculty, Proposal for Center for the Study of Race and Ethnicity in America, p. 2. By 1989, 57 percent of the current undergraduate population had taken at least one Third World or Minority Course. Sheila Blumstein, "The Brown Curriculum Twenty Years Later, January 1990," p. 57. Enhancing the course offerings of the college is only one goal of the center – instituting a faculty seminar and providing research support are also important goals.

25. *Brown University Student Handbook*, 1989–90, Office of Student Life, Brown

University, p. 64.

26. "Appendix: 1984 & 1987, Sex Survey," Office of Health Education, Brown University Health Services, *Annual Report, 1987–88,* p. 4.

27. George Carey, "A View from the Futon," *Brown Alumni Monthly* 90 (March 1990): 41.

28. Brown University, *Trustees' Report, 1988–1989,* p. 98. Brown stopped offering the option of an all-female dorm in the late eighties due to declining interest, but several dorms have all-women hallways.

29. Information on resident counselor programs supplied by Dean Karen Romer.

30. Anonymous woman faculty member interview with author, January 1991. This was also true at Yale: see Janet Lever, Pepper Schwartz, *Women at Yale* (Indianapolis: Bobbs-Merrill, 1971), p. 58.

31. Zwick Survey, anonymous student, Class of 1990.

32. Zwick Survey, anonymous student, Class of 1987.

33. Zwick Survey, anonymous student, Class of 1984; Zwick survey, anonymous student, Class of 1989.

34. Zwick Survey, anonymous student, Class of 1987.

35. Zwick Survey, anonymous student, Class of 1983.

36. Zwick Survey, anonymous student, Class of 1983.

37. Zwick Survey, anonymous student, Class of 1991.

38. Zwick Survey, anonymous student, Class of 1983.

39. Laurie Sherman, "Women at Brown University Decry Sexual Assaults," *Gay Community News,* 1 June 1985, p. 3.

40. Tracey L. Scronic, "The Evolution of the Coed Fraternity Zeta Delta Xi From the All-Male Fraternity Zeta Psi," student papers, American Civilization 190E, December 1989, Christine Dunlap Farnham Archives, Brown University.

41. "Psi U Becomes First Brown Fraternity to Abolish Pledging," *Brown Alumni Monthly* 90 (March 1990): 15.

42. Author interview with Elizabeth Zwick, December 1990.

43. See, for example, Bernice Johnson Reagon, "Coalition Politics: Turning the Century," in Barbara Smith, *Home Girls: A Black Feminist Anthology,* (New York: Kitchen Table/ Women of Color Press, 1983).

44. The Third World Center's membership has shifted radically as the minority population at Brown has shifted. African-American enrollment in universities throughout the U.S. peaked in the mid- to late-1970s and began to drop precipitously by the early 1980s. Brown's African-American population has leveled off during the 1980s at about 7.45 percent. Asian-American enrollments have climbed steadily, beginning with only 3.1 percent of the Class of 1980 and reaching 8.2 percent of the Class of 1989. Hispanic-Americans have also gained steadily in enrollments throughout the decade, beginning with 0.5 percent of the Class of 1980 and reaching 3.1 percent of the Class of 1989. Report of the Visiting Committee on Minority Life and Education at Brown University, "The American University and the Pluralist Ideal," May 1986, p. 59.

45. The TWC currently has a long list of ongoing organizations and support groups which it hosts, including distinct organizations for many of the different races represented among the Brown student body. Current organizations at the TWC include: African Students' Association, Association of Middle Eastern Students, Bi-Racial Student Support Group, Cambodian Students Association, Chinese Students Association, Filipino Alliance at Brown, Hong Kong Students Association, Latin American Students Organization, la Federacion de Estudiantes Puertorriquenos, Native Americans at Brown, and the South Asian Students Association, among others. Throughout the 80s, the TWC has had a proliferation of other types of organizations as well, many based in academic disciplines: ONYX, Black Pre-Med Society, Black Psychology Students Association, National Society of Black Engineers, Third World Gay/Lesbian Support Group, Third World Pre-Business Society, Third World Pre-Law

Society, and Minority Peer Counselors. The Third World Transition Program pamphlet produced by the Third World Center states:

At Brown, Asian, Black, Latino, Native American and multi-racial students use the term "Third World" to describe a consciousness which recognizes the commonalities and links shared by their diverse communities. Together, these groups strive for cross-cultural understanding and a unity of purpose. Students first began using the term "Third World" at Brown in 1975 as part of a move to define their own identities. They chose the term "Third World" over "minority" because of the negative connotations of inferiority and powerlessness with which the word "minority" is often associated. For these students, "Third World" represented self-definition and empowerment through linkage to the rich heritage of their ancestors. "Third World" establishes a connection between Asian, Black, Latino, Native American and multi-racial people in the United States and people of Asia, Africa and Latin America, who together make up the majority of the world population. The concept of "Third World" has special meaning for minority students at Brown. It is not to be confused with the economic definition of the term used commonly in our society today, but understood as a term that celebrates the cultures of Asians, Blacks, Latinos, and Native Americans.

46. *Watch Us Rise: An Anthology for and by Third World Women.*

47. Mastheads from 1989 and 1990 copies of *Issues* and *Brown Daily Herald.*

48. Martha Gardner interview with Hilary Binda, Class of 1989, May 1991.

49. WEB flier, circa 1989, from files of Flora Keshgegian, chaplain for women's concerns.

50. Women students involved in Hillel during the 1980s continued to be affected by the feminist rumblings of the 1970s as demonstrated by the comparatively large number of Brown women graduates who enter rabbinical school. At least nine Brown alumnae are rabbis. See Chapter 10.

51. "Appendix: 1984 & 1987 Sex Survey," Office of Health Education, Brown University Health Services *Annual Report, 1987–88*, p. 4. Note: The researchers caution that this is not "a scientifically rigorous study of sex life on our campus," but state that it "is quite *valid*" for Brown.

52. Office of Health Education, Brown University Health Services *Annual Report, 1987–88*, pp. 16–17; hereafter referred to as Health Education *Annual Report, 1987–88.*

53. "Appendix: 1984 & 1987 Sex Survey," pp. 3, 4, 6, 7.

54. Ibid., pp. 6, 7; Health Education, *Annual Report, 1987–88*, p. 17.

55. Ibid., p. 19.

56. The Brown Sex Survey revealed that in 1987 students viewed AIDS as a relatively remote threat; their attitudes displayed misinformation and lack of sensitivity towards people with AIDS. Ibid., pp. 17–19.

57. "Appendix: 1984 & 1987 Sex Survey," p. 11. It is highly likely that these statistics reflect underreporting because of the stigma associated with admitting to homosexuality. Of those who reported "equal heterosexual and homosexual orientation," males and females were equally represented. By contrast, the "exclusively homosexual orientation" category had a three to one ratio of men to women, perhaps due to the fact that men tend to be sexually active at a younger age than women, and thus explore sexual orientation sooner in their undergraduate years.

58. Anonymous student, Class of 1984, quoted in Garrett and Hitti, *Piecework,* p. 48.

59. Anonymous student, Class of 1985, quoted in Garrett and Hitti, *Piecework,* p. 47.

60. Anonymous student, Class of 1984, quoted in Garrett and Hitti, *Piecework,* p. 48.

61. Anonymous student, Class of 1985, quoted in Garrett and Hitti, *Piecework,* p. 47.

62. Author interview with Martha Gardner, Class of 1988, March 1991. In the early eighties LGBA was primarily a social organization of gay men until a group of politically active lesbians became involved. The organization remained predominantly male in member-

ship throughout the decade, but to encourage power sharing, the group began to require gender parity in its leadership positions, so lesbians became increasingly visible spokespersons. The Lesbian/Bisexual Collective, on the other hand, drew on the history of women-only organizing based at the SDWC. In the early 1980s, women at SDWC began organizing discussions for women about sexuality and lesbianism. The Lesbian Collective has provided a similar discussion and support function for lesbians as well as a network for resource development and political action.

63. Author interview with Gardner.

64. "Sixty-Five Students Face Charges of Disrupting CIA Recruiters," *Brown Alumni Monthly* 84 (December–January, 1985): 18.

65. *Cooperative Institutional Research Program*, p. 1.

66. Brown has not offered comparable training in diversity issues for the majority of the faculty and staff causing some administrators to worry that this has the effect of putting all the responsibility for racism, sexism, and other oppressions on the shoulders of eighteen-year olds.

67. Author interviews with Edee Saar, Class of 1992, and Elizabeth Zwick, Class of 1982.

68. *Ms. Magazine*, October 1983, p. 61.

69. "Women at Brown University Decry Sexual Assaults," *Gay Community News*, 1 June 1985, p. 3.

70. *Cooperative Institutional Research Program*, 1986 Follow-up of 1984 Freshmen, p. 8. "Community action" in 1984 was 30.1 percent men, 32 percent women and in 1986 was 23 percent men, 36.5 percent women; "racial understanding" in 1984 was 47 percent men, 51.9 percent women and in 1986 was 43.3 percent men, 59.8 percent women.

71. "Robin Rose to coordinate women's concerns," *Brown Alumni Monthly* 91 (February 1991): 11. For date rape as a national issue for college women, see *Time*, 3 June 1991, pp. 48–55.

72. Martha Gardner interview with Cathy Lewis, Class of 1976, May 1991, and Linda Kramer, Class of 1977, May 1991.

73. Martha Gardner interview with Wendy Becker, Class of 1983, May 1991.

74. Martha Gardner interview with Katherine Barrows, crisis intervention coordinator at the Rhode Island Rape Crisis Center, May 1991.

75. Martha Gardner interview with Donna Nesselbush, director of the Coalition against Domestic Violence, May 1991.

76. Martha Gardner interview with Natalia Peart, Class of 1988, May 1991.

77. Quoted from "The Sixth Annual Resource Scholars Program" brochure, April 1991.

78. Ibid.

79. Martha Gardner interview with Claudia Yellin, director, Resource Center, May 1991.

80. Martha Gardner interview with Carolyn Digbie, May 1991.

81. Martha Gardner interview with Peter Hocking, assistant director of the Center for Public Service, May 1991.

82. Martha Gardner interview with Gigi DiBello, coordinator, Sarah Doyle Women's Center, May 1991.

83. *Cooperative Institutional Research Program*.

84. Laurie Sherman, quoting Yuko Uchikawa, "Women at Brown University Decry Sexual Assaults," *Gay Community News*, 1 June 1985, p. 3.

CHAPTER 9

A Network of Women:
Alumnae Volunteerism in Rhode Island

by KAREN M. LAMOREE

WHEN JANE ADDAMS visited
Providence in 1910, Sarah Doyle was eager to introduce her to one of the
young Brown alumnae capitalizing on her college education with a professional career. She brought Addams to meet Margaret Bingham Stillwell,
Class of 1909, in the John Carter Brown Library. There Stillwell was
embarking on the library career in which she would become a well-known
incunabulist. Addams, however, was singularly unimpressed with Stillwell's
choice of career and exhorted her to work for change in one of the movements of the Progressive era. As a result, Stillwell used the research skills
garnered from her career to write three reports on the status of children
for Rhode Island's nascent Division of Child Welfare. Only two were published; the third on child labor was suppressed by the industrial interests,
much to her chagrin.[1]

The women of Brown University owe their educational opportunities
in large measure to the women's clubs of Rhode Island, in particular to
the Rhode Island Society for the Collegiate Education of Women (RISCEW)
and its leader, Sarah E. Doyle. Brown women have paid that debt many
times over with their volunteer services both during their schooling and
especially after graduation. From the very beginning, Brown alumnae,
students, faculty and faculty wives have been involved in volunteerism
and reform.

Women serving Brown: Gail McCann, Class of 1975, president
of the Associated Alumni; Doris Hopkins Stapelton, Class of 1928,
former executive secretary of the Pembroke Alumnae Association; and Sally Hill Cooper, Class of 1952, alumnae trustee.

National Sample of Alumnae Volunteers

A 1990 sample of Brown alumnae who graduated in the "0" and "5" years between 1930 to 1985 was divided into three cohorts: 1930–1949, 1950–1970, and 1971 to 1985.[2] A comparison of their activities reveals change over time. Sixty percent of the alumnae performing one-to-one service as counselors, servers in soup kitchens, and working in homeless shelters were from the youngest cohort. Two-thirds of those working on environmental issues were from the same cohort. Eighty percent of the alumnae working in feminist and/or women-centered activities were evenly divided between the 1950–1970 and 1971–1985 cohorts. Many of these women worked for the goals of Planned Parenthood, served as pregnancy counselors, and worked for pro-choice movements. Other women-centered activities include serving in battered women's shelters or on rape crisis hotlines, leading women's discussion groups, and volunteering as a docent in a women's art museum. Alumnae have worked for the National Organization for Women's Legal Defense Fund. An alumna from California challenged the exclusion of women from public golf courses and girls from Little League.[3]

The 1950–1970 cohort was most involved with cultural activities (55 percent of the total), church work (50 percent of the total), and education/work with children (55 percent of the total). Cultural activities have included historical societies, serving on the boards of the Rhode Island Philharmonic, an opera, and the Boston Ballet. One-half of the respondents in the middle cohort can be characterized as leaders or founders. The oldest and most experienced cohort, 1930–1949, accounted for 75 percent of the board of director positions. They also comprised one-third of the church workers and 40 percent of those involved in cultural activities.[4]

The sample also revealed that the greatest satisfactions from alumnae volunteer activities were first, helping others and second, self-improvement. Alumnae noted that volunteer work gave them opportunities to spread their wings and acquire experience. As a result they gained confidence in all areas of their lives. Time management followed by insufficient funding were the two largest sources of frustration. The greatest frustrations were felt by the youngest group. Fifty-four percent of those citing time management as a problem came from the third cohort and 70 percent of those citing funding came from the same cohort.

Early Student and Alumnae Volunteerism in Rhode Island

All over the country, Brown alumnae have been involved as community activists and reformers, but the most concentrated effect of their work has been in the state of Rhode Island. This chapter will examine the volunteer careers in Rhode Island of some representative figurative daughters of Sarah E. Doyle. College students and alumni often have an impact on their college town, but in the case of Brown women, the connection between town and gown was strengthened by the overwhelmingly local nature of the student body in their first fifty years in the university. In 1907 Dean Lida Shaw King recalled that President Elisha Benjamin Andrews often referred to the college as a "State College" because it was the people of Rhode Island who would reap the greatest benefits. She noted the accuracy of his title – at that time 80 percent of the students and 73 percent of the living alumnae resided in Rhode Island. The concentration lessened over time; by 1941, 35 percent of living alumnae resided in the state and by 1990 only 10 percent remained.[5] Although the geographic composition and types of activities grew more diverse, a common thread connecting all the generations was the ethos of community service and action inherited from and inculcated through contacts with the women who engineered women's entrance into Brown in 1891.

The Women's College encouraged its students and alumnae from its beginning to participate in the club and reform movements of the day. The Christian Association at the college had, for example, organized a Student Volunteer Band by 1907. It was through the Christian Association that most women students through the 1950s explored the volunteer activities which they would follow throughout their lives.[6] The type of community service encouraged at the Women's College fit into the traditional woman's sphere of church and children. These areas were safe by virtue of their feminine connotations. They were also overlooked or devalued by the male-dominated political and social milieu.

Women continued the nineteenth century pattern of finding in church work an acceptable outlet for their interests and a way to address problems untouched by male society. Innumerable alumnae served as church officers, most often as secretaries, in the years prior to the women's movement. Gertrude Conant, Class of 1912, held that position at St. Paul's Episcopal Church in Pawtucket for thirty-five years as well as a place on the board of the Episcopal St. Elizabeth's Home in Providence. Margaret Stone Strout, Class of 1910, served on the Board of Managers of the Baptist State Convention from 1927–1932 and as the program chair for the Businesswomen's Fellowship of the Mathewson Street Methodist Church. Marion P. Harley, Class of 1915, was a trustee of Park Place Congregational Church in Pawtucket in 1958 and Grace A. McAuslan, Class of 1928, executive secretary of the First Congregational Church. Perhaps the best known Rhode Island churchwoman was Anna Canada Swain, Class of

1911. From the First Baptist Meeting House in Providence, she became the first woman to serve on the Central Committee of the World Council of Churches. She also served as president of the American Baptist Churches, the Rhode Island Baptist Women's Mission Society, the Women's American Baptist Foreign Mission Society, and the Northern Baptist Convention. In her speeches she often lauded the contributions of women in evangelism. In one broadcast speech, "Both Martha and Mary," she argued that churches needed women both as housekeepers and lay leaders. She would become Brown's first woman trustee in 1949.[7]

Work with children was an area to which women were attracted and which was an acceptably feminine enterprise. In the first decade of the twentieth century, women received laudatory attention in Rhode Island newspapers largely for activities which related to children, later broadening to include educational and health issues.[8] College women were in the forefront of the Progressive movement, but only in certain prescribed areas. Although their talents and intellectual capabilities were honed in the still-radical world of college, they were most often involved in traditionally feminine areas of community action that utilized their role as nurturers. In addition, because of their unique perspective, women saw holes where men never thought to look.

In a 1917 description of "Volunteer Social Work in Providence" in *The Sepiad*, Doris Snow Briggs, Class of 1914, urged students to work with children and adolescents through the Children's Theatre and the Young Women's Christian Temperance Union and to perform "friendly visiting" for the Society for Organizing Charity.[9] Service through work with private associations or new, public agencies that focused on children's welfare was common for women professors, professors' wives, students, and alumnae. In the 1930s the Christian Association assisted in evening school classes in sewing, painting, dramatics, bridge, and dancing. This orientation toward child welfare as the acceptable form of volunteerism for women was institutionalized in such programs as Pembroke's Volunteer Service Bureau, established in 1946. The Bureau's projects were largely geared toward children. Under the direction of the Bureau, Pembroke students taught junior high school subjects to girls under sixteen at the Woman's Reformatory and led recreation, handicraft, dramatics, and Girl Scout troops at the Girls' Reform School.

Beyond student efforts was the work of alumnae, faculty, and the wives of faculty. They often worked together in the network of philanthropy and reform groups of the day. Annie H. Barus, wife of Brown Professor Carl H. Barus, was secretary of the Providence Public Education Association and also a leader in the Association of Collegiate Alumnae

Pembroke students making Christmas toys for the Children's Friend Society in 1937, from left: Kathryn Rau, Lucile Bowers, Barbara Campbell, and Alice Barlow, all Class of 1939.

and in mothers' clubs. Gertrude Conant, Class of 1912, was president of the Girls' Friendly Society from 1917–1920. Wilhelmina Bennett Cox, Class of 1916, was the senior president of the Rhode Island Society of Children of the American Revolution. Introducing sports to young women was Edith Davis Richard, Class of 1916, who chaired the Junior Girls' Golf for the Rhode Island Women's Golf Association. Celia Ernstof Adler, Class of 1925, spent more than fifty years engaged in social work for children and serving on the board of the Child Guidance Clinic, and Deborah Burton, Class of 1926, was executive director of the Smith Hill Girls' Club of Providence. Her role as a mother spurred the charitable efforts of Margaret Porter Dolan, Class of 1939. "Having six children," she said, "I felt keenly the need to do something for children less fortunate." She concentrated on the Guild of the St. Aloysius Home for Orphans. The Guild raised funds to purchase the "extras" the children desired. Beryl Kossove Meyer, Class of 1945, was neighborhood chair of the Elmgrove area of Girl Scouts, one of many alumnae involved in that organization.[10] In the 1960s one of the major volunteer activities for women was teaching youngsters at the Lippitt Hill Tutorial.[11]

Faculty such as biology instructor, Ada Wing Mead, A. M. 1896, provided role models for their students. As a female biology and hygiene professional, she was the logical choice to write a 1901 report on the sanitary conditions of the Providence Public Schools. The membership of the Providence Public School Association was largely female and included a number of RISCEW members, including Sarah E. Doyle.[12]

As women carved respectable niches for themselves in issues not often given the highest priorities by the political and corporate establishment, for example, child welfare and day care, the volunteer movement became professionalized. Rhode Island native Dr. Ellen A. Stone, A.M. 1896, for example, was superintendent of the Child Hygiene Division of the Providence Department of Health from 1913 to 1934, developing it into "a model for other communities." She advocated public health measures and child guidance clinics, and established a fresh air school for tubercular children as well as investigating the causes of juvenile delinquency. At the time of her death she was characterized as "a pioneer woman physician and one of the country's best known workers in child health."[13] Stone typifies the college-educated woman with a progressive agenda. Taking advantage of her education and expanding horizons, she constructed a governmental agency in an area considered highly appropriate for a woman.

Women of the Progressive era, whether as volunteers or as paid professionals, created and exploited a newly favorable social and political climate to provide services or the means of social change for those segments of society usually hidden from view. As time went on, these programs changed from private programs to bureaucracies in the alphabet agencies of the New Deal. While working as volunteers and reformers, women were usually not one-issue activists, but rather were involved in a wide variety of activities revolving around children, church, and general community welfare. This type of volunteerism – professional and with a generalist approach to community service – attracted many Brown alumnae, particularly those who graduated in the period prior to 1960. Volunteerism allowed them an opportunity to use their education in new ways to fill gaps in community services and expand their horizons beyond the limits of paid employment and home.[14]

Doris Hopkins Stapelton, Class of 1928, is perhaps best known to the Brown community for her seventeen-year stint from 1955 to 1972 as executive secretary of the Pembroke Alumnae Association. Characterizing her paid employment as "routine" and her volunteer work as "exciting," Stapelton found her challenges since the 1940s in the more than twenty different positions she has held as a volunteer.[15]

Her peripatetic career began quietly. After her 1930 marriage, Stapelton stopped working as a teacher and worked as a private tutor. She had two daughters six years apart. Although she characterized her entrance into volunteerism as "strange," in fact it was the most common method of all, volunteer work related to the maternal role. In Stapelton's case, it was the Girl Scouts. From troop leader, Stapelton went on to the district committee and from there to council and commissioner.[16]

Stapelton's Girl Scout work led to the Group Work Division of the Rhode Island Council of Community Services (RICCS). While she was chair, a council study led to the first program for senior citizens, which still exists in 1990 as the 60 Plus Club. In the network approach characteristic of volunteerism, the position of chair of the Division at RICCS led to her being elected secretary of the United Way. From 1951 to 1953, she was president of the Pembroke Club of Providence and from 1953 to 1955, president of the Pembroke Alumnae Association. She resigned that position in order to become the executive secretary of the association.[17]

Although Stapelton's volunteerism tapered off during her years of paid employment, her church work continued. As assistant superintendent of the church school, she occasionally taught an adult Bible class. She also served as deaconess, director of the senior high youth program, and director of the church's Kinderkirk. Since her retirement she has become increasingly involved in her church. Her positions have included three years as clerk and three years as moderator, the chief officer of the church. One of her greatest accomplishments was serving as chair of the Stewardship Committee, charged with raising the annual budget, now amounting to $260,000 per annum.[18]

Retirement allowed new opportunities and new foci to emerge. In 1981 she became the first woman member on the board of management of the Cranston Historical Society, eventually serving as secretary and chair. From 1972 to the present Stapelton has been a member and two-term president of the steering committee of Cranston Leisure Learning, an adult education program which she saw grow from fifty to more than three hundred members and then "decline" into the establishment of senior centers. Among her recent activities at Brown has been editing the newsletter of the Pembroke Center Associates.[19]

As with many generalists, Stapelton's skills in administration were honed in the more than twenty different positions she held. Volunteerism allowed her to change her public activities as community needs and her personal interests changed. The community network allowed an interested and capable volunteer the ability to leapfrog from organization to organization. This horizontal movement provided the opportunity for the excitement of which Stapelton spoke: "I was always learning. I was constantly challenged."[20]

The overriding characteristic of the women involved in such activities as church, child welfare, and that other major form of organized relief efforts, women's war work, was a general orientation toward community service rather than a focused intensity toward one issue. Their work filled the need of a particular moment. They belonged concurrently to a variety of organizations and operated within an interwoven network of volunteers. In weaving this pattern, students and alumnae were following the traditions created by the Rhode Island club women who helped to found the Women's College.

Establishing Volunteer Networks

The women of RISCEW and the Rhode Island Women's Club (RIWC) created and participated in the remarkable associational trend among women in the nineteenth century. RISCEW Treasurer, RIWC President, and Daughters of the American Revolution State Regent Amelia S. Knight established the Rhode Island State Federation of Women's Clubs in 1895. Beginning with Elizabeth Peckham Kinder, Class of 1895, innumerable Brown women have served on the federation and on its early parallel, the Rhode Island Federation of Colored Women's Clubs.[21]

One of the early African-American graduates of Brown University, Beatrice Coleman, Class of 1925, became involved with the Rhode Island Association of the National Association of Colored Women's Clubs in 1944 and held several posts. She served as past president of the Criterion Club and as secretary of the local branch of the National Association for the Advancement of Colored People.[22]

In 1990–1991 the International General Federation of Women's Clubs celebrated its centennial with the theme "A Past to Remember – A Future to Mold." The international president during 1988–1990 was Alice Clark Donahue, Class of 1946, of Barrington. She spoke of the connection between early women like Amelia Knight and Sarah E. Doyle and women of today: "As our founders and the leaders who followed them determined the course of action for the twentieth century, so must we determine the major issues facing society in the twenty-first century." One of the necessary subtexts to the issues of illiteracy, teen pregnancy, and natural resources was the changing nature of volunteerism itself.[23]

Like her nineteenth century predecessors and many of her contemporaries, Alice Donahue entered community work in order to "do something." In a chain of events common to professional volunteers, Donahue came to volunteerism after she resigned her positions as a speech instructor at Brown and Salve Regina College following the birth of her first child in 1948. She believed her time in the workforce was limited after her 1947 marriage to Thomas Donahue, Class of 1945, because, she said, "at the time very few married women worked," whether through desire or because of prohibitions in such professions as teaching. "I knew I wasn't the kind to want to play tennis or golf or bridge . . . that's when I became interested in organization and volunteer work. To me it was very similar to a job," she explained. Another motivator was her mentor, Sr. Mary James, the principal of her high school, St. Xavier's Academy. Sr. James was delighted that she would be attending Pembroke, but Donahue remembered her admonition that one's education is meaningful only to the degree that you share it with others.[24]

Donahue's first introduction to clubs and conventions was alumnae clubs and the Parent Teacher Association. Of greatest interest to her was the PTA's newly active interest in school board committees.[25] In 1958, after she became involved with the Barrington Junior Women's Club, she campaigned for the school board and lost. As a result, however, Donahue became active in the Democratic Party and served on the Barrington and State Democratic Committees. She also held positions on the School Survey Committee and the Child Welfare Advisory Committee.[26]

In the late 1950s and early 1960s Donahue recalled that a group of her associates thought the time had come for Rhode Island to have candidates in the government reflecting greater ethnic and religious diversity. As a result the Women's Intergroup Relations Committee was formed. One of the outcomes was a conference held at Pembroke of Catholic, Protestant, Jewish, African-American, and Hispanic Rhode Island women. Donahue considered it an "eye-opener." When she attended Pembroke with some of the African-American women, she had felt that they were like "any other student. But they had to overcome many obstacles [of which] I had no idea," she said. Out of the conferences grew a concern for fair housing. Donahue was co-chair of the "Good Neighbor Pledge." One signed a pledge stating that one was not adverse to someone of a different race buying or renting a home next to one's own. The pledges were accumulated and printed in local newspapers to demonstrate the breadth of support. Donahue was harassed for her efforts; one night a man followed her from a Providence meeting to her Barrington home. Shortly after arriving at her house, she received an anonymous phone call, warning her "You were lucky tonight. You might not be as lucky with your children." The police watched her children at the bus stop daily and she had to report her whereabouts to the police.[27]

During the 1960s Donahue began to achieve prominent positions in local organizations. In 1970 she was elected to a two-year position as president of the Rhode Island Federation of Women's Clubs. In 1978 she was elected treasurer of the worldwide federation and began the structured path to the top culminating in her 1988 election to the presidency.[28]

Donahue's primary interests in the GFWC are education and health. These combine in the GFWC programs about teen pregnancy, which she calls "one of the major concerns in the United States today." A second major initiative and interest in education is the GFWC literacy program. Of her wide variety of volunteer work, Donahue remains proudest of her GFWC presidency.[29]

The future of volunteerism of the kind exemplified by Alice Clark Donahue – professional, generalist in orientation, devoting many hours per week of unpaid labor – is in doubt. In 1972 the National Organization for Women passed a resolution condemning "traditional" volunteerism in which women serve as the unpaid conscience of the nation. The resolution urged women to work for change rather than to provide services the government should provide. Donahue, like many of her peers, argues that governmental resources are not unlimited and that the likelihood of government providing all of the services available through volunteers is slim. Equally problematic, however, is the fact that as governmental cutbacks in services in the 1980s demonstrated, women are no longer available as volunteers in the great numbers of the past. As Donahue notes, most women today hold paid jobs *and* care for a family, leaving little time or energy for wide-ranging community service. Those women who can find work that combines a salary with fulfillment of the desire for community service are fortunate.[30]

Judith Weiss Cohen, Class of 1943, A.M. 1948, was one who found employment for social change in the 1960s. After graduation from Brown, Cohen served a two year stint in the Women's Army Corps; she attained the rank of sergeant by the time of her discharge in 1946. In 1948 she earned her master's degree from Brown in political science.[31] She devoted the next several years to homemaking and her volunteer work. She especially enjoyed the presidency of the Pawtucket League of Women Voters in 1956. She wanted to continue her activities in the league and work toward the presidency of the state league, but financial pressures forced her instead to seek full-time employment.

She was fortunate to secure employment she felt would benefit society with the Blackstone Valley Community Action Program (BVCAP). Originally hired as a part time research assistant, Cohen wrote a study on poverty in Pawtucket which was instrumental in determining the direction of the agency in the future. She eventually became associate director for fiscal operations, a position she held from 1966 to 1973. In 1989 she recalled that she "helped the agency grow from tiny beginnings to a major force in the Blackstone Valley during the [1970s].[32]

The BVCAP was funded by the federal Office of Economic Opportunity (OEO) and had "almost no money" that first year. She explained that "We faced an awful lot of hostility in those days. It was hard for people to believe there was so much poverty around them. They'd say things like, "'This isn't Appalachia.'" After receiving an initial grant from the OEO, the agency began establishing programs for the poor.[33] Grant writing was a necessity and Cohen became an accomplished grant writer. In 1968 she wrote a grant for the BVCAP "for what was to be the first family planning program in Rhode Island." When local mayors threatened to close all Blackstone Valley anti-poverty efforts, the money had to be returned to the federal government. "The resulting publicity helped create a climate for family planning," she said. As part of the BVCAP, she also wrote a grant which established the BVCAP Health Center in Central Falls. The center opened in 1972 and was one of the first to serve Hispanic immigrants in Rhode Island. Another of her grants obtained funds for the area's first school lunch program for the town of Central Falls, but the town refused to accept the money. The state of Rhode Island, however, used the funds "for advocacy to push successfully for school lunch legislation."[34]

Today Cohen employs her grant-writing skills on both paid and volunteer bases. In the 1980s she served as project coordinator for the Interfaith Council of the National Conference of Christians and Jews. She wrote a grant for partial funding for a biomedical ethics conference as part of a conference program in 1989. She conducted the grantmanship program for the National Women's Political Caucus in 1973. Most recently she wrote a grant to help stem racial unrest at a Providence high school.[35]

Jane Walsh Folcarelli, Class of 1947, embarked on her career as a professional volunteer and community worker after her first child was born. Her four sons led her into involvement with the Cub Scouts and the PTA, for which she served as local president. She worked on the guild of the St. Aloysius Home for Orphans. She was also heavily involved in alumnae activities in the 1950s and 1960s, working as board member and then president of the Pembroke Club of Providence and vice-president and president of the Pembroke College Alumnae Association.[36]

Folcarelli's first expansion beyond the realm of alumnae and maternal activities was the Women's Intergroup Relations Committee in the 1960s, serving on the steering committee from 1962–1966. The committee's goal was "to promote enough racial harmony to get a fair housing law passed in Rhode Island." Folcarelli became involved in this conference as a result of beliefs and experience:

Since in Rhode Island non-Italians assume successful Italian-Americans are *mafia,* I have had my share of prejudice. It was time for women of good will to begin to bury bigotry, racial bias and ethnic myths. We all made good friends – and since it antedated [feminism, the conference] gave women in Rhode Island a start in flexing their political and social muscle.[37]

At the same time, Folcarelli also served on the board of Citizens United for Fair Housing. In 1965, the group worked successfully to pass a fair housing law. Through this work she came to know the board of Bannister House, then known as the Home for Aged Colored Women. She was attracted to it because it needed *"workers* not *noblesse oblige* white women. The need for a new facility led to the first integrated fund raising efforts – and a home for more than just "Aged Colored Women." During her tenure as president of the board from 1964 to 1974 the goal was to raise $500,000 from public and private sources to build a 160-bed facility and re-site the institution on Providence's west side to benefit the Codding Court Housing Project neighborhood.[38]

In the midst of this work to promote racial harmony, equality of opportunity, and integrated community service, Folcarelli participated in a 1968 symposium at Pembroke College, "Volunteer Voices." She commented that the current challenge was to train women in inner cities and for the education of volunteers in the areas of race relations, urban problems, and communications. Co-sponsored by Pembroke College, the Junior League, and the United Fund Women's Council, the symposium examined the status and possibilities of the volunteer in Rhode Island. Community service was in grave danger, according to the conference participants – danger from paid employment and frustrations. At the end of the symposium the discussion shifted to politics as a volunteer activity for women.[39]

Folcarelli herself had already found community service and politics consuming, if sometimes frustrating, activities. Her home town of Scituate has benefitted from her work on the Northwest Community Health Service, the Scituate Arts Festival, and the North Scituate Public Library. During her tenure as president of the library, the board raised $500,000 to construct an addition, one of the highlights of her volunteer career. Since 1964 she has served as member and chair of the Scituate Democratic Town Committee. "Scituate has had two elected Democrats in [seventy-five] years, so it's like being a missionary. . . . I beat the bushes to find seven council candidates and one school committee candidate." She ran for school committee and representative herself and like all but those two Scituate Democrats, was defeated. That such Democratic platform agendas as town improvements in housing and tax relief programs for the elderly, and zoning laws, have now become law provides her with some gratification.[40] A short list of Jane Walsh Folcarelli's community activities includes no fewer than sixteen organizations, for many of which she served as chair or president.[41]

From Community Service to Politics

The 1960s was a pivotal decade of change for alumnae active in reform. Rita Caslowitz Michaelson, Class of 1950, was interested in civil rights even before graduation. During her college years she had participated in a study investigating whether restaurants would seat and serve African-American patrons. After graduation she continued her efforts. In the late 1950s to mid-1960s Michaelson, too, served on the board and as president of the Women's Intergroup Relations Committee. She concentrated on the establishment of libraries in two east side Providence schools. The committee staffed them with volunteer librarians who soon discovered the community children's need for tutors, especially in the minority community. In response, the women founded the Lippitt Hill Tutorial program. Michaelson tutored math for seven years and served on the board of directors. She recalls that at one meeting the board was polled and seven out of ten were Brown alumnae, including Peggy Gardner Kohlhepp, Class of 1953, and Joyce Wetherald Fairchild, Class of 1947. Many of the tutors in the 1960s were Pembroke students. By 1973 the tutorial served one thousand school children per year.[42]

When the Rhode Island Coalition against Bigotry was formed in response to Ku Klux Klan incidents at the University of Rhode Island, Nazi graffiti on the Jewish Community Center in Providence, and threats against local anti-Vietnam War activists, Michaelson served on its executive board. The coalition was successful in passing a bill to make such actions felonies rather than misdemeanors. Also thanks to their efforts, the Providence Police Department began to provide bilingual dispatchers, and the Providence Fire Department made its entrance exam more responsive to the experiences of minority candidates. Michaelson chaired a Hispanic Town Meeting at the Rhode Island State House to air testimony on discrimination in housing and employment.[43]

Michaelson's background made her a natural choice for the Rhode Island Human Rights Commission. She and another woman were appointed in 1972 as the first women in the commission's history. The commission is Rhode Island's Equal Employment Opportunity state agency and, prior to 1972, administered the state laws prohibiting discrimination in employment and housing on the basis of race, color, or national origin. In 1972 the statutes were amended to include gender. Her major satisfactions after serving fourteen years on the commission include being one of the first women members and broadening the statutes to include physical handicaps. The Commission was intended to provide speedy and fair service, but Michaelson found the process becoming increasingly legalistic and "jammed up" with lawyers. Feeling the commission had lost its effectiveness, she resigned in 1986.[44]

In 1972 Michaelson also began serving on the steering committee of the Women's Political Caucus where she was responsible for lobbying to get more women appointed to state commissions and boards. In 1973, the problems were obvious; as Michaelson exclaimed, "Can you believe that until recently, there were NO women on the governor's advisory committees on day care and divorce law reform?" In 1975 Michaelson began working as a labor arbitrator. During the 1980s she concentrated her community work in the Urban League where she served on the Southeast Asian Education Task Force and at the Rhode Island Foundation.[45]

In reviewing her career, Michaelson criticized the society in which she came of age. Her college education did not, she feels, prepare her for the 1960s and beyond because it was "male-dominated, Eurocentric, white. I never had a woman professor. No readings shaped me in any way for the changing world." In 1973 she discussed NOW's resolution against volunteerism and noted that:

> there are many levels of volunteering. You can make the sandwiches for the fund-raising picnic or you can draft model legislation on fair housing. I do both. On the other hand, I was a typical woman of my generation who was educated with the idea that I would do good works and never really use my education. I have managed to find outlets that I think are worthwhile but I have great empathy for women who feel stymied.

In spite of their upbringing and education, Michaelson notes that many of her generation have been able to turn their focus to social change.[46]

Generalist volunteers with professional-level skills in administration, organization, and fund raising have the knowledge and commitment to public welfare that should characterize politicians. As women knock at the doors of politics, elected officeholding may come to replace, in part, the generalist approach to community service characteristic of women of earlier generations.

Politicians Claire Sullivan Drummey, Class of 1929, and Victoria Santopietro Lederberg, Class of 1959, Ph.D. 1966, are bridges between the generalists who began their careers in community service in order to "do something" and the focused community action efforts of other women. Like the former, they are generalists in knowledge and skills. Like the latter they have carved out and focused on specific areas of expertise. Lederberg, again like many of the latter, holds a full-time, professional job. Both moved into politics as a necessary step to accomplish their goals.

Attorney Claire Sullivan Drummey was the first woman to hold elective office in Warwick when she was elected to the city council in 1953. Her legal education and work provided the basis for her political work. In 1951 she had served on the Warwick Charter Revision Commission and later as secretary of the Rhode Island Home Rule Association. In 1958 she was a delegate to the Rhode Island Constitutional Convention. She served on the city and state Republican committees and for nine years on a state drug prevention commission.[47]

Attorney and psychology professor Victoria Lederberg is known as the most highly-educated woman to be elected to the Rhode Island legislature. She served more than fifteen years as representative and senator, but came to politics in a roundabout way. She achieved her long-time career goal in 1968 when she became an assistant professor of psychology at Rhode Island College, ten years later becoming a full professor. Along the way she had two children and became interested in the law, earning a law degree in 1976. During 1973 she carpooled to Suffolk University Law School in Boston with other Rhode Islanders and she credits that experience with broadening her political horizons. "Every single one of those [commuters] had some kind of affiliation or connection with politics or politicians. That was my first personal experience with politics and politicians – the talk going back and forth in the car pooling. And as I got familiar with what went on and who was what," it dawned on her, she said, that she was as competent as they were in the area of public service. That revelation and her campaign work for her husband, Seymour Lederberg, and state legislator Lila Sapinsley spurred her to decide to run for the state representative seat from her district in 1974.[48]

Lederberg had belonged to only one group prior to her election – the League of Women Voters. She credits the league with providing her with "a working knowledge of issues such as school finance; [it] was probably my first teacher of politically related issues." The second was working on committees and councils at Rhode Island College. As Lederberg notes, "In my view, the so-called politics of learning how to get things done can have no better proving or testing ground than on a campus."[19]

Lederberg won four two-year terms in the House. Although the position of Rhode Island legislator is a part-time job paying only $300 per year, in her first nine months on the job, Lederberg logged 540 hours. During this time she was attending law school and working as a professor.[50]

As a freshman representative she caused a stir when given the position of chair of the education subcommittee of the House Finance Committee. She was the first woman to obtain a position on that committee, which she held for nearly five years. In 1979 she was discharged from Finance and placed on the Health, Education and Welfare Committee. In 1982 she ran for secretary of state and lost by three-tenths of a percentage point, but in 1985 she won a state senate seat. She has campaigned on such education and good government issues as educational financing and opportunities, conflict of interest legislation, open meeting laws, and open records.[51]

Lederberg has found the legislature to be a "very fruitful area." She characterizes herself as an "issue person," but became involved in issues that were unpopular among legislators and the press. Her areas of expertise – educational funding and energy facility siting – are not "sexy issues that people can touch the surface and get involved with." In the area of energy facility siting, she chaired the commission and drafted a siting act which established timely, safe and environmentally responsible procedures.[52]

Lederberg is best known, perhaps, for her expertise in educational policy. Her academic background has been supplemented by work with the Department of Education on program funding, and terms as a trustee of both Brown University and Roger Williams College. In 1979 President Jimmy Carter appointed her chair of the National Advisory Panel on Financing Primary and Secondary Education created by Congress. On the state level Lederberg has served on six education commissions, chairing the efforts of the Commission to Update Educational Laws and the Commission on the Study of Public School Funding. Her success in state educational legislation includes the "Lederberg Act" on education for handicapped children. Written to enable the state to gain federal funds, the act has been used as a model in other states.[53] She also worked on bills to "promote and establish confidence in government agencies," including one requiring open meetings for public bodies and a conflict of interest law, forbidding public officials from using their offices for personal gain.[54]

While education and governmental reform have been her two main areas of interest, Lederberg has cast her net widely. She was the original proponent of patients' rights to their own records. She discovered that medical records could be subpoenaed in court and held against a patient, an action particularly troublesome to women in divorce and child custody cases. In 1978 she submitted a bill to allow women to retain their maiden names after marriage. It was prompted by a Superior Court ruling in 1977 that Rhode Island women were compelled by law to assume their husband's surname after marriage.[55]

When asked about the difference between the experiences of male and female legislators, Lederberg noted that voters tend to feel women are "less corrupt, more serious, more diligent. I feel certain that people who call me on issues would not call . . . a man. . . . Some people just feel more comfortable talking about issues and problems with a woman." She notes, however, that part of the willingness of voters to call female legislators may be a feeling that men are "too busy" to be bothered. In her freshman year, Lederberg logged fifty-eight hours on discussions. In evaluating her political career, Lederberg commented, "I think it's been moderately successful, both rewarding and frustrating. The fact that I've been able to be influential in affecting what I consider to be important policy issues is the largest benefit of it."[56]

Volunteer Lobbyist

Direct political action was not an activity in which women engaged in great numbers from the 1930s through the 1950s. Women reemerged in the 1960s as community activists in significant numbers. Spurred on by the civil rights, women's, anti-war, and anti-poverty movements, women found increasing acceptance of their political work.

Lillian Kelman Potter Goldstein, Class of 1933, is the most well-known proponent of gun control in Rhode Island. Following the 1968 assassinations of Robert F. Kennedy and Martin Luther King, Jr., Lillian and her husband, Dr. Charles Potter, decided to work intensively for gun control. This political activity was only one aspect of their busy lives.[57] Gun control became, however, the focus of her political action.

Through their involvement with the Rhode Island Emergency Committee for Gun Control, which Lillian Potter co-chaired, the Potters worked unsuccessfully for reform on a state level. After the loss in the Rhode Island State House, her activities decreased. "I felt pretty beaten down. I had no idea we'd be clobbered." In December 1970, however, her husband was killed by two escaped convicts using a stolen handgun. This senseless and personal tragedy gave her the motivation to continue to work for gun control. She said, "I am determined to dedicate myself to gather together the many people, who, because of similar tragedy, or their concern for the general safety, want to see the traffic in handguns ended."[58]

By September 1971 Lillian Potter had collected 11,000 signatures on a petition which she brought to the United States Senate Subcommittee on Juvenile Delinquency, before which she was testifying. She asserted at the time (in spite of her earlier experience) that quicker action could be achieved through local ordinances, although she believed that strict federal controls were necessary. She therefore organized a grassroots organization known as Handgun Alert, Inc.[59] On many nights, Potter could be found discussing her proposals and deflecting anti-gun control arguments in public forums. Potter's earlier experience may have prepared her for the inevitable opposition, but the gun enthusiasts who called her "Communist" and those who thought, "Poor thing! Her husband was killed and she's gone off her trolley," would become part of the landscape of her life.[60]

In April 1974 Handgun Alert lost in its efforts to have a comprehensive gun control bill passed in the Rhode Island House. All of her statistics and impressive collection of clippings citing deaths by handguns did not help her in the battle. At the time, she noted that most handgun legislation "never gets off the ground for the simple reason that the people with a vested interest make this a high priority, whereas the rest of us have other social interests." In 1974–1975 the organization intensified its public education campaign. The Honorary Board of Governors included prominent politicians. Handgun Alert succeeded in having a Firearm Safety Week proclaimed in December 1975 by Governor Philip O. Noel and by the mayors of seven towns in the state. In 1976, the organization published an information booklet, *Bearing Arms... Right or Risk?* The *Providence Journal* stopped running classified advertisements by individuals for guns. Legislative success, however, required years' more work.[61]

Finally, in 1979, the General Assembly approved the "Prepurchase Training Requirement" bill, which required handgun owners to take a four to six hour safety course and submit to a police background check before taking possession of a handgun. The gun lobby managed to "whittle away" at the bill, however, with two amendments in 1981 and 1983 which decreased the training session to two hours. Although disappointed with the diminishment of the requirements, Potter mused philosophically that the bill "was as far as we could go ahead in Rhode Island." Handgun Alert functions in the late 1980s as "a mailing list and a checking account." Largely dormant, it still responds to special calls from the national organization, Handgun Control, Inc., based in Washington, D.C.[62]

Contemporary Health Issues

At a 1990 Brown University Commencement Forum on AIDS Marjorie Jones Stenberg, Class of 1954, asked the rhetorical question, "How did I get here from there – [from] the 'silent generation' of the 1950s to being a possibly gray haired grandmother with a pocket full of condoms and a wide acquaintance with people in bars and half-gutted crack houses?"[63]

Stenberg's destination is not as surprising as it might seem; rather it is, as she said, "a logical extension of the community work that drew me in the past. It was a continuum, as... society provides us with ever more complex permutations of the same problem – injustice." Her volunteer and paid work is also a continuum because Stenberg has blurred boundaries of her public and private spheres in the same way that her predecessors did.[64]

Stenberg's original goal was to become a doctor, but she married shortly after graduation and worked as a research associate in the Brown Biology Department from 1957 to 1965, with time off for the birth of two sons. In the meantime, she became involved with Brown alumnae affairs.[65]

In 1962–1963 she helped establish the Rhode Island Congress of Racial Equality (CORE). She characterized the branch of CORE as a small group, consisting largely of African-American and white women with some men. It marked the first time that she became involved in fair housing issues. She recalled that she spent a lot of time explaining the idea of Black Power to whites, to help diminish their fear. She served as public relations director and also served as treasurer of the organization before it became an all-African-American group. Although the composition change was right for the group at the time, Stenberg felt that it could have been fruitful if CORE had aggressively promoted the change and thereby increased its membership. The group became moribund, however, and eventually died. Stenberg attributed part of its demise to its reliance on the unpaid labor of women and the failure to recognize the differing time commitments white women and African-American women in the group could make. CORE leaders found that the interested African-American women were too busy earning a living and raising children to devote large chunks of unpaid time to a cause, a foreshadowing of the future of volunteerism. At the same time, Stenberg became involved in the anti-Vietnam War movement, in part inspired by the discussions among the African-American women of CORE.[66]

She had become involved in feminist consciousness-raising groups by 1966 and worked with the Win with Women Program from 1974 to 1976 to help elect women politicians. She helped found the local chapter of the National Organization for Women and the Women's Political Caucus, but admits that by the late 1980s her contributions were largely monetary because her commitments had changed.[67]

In what Stenberg acknowledges seems to be an odd decision, she became involved with the Rhode Island Republican Party during the late 1960s. "Sounds like [a paradox], doesn't it? That you would become involved in Republican politics when you were this flaming liberal and you've got the Congress of Racial Equality on one side." She believed that the Republican Party in Rhode Island in the 1960s was the more liberal party, although she admitted to being its only anti-war and anti-Nixon member. In 1966 she became a member of the Republican State Central

Committee. She continued her concern for social justice, at one point picketing, with her children at her side, Republican Rhode Island Governor John Chafee over the issue of welfare. Laughing, she recalled, "It went over not well with the Republican State Central Committee, but I was always doing things like that."[68]

At the same time that she became involved with the Republican State Central Committee she began a four-year stint as instructor in anatomy at the Roger Williams General Hospital School of Nursing. In 1970, she helped establish the Health Task Force of the Urban Coalition, which resulted in the development of community health centers. In 1977 she obtained her present position in infection control with the Veterans Administration. One of her first accomplishments there was sharing policy information and developing an outside peer group.[69]

When AIDS started to appear in the medical literature in 1981, there was, therefore, a logical group of medical people to tap for work. In 1982 the first AIDS patients were diagnosed at the VA and Rhode Island hospitals. While the VA had the luxury to allow patients long hospital stays, there was concern that there was no support for patients outside the hospital. The length of time necessary to obtain public assistance created tragedy; it required seven months before one of Stenberg's patients received Social Security benefits. They arrived the day he died. Stenberg is concerned that the spread of the disease will stretch the resources of the community to the utmost and also that AIDS "will be predominantly a disease of minority, inner-city people and it's going to more and more difficult to get funding and to get people to work with these patients."[70]

In the summer of 1985, Stenberg became one of the founders and first president of Rhode Island Project AIDS. At the time there were only twenty reported AIDS cases in Rhode Island. She was chosen president partly, she said, because "I was a straight woman and the gay men who were in the organization did not want the organization to be a *gay* organization." Also helpful were Stenberg's political connections in the Republican Party. In the first year of the organization they wrote and received a grant for $36,000 from the Rhode Island Foundation, the largest award ever made by the agency at that time. The money was used for printing and to hire an executive director. By the time Stenberg resigned as president in December 1987, the organization was anticipating a budget of $300,000 and had hired an executive director; in 1990 the budget had grown to $1.2 million.[71]

The goals of RIP/AIDS are the education of the general public and the at-risk, intervention with those at risk or with HIV infection, and direct support for those with AIDS or HIV infection. The hotline handles six hundred calls per month. One of the organization's most successful efforts is the "buddy" program, which offers care and compassion. Stenberg decided early on that she would have to provide a model for her staff, that "I could not ask the staff to do what I myself would not do." She therefore went back to bedside nursing, which also enabled her to learn patients' needs directly. In 1990, Stenberg reported that after "years of continuous education and role modeling we have been able to get the vast majority of our employees to [provide] compassion and hassle-free care for [AIDS patients]." The provision of ethical health care has been, she feels, her greatest contribution.[72]

In retrospect, Stenberg said that she has led "a reasonably busy life, when you consider that we were called the silent generation and no one expected anything out of us. But I think if you go out into these communities and look at the accomplishments of women of my generation you might find that they're considerable."[73]

Hilary Ross Salk, Class of 1963, M.A.T. 1965, is another member of that silent generation who found her public voice in her adopted home town of Providence. Her issues are women's health and the control of nuclear power and weapons. Salk's ultimate goal in both of these areas is the empowerment of women.[74] Like her nineteenth-century foremothers, Salk acts in the belief that private issues require public activism. Like her peers in the women's movement, Salk has found that the personal is political.

She married Stephen Salk of Providence after she earned her M.A.T. and the couple moved to the Boston area, where Salk taught English for two years. There she gave birth to her daughter in 1966. One of the most personal of all life experiences – childbirth – was the "driving force that led [her] to work on improving childbearing experiences for other women." Salk therefore became involved in the natural childbirth movement through the Boston Association for Childbirth Education before moving back to Providence in 1973.[75]

By this time, Salk's interest in women's health had expanded beyond natural childbirth in a hospital setting. "As I learned more about the medical system and many of the abuses to women in other areas, I became interested in transforming the medical profession as a whole." Her work increasingly focused on educating, preparing, and assisting women in controlling their own health care. With Carol Regan Shelton and Elizabeth Edgerly, she established the Rhode Island Women's Health Collective in 1975. At the first meeting, she recalls, "I was scared to death . . . because I knew it was a terrible responsibility in some respects . . . I had never been the president of any organization . . . I knew about the model of the Health

Collective [in which] there were no presidents; they were all chiefs! and that was an extremely interesting model for me and gave me courage." The first three or four years Salk felt largely responsible for leading the group. The goal was to "change the way women's health care was provided in Rhode Island."[76]

Salk's work in advocating the replacement of obstetrical care with midwifery care for women during childbearing years consolidated her interests in childbearing and women's control of their bodies and health care. In 1976 she coordinated the Women's Health Conference and three years later wrote and oversaw a grant which included four conferences and the establishment of the Health Collective's office and hotline service. As she has grown older, her interests have expanded to include the health of older women and led to her writing the grant proposal for and chairing the Collective's Older Women's Health Project in 1988–1990. Her work in the area of women's health received national notice in the 1986 edition of *The New Our Bodies, Ourselves*, for which she contributed the chapter on "Women and the Politics of Health Care."[77]

Salk's efforts to empower women and her concern over nuclear energy led to her work as one of the original members of Women for a Non-Nuclear Future (WFNNF), shortly after Helen Caldecott of Physicians for Social Responsibility spoke in Providence. The initial focus was to end the use of nuclear power. After Ronald Reagan's election as president of the United States, however, the group widened its scope. "As Reagan began to escalate the nuclear arms race, our focus very quickly and appropriately became the reduction of the ... race and ultimately an end of all nuclear power and weapons."[78]

In 1982 the Rhode Island Citizens' Party asked Salk to run for governor. She accepted it as an "opportunity to speak out on the issues that were important to me. ... It was a great chance to broaden the critique I had and to expand my knowledge of alternative ways to solve the problems faced by Rhode Island." Rhode Island has provided Salk with roots and with her greatest satisfactions in community work. The state's small size and population and "easy accessibility to all levels of government and policy-making" allow the groups with which she is involved to have an impact. The changes in which she takes pride are incremental, however, rather than the revolutionary ones for which she hopes. The effort to retain victories, such as abortion rights, frustrates her. In 1988, she wrote, "I have found that I do have roots after all. They are here in Providence where I am involved in my extended family, a community of activists I'm part of even in the 1980s, where I have raised my children and stayed married to the same man ... and where I have developed a successful real estate business in this erratic decade. Still I am not content; there is too much misery, injustice, and poverty to escape into the bourgeois complacency we were so critical of in college even before the sixties began."[79]

Student Volunteers of Today

Complacency was not evident in the Brown women from the Sarah Doyle Women's Center who in the 1970s helped establish Sojourner House, a battered women's shelter in Rhode Island. Nor has it been evident among the students of the 1980s. A number of Brown women, for example, volunteer at Dorcas Place, an adult literacy program for women in Providence, which also provides health and consumers' rights training for its clientele. Brown women continue the tradition of community action which engineered their entrance into the university. In 1987, President Howard Swearer institutionalized that tradition when he created the Center for Public Service. In the 1980s that tradition was often directed at social action and change, particularly the empowerment of women and girls.[80]

Edee Saar, Class of 1992, volunteering at the Family AIDS Center for Treatment and Support.

Galia Siegel, Class of 1989, established the Peer Sister Program at the Urban League of Rhode Island in the spring of 1987. This program is designed to provide companionship and tutoring to pregnant and parenting teenage girls in Providence. The goal of the program is to make the girls self-sufficient and increase their self esteem. Volunteers provide tutoring and personal support. In addition, Siegel volunteered as a creative movement teacher at the Mount Hope Day Care Center in Providence in 1986, where she taught dance to four year olds. Like many students, Siegel also volunteered during school breaks. A native of Washington, D.C., she volunteered as an assistant in a day care center in her home town.[81]

Pamina Gorbach, Class of 1987, a transfer student from Johns Hopkins, came to Brown with the experience of providing an escort service for women's medical center clients harassed by anti-abortion protestors. With other young women, she determined to provide a safe passage from car to door for the Saturday clients of the Women's Medical Center of Providence. Every Saturday for the last several years, at least one woman from Brown has performed the arduous task. Different reasons exist among the women for their involvement, and not all believe personally in the moral rectitude of abortion, as might be expected. In fact, two of the young women, Nancy Peterson, Class of 1989, and Sarah Fass, Class of 1989, decided to act as escorts in order to determine their opinions on the matter. A year later, Peterson decided she did not believe in abortion, but she shared with all of her co-workers that belief that every woman is entitled to make her own decision and to safe passage to the clinic. This work is neither easy, nor glamorous, and, in fact, can be dangerous. At least two Brown students have been assaulted by pro-life protestors. Respondents to the questionnaires distributed by the Women's Medical Center to its clients often make mention of the importance of the escorts in providing safe physical passage and emotional care during these already difficult moments in a woman's life.[82]

Katie Plax, Class of 1989, is another recent Brown graduate who made a difference in Rhode Island while a student. As a freshman, she became interested in working with children because of a course about cancer in which she was enrolled. In addition, her father is a pediatrician, and her mother, the director of an early childhood center in St. Louis. Plax began working with Cancer Outreach Relief Effort (CORE) in her first year and by her senior year she was student coordinator. CORE grew out of an independent study project at Brown. It matches Brown students with children affected by cancer. Students visit their matched child independently and attend bi-weekly CORE meetings in which social workers and consultants from Rhode Island Hospital give advice. Also during her senior year, Plax became health and disabilities coordinator on the executive board of Brown Community Outreach. After graduation, she began work as volunteer coordinator for the Family AIDS Center for Treatment and Support in South Providence. FACTS House is a joint effort of St. Michael's Church and Rhode Island Hospital.

As Plax anticipated her future, she unknowingly echoed the motivations of the century of women before her, "Given that I've had all these amazing opportunities, I feel a responsibility to give something back. [FACTS] is an organization that's just starting. There's so much for me to learn . . . I'm interested in education and seeing social change happen. Education is the way to see a real democratic society. I think I can have an impact."[83]

NOTES

1. Addams's exclamation, "How can you! A young woman like you, so competent and well and strong, when there are so many people in the world who need you," in fact led Stillwell to consider accepting a job with the Women's Educational and Industrial Union in Boston. Although Stillwell declined that position, she dedicated her future civic work "as a token in memory of Miss Jane Addams." Margaret Bingham Stillwell. *Librarians Are Human* (Boston: Colonial Society of Massachusetts, 1973), pp. 29–30, 188–119; Stillwell, *Is Rhode Island a Thoughtful Father to His Children?* (Providence: Rhode Island State Board of Health, 1923) and Stillwell and Harold A. Andrews, *Fitting Rhode Island Children for School Days and Their Work in Life* (Providence: Rhode Island State Board of Health, 1920).

2. "Survey of Brown Women in Classes with Reunions in 1990," in Christine Dunlap Farnham Archives, Brown University, hereafter cited as 1990 Survey.

3. Ibid. Carol Agate, 1990 Survey.

4. Ibid.

5. Lida Shaw King, "The Women's College in Brown University," *Education* 27 (April 1907): 478; Brown University Council, *Preparing Pembroke for its Second Half-Century* (Providence: Brown University, 1936), p. 8; Laura DeGuidice to Barbara Anton, 31 May 1990, in author's possession.

6. Grace E. Hawk, *Pembroke College in Brown University* (Providence: Brown University, 1966), p. 77.

7. *Pembroke Alumna* 33 (April 1958): 46; (January 1958): 20; Pembroke College Class of 1928, *Who's Who/ Pembroke/1928* 1942 (Providence, RI, 1942), p. 12; Karen M. Lamoree, *Research Guide to the Christine Dunlap Farnham Archives* (Providence: Brown University, 1989), pp. 69–70; Anna Canada Biographical File; Anna Canada Writings File, both in Farnham Archives.

8. Karen M. Lamoree with Laelia Z. Gilborn and Susan J. Friedland "Women's Voluntarism and Institution Building in Rhode Island: An Initial Survey," research project funded by the American Association for State and Local History, 1989. In the 1910s, the National Congress of Mothers set the agenda for mothers' clubs across the country. Popular issues were child welfare, dental care for poor children, and teaching domestic science principles.

9. Doris Snow Briggs, "Volunteer Social Work in Providence," *The Sepiad*, February 1917, pp. 32–36.

10. Lamoree, *Research Guide*, p. 235; Lamoree, Gilborn, and Friedland, "Women's Voluntarism;" *Pembroke Alumna* 33 (April 1958); 46–47; Celia Ernstof Adler questionnaire in author's possession; Margaret Porter Dolan questionnaire and Dolan to author, March

1990, in author's possession.

11. Hawk, *Pembroke College*, p. 177; Brown University, News Release, #46/149; Ann Banks, "Rita Michaelson: Sandwiches and Legislation," *Brown Alumni Monthly* 74 (March 1973): 39.

12. Lamoree, *Research Guide*, p. 237.

13. Ellen Appleton Stone Biographical File, Farnham Archives, "Dr. Ellen A. Stone, Pioneer in Child Health, Dies at 82," *Providence Journal*, 19 February 1952.

14. During the 1930s women's clubs retreated from public welfare concerns. In 1934 during the Depression, the Rhode Island Women's Club created a new program, "Extra Leisure Hours Exhibit." By 1939 it had grown into a major conference exhibition. Lamoree, Gilborn, and Friedland, "Women's Voluntarism," pp. 15–17.

15. Doris Hopkins Stapelton, taped interview by Ramsey Fadiman, 26 April 1982, Oral History Collection, Farnham Archives; Doris Hopkins Stapelton to author, 11 June 1990, in author's possession; Doris Hopkins Biographical File, Farnham Archives.

16. Stapelton, interview.

17. Stapelton to author, 11 June 1990. In 1972, she received a Brown Bear award for her alumnae service. Since then she has served eleven years on the Pembroke Center Associates Council and five years on the Christine Dunlap Farnham Archives Advisory Committee.

18. Ibid.

19. Ibid.

20. Stapelton interview; Stapelton, Biographical File; Stapelton to author, 11 June 1990.

21. Lamoree, *Research Guide*, pp. 88, 236–237, 252, 254.

22. Charles Harris Wesley, *The History of the National Association of Colored Women's Clubs, A Legacy of Service* (Washington, D.C.: National Association of Colored Women's Clubs, inc., 1984), p. 198.

23. Mary Jean Houde, *Reaching Out: A Story of the General Federation of Women's Clubs* (Chicago: Mobium Press, 1988), pp. 442, 444.

24. Alice Clark Donahue, taped interview by Karen M. Lamore, 12 September 1989, Oral History Collection, Farnham Archives.

25. Donahue joined the International Federation of Catholic Alumnae in 1942. From 1948 to 1953, she was a co-founder of the Pembroke College Junior Club. Donahue oral history biographical form with Donahue taped interview, Oral History Collection, Farnham Archives.

26. Alice Clark Donahue, interview.

27. Ibid.

28. For example, Donahue was elected president of the BJWC in 1961 and director of the Junior Assembly in 1964. Donahue interview; *Brown Alumni Monthly*, 88 (October 1987): 55. See Houde, *Reaching Out*, p. 467–469 for details on the path to the presidency.

29. Donahue interview; Houde, *Reaching Out*, p. 444.

30. For an example of an in-depth response to the NOW resolution see, for example, Mary Malko and Judith C. Bartow, Committee on Hospital Volunteer Service, United Hospital Fund, New York, NY, letter to Kirsten Joslyn of NOW, 13 February 1973, in Caroline Flanders Writings File, Farnham Archives.

31. Judith Weiss Cohen, taped interview by Carol Fenimore, 25 February 1986, Oral History Collection, Farnham Archives.

32. Cohen, interview, Judith Weiss Cohen to author, June 1989.

33. Stephen M. Baron, "As Key Aide Leaves, BVCAP Faces Test," *Providence Journal*, 16 May 1973.

34. Cohen interview.

35. Cohen to author. Cohen left BVCAP in 1973 to serve as director of administrative departments at the Jewish Community Center of Rhode Island, a position she held until 1976. After her 1987 retirement, she assumed the position of editor of the *R.I. Jewish Historical Notes*. In addition she has served on many boards and committees and was consultant

to the Rhode Island Department of Community Affairs in 1975. In 1988, she worked as a consultant to the Rhode Island Housing and Mortgage Finance Corporation, where she wrote a grant to help the elderly living in subsidized housing. Judith Weiss Cohen, interview by Karen M. Lamoree, April 1990.

36. Jane Walsh Folcarelli to author, 11 June 1990; Jane Walsh Folcarelli taped interview by Julie Berman, 5 April 1988, Oral History Collection, Farnham Archives. Folcarelli noted that the Pembroke alumnae activities were an anomaly in her volunteer work because they were social and public relations duties.

37. Folcarelli letter to author, 11 June 1990.

38. Ibid., Folcarelli interview; Bannister House 1974 fund raising pamphlet. Citizens United for Fair Housing; Barry A. Marks to Folcarelli n.d., in personal collection of Jane Walsh Folcarelli.

39. Jane Walsh Folcarelli, "A Volunteer's Challenge," *Pembroke Alumna*, 43 (July 1968): 24; Pembroke College, "Volunteer Voices, A Symposium, Thursday, April 5, 1968," (Providence: Pembroke College, 1968), pp. 42–44, Farnham Archives.

40. Folcarelli to author, 11 June 1990; Folcarelli personal collection; Folcarelli interview. She also served on the organizing committee of "McGovern for President" in Rhode Island.

41. In addition, Folcarelli, served on the Providence-Cranston District National Council of Catholic Women, Legislative Committee of the Rhode Island Fine Arts Council, committee to reelect Senator Claiborne Pell, Citizens' Advisory Committee of the Scituate School System, and on the Regents Advisory Committee. Jane Walsh Biographical File, Farnham Archives.

42. The women on the board, according to Michaelson, noted that while Brown alumnae tutors and administrators and student tutors provided a presence and services to the nearby neighborhoods, the university itself did not. Rita Caslowitz Michaelson interview by Karen M. Lamoree, 17 June 1990; Michaelson to author, March 1990; Banks, "Rita Michaelson," p. 39.

43. Michaelson interview; Rita Caslowitz Michaelson personal collection.

44. Banks, "Rita Michaelson," p. 39; Michaelson interview.

45. Banks, "Rita Michaelson," p. 39; Michaelson interview; "With Liberty and Justice for All," Rhode Island Foundation conference program, April 20–21, 1986, Michaelson personal collection.

46. Michaelson interview; Banks, "Rita Michaelson," p. 39.

47. Claire Sullivan Biographical File, Farnham Archives.

48. Victoria Santopietro Lederberg, taped interview by Emily Stier Adler, 12 May 1986 and J. Stanley Lemons, 6 June 1986, in personal collection of Adler and Lemons. See also: Adler and Lemons, *The Elect: Rhode Island's Women's Legislators, 1922–1990* (Providence: League of Rhode Island Historical Societies, 1990).

49. Lederberg's community involvement expanded to include Hadassah, Women's Political Caucus, Common Cause, Temple Beth El Sisterhood, Miriam Hospital Women's Association. Lederberg's academic committee experience was impressive. A short list includes the following: member of the Council of RIC and its Executive Committee 1972–73; member of Major Academic Planning Committee, 1969–70; member Educational Policy Committee, 1978, chair of the Educational Studies Curriculum Task Force, 1970–72; and chair of RIC's Committee on Committees, 1969–70. Victoria Santopietro Biographical File, Farnham Archives; Lederberg interview.

50. M. Charles Bakst, "Part-time Is Lots of Time, Rep. Lederberg Finds," *Providence Journal*, 7 September 1975, p. F-2.

51. "She Out-Degrees House," *Providence Journal*, 6 September 1976; Lorraine Hopkins, "Professor Shines as a Freshman," *Providence Journal*, 12 May 1975; Lederberg interview.

52. Lederberg, interview; Lederberg Biographical File.

53. As chair of the National Advisory Panel, Lederberg directed the seven million dollar research budget which resulted in educational policy recommendations to the President and

Congress. Mark Patinkin, "It's a Modest Intention for Such a Big Bash," *Providence Journal*, 10 March 1978; Lederberg interview; Lederberg Biographical File.

54. Ibid.

55. Ibid.; "Mrs. Lederberg Files Maiden Name Use Bill," *Providence Journal*, 22 February 1978.

56. Lederberg, interview; Bakst, "Part-time." In 1990, Lederberg was defeated as a Democratic primary candidate for mayor of Providence.

57. Goldstein had been a biology teacher in Lincoln, Rhode Island, since the early 1960s. Since the 1940s, she campaigned for a less political school committee in Providence. She was a past president of the League of Women Voters. During her tenure as first president of the Friends of Roger Williams Park Museum, she led a drive that raised $10,000 for a planetarium. C. Fraser Smith, "I Feel I Have to be Doing This," *Providence Journal Sunday Magazine*, 15 December 1974, p. 9.

58. Marlene Cimons, "Slaying of Husband Spurs Her Fight Against Handguns," *Los Angeles Times*, 24 October 1971, p. 3; Smith, "I Feel," p. 8; Martha Gagliardi, "A Widow Battles Handguns, 'A Man-Made Plague,' " *Virginian-Pilot*, 28 September 1971, p. A9; Hamilton E. Davis, "Senators Hear Mrs. Potter's Plea," *Providence Evening Bulletin*, 14 September 1971, p. 24; all in Scrapbook of Lillian Kelman Potter Goldstein in her possession.

59. "Hits Sale of Handguns," *Chicago Today*, 17 October 1971, p. 28; James J. Brown, "Grassroots Fights on Handguns," *Fresno Bee*, 10 September 1971, in Goldstein Scrapbook.

60. Anthony R. Lioce, Jr., "Mrs. Potter Shoots Down Pro-Handgun Line," *Providence Evening Bulletin*, 30 November 1973, Goldstein Scrapbook. In 1989, Potter Goldstein would discover essentially the same proposal on the Op-Ed page of *The New York Times* and wasted no time in writing to the author, Joel Joseph, to break the news that his idea was not a new one, but had in fact been proposed by gun-control advocates for years. Lillian Kelman Potter Goldstein interview by Karen M. Lamoree, 7 August 1989; Smith "I Feel," p. 6.

61. Christy Bowman, "Lillian Kelman Potter '33, 'Fighting the Menace of Handguns,' " *Brown Alumni Monthly* 75 (May–June 1974): 33. Part of this prioritization, she asserts, is that the gun enthusiasts pay professional lobbyists to work every day in the State House, while reform efforts are conducted by volunteers in their spare time. Goldstein interview; Smith, "I Feel," p. 8; Handgun Alert, Inc., *Newsletter*, December 1974, proclamations and booklet; *Providence Journal*, 22 June 1981, Goldstein personal collection.

62. *Providence Journal*, 24 July 1980; Goldstein interview.

63. Marjorie Jones Stenberg, untitled speech, Brown University Commencement Forum 1990, "The Human Face of AIDS: Brown on the Front Lines," personal collection of author.

64. Marjorie Jones Stenberg to author, 26 May 1990.

65. As a Brown alumnae, Stenberg helped plan class reunions and served on the editorial board of the *Pembroke Alumna* from 1964 to 1970. Marjorie Jones Stenberg, taped interview by Julia Hyun, 16 April 1988, Oral History Collection, Farnham Archives.

66. Ibid.; oral history biographical form, Farnham Archives.

67. Stenberg's feminism asserts itself politically in her career and in her involvement with her alma mater, particularly regarding the effects of the 1971 merger. Ibid.; Marjorie Jones Stenberg, personal collection.

68. Stenberg interview.

69. Ibid.

70. Stenberg untitled speech; David A. Eligator, "Rhode Island Project/AIDS: A Community Organization is Born," US187c Final Paper; Professor H. Silver, 7 December 1987, p. 2, personal collection of author; Stenberg interview.

71. Ibid., Stenberg letter; Eligator, "Rhode Island Project AIDS," pp. 7, 10–11.

72. Stenberg interview; Eligator, "Rhode Island Project AIDS," p. 1, 14–15; Stenberg untitled speech.

73. Stenberg interview.

74. Hilary Ross Salk to Karen M. Lamore, 24 May 1990, personal collection of author.

75. Hilary Ross Salk, taped interview by Karen M. Lamoree, August 1988, Oral History Collection, Brown University.

76. Salk interview; Salk letter to author, 24 May 1990.

77. In 1986 she organized the Providence chapter of Tough Love, inspired by her experiences with her son, Daniel. She has also been involved in The Friday Group from 1975, a Providence-based alternative Jewish group. She wrote and acted as part of the Rhode Island Feminist Theatre's 1975 performance of "Persephone's Return." Ross Salk, interview.

78. Salk letter to author, 24 May 1990.

79. Hilary Ross Salk, in Judith Neal Murray, ed., Brown University Class of 1963, 25th reunion yearbook, (Providence, RI: Brown University, 1988), p. 123.

80. Dorcas Place Co-Director Deborah Thompson, interview by Karen M. Lamoree, 16 November 1989.

81. Galia Siegel, taped interview by Karen M. Lamoree, 7 March 1988, Oral History Collection, Brown University.

82. Women's Medical Center Escort Service, taped interviews by Karen M. Lamoree, 15 April 1988 and 25 May 1989; Oral History Collection, Farnham Archives; Women's Medical Center Escort Service, Records, Farnham Archives.

83. Christopher F. Lemly, "After Brown," Brown Daily Herald, Commencement edition, May 1989, p. 13; "Student Volunteers...for Babies and Children Exposed to AIDS," Brown Alumni Monthly 91 (February 1991): 12–13.

A Wider World:
Careers of Brown Alumnae

by CHARLOTTE LOWNEY TOMAS

Barbara kirk (andrews) hail, Class of 1952, now curator and associate director of Brown's Haffenreffer Museum of Anthropology, spoke at a Pembroke Center Alumnae Forum in Spring 1990 about the newspaper career, travels and collections of Emma Shaw Colcleugh, a Providence newspaper woman and subarctic traveler at the end of the nineteenth century. Hail began with the following quote from a newspaper article written in 1898 by Colcleugh:

> The Coming Woman, the "new woman" and kindred expressions have lately come to be used . . . as if there was a general expectation that from some long-hidden chrysalis a radiant, winged creature was expected to emerge, dazzling all about her with the brilliancy of her attainments as she soared high above the heads of less ambitious onlooking sisters. . . . Is it a new woman, or has the world progress so changed the conditions environing her that new avenues are open to her and new duties required of her? . . . The world moves, and men with it. Must not their wives and sisters keep pace?[1]

The sentiment might well have been written ninety years later. In order to show how Brown women have moved forward with the times, this chapter brings together information about women who were Brown/ Pembroke undergraduates and their subsequent careers and life choices. Of necessity, it is mainly an impressionistic account of *some* successful

Social work, librarianship, business, teaching, and college and school administration are careers held by these reuning members of the Class of 1937; from left: Anna Tamul Ferrara, Esther Feiner, Rose D'Avanzo Ciciarelli, Mary Cochran Lynch, Dorine Laudati Linnane, Erika Schnurmann (in back), Dorothy Pickett Priestman, Emma Warner Kershaw, Gala Swann Jennings, Mary Louise Hinckley Record, and Marion Sittler.

women graduates of six decades, and is based on alumnae who replied to our survey questionnaire and/or who have been active with the university in other ways.[2] It cannot be inclusive or regarded as a formal historical record. It is hoped, however, that the information will prove to be representative of the larger body of alumnae and will provide a beginning for a future history of the careers of women graduates of Brown.

The women surveyed for this chapter on life and career information after Brown have been divided into three groups, clearly identified by historical developments, both at the university and world levels. Those three groups of alumnae are:

> *1949 and before* – those who attended Brown when its student body was mostly local and through the last entering class just after the end of World War II.

> *1950–1970* – those alumnae who were recruited as students from a much wider geographic base and, in the latter 1960s, experienced the beginning of the women's movement.

> *1971–1989* – the years after the merger of Pembroke and Brown which have seen the largest number of women graduate from Brown, comprising 59 percent of all living alumnae and representing a great surge forward in opportunities in business and the professions, which had previously admitted only small numbers of women.

The numbers of living alumnae for the three periods are:

	Living Alumnae	*Percent of Total*
1949 and before	3,031	17.4
1950–1970	4,114	23.6
1971–1989	10,232	59.0

The alumnae survey asked the graduates to list the major decisions in their lives. Results showed that the sixty-year class, 1930, labelled their turning points in much the same way as those who came along forty and fifty years later. The four major turning points which were identified by all alumnae as most important life junctures were: (1) attending and graduating from Brown; (2) settling down, including a somewhat permanent geographic location, and/or marriage and children; (3) travel and/or move to a new environment; and (4) graduate school and/or choice of career. Not surprisingly, the most important second turning point for the youngest cohort was graduate school or career choice.

The survey tried to identify the larger changes, as well as some of the stated reasons for satisfactions/frustrations with their lives, and where those changes were the result of their differing kinds of education at Brown (class size, pre-merger, post-merger), the realities of life after Brown in the larger society; and, always present, the obstacles presented by health, geographic location and other personal factors. Many of the same factors had an impact on the lives of the male graduates at Brown, but it is clear from the responses that the women have had to make all of their decisions in the context of family plans, or *against* family considerations, with resultant personal readjustment, if not anguish.

There were two questions on the survey which were meant to elicit responses reflecting the undergraduate years as a basis for the future. The first was, "How did your experience at Brown contribute to your life?" Of the total respondents, 21.8 percent indicated that Brown had given them a broader perspective on themselves and the world; 20 percent indicated they had learned analytical skills which helped to open post-graduate career doors; 14.5 percent mentioned the maturity and confidence they gained; and 11.8 percent cited specifically the long-lasting friendships they had made.

It is obvious that in many fields, an A.B. or Sc.B. alone was not enough and that an advanced degree was necessary. Figures provided for the study from the Brown Alumni and Development Information Services (ADIS) indicate that of the 17,377 women graduates through June 1989, 5,244, or 30 percent, have earned graduate degrees, plus 856 who reported enrollment in graduate programs when they responded. These figures included 27 Ph.D.s and 11 M.D.s in the earliest group; 151 Ph.D.s and 46 M.D.s in the middle group; and 185 Ph.D.s and 444 M.D.s thus far for the youngest group.

For alumnae with a sure direction and the funds or fellowship to pay for it, graduate study followed the undergraduate degree quite soon after graduation for alumnae in all three of the eras. For others, the path has been to earn the advanced degree at age thirty-five or older when children were launched and a period of preparation for reentry into the job market was possible. Threaded through the responses from alumnae in the two early eras are some examples of women who have retooled for the times with new study and training after bringing up families; some who have returned successfully to the business world; late degrees even after long service in the same field. Examples include Barbara Bliss, Class of 1940, who earned an M.S. in guidance and counselling in 1973; and Beverly Moss Spatt, Class of 1945, who completed her Ph.D. in 1976 in urban planning. One alumna from the middle era is now completing a Ph.D. at age forty-six, but even in the 1980s, she reported having had little strong encouragement, saying, "With 790 out of 800 on the Graduate Record Examination, I was advised not to apply to certain universities because they take few women and no older people." Another "returner" is Barbara Kirk (Andrews) Hail, Class of 1952, whose scholarly work is quoted at the beginning of this chapter. She transferred to Cornell because of marriage, and earned both a B. A. and M. A. at Cornell in history, followed by teaching and family years. After her first husband's death, she studied history at Columbia with a Danforth Fellowship before moving to Rhode Island, where she did further graduate work in anthropology.

The context in which the women attended Brown had a significant bearing on their choices and chances. The life paths of the alumnae surveyed prove that there is room for the diversity which comes in a woman's life in whatever pattern: work/family/family-volunteer; work/family/work; or work/work and family/and more work! When a woman graduated between 1930 and 1949, she was expected to work in one of the "womanly" professions for college-educated women, but then to call a halt to work outside the home until her children were raised. In most cases, she was not expected to resume an outside career, but to devote the major portion of her time and energy to being a full-time wife, homemaker, and volunteer in the community. The class profiles show that the middle group in the survey were aware of the opportunities for outside involvement and were very much part of that world, before, during, and after the intense, child-rearing family years. The youngest group in the study, those who graduated after 1970, showed a tremendous surge of accomplishment in business and the professions, but also expressed the common frustration about the inability to "have it all," sometimes opting out of having children or postponing them to a later age, or deciding that personal satisfaction could best be found in the family context and not in the professional world. The biggest difference between the earlier and the later generations of Pembroke/Brown alumnae is that women have the choices now.

Of the 17,377 alumnae in the larger statistical count (to 1989), 39 percent of the oldest group self-labelled themselves "homemaker" for record purposes; 29 percent of the middle group did so; and only 2 percent (166 out of 10,232) in the youngest group did so. Even allowing for the fact that many of these younger people have not yet settled into a permanent life routine, the changes in percentage are startling.

The following sections describe general trends for the three alumnae cohorts followed by information about some specific career fields which have attracted Brown alumnae.

Group One: The Classes from 1930–49

The women who attended Brown as undergraduates between 1926 and 1945 comprised the first cohort for the study. These women were enrolled when the student body had many local students and included those who graduated between the beginning of the Great Depression and the end of World War II.

Thirty-eight percent of alumnae in this first cohort completed further study after Brown, including R.N. diplomas and graduate degrees. Of that larger group of 3,031 alumnae, 877, or 28 percent, earned their advanced degrees at Brown.

The two earliest classes included in the survey were the Classes of 1930 and 1935.[3] In some ways, the lives of these women were the most exciting to uncover because many were listed in alumni records as "retired," telling us very little. Their choice of undergraduate field was, to a large extent, determined by the times. Because the women in these two classes graduated during the Depression, many found it necessary to develop saleable skills and to go to work immediately in the careers open to them. Teaching, librarianship, and social work were the first opportunities. As their careers progressed, many class members made the most of their opportunities or later developed special interests. Seventy percent of the respondents from the Classes of 1930 and 1935 reported such working careers as teacher, social worker, statistical analyst, administrator, librarian, owner of own business, radio producer, investment advisor, with the others reporting a variety of careers in voluntary service.

Respondents from the Class of 1930 included Helen Smith Magee, who taught for ten years, then became a statistical analyst in sonar research for three years during World War II. Since 1960, Magee has been a professional artist and has exhibited in several galleries and competitions. Honor McCusker earned a Ph.D. from Bryn Mawr in 1937. She spent her career with the State Department as director of library service for Africa, Athens, New Delhi, Rome and The Hague, earning a Meritorious Service Medal from the U.S. Information Service. Verna Follett Spaeth earned an M.A. from Brown in 1931 and married a Brown classics professor, John W. Spaeth, Jr. Her husband's career took them to Wesleyan University where she tutored in Latin, English and psychology. She also started, with her husband, the Wesleyan University Archives. Gertrude Rosenhirsch Zisson is an early example of reentry to the professional world. Twenty-nine years after her Brown graduation, she earned an M.A. in history (her undergraduate field) in 1959 at Columbia. She taught for several years right after college and again from 1956 to 1966.

Varied career patterns from the Class of 1935 include Sara Bloom Paul who went back to work after thirty-five years "at home" and has had a late career as manager of a brokerage office. Virginia Kempton Connor began her career with the East Providence Library system when that library was one room in a house lived in by others, then by Connor with her family for a period of time, and, finally, saw the library through a transition to a modern, up-to-date building. At her retirement after forty-one years, the children's room there was named for her.

The responses from the Class of 1940[4] and their own 1990 reunion survey show that graduating at the beginning of World War II had a profound effect on their lives. Almost all of the women reported that they had worked at one kind of job or another for a number of years; others moved family and household a number of times to be near family during military career changes. Those women who married soon after graduation held themselves and their families together during those difficult years, and were happy to be able to settle back into home and family surroundings and responsibilities after the end of the war.

The summary of the Class of 1940 compiled for their fiftieth reunion in 1990 reveals that nearly half of the women in the class saw their careers as homemaker/volunteer, but most of the women have had very productive volunteer careers. Of class members describing careers, nearly one-fifth of them were in education. Phyllis Riley Murray spent her professional career as a teacher of emotionally disturbed children and then, after retirement, volunteered for the Family Court's Special Advocate Program for abused and neglected children. Shirley Roberts Barbour recalls her fifteen-month stint with the Red Cross overseas during World War II as a major turning point which expanded her horizons greatly. Barbour worked for several magazines on the West Coast after the war and then found her niche as long-time art editor for the American Mathematics Society.

The 160 women who were in the Class of 1945[5] have a story of their own to tell. The United States entered World War II just after they entered college, and it was not long before Brown lost a good number of its male students to the service. Women were integrated with male students in classes more quickly than might have been the case under ordinary circumstances, and opportunities opened up for women because of the shortage of men for appropriate openings. Florence Asadorian Dulgarian was one of the Pembroke undergraduates awarded Pratt & Whitney scholarships for undergraduate study and, in return, asked to work for that company afterward. Jean Tanner Edwards served as an Ensign in a U.S. Naval Reserve communications intelligence unit during the war. After marriage and children, Edwards followed a more traditional career as a librarian and media specialist.

It is clear that a number of the members of the Class of 1945 followed a post-graduate pattern of becoming wife, mother, and homemaker. There are many exceptions, however, including Shirley Gallup, who was in the first class of women at Harvard Medical School, and Elizabeth Jackson Phillips, a professor of social work at Wayne State University. Speaking at a 1990 Brown Commencement Forum on careers sponsored by the Pembroke Center, Phillips described a very different experience at Pembroke from what is remembered by most alumnae. She was the only African-American in most of her classes. Brought up in Providence by parents who taught her that she must "pull her weight" and be responsible, but sheltered in a very protective way, she reports that her introduction to the outside world came when her family allowed her to move to Pittsburgh to earn a Master of Social Work degree. Phillips is the first African-American woman to serve on the Brown Corporation.

Group Two: Classes of 1950–1970

The middle group of alumnae surveyed included the women who entered Brown in 1946 immediately after World War II, those who studied there during the purportedly passive fifties, and those who came to Brown in the sixties as the civil rights and women's movements were under way. When the Class of 1950 entered Pembroke, they found that women made up one-third of the undergraduate student body and that the male two-thirds was a mixture of men of usual college age and a great many older men who had returned from war service and were welcomed to Brown through the Veterans College. A few of the women were veterans, too, and the campus emphasis was on a return to normalcy.

The Classes of 1950 and 1955 reported career information including: urban planner; special librarian; actress; labor arbitrator; teacher at elementary, secondary or college level; judge; former librarian and now mother of four, grandmother of four and deacon in the Presbyterian Church; protein chemist; teacher and creator of quilts; editor, TV magazine; free-lance photographer and exhibitor; psychiatric review specialist; chair of a Quaker meeting; vice president, Chase Manhattan Bank.[6]

Which of these people is typical of the "passive Fifties"? In Brown's *George Street Journal* for March 31, 1990, Leslie Travis Wendell, Class of 1955, a psychology major who is now a marketing and communications consultant, describes her memory of how she and her classmates thought about the future in the early 1950s, saying, "We (the women) would graduate, work for one year in a glamorous job, probably in New York. We'd get married, move to the suburbs and drive around in a station wagon with the dog and kids in the back seat." There were some in the fifties who had that dream. Others knew that real life for them began right after graduation with self-support and a job as necessity, not time-filler. The important difference was that in those years, graduating women, and the men who married them, expected them to stop working when they married and fulfill the American dream by having a family and making a home.

By 1946, when the Class of 1950 entered, all classes were coeducational with the exception of sections of introductory courses in fields such as English and languages. Pembroke campus activities still included (through the fifties and into the sixties) an active athletic program, singing groups, a newspaper, and a yearbook. Survey responses by the women on campus in the fifties mention frequently that a lifelong benefit of Pembroke was the cohesiveness brought about by their extracurricular activities and the friendships they formed, especially in small freshman dormitories.

Responses from members of the Classes of 1950 and 1955 included 84 percent who followed the pattern of the times by marrying soon after graduation, having children, becoming involved with church, school and community. Unlike the women often depicted in this era, a full 68 percent returned to the permanent work force after ten to fourteen years of being a full-time mother and homemaker. In some ways, these women had something new going for them. By the time their children became semi-independent, the women's movement was in full swing and women were being told it was acceptable to leave their kitchens and re-engage with the world. For many, a return to school for a professional degree was the answer. Marcia Finberg Goldfarb, Class of 1955, graduated with a major in international relations after she was carefully steered away from the sciences by her well-meaning advisors. Science turned out to be her strength, she learned belatedly; she returned to college (after marriage and three children) in 1970 to study chemistry, and is now a protein chemist with her own company.

Fifty-eight percent of the respondents from the Classes of 1950 and 1955 earned advanced degrees, including a number who did so after their children had grown. Curious about how the women's movement of the sixties was remembered by their peers, the Pembroke Class of 1958 included two questions in a 1958 reunion survey with some interesting results as summarized by Patricia Patricelli. She reported: "Almost none of us were active in the women's movement, but almost all of us think it is the single most important event to have happened in the last thirty years. About 95 percent like the changes, but there is some concern about our daughters' capabilities of handling the range of options now open to them."

It is thought-provoking and a cautionary tale to report that 46 percent of the respondents from the classes of 1950 and 1955 are single, divorced, or had a spouse who has died or had an incapacitating accident. It's a far cry from the carefree station wagon life that might have been imagined by that age group when they were Pembroke students. The tenor of the responses from the women of the fifties was upbeat, however. The respondents have clearly all had their battles with life and circumstances, but they indicate, on balance, that they have had their place in the world and have contributed significantly to it. They remember their undergraduate years very positively and Fredi Kovitch Solod, Class of 1950, summed it up in a brochure she wrote entitled "Letter to My Daughters and Their Friends...: "Learning to be flexible in college may be your most valuable curriculum."

The students in the Classes of 1960 and 1965 lived what, in retrospect, seems to have been a traditional campus life in single-sex dormitories with quiet hours, dormitory closing times and served, sit-down dinners.[7] As benefits of their undergraduate years at Pembroke, several mentioned the small freshman house system as fostering lifelong friendships. Yet, some alumnae remember feeling stifled by the way in which women were treated differently from the men and were sheltered much more than necessary from the real world.

The women of the 1960s combined professions and volunteer careers, careers and family responsibilities, careers and compelling avocational interests. Several have gone on to second careers in very different fields from those for which they had educated themselves initially. An example is Bernadine Courtright Barr, Class of 1965, who earned an M. F. A. in 1967 at the University of Chicago and in 1990, after several years of family life in several locations with her husband and two children, was completing a Ph. D. in child and adolescent development.

More than half of the Class of 1965 respondents to the survey reported graduate study, and the responses represent the following areas: art, biology, classics, economics, education, English, history, library science, medicine, and law. The variety of fields is representative of the time, when so many opportunities were opening to women in graduate school and in professional fields. It wasn't always easy, though, and Barbara French Pace represents the transitional year in which this Class of 1965 graduated. As a magna cum laude graduate with a Phi Beta Kappa key, she applied to Princeton for graduate study and was told, "We are sorry to have to tell you that we do not admit women." She went on to complete graduate study at Johns Hopkins School of Advanced International Studies and now, after years of successful experience in several countries, is head of a major research desk for a federal agency.

It might be expected that a reader of this chapter might say, "Oh, only the stars respond to such inquiries; the rest are malcontents or also-rans." Not so. The combined Brown-Pembroke Class of 1965 had its twenty-fifth reunion in 1990 with seventy-two Pembroke women (more than one-third of the Pembroke class) in attendance at their reunion activities. The combined class published an anniversary yearbook that reveals fifty-five more master's degrees, thirteen more doctorates in the fields of biology, communications, education, history, mathematics, political science and psychology, four more lawyers, another medical doctor, a veterinarian, a nurse, an alumna who went on to retool and earn a second bachelor's degree in mathematics in order to teach in the public schools; and wonderful and varied volunteer service of great value to their communities.

The women of the Class of 1970[8] entered Brown in 1966 when there was still a structured curriculum and single-sex housing on the Pembroke campus. Before they graduated, all that had changed. The Brown curriculum was substantially revised in 1969 after a year-long study by a combined faculty-student committee. In addition to the curricular revision and campus unrest at Brown, as elsewhere, surrounding the Vietnam War, the Cambodian invasion, the pressure for more minority students, and the move against the Naval ROTC unit on campus, there was a continuing attempt from 1966–71 to bring about an end to the residential and social inequities between men and women on campus. The move was at first pressed by the *Brown Daily Herald* as an attack on parietal rules on the Pembroke campus, and then greatly enlarged as Brown suffered a severe financial deficit and a merger came to be perceived by key administrators as a cost-cutting measure. President Hornig appointed a year-long study committee of corporation, faculty, administration and students, and their report formed the basis for the Brown-Pembroke merger in 1971.[9]

Cynthia White Hesel, Class of 1970, said of her time at Brown, "Our class represented a transition between more restrictive roles for women in society and more freedom of choice. I think Brown helped set these changes in motion without giving us guidance in ways to deal with them." Those active in university administration in those years were all too aware that students, faculty, administration, and the public at large, were living in an era where all ground rules were changing so rapidly that there was no blueprint to hand on to the new generation. They were making the ground rules themselves.

Respondents echo the tenor of the times in mentioning their campus activities and undergraduate interests. They were idealistic; they felt they had much to contribute to the real world and were anxious to get on with it. Respondents included lawyers and a judge, doctors, clinical psychologists, an urban planner, an architect, several in banking and finance, two who are self-employed in businesses, a museum archivist, a computer scientist, a graphic artist, several women in college/university teaching, a librarian, and several in elementary, secondary and international education. One-third of the respondents have earned advanced degrees; the choices they have made *within* the fields seem to represent clearly the time in which they came of age and began to question the world around them. Laurie Davison said, "I learned concern for the larger society – civil rights, anti-war activities, police brutality, poverty and its impact." Catherine Laughlin earned a Ph.D. in microbiology and is now at the National Institutes of Health doing antiviral research. She feels good about "being in a position to have a positive impact on the development of effective therapies for viral diseases."

On the personal side, several respondents mentioned divorce, including one who reported that her husband had always said that when "they" finished putting him through law school and he was launched on a career, it would be her turn for graduate school. Many indicated that they found the balance between family and professional life to be more stressful than satisfying, but the hard decision is perceived by many to be worthwhile. Catherine Nicholson Donnelly, senior conservator at the National Archives, is proud of her career with international ties and her several publications, but admits that "having a child at age 38 turned my neat little world upside down and added immensely to it." Carol Landau earned a Ph.D. in psychology and has a practice of her own as well as being director of psychological services for Women's Health Associates in Providence. She has written a number of articles on behavioral medicine and the psychology of women.

Christine Sweck Love's undergraduate and professional careers have spanned the many changes at Brown in the last two decades. After graduation, she became a Pembroke admission officer, moving to the Brown Admission Office in 1971 at the time of the merger of the two colleges. After a degree from library school in North Carolina, she served as director of the Middletown (RI) Public Library. She returned to Brown in 1987 as associate director of the Brown Annual Fund and was promoted in 1989 to director of alumni relations, providing leadership to Brown's 60,000 alumni.

Group Three: Classes since 1971

The merger of Pembroke and Brown went into effect in 1971. The ratio of women to men undergraduates, which had been one-third women/two-thirds men for many years, was abandoned and the new goal of the Admission Office was equal representation of women and men. Women of the Class of 1975 were the first to be recruited by the Admission Office as part of a totally integrated student body. For more than seventy-five years, and particularly during the 1950s and 1960s, Pembroke had been promoted as "the best of both worlds," a chance for coeducational classes, research, excellent university faculty, but also separate housing and student activities which would foster a spirit of independence among women and give women a chance for leadership of their own organizations. Now what to say? In some ways, the text had already been dictated by the success of women in coeducational activities on the main Brown campus.[10]

ADIS records show that there were 10,232 alumnae of the classes of 1971–89, and of that number, 32 percent have reported either completed advanced degrees or were continuing graduate study in a wide range of fields.[11]

The survey responses from this youngest cohort also shows a marked contrast in marital status as reported five, ten, and fifteen years after college compared with the usual pattern for graduates in the two earlier groups. Of the Class of 1975, 73 percent of the respondents indicated that they were married; 9 percent have been divorced and remarried; another 9 percent have been divorced and 9 percent are single. Of the Class of 1980, 59 percent of the respondents are still single or are married, but without children as yet, a far cry from the norm in the 1950s. Five years out of college, only 41 percent of the respondents from the Class of 1985 were married.

Full-time professional employment was reported by 73 percent of the Class of 1975 respondents.[12] Advanced degrees were reported by half of the class, including master's and Ph.D. degrees in academic subjects, business, public health, medicine, and law. One class member who earned the degree of Master of Public Health combined important social service with her specialized area. Susan Greathouse earned an undergraduate degree in comparative literature with Spanish as her second language, little realizing how she would use her knowledge of Spanish. She is now a registered dietitian and instructor at a state university. Her greatest satisfaction has been "empowering women through support and education to make better use of available resources and better choices for their and their family's health." She has had two publications thus far, one on nutrition and another in Spanish on "Lactation and the Premature Infant."

The survey responses from the Class of 1980[13] represented a wide gamut of professional interests from archeology to zoology and from the most high-pressure career person to the alumna who has opted out of the professional world altogether. What definitely does not come through is the self-centered "me" generation so much ballyhooed by the press about the 1980s. There were the expected doctors, lawyers and M.B.A.s, but there were also responses from those who have chosen to work for social causes. Examples are Cynthia Harding, who earned a Master of Public Health degree in epidemiology, and is now with the L. A. County AIDS Program; and Sally Friedman, who worked from 1985–88 for the Coalition to Free Soviet Jews, and earned a law degree to buttress those efforts. Marcie Cohen, with an M. A. in history and museum studies, was formerly with Plimoth Plantation. She is currently assistant director of international programs with Elderhostel. Two of the class members who received doctorates in psychology are Terry Bensinger, who is now a counselor/therapist and Elizabeth Roberts, who heads a learning diagnostic center in Boston. A third, Alison Kane, is a psychotherapist at Whitman Institute and a Ph. D. candidate at Fordham University.

To demonstrate the variety of careers represented in this class, it should be added that Tobi Casselman is benefit systems specialist for Playboy Enterprises; Cynthia Easton is a registered pharmacist; Javette Pinckney Laremont is a marketing consultant for IBM; and Kimberly Davis, formerly an assistant attorney general in Massachusetts, is an associate with a law firm in Boston. Laura Greenfield Martin has started her own company, Colorful Cloths, after working as a corporate director of marketing.

Five years after graduation, all the respondents from the Class of 1985 reported full-time careers.[14] There are doctors, lawyers, engineers, computer scientists, women in theatre, real estate, government, finance, educational administration and carpentry, the last-named showing the power of a liberal arts degree to let you do what you want most to do. The group also includes several women who have been successful with writing, journalism and editing careers.

Elizabeth Ann Cullen combined her undergraduate concentration in women's studies with an interest in law. With the help of a Marshall Fellowship, she went to law school at New York University and also earned a Master of Public Administration degree from Columbia. Cullen says, "At Brown I became greatly involved with women's issues, politically and academically – a focus which I have maintained over the years." She has been active with the NYU Battered Women's Program, and the St. Vincent's Rape Crisis Program. When she responded to the survey, Cullen was a legal intern with the NOW Legal Defense Education Fund. Another class member who has made a unique contribution, both as undergraduate and now lawyer, is Grace W. Tsuang, who has been active in the fight against racial discrimination in college admissions for Asian Americans. She testified on Capitol Hill in 1988 and has lectured extensively on the issue. Tsuang says she is "pleased to see that many colleges and universities, especially Brown, have now taken measures to address this problem. It's been satisfying to see changes as a result of one's efforts."

Nearly two-thirds of the respondents found graduate school necessary for professional advancement. In addition to those in medicine and law mentioned above, a number are still in graduate school in a variety of academic fields: history, biology, business administration, education, engineering, theatre, journalism, public health, marriage and family therapy.

Most of those who did not attend graduate school are in fields which are personally creative and/or highly competitive in a non-scholarly world – advertising, computers, video production, music. Alicia Svigals, who completed an ethnomusicology concentration (a new academic field at Brown in the 1980s), earns a living by serving as executive secretary for Yivo Institute for Jewish Research, but has, in addition, become very successful in her own brand of ethno-music. Her Jewish ethnic music band, the Klezmatics, was featured in a music note in a July 1990 issue of the *New Yorker*. They have recorded two albums, and have toured Europe three times, with future trips planned to the USSR and South America. Anne W. Fischer, who completed concentrations in both Latin American studies and art, is a pre-vocational coordinator for La Alianza Hispana in the Boston area, a clubhouse model rehabilitation program for Hispanic adults with chronic mental illnesses. She balances her career with quilt-making and exhibitions. Marta Hanson, who did undergraduate concentrations both in health and society and in Chinese studies, spent two spring semesters in Nanjing, China, and has published two papers on the history of Chinese medicine.

The women's movement, with its emphasis on women's rights, including birth control, and societal expectations and norms has surely had its effect on this generation. Rather than representing the norm, as it would have in an earlier decade, it took a special kind of courage for one woman from the Class of 1980 to write that her major accomplishment was "Against many odds, staying at home to raise our children; totally rebuilding (with my husband) a 150-year-old home; growing in a beautiful marriage; spending time with four loving children." Her comment points up the painful decisions that may be necessary now that options and opportunities for women have broadened so much.

Resumed Undergraduate Education Program (RUE)

In 1972, Brown was one of the earliest private liberal arts institutions to begin a formal resumed education program for people whose formal education had been interrupted for five years or more. The program (for both women and men) has been particularly valuable for women who had been good students academically, but had to interrupt their educations, usually for marriage, children and/or a change of location caused by their husband's job. From 1973 through 1989, 117 women completed degrees through this program. From the beginning, there have been a number of Brown and Pembroke non-graduates who have been "folded into" the program after readmission. One of the key elements of the program has been the availability of part-time study for those whose family and/or employment obligations precluded a full-time program.

The 117 women who earned their degrees through the program include some who have gone on to medical school and graduate study in the liberal arts, to professional positions in teaching and administration, human resources, health services organizations, and museum work, as well as others who have entered, or reentered employment in business, finance, and real estate.

Two RUE alumnae are presently completing Ph.D. programs in anthropology, one at Brown after an "earlier" life as a registered nurse and mother of several children and stepchildren; the other now at Yale after a banking career in the Virgin Islands followed by entry to Brown as a full-time forty-year-old freshman. Lydia English, Class of 1985, reported: "Brown was a pivotal experience in my life... I learned many academic subjects, but I believe the more meaningful experiences centered around learning about the life of the mind... and the intellectual and emotional experiences of the academic community. My experiences at Brown were the experiences of a lifetime and the inspiration for pursuing my doctorate."

Three Pembroke returners who have taken advantage of this unique support system are Mary Klohr Merrill, Class of 1942, who commuted from her home in Boston in 1981–82 and received her A. B. degree in 1982, the year of the fortieth reunion of her original class; Julia Foster Paxton, Class of 1965, who received her degree in 1981 and is now a newspaper editor; and Diane Waldman Kleinmann, Class of 1955, who commuted from New York to complete her "unfinished academic business" in 1987.

Career Choices of Brown Alumnae

The careers of the alumnae body at large, the 17,377 living alumnae through the Class of 1989, represent a movement toward fewer restrictions of opportunities in all areas, fueled in a very real sense by the Civil Rights Act, Title VII (1964) followed by the appointment of the Equal Employment Opportunities Commission. The women's movement was in full swing, and those alumnae who were among the organizers of chapters of

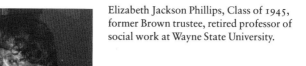

Elizabeth Jackson Phillips, Class of 1945, former Brown trustee, retired professor of social work at Wayne State University.

Betsy August, Class of 1980, M.D. 1984, an obstetrician in Massachusetts.

the National Organization for Women (NOW) in 1966 had no small part in getting unfair practice recognized. By the 1960s, it had become impossible to regard women candidates as "invisible," and women began to be hired as something more than "go-fers" in radio and television, on newspapers, in advertising, banking and insurance, in government, higher education, and in the professions.

In the career information part of the survey, alumnae were asked to list their major satisfactions, as well as their greatest career frustrations. As accomplishments, establishing a career and reaching their goals were listed by 34 percent of the respondents, with the earning of an advanced degree as the second most important accomplishment. Company politics led the list of career frustrations, with 24 percent of the youngest mentioning that factor, and a smaller percentage of the two other groups. Frustrations related to sexism on the job were mentioned by 12.2 percent of the respondents, the same percentage for both the middle and younger groups.

The aim of this section is to describe several fields which have shown large increases in the numbers of alumnae represented and/or real breakthroughs in opportunities for women.[15] There have been increases in numbers of alumnae going into medicine, law, higher education, business, industry, and engineering. The number of alumnae representing all of the communications fields, writing, editing and producing for newspapers, radio and television has also increased.[16] There has been a decrease in the number of alumnae going into elementary and secondary education and library work, perhaps as a result of enlarged opportunities now available for women graduates in other areas. The fields described below, therefore, are representative, but cannot pretend to describe fully the broad array of careers of the total body of Brown alumnae.

Medicine

One of the strongest professional fields among Brown alumnae is medicine, with nearly eight hundred women reported as practicing physicians. Even though the opening of the Brown medical program helped to accelerate the number, Brown women have always chosen medicine as a field. The proportion of living alumnae physicians is 1 percent of the oldest survey group, 2 percent of the second cohort and 5 percent of the most recent group.[17]

In September 1990, the Brown Medical Program Public Affairs Office listed 593 women physicians who were undergraduates at Brown and who attended other medical schools; 183 women physicians who have both Brown undergraduate and medical degrees; and, in addition, 344 women physicians who have medical degrees from Brown after undergraduate work elsewhere.[18]

Among the factors determining their decisions about specializations are being able to control the schedule of hours to be somewhat compatible with family life, and encouragement or lack of support for entrance into a specialty. The women in the survey sample are in the following specialties: anesthesiology, community and family medicine, gastroenterology, hospital emergency room, internal medicine, neurology, obstetrics and pediatrics, physical medicine and rehabilitation, and psychiatry/psychoanalysis.

The oldest physician to respond to the survey was Sophie Trent Stevens, Class of 1939, who graduated from Yale Medical School in 1943 and practiced in Tennessee, Puerto Rico, Florida, Maryland, and the Virgin Islands in pathology and tropical medicine before settling in Connecticut. Jeanne Rafsky Jaspan, Class of 1945, went on to New York University School of Medicine and has been in practice in New York City since then in gastroenterology.

The second cohort of respondents, from the classes of 1950–70, included some women who were enrolled in the Brown Program in Medicine from the time of it beginning in 1962 as the Master of Medical Science program. Beginning at that time, entering freshmen were preselected for the medical program at admission, thus giving already-decided students a head start on their careers. The percent of women in those classes averaged much higher than the national figures for the same time period, 23 percent at Brown as opposed to 10 percent nationally.[19] Survey respondents from doctors in the Class of 1965 included Estelle Pisetsky Bender, M.D. Columbia 1968, who is in practice in New York City in psychiatry and psychoanalysis, and Suzanne Solomons Love, M.D. Vanderbilt 1975, who now works in emergency medicine at the Virginia Beach General Hospital.

The next medical respondent was from the Class of 1975, ten years later. After completing her M.D. at Brown, Sharon Akrep Crough moved with her husband and children to Great Falls, Montana, where she is an anesthesiologist at two hospitals. Cheryl Soled Reid, also Class of 1975, earned her M.D. from Rutgers and is assistant professor of pediatrics and head of the Division of Genetics at Robert Wood Johnson Medical School. She started the clinical genetics service for southern New Jersey and the regional birth defects program there.

The third cohort in the survey included a number of women who were at Brown when the university began the full M.D. program in 1972. One of the early graduates of that group was Deborah DeHertogh, Class of 1974 and M.D. 1977. Speaking about her undergraduate years at Brown, she said: "At Brown I was given the opportunity to be the best that I could be, regardless of the fact that I was a woman. Brown gave me a love for being challenged intellectually which I will always treasure." DeHertogh, who is assistant chief of medicine at Mount Sinai (CT) Hospital, has been aware of a real problem in moving up the academic ladder (in a medical school faculty) without a mentor, citing as examples "not having your work recognized at times by Chairmen; not being told about meetings or having those meetings scheduled at times which are very difficult for working mothers to come, the latter despite pointing out to the committee chairman that there were 3 women faculty members with young children who found 7:30 a.m. meetings tough to get to!"

Betsy August, Class of 1980, M.D. 1984, is now an obstetrician with a community health center. August said that one of the turning points of her early life was working in Puerto Rico during medical school years and organizing a family planning clinic. Because August is bilingual, she has found great satisfaction in working with an immigrant population and has been involved in planning for better approaches to the problems of a multinational patient population.

Law and Judiciary

The number of Brown alumnae entering the legal profession increased from only ten of the 3,031 in the earliest group to 145 (3.5 percent) of the 4,114 in the middle group; then to 577 (5.5 percent) of the 10,232 in the most recent group. The survey sample included six lawyers from the Classes of 1950–70 and sixteen of the youngest group.

The fields in which alumnae have reported their legal careers are state and federal government agencies and courts, public interest organizations and administrative and teaching positions in law schools. Some few who have become associates or partners in law firms have specialties in health, safety, and environmental concerns. No wheeler-dealers are using their law degrees in high finance or business positions. Perhaps it is too early in the "co-ed law" game to attribute that absence to a lack of interest in high dealing or a purposeful shutting out of women from those areas, but the void is striking. The Massachusetts Bar Association in 1990 reported that women with equivalent experience, earn only 80 percent of the earnings of similar male lawyers.[20] It would seem from this admittedly limited sample that the discrepancy may not result entirely from hidden discrimination, but may bear some direct relationship to the areas of law into which women law school graduates are moving.

Of the six in the survey sample from the middle group, four entered law school soon after Brown graduation. Antoinette Loiacono Dupont, Class of 1950, who is now a chief judge of a state appellate court; Nancy L. Buc, Class of 1965, who has been in both federal government and private practice, in food and drug legislative matters; Laurie N. Davison, Class of 1970, who was an attorney for a legal aid society for seven years, and is now litigation director for a non-profit, statewide legal assistance program; and Beverly Hodgson, Class of 1970, who is now a judge of the Connecticut Superior Court. Hodgson reported that her greatest legal satisfaction has come from winning civil rights cases that helped women, minorities, and the elderly. The other two respondents had more traditional family lives until somewhat later. A. Patricia Pepper, Class of 1965, earned a J.D. in 1981 and is now an assistant general counsel with a state department of environmental regulation. Cathryn Cummings Nunlist, Class of 1970, completed her law degree in 1990 and was serving as a law clerk when she responded to the survey.

Carol Agate, Class of 1955, enrolled in law school in 1970, fifteen years after college. After completing the J.D. in 1973 at the University of Connecticut, she served in private practice for a time and then in 1980 became a clinical professor of law at UCLA. She became a traffic hearing officer in Los Angeles and in 1988 was appointed an administrative law judge. Agate counts as one of her major accomplishments the winning of a U.S. Supreme Court case requiring Rotary clubs to admit women and, while still in law school, successfully challenging the exclusion of women from the public golf course and girls from the Little League.

Nancy L. Buc of the Class of 1965 was one of the seven women of 250 graduates in her class at the University of Virginia Law School. She has alternated between serving in government and working in her law firm as presidential administrations changed, all moves which, Buc says, are taken for granted for men of her age and experience, but ones that are questioned when women make similar moves for similar reasons. Buc's positions have been largely "firsts:" first professional woman in the division of consumer credit at the Federal Trade Commission, first woman assistant bureau director at the FTC, then first woman partner at her law firm, first woman chief counsel at the Food and Drug Administration. She says that she was "often the first woman lawyer a colleague, an adversary or a client had ever worked with or against." Buc is one of two women on the Brown Board of Fellows.

Responses came from sixteen people in the youngest group of alumnae, 1971–89, who had earned the J.D. or were enrolled in law school. Two of the lawyers in the Class of 1975 have become partners in law firms. Gail McCann reported that she was the first woman partner in the corporate department of her firm. Another, Judith Curchin Preston, has received professional satisfaction from the *pro bono* cases on domestic problems she has been able to handle. Preston also indicated some frustration with sexual discrimination in the workplace: "women are given boring cases, less responsibility."

The greatest number of respondents in the field of law were from the Class of 1985. Among the comments:

"Oddly, my greatest career satisfaction is that I have pulled myself off the fast track, which was harming my personal life, by not applying for a Supreme Court clerkship."

"At Brown I became greatly involved with women's issues, politically and academically – a focus which I have maintained over the years."

"I become frustrated when I realize the limitations of our justice system and the inequities that continue to exist."

"I initiated both a recycling program at law school and an ethics discussion group."

While in law school, Amy Reiss raised $85,000 to help her law school buy equipment for blind students, and established a blind students' scholarship fund. She also guided a blind runner in the NYC marathon for the full 26.2 miles, proof certain of her commitment to the cause she espoused! Suzanne Goldberg, J.D. Harvard 1990, is now an associate with the ACLU Women's Rights Project. While a student at Brown, she was active with the campus Committee on the Status of Women and then, after winning a Fulbright, postponed law school for a year to allow study in Singapore.

"Working for Social Change" was the title of a Pembroke Center/Sarah Doyle Alumnae panel discussion in March 1982 and is a good example of several ways in which our alumnae have made contributions to society. Speakers were Doris Stearn Donovan, Class of 1959, who developed the Providence Head Start Program and is now with the Rhode Island Foundation; Catherine J. Lewis, Class of 1975, then coordinator of the Rhode Island Council on Domestic Violence and a staff member of the RI Committee on Occupational Safety and Health; Rogeriee Thompson, Class of 1973, an attorney (now judge) who works in the area of family law; and Polly Welts Kaufman, Class of 1951, who trained and assisted community women in opening and developing libraries in 120 Boston public schools during the desegregation period.

Gretchen Reiche Terhune, Class of 1956, responded to the needs of the local school system when her children were young. After several years as coordinator of volunteers for Darien High School, she was named executive director of the Darien (CT) United Way and Community Council in 1982. Cynthia Burdick-Brill Patterson, Class of 1965, has combined outstanding volunteer responsibilities with hospitals, schools, libraries and family planning organizations with a diverse career as a paid executive for several organizations. Formerly director of development at Lincoln School, she is now director of development for the Audubon Society in Rhode Island. Her classmate, Gail Fowler Mohanty, has developed a unique career out of her combined interests. Mohanty earned an M.A. at Brown and then both an M.A. in anthropology and a Ph.D. in American civilization from the University of Pennsylvania. She has developed a special interest and expertise in the field of industrial weaving and textiles and has written many articles in the field. After twelve years of preparation, the Charles River Museum of Industry opened in 1986 with Mohanty as executive director and curator.

Kathryn Scott Fuller, Class of 1968, is now president of the World Wildlife Fund, the first woman to lead such a major international environmental membership group. Her life pattern, looked at from this vantage point in her career, points up the way in which she has woven the strands together successfully. Long interested in wildlife, she lived in a tent on Tanzania's Ngorongora Crater in the Serengeti studying wildebeest in 1972. After marriage and children, she graduated from law school and then went to work for the U.S. Justice Department in its new Wildlife and Marine Resources Department, helping to explain and enforce international wildlife laws which were at that time neither consistent nor well organized. Her next challenge came in 1985 when she became vice president and general counsel for the fund and then president in 1989.[21]

In the early years of this century, one of the fields open to women college graduates was social work. Jobs were available to them, often without graduate work, because college graduates were still such a minority in the population. ADIS figures show ninety-one alumnae social workers among the graduates of 1930–1949. The number for the larger middle cohort, 1950–1970, shows a percentage decrease from the earlier era, and the sixty-nine social work respondents from the much larger youngest group is a dramatic downturn in people self-identifying with that label. But because there are now a number of different career tracks within the larger profession, there is not an actual decrease in the number of women entering the field. Those listed in human services, hospital administration, public health, as well as many of those graduates who have entered such fields as medicine, law, and the clergy, are helping to solve community problems of housing, AIDS, birth control and prenatal health, homelessness, and hunger.

One outstanding example of a successful career in social services is Helena Hogan Shea, Class of 1930, who earned both B. A. and M. A. in psychology at Brown and spent her career as a social worker, then as an alcohol research administrator, for private agencies and for the State of Rhode Island. In 1973 the Associated Alumni awarded her a Brown Bear in honor of her extensive activities as class officer, fund raiser, and officer of the Pembroke Club of Providence.

Respondents from the middle cohort in the survey sample included Erna Hoffner Gill, Class of 1950, who earned an M.S.W. from Simmons and is now a staff associate with the National Association of Social Workers; Ursula Heineman Rickenberg, also Class of 1950, who earned an M.S.W. from Smith College and has been a caseworker in private practice and child care centers; and Margaret Millspaugh Moore, Class of 1955, who earned an M.S.W. at Smith in 1981, and has found great professional satisfaction in "bringing quality care to public mental health clients."

The career of Mary Lou McMillan, Class of 1985, is another illustration of the change of focus for a recent graduate who might in the past have been expected to go into social work. After Brown, she earned a Master of Public Health degree and then returned to Brown to work for the University Health Services as a health educator. She has written a number of publications on sex and health education and in 1990 facilitated a program at Brown entitled, "Issues of Sexuality," a serious college issue in these days of AIDS and real questions about sexual identification and activity.

Women have had a place in religious history as lay workers, missionaries, and teachers, but it is only in recent years that women have been accepted as full religious leaders of some branches of organized religion in the United States. The Disciples of Christ, Presbyterians, and Methodists voted full participation in church leadership to women in the 1950s, and seminaries, including Harvard Divinity School, began to admit women. As late as 1972, however, less than 1 percent of clergy in those churches were women, and very few even of this small number served parishes or were pastors.[22] ADIS figures show fifty Brown alumnae who are ministers or rabbis, more than half of whom graduated after 1970. A separate listing provided by the Brown Chaplain's Office in 1989 of women with careers in religion shows that all of the women listed in the oldest and middle cohorts were Protestant or Roman Catholic and the twenty-six in the youngest group included seventeen in Protestant denominations and nine in Judaism.[23]

Alison Palmer, Class of 1951, is one of the best known Brown alumnae in religion because she was a trail-blazer for women in the Episcopal Church in America. She was ordained in Washington, D.C. in September 1975 in an extra-canonical ceremony in advance of the Fall 1976 vote by the national body, which came fifty-seven years after the Episcopal Church in America appointed a study group on the subject of ordaining women to the priesthood. The move was just about inevitable, however, after the Episcopal Theological Seminary first admitted women for the full course of study in 1958 and those fully-qualified women then moved into positions as lay assistants and as deacons.

Women were also making major advances in those years in Judaism. In 1972, the first woman was ordained from the Reform rabbinical seminary and a Brown alumna, Laura Geller, Class of 1971, was ordained shortly afterward. (She is now executive director of the American Jewish Congress in Los Angeles.) Jewish women on the Brown campus had begun to have prayer services of their own since they were still excluded from participation in the major prayer services with men, and Naomi Janowitz, Class of 1977, and Margaret Wenig, Class of 1978 (and M.A. at Brown in 1984), developed an inclusive prayer book for women in Judaism while on the campus. Janowitz has since gone on to become a professor of religious studies at the University of California at Davis and Wenig to become a rabbi at Beth AM, The People's Temple, in New York City.

While African-American churches have had a strong and distinctive tradition of women's participation in church matters, those churches have been slow to recognize women as ordained preachers and ministers. Brown alumnae who have advanced in the African-American churches include Debra McGill Jackson, Class of 1976, who is associate minister of a Baptist church in Virginia, and Jewelnel Davis, Class of 1979, a chaplain at Carleton College.

The Roman Catholic Church has found it appropriate to include women as teachers and counselors, but not often in leadership positions, except in women's religious orders. One of the fields open to advanced study and administration by women is with church-related colleges and universities. Mary O'Rourke, Class of 1940, now Sister Mary Christopher of the Sisters of Mercy, has had a varied career within the church. She earned a Ph. D. in sociology from Notre Dame and served as a college teacher for a number of years. She then served as president of Salve Regina College for several years in the early sixties, including the time of the difficult decision by the order to allow men to enter Salve Regina and thus make it coeducational.

Not surprisingly, many of the women who responded to the opportunities available to them in the 1960s and 1970s were women who had been out of college for several years and had either established themselves in another career first or raised a family while doing lay religious work in their local churches. Beverly Flather Edwards, Class of 1969, returned to Pembroke to finish her undergraduate work after her children had entered school and thirteen years after high school graduation. She served for several years in the chaplain's office at Brown as lay advisor and associate chaplain. Many Pembroke/Brown women from the late 1960s and early 1970s will remember her from the informal women's caucus which developed on campus to discuss renewed approaches to feminism, and her work to help start the Sarah Doyle Women's Center. Edwards received the Bachelor of Divinity degree from Andover-Newton Theological Seminary in 1976, and was ordained in the Church of Christ. She is now pastor of the United Congregational Church in Little Compton, RI.

The oldest survey respondent in the field was Harriet Streeter Gray, Class of 1935. Daughter of Christian missionaries in Burma, Gray teamed with her first husband, a Congregational minister, for forty-seven years, often preaching for him. In her lifetime, she has, to use her words, "shared in the joyous ministry of eight parishes." After her first husband's death, she herself was ordained to the Christian ministry in 1985 at age seventy-two. She is now remarried to another minister and is minister of visitation for a church in Maine.

In the past, many women gave unpaid assistance to husbands who were ministers. Now some women have parishes – *and* husbands and children. They are not often part of the well-paid, fast-track population who can easily arrange for domestic help, and most are trying to "do it all." They have, however, entered the mainstream of American religious life, and it can be expected that the momentum will continue.

Education

There have been some distinct changes in the numbers of Brown alumnae going into the field of education, showing a drop in the percentage of those going into elementary and secondary education and an increase in the number of women going into higher education. New opportunities for teaching at the college level and in educational administration have altered the career goals of many of the more recent graduates who, in the past, might have gone into a career in teaching at the secondary level. Alumni records for the larger body of women graduates indicate that 6 percent of the oldest cohort[24] and 8 percent of the middle cohort have given elementary or secondary teaching as their career field; only 2 percent of the youngest group have done so.[25] In the survey sample, more than 17 percent of the respondents in the earliest group replied that elementary or secondary education was their career, 13 percent of the middle group did so; and 7 percent of the youngest group of respondents, both surveys indicating a decrease.

There are some outstanding elementary and secondary teachers among our graduates, and the downward trend of numbers should not obscure the fact that 707 Brown alumnae, 4 percent of the entire reported alumnae group, are teachers.[26] It is impossible to list the large numbers of alumnae who have made important contributions in the field, but, as representatives of their eras, two alumnae might be cited: Teresa Gagnon Mellone, Class of 1939, who spent her early career in secondary education and the last twenty-four in elementary education, earning a master's degree from Brown in 1962 in linguistics and education twenty-three years after her undergraduate work; and Susan Adler Kaplan, Class of 1958, M. A.T. 1965, a secondary teacher who was named "Teacher of the Year" in 1983 – 84 by the Providence Public Schools.[27]

In the younger group of respondents in the survey sample, there were replies from two alumnae with interesting private school teaching careers. Evelyn Christoph, Class of 1975, completed an M. A. and further graduate work at New York University and then went to Phillips Exeter Academy to teach French. She counts as a major accomplishment finding "the job of my dreams." Karen Murphy, Class of 1980, earned a Master of Education degree at Lesley College, and is now administrator and upper school coordinator at Belmont Day School.

A growing number of women have gone on to college or university level teaching after Brown. ADIS figures show less than 1 percent of the oldest alumnae in the field of college/university teaching and 3 percent of the middle group.[28] In the survey, the oldest respondent in the field is Kuo Ping Chou, Class of 1935, who earned an M.A. from Yale in linguistics and a Ph.D. in that field from the University of Michigan. She was a faculty member at the University of Wisconsin from 1952 until her retirement, and served as chair of the East Asian Language and Literature Program.

The career of Temple Fawcett, Class of 1950, bridges the age levels. Beginning as an elementary teacher and then certifying later as a teacher of art, she developed a career as a teacher of teachers, and has been a member of the faculty of Roger Williams College in early childhood education since 1977. She has published a book about supervision in early childhood education and also counts as a major career satisfaction the fact that she has been in positions which allowed her to develop new programs, especially for low-income populations.

Deborah Allen Thomas, Class of 1965, earned her Ph.D. from the University of Rochester in English in 1972, and now, after a long scholarly road, has a tenured position as associate professor of English at Villanova University. She is a recognized Dickens authority and her upcoming book, *Dickens, Thackeray and Slavery,* is her third, added to many articles and reviews. She is an active member of the Victorian Studies Association and has lectured on Dickens in Japan. Thomas says her greatest professional frustration was trying to find a tenure-track position within commuting distance of her husband's position, after receiving the Ph.D. in 1972 during a tight job market for humanities faculty.

Claudia Strauss, Class of 1975, earned a Ph.D. in 1988 from Harvard in cultural anthropology, and was appointed to a tenure-track position at Duke in 1990. Her professional progress was slowed by seven months in India doing requisite research for her thesis and by marriage to a university faculty member, and a child. She considers her major accomplishment to date "finishing [my] doctoral dissertation and receiving the Stirling Award for the best paper in psychological anthropology." Nalina Nadkarni, Class of 1976, is a scientist with a career in the treetops. She did field work as a Brown biology concentrator and in the years immediately after Brown in the area of forest ecology. She then earned a Ph.D. in forestry at the University of Washington and has become a treetops specialist, giving her a unique spot in our listing of alumnae professions. She is an avid tree-climber and field worker, but has also developed computer programs and graphics to study the forest canopy. She teaches at the University of California in Santa Barbara.[29]

Now opened, it is hoped that this window of opportunity will not close. Women are advancing in the number of years of service in college and university positions required to earn tenure and the future for them is very bright. What is not clear, however, is that their family responsibilities are correspondingly less complicated. The scholarly life requires a commitment of free "think" time not always available to prime care-givers, so the road will not be easy. Perhaps it never has been, for women or for men, but at least it is now open to both.

The Arts

The creative and performing arts have always had a large and devoted group of undergraduates and a loyal body of alumni, both those who perform and those who are active in fields allied to the arts. ADIS figures are reported separately for a great many categories within the field, so those mentioned here cannot represent the total number of alumnae in the arts.

ADIS lists seventeen artists and sculptors in the earliest cohort, forty-eight in the middle group and twenty-seven in the youngest group. In a separate category, creative arts and design includes thirteen people in the oldest group, forty-one in the middle group and sixty-two in the youngest cohort. Museum and arts administration shows five in the first group, nineteen in the middle group and twenty-nine in the youngest group. In the field of architecture, based so much on an arts-related background buttressed by necessary science and technical courses, ADIS figures indicate that there are two alumnae from the oldest group in architecture/city planning, eleven from the middle group and thirty-five in the youngest group. ADIS records show that 154 living alumnae are in entertainment or the performing arts, and in the field of music.

The survey elicited some interesting and enviable responses from alumnae who are artists, dancers, actresses, producers. Some began their emphasis on art in undergraduate college or before and some admit to continuing against great odds. One alumna from the Class of 1980, Yu-Wen Hwang Wu, earned an Sc. B. in psychology before she accepted art as a necessity, not a luxury, in her life. She earned a diploma from the Boston Museum of Fine Arts in 1987, and was named a traveling scholar for that institution in 1988.

An earlier alumna, Carolyn Sylvestre Martin, Class of 1955, concentrated in art as an undergraduate and has had a successful career in photography. She now reports the joy of "finally owning a Hasselblad and creating images that I had before only dreamed of." Jamie Evrard, Class of 1971, concentrated in both art and anthropology at Brown, where she greatly appreciated the encouragement of Professor Hugh Townley, but would have liked to have had female role models in the Brown Art Department.[30] Speaking in 1989 at a Pembroke Center Friday Forum on the Brown campus about her career, Jamie said that she is invariably asked the question, "Are you successful?" The questioner means, of course, "Do you make money?" Evrard's answer, "An artist is never poor."

In theater, the alumnae who are mentioned here represent only a token of the many graduates who have gone on in theatre, both on the stage in New York and in films and television, and in community-based theaters across the country. Ruth Hussey Longnecker, Class of 1933, had a long and successful career on the stage and in Hollywood. She was nominated for an Oscar in 1940 as Best Supporting Actress for her role as the newspaper reporter in "The Philadelphia Story." She was awarded an honorary degree at Brown in 1950 at the time of the installation of Nancy Duke Lewis as dean of Pembroke College.[31]

June Brenner Judson, Class of 1950, has spent more than thirty-five years as actress, director, and producer in the Boston area and in New

LEFT: Ruby Shang, Class of 1971, founder of Ruby Shang and Company, Dancers, New York City.
ABOVE: Linda Mason, Class of 1964, executive producer for CBS *Sunday Morning* and weekend editions of CBS *Evening News*.

York City, London, and Berlin. Judson is currently artistic director of Theatre-in-Process in Boston and her greatest career satisfaction was writing, directing and producing her own play about the anti-slavery heroines, the Grimkes, called *Freedom and Angelina*. Her greatest frustration is the difficulty in finding money, especially for the development of new plays.

Kate Burton, Class of 1979, successfully combined her theater participation while at Brown with concentrations in European history and Russian studies. She earned an M. F. A. at Yale in theatre arts and has since appeared in five Broadway shows, many shows Off-Broadway, and feature films and television shows. She has played in "Some Americans Abroad," "Measure for Measure," Wild Honey," "Doonesbury," and "Present Laughter." Echoing other alumnae, she finds her greatest satisfaction (and her greatest demands) in combining marriage, son, and work. Other alumnae who have been successful with acting careers include Amy Van Nostrand and Bess Armstrong, both Class of 1985, and M. Jobeth Williams, Class of 1970.

In dance, Ruby Shang, Class of 1971, concentrated in art history at Brown and conducted an informal concentration of her own in dance at the same time. She was a featured dancer with the Paul Taylor Dance Company for several years and has received many awards for her contributions to the arts. In 1980, she began her own company, Ruby Shang and Company, Dancers, and that groups creates site-specific events "which, sometimes political and always celebratory, . . . recall the beginnings of dance when it was not merely entertainment, but a ceremonial . . . function marking events in people's lives."[32] Her projects involve dancers, arts organizations, city, state, and national governments and reflect the company's goals for better understanding between nations and cultures.

Actress Jeree Palmer Wade, Class of 1983, who came to Brown through the Resumed Undergraduate Education Program, has performed at Brown for theater students and the Pembroke Center. Her one-woman show based on the life of Billie Holliday had a commercial run in Providence in fall 1990 with fine reviews. In music, country/folk singer and songwriter Mary Chapin Carpenter, Class of 1981, has several hit recordings.

Business and Industry

The women described here represent only a small segment of Brown alumnae who have been successful in the mainstream of American business and finance, most since the 1960s. Because it is so difficult to categorize those fields in a meaningful way, this section highlights some careers in the following fields: accounting, insurance, statistics, advertising, retailing, engineering, manufacturing, and computers in an arbitrary way based on production of information or material goods vs. human services. If looked at that way, 25 percent of the alumnae group who responded to our survey were in those fields. The following information represents a mixture of those who have been successful in business with or without an advanced degree in the field.[33] A number of women respondents indicate partnership with their husbands in various business firms, lumber, storage services, retailing, manufacturing, even tombstone sales. Others have gone into business on their own, some in cloth design and sales, real estate, architecture and travel agencies.

An example of an early M.B.A. is Marie J. Langlois of the Class of 1964. Langlois was one of eleven women (and 700 men) in the Harvard Business School Class of 1967, the third class to admit women to its two-year program. She worked for a large Providence bank for many years, advancing to the position of senior vice president, before moving to her present position with a private investment firm. She is treasurer of the Brown Corporation and also chair of the Pembroke Center Endowment Campaign.[34]

Carol Greenwald, Class of 1965, earned an M.A. in economics from Brown and a Ph.D. from Columbia. She has had an outstanding career in the field of economics, including the Federal Reserve Bank of Boston, a stint as a faculty member at Harvard Business School, a period as a bank president and now as president of the Washington Financial Group. She is happy that she was introduced to the field of economics at Brown, but thinks Brown should provide more career counseling about what a career path is and how to plan for it. The one respondent from the middle group of respondents indicating an M.B.A. was Susan Friedman, Class of 1970, who concentrated in economics at Brown and worked in business before earning an M.B.A. at Harvard in 1977. She is now vice president of Alliance Consulting in Boston. One alumna who has been successful in the banking field without an M.B.A. is Judi Rappoport Blitzer, Class of 1970, who has worked for Chase Manhattan Bank since her graduation. She is now vice president and senior project manager for the bank.

Computers have found a place at the center of activities in all career fields, and it is interesting to note the variety of ways alumnae have moved into the field. Learning new skills after her children had grown, Ellen Yankauer Seibel, Class of 1955, worked first for a publisher, then moved to Chase Manhattan Bank in 1978, advancing to the rank of vice president. She has developed home banking systems and designed the conversion of credit card portfolios to Chase's computer systems.

Several alumnae mentioned above are using their M. B. A. training in the computer field. An example of Eileen Rudden, Class of 1972, who earned a Harvard M. B. A. and is now general manager for Lotus 1−2−3, marketing Lotus software for business applications. Full-time and full of energy, yes, but also married and with three sons. Rudden served as chair of the Pembroke Center Associates Council and also chaired a Brown 1990 Commencement Forum on feminism sponsored by the center. Survey respondents from the Class of 1975 applied their business skills in a variety of fields. Sally E. Goldin earned a Ph. D. in psychology, and is using that background in her own software engineering firm as vice president of Goldin-Rudahl Systems, Inc.

Respondents from the 1980s represent market research, financial analysis, advertising, pharmaceuticals, real estate and tax accounting. The diversity is proved by two examples: Jacqueline Brown Wolpert, Class of 1980, who majored in geology and worked in that field before earning an M. B. A. and becoming a tax accountant; and Lara Livingstone, Class of 1985, who earned an M. A. in international studies and Chinese, then an M.B.A. She is now a trainee for Otis Elevator Company. Alice Wheelwright, Class of 1981, is field marketing manager for the Southeast region of Coca-Cola USA. She admits what many of the women in this chapter would echo: she likes having the monetary reward and the independence which goes with being successful in a competitive business career.

Respondents from the Class of 1985 have also been successful in the technical development of computer applications: Priscilla Feinberg Bauersfeld is a computer interface engineer with Apple Computer; Rosemary Perera is a software design engineer for Microsoft Corporation; Karen Smith Catlin works for Brown in the computer science research area developing software; and Grace M. Kim works with a small, independent computer company started by several Brown graduates.

Engineering

The number of women successfully completing an engineering program at Brown has increased after many years of token representation. ADIS records show none in the earliest group studied; eight in the middle era and 127 in the youngest group. The first woman engineer received her degree in 1947, the second in 1951, and the third in 1959. Then ten years later, there were two in 1969 and two in 1970. There were none in the classes of 1971−73, only one in 1974 and 1975 and then a steady increase to twenty in 1984 and again in 1989.[35] Seven of the engineers in the youngest group responded to the survey; their careers show the diversity among them. Several mentioned that they would have benefited from having more female role models on the Brown faculty.

Annette Breingan, Class of 1975, was one of two women engineering concentrators in her class. With an Sc. B. in electrical engineering and an M.S. in the same field from Stanford in 1980, she moved into software engineering for the computer industry in California where she developed software for medical imaging and a digital radiography system. Her career was firmly established before her children came along and she has been able to continue on a part-time basis since then.

Jean Baglione Panos, Class of 1980, worked for General Electric after receiving her Sc. B. from Brown and then earned an M. S. degree in mechanical engineering from Massachusetts Institute of Technology in 1984. She worked for Westinghouse from 1984 to 1987 and since then has been with an engineering firm in Colorado. She says "I am a specialist in mechanical design of high-speed rotating machinery, including turbo machinery." She reports her greatest satisfaction as "seeing the built, finished product of something I've designed." Her greatest frustration: "I would like to have a management/supervisory position – not possible in my present, very small, old-boy's network company – and time is 'running out' to establish myself elsewhere in a management track." She has been active with the Society of Women Engineers and admits to some frustration "that women don't understand what power we have as a group (and what power we *need*)."

All five of the engineers who responded from the Class of 1985 went on to earn Master of Science degrees and are in a variety of interesting areas: Angela Harris is on the technical staff of an aircraft company; Tracy Kelly Lindsay is in lithography development for a large computer firm; Eva Manolis is in electrical engineering with a silicon graphics company; and Marian Schmier is in a Ph.D. program in textiles and polymer science. Nancy Lanzarone, a civil engineer, learned to speak German after becoming involved with an environmental engineering project which helped to clean up the Rhine River in Switzerland after a spill, and she is now in a position with a firm which combines environmental engineering and law.

Radio, Television and Journalism

The stories of individual Brown alumnae who have been successful in the communications fields show the great changes which have taken place in official (and legal) attitudes toward the employment of women. ADIS records show only two people in radio-TV from the oldest group, eleven in the middle group, and ninety-four in the youngest group.

Carolyn Troy Watts, Class of 1935, is the earliest of the respondents to report a career in radio. She was assistant manager and music producer for a public classical music radio station in Cincinnati from its beginning days in 1960 to 1980. She reports her satisfaction at having the chance to help the station to become one of the top classical stations in the country, winning two national awards. In linking her Brown background to her career, she said, "It was my studies in music and romance languages that made my radio and TV career in the 50s, 60s and 70s possible. Those courses made me uniquely qualified for what was to become a tremendous move toward music in the communications field."

Linda Mason graduated from Brown in 1964 before the dramatic changes in life styles and turmoil of the late 1960s but at the time of the passage of the historic Civil Rights Act of 1964. She credits her international relations concentration and her honors thesis in history with giving her an excellent background for her future career. Mason joined CBS News in January 1966, and progressed through the ranks of writer, associate producer, field producer for the CBS *Evening News* with Walter Cronkite, senior producer for the same show and then a senior producer with Dan Rather. In 1986, she was made executive producer of the *Weekend News* and the next year was made executive producer of *Sunday Morning* as well. Luck? No! Hard work? Yes! Mason says: "In all of these moves, I was the first woman to hold the job. I was not fighting the feminist fight, I was doing what I loved to do, and there were just a lot of men. . . . Not only was I the first woman in all these jobs, but I was the first mother as well."

Ten years later, Elizabeth B. West, Class of 1973, majored in English and film and then went on to Syracuse for an M.S. in Communications. West went to work for ABC Radio in New York City in 1975 and then to ABC-TV in Chicago. She has been a writer and producer for that network in London and New York and in 1989 became senior broadcast producer for ABC *News Prime Time Live*. She has produced ABC *Nightline* programs in South Africa, Israel, and the USSR. She says that it has been important for her career not only to have the ability and the appropriate training, but to be available for assignment to a variety of locations as the opportunities arose. She notes that being a woman had its advantages in some foreign paternalistic societies. She was able to gain access or get quotes often where men were not allowed, whether because she was non-threatening (as a woman) or not taken seriously enough. For whatever reasons, and wearing a makeshift outfit covering head and body, she was granted the first live TV interview in Teheran after the end of the 1984 embassy takeover.

Brown women graduates of the 1980s have become successful in the highly competitive field of radio and television, and Allison Chernow, Class of 1980, is a representative of that younger group. Chernow earned an M.A. in journalism from New York University in 1983. She had a succession of jobs with WNYC Public Radio culminating in her appointment in 1989 as production director for AM and FM radio for that station. She is now one of the highest-ranking female managers in public radio and has received national awards for her performance. She is the producer of a weekly live cabaret program which broadcasts from cabaret revues around New York City. She states as an important career satisfaction the "feeling that I have developed a uniquely female management style that combines humor and compassion with directness and firmness, when needed."

Other respondents from the classes of 1980 and 1985 are Katherine Freed, Class of 1980, producer for *ABC World News Tonight;* Laura Barnett of the Class of 1985, who is casting director for a New York City TV station as well as project director for a small theatrical company; Audrey Laganas, Class of 1985, who is an anchor/reporter for a cable television station in New Hampshire; and Susan Smith Margolin, also Class of 1985, who has started her own video company "to edit trailers, TV spots and sales/promotional reels."

Journalists, Editors

Brown has had an increasingly successful group of alumnae move into responsible positions in mainstream publications, including V. Annette Grant, Class of 1963, who is editor of *Weekend Magazine* for the *New York Times;* Cathleen M. McGuigan, Class of 1971, who is the general editor of *Newsweek;* Wendy J. Strothman, Class of 1972, who is the director of the Beacon Press; Anne Hinman Diffily, Class of 1973, who is managing editor of the *Brown Alumni Monthly;* and Mary Haus, Class of 1983, who is managing editor of *Art News.*

Respondents from the Class of 1980 in journalism are Debra Bradley, who is news director for Smith College; Nan Silver, who is editor-in-chief of *Health* magazine; and Andrea Neal Schmelzer, who is assistant city editor of *The Indianapolis Star* and author of a bi-monthly column, "My Generation," about women's issues. Schmelzer counts as her greatest satisfactions, "My two-and-a-half-year-old son. My column."

Representing the class of 1985 in the field are Stephanie Brommer, who is a reporter for the *Los Angeles Daily News* and Leslie Elmas, who is a business editor for the *Syracuse (NY) Herald.* Jill Blanchette, Class of 1985, who is a reporter/editor for *The Westerly (RI) Sun,* serves appropriately as representative of most of her peers when she says, "I take great pride in the fact that I write for a living – that I write every day and I even get paid to do it."

Conclusion

There is a natural progression, whatever the era, from college graduation to career, family (or some combination of the two), and retirement. It is that middle "passage" which provided much of the material for this chapter. For "family," read husband, children, partners, and own parents. Not one of the respondents was free of family responsibility of one kind or another during their active lives. For "career," read paid or volunteer, and, here again, there were no respondents who had neither. When comparing the chances and choices of Brown women graduates from the three eras, the dramatic difference is that of expectations. Women who entered a four-year liberal arts college in the years between 1925 and 1946 were self-selected as people who would actively use their education in later life. Whether that use was on a paid or volunteer basis was, to some extent, irrelevant. They were expected, and themselves expected, to participate in community life, if not in a paid, professional career.

Women who entered Pembroke/Brown in the middle era, 1946–1956, were self-selected in the sense that they were bright, excellent students whose families, in the majority of cases, could afford to send their daughters to a liberal arts college.[36] Their families expected them to do well and to graduate, and they were then applauded warmly when they married and went where and when their husband's career dictated. Even when they attended graduate school immediately after graduation, it was a rare husband who went where his wife's career took her. It was the wives, Brown alumnae, who adapted. Those women who formed their own major career goals without regard for family considerations were rare.

After the 1950s, the range of expectations began to change. As opportunities in professional fields and in business and industry opened to women, they expected, and were expected, to enter those fields. Indeed, some felt apologetic and/or defensive if they made family considerations their first priority. The expectations of husbands also changed, and it is now anticipated, if not required, that married women will contribute to the family income in a major way. It now seems evident that a two-income family is a necessity for the future, not a luxury, for those families who hope to live reasonably well and, especially, to send their children to selective colleges.

This small sample of alumnae reflects a much slower rate of marriage after college for those in the youngest cohort. That response may reflect the wider "acceptable" living options for women and men, and also the fact that the climate of opinion in the 1980s and 1990s does not force young people to make too-early choices of lifetime commitment. The cost of a university education, and the debt with which so many recent graduates have left Brown, also has had its effect on post-college plans for those who must repay large college debts.

The frustration expressed most often by alumnae of all the classes, and especially by the younger women, was the shortage of time and strength for personal, family, and career involvement. They, at all ages, seem well aware that no one can "have it all" without great sacrifice as well as excellent ability and availability of opportunities.

The one strong conclusion reached from the wonderfully varied and honest responses received is that Pembroke/Brown women have fulfilled the charge of the Brown Charter for "lives of usefulness and reputation," and have done so in a much wider field of endeavor than ever could have been imagined in 1891 for women graduates. They have accomplished much and have done it with confidence and panache.

NOTES

1. Colcleugh, Emma Shaw, 1875–1940 Papers. Vol. II: 48, Haffenreffer Museum, Brown University. The quote is from a Colcleugh scrapbook located after publication of Barbara A. Hail and Kate C. Duncan, *Out of the North: the Subarctic Collection of the Haffenreffer Museum of Anthropology* (Brown University, 1989).

2. Questionnaire mailed in 1990 to alumnae classes of 1930–85 having reunions in 1990. Additional sources include the records of the Alumni and Development Information Services (ADIS), Brown directories, the *Brown Alumni Monthly* and the *George Street Journal*, as well as information from some non-reuning alumnae where relevant. Thanks to Marilyn Hines, Class of 1990, who analyzed the alumnae questionnaires. See Chapter 9 for volunteer careers.

3. Fourteen percent of the 56 women of the Class of 1930 and 27 percent of the 78 women of the Class of 1935 responded to the survey.

4. Survey responses were received from 14 percent of the women in the Class of 1940.

5. Nine percent of the women of the Class of 1945 responded to the survey.

6. Survey responses were received from 13 percent of the 203 women of the Class of 1950 and from 8 percent of the 169 women of the Class of 1955.

7. The survey could not include the 219 women of the Class of 1960 because they were doing a reunion survey of their own. Their results were not separated by sex, so the figures could not be helpful for our current purposes. Responses were received from 11 percent of the 205 women in the Class of 1965.

8. Survey responses were received from 10 percent of the 237 women in the Class of 1970.

9. See Chapter 3.

10. Part of the reason for the success of the merger plan in 1970–71 was the attitude of the student body, men *and* women, who strongly favored the merger or did not care except that it gave women social freedom.

11. These are ADIS figures. The largest number of this young cohort reported medical degrees, 444 (of whom 208 are reported as having their M.D. from Brown), followed by 384

with law degrees, 226 holding M.B.A.s, 163 Ph.D.s and 730 listing master's degrees. These figures, as high as they sound, must be considered very conservative because 1,899 graduates in this group were reported by ADIS as "not classified."

12. Survey responses were received from 5 percent of the women in the Class of 1975, the lowest percentage in the study, and several responses from this class show clearly the ambivalence between full-time professional employment and family concerns.

13. Responses were received from 7 percent of the 595 women in the Class of 1980.

14. Responses were received from 8 percent of the 660 women in the Class of 1985.

15. No real percentages of the total alumnae body can be cited in specific fields because many alumnae reported themselves as retired, gave titles which were too unspecific to include in a larger field, or did not reply.

16. Communications as a field is hard to isolate because it includes women in many fields, including public relations for business, industry, education, non-profit organizations.

17. ADIS records.

18. Our thanks to Ruth Sauber, director of medical student affairs, and Judi Chambers, director of medical public relations, Brown, for information and lists provided for this chapter in September 1990.

19. Stephen R. Smith, M.D., M.C.H., "Continuum Medical Education at Brown University: Retrospective" (internal document), 1989, pp. 19–20.

20. MBA and Massachusetts Lawyers Weekly survey quoted in an Associated Press article in the *Providence Journal Bulletin*, 24 September 1990, p. B-3.

21. Information from *Brown Alumni Monthly* 89 (October 1989): 38–41.

22. General information, dates and names of committees are from Rosemary Ruether and Eleanor McLaughlin, *Women of Spirit: Female Leadership in the Jewish and Christian Traditions*, (New York: Simon & Schuster, 1979).

23. Information from Flora Keshgegian, associate chaplain at Brown and herself an ordained member of the Episcopal clergy. She graduated from Philadelphia Divinity School in 1974 and was ordained to the priesthood in January 1977.

24. Probably would be higher except that a number of older alumnae now list themselves as homemaker or retired.

25. ADIS lists 824, 8 percent, of the youngest group, as "Education-student" so some of those people may be preparing for teaching at elementary or secondary level.

26. ADIS figures.

27. Kaplan has served as an alumna trustee of the Brown Corporation and as chair of the Centennial of Women at Brown being celebrated in 1991.

28. Only 110, or 1 percent, of the youngest group are so listed; a great many are still studying at the advanced level.

29. *Boston Globe*, 9 November 1987.

30. The climate in that department has changed greatly since Evrard's years there; in 1990, the chair of the department was Professor Wendy Edwards, a painter, and there are other talented women faculty members on that staff.

31. Jay Barry and Martha Mitchell, *A Tale of Two Centuries*, published by the *Brown Alumni Monthly*, 1985, p. 177.

32. Information from Ruby Shang and Company, Dancers, June 1990.

33. Solid figures on numbers of alumnae going on to business school for the M.B.A. degree were not available because alumnae often go to business school after initial employment, whether from a bank or investment firm or from a non-profit area.

34. Teresa Gagnon Mellone, "Marie J. Langlois, First Woman Treasurer of Brown University," *Pembroke Center Newsletter* 5 (Spring 1988): 5.

35. Information from the Brown University Division of Engineering in October 1990.

36. The continuing exception is that of students accepted on financial aid through all three eras, but the post-college expectations were the same.

KAREN J. BLAIR, associate professor of history at Central Washington University, Ellensburg, is the author of *The Clubwoman as Feminist: True Womanhood Redefined, 1868–1914* (1980) and *Women's Voluntary Organizations in History, 1810–1960: A Guide to Sources (1989)*. She is currently writing a history of the efforts of women's organizations to help college women. A graduate of Mount Holyoke College, Blair's Ph.D. is from the State University of New York at Buffalo.

LINDA EISENMANN, a graduate of Connecticut College, is the assistant director of the Mary Ingraham Bunting Institute at Radcliffe College. Her dissertation for her Ed.D. at the Harvard Graduate School of Education in 1987 was a study of women at Brown University: "Women at Brown University, 1891–1930: 'Academically Identical, But Socially Quite Distinct.'"

MARTHA N. GARDNER, Class of 1988, a women's studies major, is a policy aid for the wife of the governor of Rhode Island, specializing in issues about incarcerated women and their children.

CINDY HIMES is an assistant professor of history at Towson State University, Baltimore. Her interest in women's sports history began as an undergraduate at Vassar where she played on the varsity basketball team and was student director of the women's and coed intramural sports programs. She is working on *The Female Athlete in American Society: 1860–1940*. She holds a Ph.D. in history from the University of Pennsylvania.

JEAN HOWARD, Class of 1970, a professor of English at Columbia University, is a former member of Brown's Board of Trustees and past chair of the Pembroke Center Associates Council. As chair of the Corporation Committee on the Status of Women, she oversaw the task force that evaluated how coeducation was working at Brown and helped write the final report: *Men and Women Learning Together: A Study of College Students in the late 70's* (1980). She is the author of *Shakespeare's Art of Orchestration: Stage Technique and Audience Response* (1984) and co-editor of *Shakespeare Reproduced: The Text in History and Ideology* (1987) and holds a Ph.D. in English from Yale.

POLLY WELTS KAUFMAN, Class of 1951, is a former editor of the *Pembroke Alumna*. The author of *Women Teachers on the Frontier* (1984), she has recently completed a book on women and national parks. She teaches women's history at the University of Massachusetts at Boston and is currently a visiting professor at Bowdoin College. She earned an M. A. in history from the University of Washington and an Ed. D. in educational leadership and American studies from Boston University.

KAREN M. LAMOREE is the former archivist of the Christine Dunlap Farnham Archives which is devoted to collecting materials related to the history of women at Brown and in Rhode Island. Serving from 1986 to 1990, she prepared the *Research Guide* to the archives (1989) also including sources about women in collections throughout the Brown libraries. A graduate of Clark with a master's from the State University of New York at Albany, she is currently the collections development archivist at the State Historical Society of Wisconsin.

SHELLEY MAINS, Class of 1982, works in Boston as an adolescent health educator. She is a feminist activist and occasionally writes for *Sojourner* and *Gay Community News.*

SANDY MARTIN, Class of 1982, is a feminist activist and co-coordinator of the Women's Studies Program at the Massachusetts Institute of Technology. She is writing a thesis on women and social change.

LOUISE NEWMAN, a graduate of Harvard University, is completing a history dissertation at Brown to be titled: "Different But Equal: The Problem of Sexual Equality in the United States, 1870–1930." She is the editor of *Men's Ideas/Women's Realities: Popular Science, 1870–1915* (1984) and teaches in the History and Literature Program at Harvard University.

JOAN W. SCOTT is the founding director of the Pembroke Center for Teaching and Research on Women and was the Nancy Duke Lewis Professor at Brown from 1980 to 1985. She is currently professor in the School of Social Science at the Institute for Advanced Study in Princeton, NJ. Her most recent book is *Gender and the Politics of History* (1988). She is a graduate of Brandeis with a Ph. D. from the University of Wisconsin.

LYDE CULLEN SIZER, a graduate of Yale University, is currently working on her Ph. D. in history at Brown. The title of her dissertation is "Between the Lines: Gender, Race, and the Politics of War in Northern Women's Writing on the American Civil War."

CHARLOTTE LOWNEY TOMAS, Class of 1957, M. A. 1965, has spent most of her career at Brown, serving first as director of career planning and associate dean at Pembroke. As associate dean of The College from 1973 to her retirement in 1990, she participated in the development of the Resumed Undergraduate Education Program.

THE SEARCH FOR EQUITY
Women at Brown University, 1891–1991

was designed by Melissa Moger Gilbert,
Gilbert Associates and printed by Eastern Press.
The typeface is Sabon, a variation of Garamond.
2500 softcover and 500 casebound copies
on the occasion of the 100th anniversary of
women at Brown University